The Organization of Information

THE ORGANIZATION OF INFORMATION

Second Edition

Arlene G. Taylor

Library and Information Science Text Series

LIBRARIES UNLIMITED

A Member of the Greenwood Publishing Group

Westport, Connecticut • London

Library of Congress Cataloging-in-Publication Data

Taylor, Arlene G., 1941–
   The organization of information / Arlene G. Taylor — 2nd ed.
     p.   cm. — (Library and information science text series)
   Includes bibliographical references and index.
   ISBN 1–56308–976–9 (alk. paper) — ISBN 1–56308–969–6 (pbk. : alk. paper)
   1. Information organization. 2. Metadata. I. Title. II. Series.
Z666.5.T39 2004
 025—dc22   2003058904

British Library Cataloguing in Publication Data is available.

Library of Congress Catalog Card Number: 2003058904
ISBN: 1–56308–976–9
     1–56308–969–6 (pbk.)

First published in 2004

Libraries Unlimited, Inc., 88 Post Road West, Westport, CT 06881
A Member of the Greenwood Publishing Group, Inc.
www.lu.com

Printed in the United States of America

The paper used in this book complies with the
Permanent Paper Standard issued by the National
Information Standards Organization (Z39.48–1984).

10 9 8 7 6 5 4 3

*To Wayne, who makes life easier
and much more enjoyable*

CONTENTS

LIST OF FIGURES

PREFACE

I began the preface to the first edition of this book as follows:

> As I began work on the ninth edition of *Introduction to Cataloging and Classification* I became more and more aware that another work was needed that would precede the cataloging text. Core courses in many schools of library and information science now include a course in organizing information. These courses typically cover much more than cataloging and classification. They discuss the concept of organization and its role in human endeavors; many kinds of retrieval tools, such as bibliographies, indexes, finding aids, catalogs, and other kinds of databases; encoding standards, such as MARC, SGML, various SGML DTDs, and XML; creation of metadata; all kinds of controlled vocabularies, including thesauri and ontologies, as well as subject heading lists; classification theory and methodology; arrangement and display of metadata records and physical information-bearing packages; and system design. *The Organization of Information* addresses this need, leaving *Introduction to Cataloging and Classification* as a textbook for courses devoted to the specifics of cataloging and classification.[1]

This statement is as true now as it was when I wrote it four-and-a-half years ago. Changes have come in degree, however. More schools of library and information science now include organizing information as a core course. Encoding standards, metadata standards, and systems continue to evolve, and new ones have been developed. New information organizing concepts (or some would say old concepts with new names) have become useful additions to the discussion of organization of information—concepts such as information architecture, knowledge management, portals, and taxonomies.

The goal of this edition remains to enable students, practicing librarians, and others interested in organizing information to understand the theory, principles, standards, and tools behind the organization of information in all types of environments. As with the first edition there is still more about libraries than about other types of environments. This is at least partly because the weight of history means that there are many centuries of accumulation of theory, principles, and practice behind organization of information in libraries, while archives have not quite two centuries of accumulation, and the other environments have only decades, or in some cases, less than a decade, of history.

In order to accomplish the book's goal effectively, it was necessary to make some rather major changes in the structure of the work. The first four chapters continue to cover the same concepts as in the first edition but with extensive updating. Chapter 1 looks at our basic human need to organize and how it is approached in various environments. A new section discusses the nature of information, and new environments included are digital libraries, information architecture, and knowledge management. Chapter 2 is concerned with the formats and functions of basic retrieval tools that have been developed. New sections are included for pathfinders and for search engines and directories. In Chapter 3, I ask, "How did we arrive at this state of organization?" and discuss the history of basic principles that have developed over the centuries. Chapter 4 continues to deal with encoding standards, but is considerably expanded to give much more attention to XML and XML schemas. A new section on frameworks discusses RDF, METS, and the Semantic Web.

The concept of systems and system design has changed significantly in the last five years and has become much more central in organizing information. It now must be considered as an integral part of the organizing process. Therefore, I moved the former "System Design" chapter from the end of the book to become Chapter 5, "Systems and System Design." The concepts discussed here permeate and underlie discussion of concepts in later chapters. The chapter is completely rewritten and updated. New concepts covered include discussion of databases (including bibliographic networks and integrated library systems), searching and retrieval models, meta-searching, user-centered system design, and authority control integration.

A completely new addition is Chapter 6, "Metadata." It gives an overall introduction to the area of metadata, discussing its basic characteristics and purposes, its relationship to cataloging, and types of metadata, including administrative, structural, and descriptive. Finally, it discusses several of the newer metadata management tools, including application profiles, metadata registries, crosswalks, harvesting tools, and templates.

Chapters 7 and 8—updated versions of the first edition's Chapters 5 and 6—continue discussion of metadata, covering descriptive metadata in depth in Chapter 7, and covering access points and authority control in Chapter 8. New material in these chapters includes discussion of entities as defined in International Federation of Library Associations and Institutions's *Functional Requirements for Bibliographic Records*, AACR2R's new concepts of continuing resources and integrating resources, and bibliographic relationships. New metadata schemas included are MODS (Metadata Object Description Schema), ISAD(G) *(General International Standard Archival Description)*, CIMI's XML Schema for SPECTRUM, and ONIX (ONline Information eXchange).

Subject approaches to organizing information are covered in Chapter 9, "Subject Analysis," Chapter 10, "Systems for Vocabulary Control," and Chapter 11, "Systems for Categorization." These are updated and rewritten versions of Chapters 7 and 8 from the first edition. It seems useful to separate the challenges and concepts involved in determining the "aboutness" of an information package from the concepts of using vocabulary and/or categorization to express such "aboutness." This is now covered in Chapter 9. Chapter 10 discusses, first, the concepts involved in creating controlled vocabularies, which are then followed by discussion of applying controlled vocabularies, including descriptions of several of the most used existing vocabularies. Chapter 11 covers theory of categorization and how this translates into classification. It includes new sections on bibliographic classifications and on taxonomies. Because arrangement and display of information is so important to users' retrieval of information, Chapter 12 is devoted to theory and practice in this area.

NOTE

1. Arlene G. Taylor, *The Organization of Information* (Englewood, Colo.: Libraries Unlimited, 1999), p. xvii.

ACKNOWLEDGMENTS

Many people have contributed to the existence of this book. To begin naming is always a danger, because one risks inadvertently omitting someone who actually contributed greatly. I would like to try, though, to acknowledge at least some of them. First, I again acknowledge my mentor and cataloging professor, Kathryn Luther Henderson, Professor, Graduate School of Library and Information Science, University of Illinois at Urbana/Champaign, who inspired me to understand the "why" behind all the practices involved in cataloging. This approach has assisted me greatly in making all the transitions that have been necessitated by the move from a paper environment to an electronic environment during the course of my career.

Three people were particularly helpful in advising me during the writing of the first edition about organization of information in particular environments. Their ideas continue to be expressed in this edition. Bernadette Callery, Museum Librarian, Carnegie Museum of Natural History, assisted with discussions of the museum environment. Patrice Clemson, Instructor, School of Information Sciences and Technology, Pennsylvania State University, Beaver Campus, gave me assistance with office environments. Elizabeth Yakel, Assistant Professor, School of Information, University of Michigan, was an immense help with my understanding of organization in archives. Any errors that might be found in the discussion of these areas are, of course, my responsibility, not theirs.

For this edition, the person who has made such immeasurable contributions that it is difficult to enumerate them all is Daniel N. Joudrey, doctoral student, School of Information Sciences, University of Pittsburgh. He wrote the first drafts of what are now Chapter 5 (systems) and Chapter 6 (metadata) as papers for doctoral seminars, one under my direction, and the other under the direction of Hong Xu, formerly Assistant Professor in the school, and now Head of the East Asian Library of the University Library System, University of Pittsburgh. As my teaching fellow for a year and then an instructor teaching sections of the core organizing information course for the last two years, Mr. Joudrey made numerous suggestions for additions and changes needed in the text. Finally, he read every chapter in manuscript form and made many extremely helpful suggestions for improvements in clarity, material for inclusion, organizational structure of the text, and other such contributions. Without Mr. Joudrey's expertise, this project would have been considerably delayed.

Other people have made extremely useful contributions. Some are colleagues who have used the first edition as a textbook, and, in the process, noted, for my benefit, changes they would like to see in the text in the future. David Bawden, Senior Lecturer, Department of Information Science, City University, London, liked the book so much that he built a course around it. In the process, he shared with me materials that he developed for the course, and these have been quite helpful. Marcella Genz, Assistant Professor, School of Information Studies, Florida State University, spent time assisting me in making a list of lacunae from the first edition and desiderata for the next edition, all of which are now included in this edition. Numerous other colleagues have called to my attention one point or another that needed improvement. I hope that I managed to incorporate all of these, and I am extremely grateful to all these colleagues for their attention to detail and for caring enough to try to assist in the improvement of this text. I am also grateful to all the colleagues who have adopted the book as a text and have passed on to me the favorable comments of students who find it readable and helpful in understanding this material.

All the students I have ever taught can take credit for contributing, because they have been my "guinea pigs" in the process of explaining theory and mixing it with practice. In addition, over the years, many colleagues, too numerous to mention individually, have contributed to my understanding, first, of cataloging, and then, of broader organizing issues. I wish them to know how much I appreciate their input.

I would like to thank the ALA committee who chose the first edition of this book to receive the 2000 ALA/Highsmith Library Literature Award. The encouragement gained from such recognition has provided impetus needed to keep working when I might rather have taken some time off.

I truly appreciate the staff of Libraries Unlimited for their work in producing the book. I wish to thank Martin Dillon, with whom I worked during the writing of most of the text. His suggestions for additions and changes have contributed greatly to the completeness of this edition. (Dr. Dillon served, many years ago, on my dissertation committee at the University of North Carolina, and was also quite helpful to me then.)

And last, but absolutely not least, I thank my husband, A. Wayne Benson, whose love, understanding, and culinary skills have sustained me through many deadlines. This book's existence is largely attributable to him.

Arlene G. Taylor
Pittsburgh, PA
July 2003

CHAPTER 1

ORGANIZATION OF RECORDED INFORMATION

This chapter gives an overview of the field of the organization of recorded information. Terms used here that might not be readily familiar to the person new to the field of organizing information will be explained in later chapters. In the meantime the reader will find definitions of most unfamiliar terms in the glossary of this book.

THE NEED TO ORGANIZE

There seems to be a basic drive in humans to organize. Psychologists tell us that babies' brains organize images into categories such as "faces" or "foods." Small children do a lot of organizing during play. With some individuals the need is much stronger than with others. Those who operate on the maxim "A place for everything and everything in its place" cannot begin to work until the work surface is cleared and every stray object has been put in its place. That is, such a person has to be "organized" before beginning a new project. But even those whose work spaces appear to be cluttered or chaotic have some organization in their heads. Such persons usually have some idea, or perhaps certain knowledge, of what is in the various piles or collections of "stuff." Regardless of one's personal style, however, human learning is based upon the ability to analyze and organize data, information, and knowledge.

We organize because we need to retrieve. Kitchens are organized so that cooking equipment is easily accessible and foodstuffs and spices can be used as needed. Workplaces are organized so that appropriate records are retrievable and work can be done. Learning processes are organized so that relationships among ideas can be used to assist the learner in recalling the learned material.

Retrieval of information is dependent upon its having been organized. Information is needed in all aspects of life—for example, for health reasons, to understand each other, to learn about one's relationships, to fix things that are broken, or simply to expand our knowledge. Some of this information has already been assimilated and is in one's knowledge store, while other information has to be sought. If it is not organized, it is difficult, if not impossible, to find. So we have all kinds of tools that are organized to aid in the process of finding information that we need: telephone books, directories, dictionaries, encyclopedias, bibliographies, indexes, catalogs, museum registers, archival finding aids, and databases, among others.

Organization of information also allows us to keep usable records of human endeavors for posterity. Libraries, archives, museums, and other types of institutions have been doing this for many years. (This book does not deal with organization in commercial enterprises that have put together collections for the purpose of sale, rather than collecting for posterity.)

THE NATURE OF INFORMATION

I have sometimes given students the following list of terms and then asked them to place the terms in order from the lowest level of thinking to the highest: understanding, data, knowledge, wisdom, information. Clifford Stoll, in his book *Silicon Snake Oil: Second Thoughts on the Information Highway,* discussed these words that we use to indicate different levels of comprehension of symbols.[1] His order, indicating symbols from the least meaningful to the most meaningful, is: data, information, knowledge, understanding, wisdom. Which of these are we organizing in libraries, museums, archives, and the like? There is a running argument between those who believe we are organizing information and those who believe we are organizing knowledge. My prejudice is evident from the title of this book. It seems to me that I can use my knowledge to write a book, but until you read that book, understand it, and integrate it into your own knowledge, it is just information. That is why I believe we organize information—so that others can find it, read or otherwise absorb it, and use it to add to their own store of knowledge.

Notice that in the preceding paragraph, I said that you read, understand, and then integrate into your own knowledge. So I'm not sure about Stoll's putting understanding after knowledge. I think those two may be intertwined. You need to have some understanding in order to incorporate something into your knowledge, but you must have a certain amount of knowledge in order to understand new things.

According to several dictionaries, *knowledge* exists in the mind of an individual who has studied a matter, understands it, and perhaps has added to it through research or other means. The same dictionaries indicate that *information* is the communication or reception of knowledge. Such communication occurs in great part through the recording of the knowledge in some fashion. People write, speak, compose, paint, sculpt, and in many other ways attempt to communicate their knowledge to others. This book, for example, is a representation of my knowledge; but it is not a complete representation of my knowledge of this subject. It is, no doubt, an imperfect representation, in the sense that some concepts may not be explained as clearly as I truly understand them. However, it is not a representation of the reader's knowledge until the reader has read and understood it. That is, it is information that can be placed into a scheme of organization from which it can be retrieved for study by those interested in increasing their knowledge of the subject.

Thus I have chosen to use the term *information* rather than *knowledge* as my expression of what I believe we organize when we organize for the benefit of other people. This is not a rejection of "organization of knowledge," however. The knowledge existing in the brains of people is being harnessed in many situations. I work on organizing my own knowledge every time I write. The knowledge of reference librarians is used in an organized way when they assist patrons in answering questions. "Knowledge management" has recently come into use in the administration of organizations and is discussed below.

THE NATURE OF THE ORGANIZATION OF RECORDED INFORMATION

As mentioned earlier, this book addresses the organization of recorded information, as other means are necessary to "organize" information that has only been spoken, heard, or thought about. Recorded information, however, includes much more than text. Video and audio recordings, pictures, cartographic representations, and Web pages are all examples of recorded information that is not just "text." Therefore, instead of using words such as *book* or *item* to refer to the organizable unit of information, the term *information package* is used in this book.

Ronald Hagler, in his book *The Bibliographic Record and Information Technology,* has identified six functions of bibliographic control.[2] His listing reflects the purpose of his book—that is, the emphasis is upon the work of librarians. However, the list, presented and elaborated below, with wording altered to be inclusive of all recorded information, reflects the major activities involved in the organization of recorded information.

1. *Identifying the existence of all types of information packages as they are made available.*

   A book may be published or a Web site may be established, but if no one knows of its existence except the person(s) involved in its creation, it will be of no informational use to anyone. Existence and identity can be made known in many ways: publishers' announcements, e-mail announcements, reviews, subject-related listings, to name a few. Most publishers create catalogs listing their products along with abstracts for them. Reference tools such as *Books in Print* are products of this activity. Some online journals send regular e-mail announcements, outlining contents, to let readers know when a new issue is available. Some news organizations allow people to sign up to receive e-mail announcements about new information available at the organization's Web site or about how to order recordings of special programs, and so on.

2. *Identifying the works contained within those information packages or as parts of them.*

   In the majority of cases one information package is equal to one work. However, a collection of short stories or a grouping of artistic works may be considered to be an information package as a whole, or each individual story or artistic work may be considered to be an information package. It depends upon how much *granularity* is desired. A Web site that is all about a famous person may have individual digitized works of the person, biographical material, accounts of the person written by contemporaries, accounts of events contemporary to the person's life span, and other parts. The writings about the person and the events may be important works in their own right and may need to be identified separately.

3. *Systematically pulling together these information packages into collections in libraries, archives, museums, Internet communication files, and other such depositories.*

The activity of creating collections has been thought of traditionally as the province of institutions such as libraries, archives, and museums. But collections have always been created in many other situations: for example, personal collections made up because of an intense interest in a particular kind of information, office collections of internal information and information needed to carry out the work of the office, university departmental collections of materials needed for teaching in a particular discipline, and so forth. Now that it is easy to make these collections known publicly, lists are being provided at Web sites.

Collections often include electronic resources not held locally. Many institutions purchase the right to allow the users of their collections to search a resource online. Some resources are accessible only online. Others are also available in print. Part of the organizing process is determining whether such resources need to be added to one's collection in some permanent way.

4. *Producing lists of these information packages prepared according to standard rules for citation.*

Lists created in the process of describing information packages include bibliographies, indexes, library catalogs, archival finding aids, museum registers, and Web directories. These are important to the retrieval of individual information packages, because if one is looking for a known item, especially a tangible one that needs a physical location, it is necessary to find it listed somewhere. Such lists may be in print or electronic form.

5. *Providing name, title, subject, and other useful access to these information packages.*

The activity that adds the most value to the usefulness and retrieval potential of a collection is the provision of authority-controlled name, title, and subject access points to the descriptions of the information packages. Keyword access can be provided more or less automatically and "on-the-fly"—that is, any information in electronic form can be found by searching for a word that appears in the electronic information package. However, as the size of the collection being searched increases, results of keyword searches become less and less satisfactory. More satisfactory retrieval comes from being able to search for names, titles, and controlled vocabulary that have been created under authority control, usually by humans. If a person has been identified by different forms of name, and if that name is brought under authority control, then a search for one form of the name will retrieve information packages related to the person regardless of which form of name appears in a particular package. If a work has been given different titles in its different manifestations, a search for one of the titles will retrieve all. If a system uses controlled vocabulary, a search for a word with more than one meaning (which encompasses most English words) will allow differentiation among the various meanings and will direct one to broader, narrower, and related terms. It will also bring together under one term all the synonymous terms that may be used to express a concept.

Authority-controlled access is of little use unless systems are designed to take advantage of it. Therefore, a major part of organizing information is designing systems for searching and display that will allow information-seekers to find easily what they need and want.

6.   *Providing the means of locating each information package or a copy of it.*

Location of information packages has been, for at least a century, a value added by institutions with collections. The catalogs or other lists created in these institutions give information on the physical location of the information package, if it has not been taken out by a patron or is not being used by someone on the premises. In many library online catalogs, circulation information is available so that if an item has been taken out of the library, that information is available with the location information. Bibliographic networks (e.g., OCLC, RLIN) allow one to find out which locations physically own a particular item. Many library, museum, and archival catalogs are available on the Internet. One can learn from these which locations own an item, whether it is on loan at a particular location (usually a library, as archives and museums generally do not circulate items from their collections), and often whether an item is on order and when it is expected to arrive.

Traditionally, bibliographies and indexes have not given location information. Bibliographies list information packages that exist somewhere, but seldom tell where. Indexes give the larger work in which a smaller work being listed can be found (e.g., in which journal an article can be found), but do not give the physical location of the larger work. All of this is still true for tangible resources, but for electronic resources found on the Internet, it is becoming more common to give the location (e.g., the URL) in any listing that includes the electronic resource. However, the instability of URLs makes it difficult to keep them current.

ORGANIZATION OF INFORMATION IN DIFFERENT ENVIRONMENTS

There are many environments in which there is a desire to organize information so that it will be retrievable for various purposes and so that at least some of it will be kept for posterity. The ones to be discussed here are libraries of all types, archives, museums and art galleries, the Internet (including digital libraries), data administration environments, and knowledge management environments.

Libraries

We consider libraries first because they have the longest tradition of organizing information for the purpose of retrieval and for posterity. As mentioned earlier, the process begins with collections. Collections in libraries are created through the process called collection development. Collections of tangible information packages are developed most often in three ways: (1) librarians learn about existence of new works through reviews, publishers' announcements, requests from users of the library, and the like, and then order appropriate materials; (2) gifts are given to the library; and/ or (3) approval plans, worked out with one or more vendors, bring in new items according to preselected profiles. And, of course, journals keep adding to the collection's size unless subscriptions are dropped.

When new materials arrive for addition to the collections, physical entities have to be arranged in some fashion. They may be placed on shelves in the order in which they come in, or they may be placed in some more meaningful order. They could be placed in alphabetical order, the way that many fiction and biography sections are arranged. Most, however, are arranged by classification.

Classification of materials is part of the process of cataloging, which is usually the first activity following receipt of the materials. Cataloging of individual items involves creating a description of the physical item; choosing certain names and titles to serve as access points for getting to the description in the catalog; doing authority work on those names and titles; doing subject analysis of the content of the work in the item; choosing subject headings and classification notations to represent the subject analysis; and creating call numbers (location devices), usually by adding a Cutter number to the classification notation to make a unique set of letters and numbers to identify the particular physical item. Most records thus created are encoded with the MAchine Readable Cataloging (MARC) format so that they can be displayed in the Integrated Library Systems (ILSs) that most libraries have.

Finally, physical items have to be "processed" so that they can be housed with the collections. This involves removing or adding book jackets, placing security strips in or on items, placing call number labels and barcodes on the items, sending an item to the conservation/preservation department if it is an older item that is not in good shape, and so forth.

The two major results of the cataloging process are arrangements of collections and the creation and maintenance of the catalog that provides the major access to the collections. The catalog is able to show what exists in the collection written by certain authors, having certain titles, or on certain subjects. It also collocates (i.e., brings together) all of the works of an author and all the editions of a work, and all works on a subject, even though they might not be brought together in the collections.[3] Finally, the catalog provides some kind of location device to indicate where in the collection the item will be found, assuming it is not circulating to a user.

Before online catalogs existed, the library's main card, book, or Computer Output Microform (COM) catalog typically was supplemented by other catalogs. Catalogs for departmental libraries, serial record holdings, special formats catalogs, and shelflists containing location information for specific copies of an item were the most common. All of these have been incorporated into one database in most online catalogs. In addition, most online catalogs are part of integrated systems, which means that circulation information can accompany each catalog record.

Until recently the online catalog continued to contain records only for items physically held by the library system. As libraries have entered into cooperative relationships, this principle of telling "what the library has" has eroded. In union catalogs that contain records from libraries of more than one institution, the concept was expanded to "what at least one of the cooperating libraries has." More recently, the addition of Internet records has meant that a number of catalogs now contain records for "what the library can give access to," including "what the library has."

Online catalogs also can be gateways to outside systems such as bibliographic networks (e.g., OCLC, RLIN) that can tell where an information package may be found if it is not in the local catalog. The item can then be requested through interlibrary loan (ILL). In addition, bibliographic and text databases can be accessed from a catalog gateway. Many of these have become document delivery systems. A major addition to online catalogs has been access to the World Wide Web (referred to hereinafter as the Web). Many libraries are cataloging Internet resources that seem to be important for the users of that catalog, and a URL in a catalog record can be hyperlinked to the Web for immediate access to the information package represented by the catalog record. As mentioned earlier, a major challenge has been keeping the URLs up-to-date.

Another influence on the organization process in libraries is found in the reference process. Libraries are organized so that information can be retrieved. In the reference process the success of the organization is tested. If it is found to be difficult to use, some of the organization process must be redone. Administrative services in libraries also must be concerned with the organization of information. Administrators are responsible for technological decisions that are directly affected by the organization of the recorded information in that setting. Conversely, administrators' decisions affect the future, in which electronic chaos will result if organization of information is not supported.

Archives

Libraries became more and more standardized throughout the twentieth century, with many information resources in a library being duplicates of resources in another, but this is not the situation in archives. Archives usually consist of unique items. Therefore, it once was thought that standardization was unnecessary. Archives could not take advantage of copy cataloging (i.e., using catalog records created by other agencies) because they were not cataloging materials that were also owned elsewhere. More recently, however, archives have seen significant standardization movements.

Archives preserve records of enduring value that document organizational or personal activities accumulated in the course of daily life and work. Organizational records consist of such things as annual reports, correspondence, personnel records, and the like. Personal records might consist of such things as correspondence, manuscripts, and personal papers, or might be a collection of memorabilia or a scrapbook. Even though materials in archives often are thought to be "old," this is not necessarily so. Further, archival materials can be in many different formats: texts, graphic images, sound recordings, moving image recordings, on paper or in analog or digital formats.

Archival materials have been organized for centuries. Unlike library materials, archival materials are arranged and described in groups. Until the last few decades, each archives chose its own way to organize the information, particularly regarding level of control and depth of description. There have been several major schools of thought through the years as to how organization of archival information should be done. The one that seems to have prevailed states that the basic principles of organization are provenance and original order. *Provenance* is the originator (i.e., the corporate body or individual) that created, gathered, and maintained the collection before it was sent to the archives. The term *provenance* is also used to show the ownership history of a particular artifact or collection of archival information. *Original order* is the order in which the originator of an archival collection kept or created the collection. Most archives now keep the contents of individual collections within the archives as a whole in original order, and the collections are maintained according to provenance.

Standardization and cooperation have come to the archival world in part because of increased interest in research involving documents and archival collections housed all over the world. In addition, interest has grown, especially in the academic community, in entering descriptions of archival collections into the same databases with library catalog records. It has now become possible to easily share knowledge of the existence of these collections on the Internet.

Descriptions of archival materials can take one or more different forms. An *accession record* summarizes information about the source of the collection, gives the circumstances of its acquisition (which are more fully treated in the donor file), and briefly describes the physical data and contents for a collection. A *finding aid* gives a detailed contents note of the historical and organizational context of the collection and continues by describing its context, perhaps providing an inventory outlining what is in each box. It may also contain physical details such as the presence of brittle or fragile materials. A *catalog record* is a much shortened version of a finding aid.

Archival materials are generally housed in closed stacks, accessible only to staff. There is no public browsing and so the arrangement does not need to be classified as is usually true in an open stacks library. Any classification given, in any case, would be so broad as to be almost useless, due to the varied nature of each collection.

When the archival world became interested in placing its catalog records into bibliographic databases in the 1980s, a MARC format for archival and manuscript control (AMC) was developed (MARC-AMC). Despite some lingering problems, the format continues to be used to code archival catalog records (now with the name "mixed materials" instead of AMC). In the last few years the SGML/XML-based Encoded Archival Description (EAD) standard has been developed for the purpose of encoding finding aids so that they can be displayed on the Web.

The organization of archival information is necessary for use, whether that use is for administrative, historical, or personal reasons. It is also useful for archives that wish to mount exhibits either in something like an academic setting or perhaps on the Web. If collections are well organized and documented, an exhibitor can use this to find appropriate additions to the exhibit.

Museums and Art Galleries

Museums and art galleries are combined here, because the kinds of art galleries that are being discussed (e.g., National Gallery of Art) operate in ways similar to museums. Art galleries that display art for the purpose of sale are not covered in this book.

Although libraries and archives both contain some visual material, the vast majority of the collections of museums and art galleries consists of visual material in two- or three-dimensional form. These collections traditionally have been organized for internal use only, but recently research needs have been given attention. Even when the needs of distant researchers are taken into account, curators may be reluctant to contribute some data because it may represent data created by individuals in the course of their research and may not yet be published.

Museum or gallery art works or artifacts are acquired through an institution's acquisitions department. As is done in archives, accession records are created, although the practice in natural history museums differs somewhat. In natural history museums, artifacts are acquired largely from fieldwork, and a preliminary field record is made. If it is decided to keep the objects in the collection, accession records are created. In some cases groups of similar objects are described as a single lot that is given a single accession number. Curating of individual objects, which may not happen for some time, results in departmental-level catalog records with their own numerical sequences.

In museums other than the natural history type, items are registered after being accessioned. Registration is a process much like cataloging in libraries and archives. The register serves as a catalog in that it establishes the organizational control over the art works and artifacts. A fairly recent development is the use of bibliographic utilities for the organizational control of art and artifacts, although records thus created are still not necessarily accepted in the museum community.

In museums, as in archives, provenance is important information and is essential in determining the name of the object. Both provenance and condition must appear with all other information about the object in the catalog or registration record. An aspect of creating records for museum objects and art that is very different from creating records for text is that the objects are often imperfectly known at the time of accessioning and registering. There may be an accumulation of conflicting information over time.

Description of visual material is often more difficult than description of textual material. There is more reliance on the perceptions of the person doing the describing. Often there are no words associated with items at all; it is necessary for the describers of such items to use their own words. A single record has many more fields than does the usual library catalog record. Some fields that might be needed for art objects that are not used in libraries are: Material content, Technique(s), Studio of origin, Type of equipment used, Color(s), Texture, Design symbolism, Provenance, Exhibition history, Installation considerations, and Appraised value. Even with additional fields, it is not possible to anticipate all the uses a researcher might find in art or artifacts. A street scene from a century ago may be useful to historians, architects, urban planners, cultural historians, medical researchers, sociologists, students of photography, or others. Systems are being developed that start with queries that use the text of the description; then query results allow the searcher to browse surrogate images.

Subject analysis is also more difficult for visual materials—an image does not tell in words what it is about. Additionally, the line between description and subject analysis is harder to draw. One might describe a work of art as being a painting of a woman in a blue dress holding and looking at a baby—this is a description. But if one gives the subject of the work as "Mary and Jesus," one has crossed the line into interpretation (unless this is in the title of the work given by the artist). And if one uses a description like "love of a mother," one is definitely interpreting.

A barrier to cooperative cataloging has been the firmly held notion that museums hold unique objects. This is perhaps less true of natural history collections than other museum and art collections. Although each specimen of a bug or bird is unique, each represents a class of organisms that can be identified to the genus and species level. There would have to be copy-specific notes, but this does not preclude the idea of cooperative cataloging for cooperative access. However, as was true of libraries when cooperative cataloging was first introduced, museum curators fear a loss of individual control and level of detail. They have been reluctant to give up their local terminology and organization in order to participate in a bibliographic utility. This is changing, however. Chapter 7 describes some cooperative museum projects currently under way.

Besides its major collections, the museum or art gallery can also have an archive, a records management program, and a library. The library may contain published materials that document or relate to the museum or art gallery collections. As with archival materials, the museum/art gallery collections are accessible only to staff. Much of the collection is stored behind the scenes while only some of it is on display at any one time. Behind the scenes, the items are numbered in a way so that they can be retrieved as needed. Persons responsible for the exhibits must make heavy use of the system of organizational control. In addition, these collections are increasingly being used for research by persons with diverse research needs.

The Internet

The Internet has been likened to a library where all the books have been dumped on the floor and there is no catalog. For several years efforts have been made to find a way to gain some control over the Internet; however, one cannot yet say that it is organized. There is so much change so fast that efforts begun may be out of date in a few months. At the end of the 1990s, it was estimated by a number of Internet specialists that a Web year was six to nine weeks. In other words, the amount of change that happens in society in a year happened on the Web in six to nine weeks. With the fall of the "dot com" milieu and with other stabilizing factors, the rate of change has slowed. Nevertheless, getting a handle on organization is still a challenge.

Several different approaches are being taken in the attempt to organize the Internet. Libraries have attempted to use traditional means for the organization. Some librarians, for example, have compiled bibliographies of Web sites. Some of these bibliographies eventually have become "gateways" to the Internet. Librarians have been part of the team of people who have been working on a metadata standard called the Dublin Core. OCLC, a major library-oriented bibliographic network, established CORC (Cooperative Online Resource Center) in the late 1990s in order to provide a way for libraries to catalog online resources cooperatively and to have ready access to a database of metadata describing important Web resources. CORC has now been absorbed into OCLC's Web interface for cataloging— called Connexion. In Connexion, cataloging can be done either in traditional MARC/AACR2 format or in Dublin Core format. An important feature of Connexion with regard to organizing the Internet is its provision for development of pathfinders for certain subjects.

Much work on organizing the Internet has been done by persons other than librarians. Search engines, for example, have been developed by computer and programming specialists. Most people appreciate search engines, even though they may be frustrated that the search engines are not more selective and precise. Most programs or agents (e.g., robots, spiders, etc.) sent out to find sites to add to the indexes of search engines are able to index text only; graphics and pictures can be recognized as such, but cannot be interpreted unless they have textual labels. In addition to that, these programs cannot analyze a site's purpose, history, policies, and so forth. In order to improve the situation, work on various kinds of metadata (i.e., information about information) is ongoing and important; appropriate information could be gleaned by robots from metadata that has been added to a site by its author or by someone trained in describing and analyzing information packages, although at this time, misuse of metadata (e.g., addition of keywords that are popular words but have nothing to do with the content of the site) has kept search engines from making use of it. Properly used, though, metadata can include information about nontextual parts of a site, information about the site's purpose and history, information about the contents of the site, and the like.

There is software that automatically classifies and indexes electronic documents, but automated tools categorize information differently than people do. The search site Yahoo! classifies by broad subject areas using human indexers. This approach has been popular, although not completely successful as a classification. A research project at OCLC is improving an approach to automatic classification using the Dewey Decimal Classification. Researchers for "Infomine" (digital library) are developing systems to automatically assign Library of Congress Classification and Library of Congress Subject Headings.

Although some believe that organizing the Internet is impossible, the parts of it that are important for retrieval and for posterity will be brought under organizational control. It is human nature, and the principles learned over centuries of organizing print information can be used to speed the process of organizing electronic resources. The current effort to create a "Semantic Web," wherein data on the Web will be defined semantically and linked to relevant data for the purpose of more effective discovery of information, is a case in point.

Digital Libraries

The Internet has given us the means for creating digital libraries and for making them accessible. Digital libraries vary greatly in content and methods of organization; all have some kind of organization, although not necessarily traditional library organization. Just exactly what can be called a "digital library" has been a matter of debate. Throughout the 1990s there were many experiments that were referred to as digital libraries. For example, at the simplest level were collections of links to resources related to a particular subject; sometimes, such "collections" (really bibliographies) were coordinated among individual librarians at cooperating institutions in such a way that a particular library would agree to cover certain subject areas, and then the locations of all the collections of URLs were brought together on reference Web pages at each institution. But "digital library" quickly came to mean collections in which a site provides digitized information resources with an architecture and a service for the retrieval of such resources. By the mid-1990s it was recognized that a digital library must contain an organized collection, which may be partly physical, but is at least partly or wholly electronic; it is not exclusively a set of pointers to other material; and it must be created for a particular audience, group of users, or community.

Moving into the twenty-first century, Christine Borgman stated: "Digital libraries are an extension, enhancement, and integration both of information retrieval systems and of multiple information institutions, libraries being only one. The scope of digital libraries' capabilities includes not only information retrieval but also creating and using information."[4] She emphasized that digital libraries are for communities of users and that they are really extensions of the physical places where resources are selected, collected, organized, preserved, and accessed, including libraries, museums, archives, and schools.[5] This is echoed in a white paper sponsored by Sun Microsystems that defines a digital library as "the electronic extension of functions users typically perform and the resources they access in a traditional library."[6] This paper emphasizes the importance of digital libraries in the growth of distance learning. Distance alternatives for lifelong learning require that libraries evolve to fit this new paradigm or become obsolete. The authors liken the use of "digital library" to the use of "horseless carriage" and state that digital library technologies are becoming essential enablers of the provision of information services, extending and enhancing the traditional provision of these services in society.[7]

During the 1990s many experimental digital library projects were funded by such agencies as the U.S. National Science Foundation and the U.K. Joint Information Systems Committee. They worked to remove technical and distance barriers from the provision of access to all kinds of information and irreplaceable artifacts. The British Library's "Electronic Beowulf Project" digitized the eleventh-century manuscript of *Beowulf.* Elsewhere, specialized cameras with filters (developed by Eastman Kodak for the space program) were used to create images of the Dead Sea Scrolls and to reveal characters in those manuscripts that were previously invisible due to deterioration. Audio recordings of historic speeches or exotic sounds from nature, along with video clips from television and movies, advanced geospacial data renderings, and so forth, can now be accessed by students and researchers from their desks. These new capabilities were collected into digital libraries and organized. Issues of digitization, rights management, preservation, and metadata encoding were addressed.

The first digital libraries were custom developments, as there were not yet any off-the-shelf software packages. For example, the University of California at Berkeley has had several projects that have contributed to digital library innovations. One project created specifications for encoding electronic finding aids for special collections and archives. This project was the basis for what has become the Encoded Archival Description (EAD). Another project was the Making of America II project, proposing a standard encoding for digital objects. This has evolved into the Metadata Encoding and Transmission Standard (METS).[8]

Another example is Cornell University, which has been recognized for having undertaken an aggressive digitization program, digitizing such items as primary sources of nineteenth-century American culture and history, audio recordings of rare birdcalls, and works drawn from the university library's rare book collection. The digital library program is establishing a central repository for all these digitized resources with the aim of supporting the total lifecycle of those resources.[9]

"Infomine" is an example of a digital library created by cooperating librarians from several academic libraries.[10] At its Web site, Infomine is described as a "virtual library of Internet resources," although it includes resources on CD-ROM in its retrievals. The system has nearly 170 librarians who create "expert created records." The system also has automatic and semiautomatic metadata generation of records retrieved by Web crawlers.

As mentioned above, development projects include work toward automatic assignment of Library of Congress Classification and Library of Congress Subject Headings.

Another example of a cooperative project is the program of the museum community that resulted in the Art Museum Image Consortium (AMICO). As museums increased their digitizing projects, they found that they needed help with the increasing amounts of time required to meet demand from students and researchers. AMICO operates a digital library that includes multimedia objects that portray fully documented works of art from member institutions.[11]

As the emphasis is shifting from experimentation to mainstream implementation, focus is changing to emphasize standardization, organization, usability, and production of commercially available packages to be used by institutions just entering the digital library arena. Several library automation companies offer digital library solutions, and some multimedia management technology companies offer packages that include distance education course development (with inclusion of the means to create digital library support for a course or set of courses). For example, Endeavor Information Systems, creator of the "Voyager" integrated library system, offers "ENCompass," a package including the means to accomplish object management, collection management, license and rights management, linking, and search and discovery.[12] Similar products are offered by Ex Libris, Sirsi, and VTLS.[13] An example of a generalized multimedia management system's product is Artesia Technologies' "TEAMS" product, which is described as a "digital asset warehouse." It allows the integration of media files with Web content management, digital rights management, customer relations management, and e-learning.[14]

Organization of digital libraries is being accomplished with such tools as metadata, XML/RDF schemas, ontologies, and taxonomies. These are described in later chapters of this book. Provision of access to digital libraries is increasingly through "portals" that give access through a unified user interface to disparate sets of information sources. Portals provide users with a way to locate all the information content that they have the authority to access. The portal server presents an authentication screen to the user; if the user name and password are accepted, the user can have access to whatever resources are allowed by the user's status. An academic institution, for example, may have licenses for its users to access many different digital databases. Formerly, one had to learn the access protocol for each database and enter a different user ID and password. Through the controlled access of a portal, an authorized user may be able to search these databases by just clicking to enter them, and may even be able to search several of them at once. A library portal may have access links for local resources, remote resources, reference help, and personal patron information, for example. Local resources may be divided into books, journals, databases, digital collections, and course reserves, and all of these may be accessible through searching the catalog. Remote resources may contain links to other libraries, subscription databases, remote digital libraries, or Web-accessible resources. Reference help may include online reference tools, links to online search engines, and a virtual reference desk with either real-time or e-mail access to a reference librarian. Personal patron information may include lists of materials borrowed, saved searches, and personalized alerts.

Information Architecture

Just as architects must determine the needs of the people who will use a space and then create a pattern that will fulfill those needs in order to design buildings or other structures that will serve people's needs in addition to being beautiful, so must information architects determine the uses to which information will be put and create patterns for paths to finding needed information in addition to creating attractive interfaces to the information. Information architecture, then, is much more than Web design, but its development and emergence as a "field" is closely associated with the creation of Web sites. Andrew Dillon defines information architecture as "the term used to describe the process of designing, implementing and evaluating information spaces that are humanly and socially acceptable to their intended stakeholders."[15] He says he purposely leaves the definition "open so that we cover the organizational, blueprinting, and experience aspects, and allow for IA [i.e., information architecture] roles to cover these aspects."[16] There is still disagreement in this emerging field about what is covered, but there does appear to be some agreement upon a desire to manage documents and provide easy access to information based upon a design of user experience, including interface and navigation systems as well as useful and pleasing graphic design.

Information architects reject the notion that information architecture is a new approach to the organization of information that has been practiced in libraries, archives, and museums for a long time. But the parallels are striking. Librarians have long understood the necessity of selectively acquiring information packages and then organizing them in ways that will aid users in gaining access to them as needed (even though one may not know all future uses to which the information may be put). In 1998 Louis Rosenfeld and Peter Morville identified the following as the job of the information architect:

- Clarifies the *mission* and *vision* for the site, balancing the needs of its sponsoring organization and the needs of its audiences.

- Determines what *content* and *functionality* the site will contain.

- Specifies how users will find information in the site by defining its *organization, navigation, labeling,* and *searching systems.*

- Maps out how the site will accommodate *change* and *growth* over time.[17]

By 2002 the situation had evolved enough that Rosenfeld and Morville expanded their explanation to say that the process of information architecture must go through the following phases: research, strategy, design, implementation, and administration.[18] *Research* includes a review of background materials, gaining an understanding of the goals and context of the organization, examining the existing information architecture, content, and intended audiences, and finally conducting studies necessary to explore the situation. *Strategy* arises from contextual understanding developed in the first phase and defines the top levels of the site's organization and navigation structures, while also considering document types and metadata schema. *Design* involves creating detailed blueprints, metadata schema, and the like, to be used by graphic designers, programmers, content authors, and the production team. *Implementation* is where designs are used in the building, testing, and launching of the site—organizing and tagging documents, troubleshooting, and developing documentation occur in this phase. *Administration* involves the continuous evaluation and improvement of the site's information architecture. The strategy and design phases are the ones that require a thorough understanding of the theoretical underpinnings of the organization of information, including understanding of metadata; provision of access points with all the attendant relationships among them; subject approaches by categories, classification, or alphabetical labels; and the system design that will allow display of results in a logical and usable fashion (i.e., the principles covered in the rest of this book).

Data Administration

Data administration is the terminology applied to the control of the explosion of electronic information in offices and other administrative settings. It has its roots in the office filing systems that developed throughout the twentieth century. These systems have been highly affected by developments in technology—typewriters, photocopiers, and computers (starting with sorters and collators)—and are often referred to as records management systems. Records management systems are often related to archives, as that is where an organization's records may be deposited when their useful operating life has passed.

As was true in other parts of our society, data administration once involved the keeping, filing, and maintaining of paper records. It was a simpler time, but also a frustrating time, because usually only one copy of a record was filed in only one place. The file labels of one records manager were not necessarily logical to the next. As information began being entered and stored in electronic files, access points (the file labels) became invisible. This was not an immediate problem as long as the people who developed the electronic files documented what was contained in them. The situation became more complicated when powerful personal computers began to allow persons to store and file their own information on their desktops. A problem of continuity developed when these personal files were abandoned.

For many years various operations were automated, each with its own system. For example, payroll, general ledger, accounts payable, inventories, and other such systems were automated separately. During the 1990s, integration of these systems took place with the result that the systems had many redundant data fields with little documentation of their content. These fields seemed to be meant to contain the same information, but what was actually there was often different (e.g., name given in full in the payroll file, but middle name shortened to an initial in the faculty file). The situation is being solved by database management systems such as Oracle, which has software that accomplishes data warehousing, data integration, security, and more.[19]

Data administrators have dealt with their information explosion by using principles of organization of information. The units that need to be organized in the administrative electronic environment are such things as directories, files, programs, and at another level, such things as field values. Organization can be by system (e.g., payroll, budget) or by type of record (e.g., person names, registration records). Data administrators must keep track of information that crosses system boundaries (e.g., person names cross boundaries when the same names are entered into several different files). There must be methods for handling concepts that have the same names but different purposes (e.g., the concept of "part-time" in a university can have different definitions depending upon whether one is talking about payroll, faculty, graduate students, or undergraduate students).

Keeping all these things straight is often done through a process called "data modeling." It can either be used as a precursor to database design or as a way to integrate the myriad systems developed over time by persons who are no longer with the corporate body. Data modeling designs a system using a series of related models. The process is to develop a conceptual model of the records management activity in the particular setting; then a logical model is developed that includes more detail; and finally, the logical model is translated into a physical data model that can be implemented as a database management system. If the data model is updated and adjusted to fit changes in the conceptual model, it can serve for a long time as the basis for the organization of information in an organizational setting.

A person's individual office organization is another matter. A major factor in one's personal office organization seems to be the use to which particular information packages will be put or have been put. For example, if an item is to be referred to in order to write a letter in the immediate future, it will be located at hand; items that have just been finished with will be filed. Also, the form of the package can be a determining factor: books may be shelved, while papers relating to the books may be placed in file folders. In one's electronic information store, it is necessary to develop electronic folders, subfolders, and so forth, if one is to be able to find a particular file again in the future. An important aspect of office organization is that some such office collections will be deposited in archives for posterity.

Knowledge Management

Everyone has heard the phrase "Knowledge is power." Originally, the phrase applied to individuals and implied that persons who increased their knowledge would be able to increase their power in society. During the 1980s it came to be understood that the same idea applied to organizations. At that time, there was much "downsizing" of organizations in order to reduce overhead and increase profits. In the process it became obvious that the organizations lost important knowledge as employees left and took their accumulated years of knowledge with them. In the same period there was much technological development that was seen at first as a way to save costs by replacing human workers. Again, though, the knowledge held and applied by the humans was not all replaced by the machines. For an organization to survive, knowledge is brought to bear in the challenges the organization faces. Management of that knowledge increases its "power."

Knowledge management came into being as an attempt to capture employees' knowledge with advanced technology so that the knowledge could be stored and shared easily. As people became overwhelmed with the increased availability of information through rapid technological developments such as the Internet, knowledge management took on the additional role of coping with the explosion of information. This same technology makes possible global sharing of the "managed knowledge" among dispersed subgroups of an organization.

Managing knowledge requires a definition of *knowledge,* a concept that has been discussed by philosophers for years without complete resolution. It has been characterized in several ways—for example, as residing in people's minds rather than in any stored form; as being a combination of information, context, and experience; as being that which represents shared experience among groups and communities; or as a high-value form of information that is applied to decisions and actions. R. D. Stacy makes the following observation: "Knowledge is not a 'thing,' or a system, but an ephemeral, active process of relating. If one takes this view then no one, let alone a corporation, can own knowledge. Knowledge itself cannot be stored, nor can intellectual capital be measured, and certainly neither of them can be managed."[20]

Dave Snowden observes that knowledge management started in 1995 with the popularization of ideas about tacit knowledge versus explicit knowledge put forward by Ikujiro Nonaka and Hirotaka Takeuchi.[21] Nonaka and Takeuchi postulated that tacit knowledge is hidden, residing in the human mind, and cannot be easily represented via electronics; but it can be made explicit to the degree necessary to accomplish a specific innovation.[22] They were describing a spiral process of sharing tacit knowledge with others through socializing, followed by listeners internalizing the knowledge, and then new knowledge being created to, in turn, be shared. Snowden says that it does not follow that all knowledge in people's minds could or should be made explicit. However, early knowledge management programs "attempted to disembody all knowledge from its possessors to make it an organizational asset."[23] Software programs were created and are being used for this purpose. For example, Knowledge Management Software from Novo Solutions claims to document internal procedures, provide a training tool for new employees, transfer employee knowledge, and create and update categorized and searchable knowledge management articles, among other things.[24] Lotus software from IBM claims to "capture, manage, evaluate, and reuse knowledge—driving responsiveness, innovation, efficiency and learning to make better decisions faster."[25] These and other such programs work to accomplish the following objectives: create knowledge repositories, improve knowledge access, enhance the knowledge environment, and manage knowledge as an asset. Core issues of concern to people in the organizing information business are those of describing, classifying, and retrieving what has been stored. In the context of knowledge management, this means that the organization's knowledge must be sorted out, labeled (i.e., described), and classified into different "subjects" or groups if it is to be retrieved when needed.

Most knowledge management so far has consisted of *content* management, which tends to focus on knowledge that has been made explicit without necessarily knowing what tacit knowledge is still "unmanaged." In order to move into the next generation of knowledge management, Snowden says we must recognize that knowledge can only be volunteered, not forced out. There is always more than can be told, and most important, human knowledge is contextual—that is, knowledge is triggered by circumstance. Snowden believes that the next stage of knowledge management requires understanding the *context* as well as the content.[26]

CONCLUSION

This chapter has discussed basic needs to organize, defined organization of information, and presented an overview of a number of different kinds of organizing environments. The following chapters discuss in more detail the processes that have been developed for the organization of information, those that are being worked on, and the issues that affect their implementation.

NOTES

All URLs accessed June 2003.

1. Clifford Stoll, *Silicon Snake Oil: Second Thoughts on the Information Highway* (New York: Doubleday, 1995), p. 193.

2. Ronald Hagler, *The Bibliographic Record and Information Technology,* 3rd ed. (Chicago: American Library Association, 1997), p. 13.

3. Charles A. Cutter, *Rules for a Dictionary Catalog,* 4th ed. (Washington, D.C.: Government Printing Office, 1904; reprint, London: The Library Association, 1962), p. 12.

4. Christine L. Borgman, *From Gutenberg to the Global Information Infrastructure: Access to Information in the Networked World* (Cambridge: MIT Press, 2000), p. 48.

5.   Ibid., p. 42.

6.   *Digital Library Technology Trends* (Santa Clara, Calif.: Sun Microsystems, 2002), p. 3. Available: http://www.sun.com/products-n-solutions/edu/whitepapers/pdf/digital_library_trends.pdf.

7.   Ibid., p. 35.

8.   Ibid., p. 28.

9.   Ibid., pp. 25–26.

10.   "Infomine: Scholarly Internet Resource Collections." Available: http://infomine.ucr.edu/.

11.   Ibid., p. 25.

12.   Information available at Endeavor's Web site: http://www.endinfosys.com/.

13.   Web sites for these vendors are: http://www.exlibris.co.il/, http://www.sirsi.com/, and http://www.vtls.com/.

14.   Artesia [Home page]. Available: http://www.artesia.com/.

15.   Andrew Dillon, "Information Architecture in JASIST: Just Where Did We Come From?" *Journal of the American Society for Information Science and Technology* 53, no. 10 (2002): 821. Also available: http://www.gslis.utexas.edu/~adillon/publications/jasisintro.pdf.

16.   Ibid.

17.   Louis Rosenfeld and Peter Morville, *Information Architecture for the World Wide Web* (Sebastopol, Calif.: O'Reilly, 1998), p. 11.

18.   Louis Rosenfeld and Peter Morville, *Information Architecture for the World Wide Web,* 2nd ed. (Cambridge, Mass.: O'Reilly, 2002), p. 212.

19.   Oracle. Available: http://www.oracle.com.

20.   R. D. Stacy, *Complex Responsive Processes in Organizations: Learning and Knowledge Creation* (New York: Routledge, 2001), as quoted in Dave Snowden, "Complex Acts of Knowing: Paradox and Descriptive Self-Awareness," *Bulletin of the American Society for Information Science and Technology* 29, no. 4 (April/May 2003): 24.

21.   Snowden, "Complex Acts of Knowing," p. 23.

22.   Ikujiro Nonaka and Hirotaka Takeuchi, *The Knowledge-Creating Company* (Oxford: Oxford University Press, 1995).

23.   Snowden, "Complex Acts of Knowing," p. 23.

24.   "Knowledge Management Software," Novo Solutions. Available: http://www.knowledgebasesolutions.com/i_knowledge_management_software.html.

25.   "Knowledge, Expertise, and Content Management Software," IBM. Available: http://www.lotus.com/lotus/offering4.nst/wdocs/knowledgehome.

26.   Snowden, "Complex Acts of Knowing," p. 24.

SUGGESTED READINGS

General

Clayton, Mark. "Library Stacks? No, That's My Office." *Christian Science Monitor* (July 16, 2002). Available: http://www.csmonitor.com/2002/0716/p16s01-lehl.html.

Gladwell, Malcolm. "The Social Life of Paper: Looking for Method in the Mess." *The New Yorker* (25 March 2002). Available: http://www.newyorker.com/printable/?critics/020325crbo_books.

Organization of Information in Libraries

Crawford, Walt. "The Card Catalog and Other Digital Controversies: What's Obsolete and What's Not in the Age of Information." *American Libraries* 30, no. 1 (January 1999): 52–58.

Hagler, Ronald. *The Bibliographic Record and Information Technology.* 3rd ed. Chicago: American Library Association, 1997. Chapter 1: "The History and Language of Bibliography."

Taylor, Arlene G. "The Information Universe: Will We Have Chaos or Control?" *American Libraries* 25, no. 7 (July/August 1994): 629–632.

Organization of Information in Archives/Manuscripts

Ellis, Judith, ed. *Keeping Archives.* 2nd ed. Port Melbourne, Australia: Thorpe, in association with the Australian Society of Archivists, 1993.

Fox, Michael J., and Peter Wilkerson. *Introduction to Archival Organization and Description: Access to Cultural Heritage.* The Getty Information Institute, 1998. Sections entitled "Theory" and "Workflow." Available: http://www.schistory.org/getty/index.html.

Miller, Fredric. "Archival Description." In *Reference Services for Archives and Manuscripts,* edited by Laura B. Cohen. Binghamton, N.Y.: Haworth Press, 1997, pp. 55–66.

Organization of Information in Museums/Art Galleries

Bearman, David. "Functional Requirements for Collections Management Systems." *Archival Informatics Technical Report* 1, no. 3 (Fall 1987): 1–87.

Bierbaum, Esther Green. "Records and Access: Museum Registration and Library Cataloging." *Cataloging & Classification Quarterly* 9, no. 1 (1988): 97–111.

Buck, Rebecca A., and Jean Allman Gilmore, eds. *The New Museum Registration Methods.* Washington, D.C.: American Association of Museums, 1998.

Organization of Information in the Internet

Berners-Lee, Tim, James Hendler, and Ora Lassila. "The Semantic Web." *Scientific American* 284, no. 5 (May 2001): 34–38, 40–43. Available: http://www.scientificamerican.com/article.cfm?articleID=00048144-10D 2-1C70-84A9809EC588EF21&catID=2.

Oder, Norman. "Cataloging the Net: Can We Do It?" *Library Journal* 123, no. 16 (1 October 1998): 47–51.

———. "Cataloging the Net: Two Years Later." *Library Journal* 125, no. 16 (1 October 2000): 50–51.

Organization of Information in Digital Libraries

Arms, William Y. *Digital Libraries.* Cambridge: MIT Press, 2000.

Borgman, Christine L. *From Gutenberg to the Global Information Infrastructure: Access to Information in the Networked World.* Cambridge, Mass.: MIT Press, 2000. Chapter 2: "Is It Digital or Is It a Library?", Chapter 5: "Why are Digital Libraries Hard to Use?", and Chapter 6: "Making Digital Libraries Easier to Use."

Digital Library Technology Trends. Santa Clara, Calif.: Sun Microsystems, 2002. Available: http://www.sun.com/products-n-solutions/edu/whitepapers/pdf/digital_library_trends.pdf.

Hodge, Gail. *Systems of Knowledge for Digital Libraries: Beyond Traditional Authority Files.* Washington, D.C.: Digital Library Federation, Council on Library and Information Resources, 2000.

Lynch, Clifford. "The Battle to Define the Future of the Book in the Digital World." *First Monday* 6, no. 6 (June 2001). Available: http://www.firstmonday.org/issues/issue6_6/lynch/index.html.

Organization of Information in Information Architecture

Dillon, Andrew. "Information Architecture in JASIST: Just Where Did We Come From?" *Journal of the American Society for Information Science and Technology* 53, no. 10 (2002): 821–823. Available: http://www.gslis.utexas.edu/~adillon/publications/jasisintro.pdf.

Robins, David. "Information Architecture, Organizations, and Records Management." *Records and Information Management Report* 17, no. 3 (March 2001): 1–14.

Rosenfeld, Louis, and Peter Morville. *Information Architecture for the World Wide Web.* 2nd ed. Cambridge, Mass.: O'Reilly, 2002.

Wyllys, R. E. "Information Architecture." Reading prepared for Information Technologies and the Information Profession, Graduate School of Library & Information Science, University of Texas at Austin, 2000. Last updated 28 June 2003. Available: http://www.ischool.utexas.edu/~wyllys/ITIPMaterials/InfoArchitecture.html.

Organization of Information in Data Administration

Atherton, Jay. "From Life Cycle to Continuum: Some Thoughts on the Records Management-Archives Relationship." *Archivaria* 21 (Winter 1985–1986): 43–51.

Ince, A. Nejat, Cem Evrendilek, Dag Wilhelmsen, and Fadil Gezer. *Planning and Architectural Design of Modern Command Control Communications and Information Systems: Military and Civilian Applications.* Boston: Kluwer Academic, 1997, pp. 90–98.

Kwasnik, Barbara H. "How a Personal Document's Intended Use or Purpose Affects Its Classification in an Office." In *Proceedings of the 12th Annual International ACM SIGIR Conference on Research and Development in Information Retrieval.* New York: ACM, 1989[?], pp. 207–210.

Mullins, Craig. *Database Administration: The Complete Guide to Practices and Procedures.* Boston: Addison-Wesley, 2002. Chapter 1: "What Is a DBA?" and Chapter 3: "Data Modeling and Normalization."

Shepherd, Elizabeth, and Geoffrey Yeo. *Managing Records: A Handbook of Principles and Practice.* London: Facet Publishing, 2003.

Weldon, J. L. "A Career in Data Modeling." *Byte* 22, no. 6 (June 1997): 103–106.

Organization of Information in Knowledge Management

Bhatt, G. D. "Knowledge Management in Organizations: Examining the Interactions Between Technologies, Techniques, and People." *Journal of Knowledge Management* 5, no. 1 (2001): 68–75.

Snowden, Dave. "Complex Acts of Knowing: Paradox and Descriptive Self-Awareness." *Bulletin of the American Society for Information Science and Technology* 29, no. 4 (April/May 2003): 23–28. Available: http://www.asis.org/Bulletin/Apr-03/BulletinAprMay03.pdf (this version is extracted and condensed from one that first appeared in *Journal of Knowledge Management* 6, no 2 [May 2003]: 100–111; a copy of the original is also available at http://www-1.ibm.com/services/files/complex.pdf).

CHAPTER 2

RETRIEVAL TOOLS

This chapter discusses retrieval tools, which are basic building blocks in the organization of recorded information, addressing the following questions: Why do we need retrieval tools? What are the basic retrieval tools, their formats, and their functions?

THE NEED FOR RETRIEVAL TOOLS

Retrieval tools are systems created for retrieving information. They contain records that are surrogates for information packages. That is, each surrogate record (also called a *description* or *metadata*) gives enough information, such as author, title, and date of creation, so that it can serve as a short representation of an information package. Surrogate records are arranged or retrieved by *access points*. An access point can be a name, title, or subject term chosen by an *indexer* (also called a *cataloger* in some settings). In online systems an access point can be almost any word in a record if keyword searching of every word (that is not a stopword) is allowed.

Retrieval tools are essential as basic building blocks for a system that will organize as much of the world's recorded information as possible. A dream of being able to provide access to all recorded information has existed since 1892, when Paul Otlet and Henri LaFontaine organized a conference to create Universal Bibliographic Control (UBC). They wanted to create a central file that would include surrogate records particularly for scientific articles in all the scientific journals of the world. The magnitude of the undertaking meant that new techniques different from conventional library practice had to be developed. As UBC evolved throughout the twentieth century, it came to mean that each country of the world would be responsible for creation of surrogate records for its information packages and would share those surrogate records with all other countries. The concept was extended also to authority control of the headings for names used as access points. A program of the International Federation of Library Associations and Institutions (IFLA) combined the ideals of UBC with the concept of making the records machine-readable. The many retrieval tools that have been developed as a result of Otlet and LaFontaine's dream have brought us closer to UBC.

THE BASIC RETRIEVAL TOOLS, THEIR FORMATS, AND THEIR FUNCTIONS

The basic retrieval tools discussed in this chapter are:

- bibliographies
  - pathfinders
- catalogs
- indexes
- finding aids
- registers
- search engines and directories

Databases and bibliographic networks have distinct roles in housing retrieval tools. They are discussed in Chapter 5, which addresses the topics of systems and system design.

Bibliographies

Bibliographies basically are lists of information packages. Bibliographies are essential to scholars and to those involved professionally with books and other sources of information (e.g., collectors, dealers, librarians), and are also useful sources of information for all serious readers. They bring together lists of sources based on subject matter, on authors, by time periods, and the like (see the more detailed list of these below). Some bibliographies include *annotations,* that is, brief notes indicating the subject matter or commenting on the usefulness of the information.

Bibliographies can be attached to a scholarly work and consist of the information packages that were consulted by the author of the work, or they can be completely separate entities—works in their own right. Each information package represented in the list has a short *description* (not to be confused with *annotation*). A typical description includes author, title, edition, publisher, place, and date of publication for a book or other such whole entity. For a part of a work, such as a journal article or a poem, one typically includes author, title, name of the larger work, volume (if applicable), date, and page numbers or other part designation. Some descriptions also include physical characteristics in the description.

In a bibliography each description usually appears in only one place, usually under the author of the work. The descriptions may be constructed according to various styles, one of which is chosen by the creator of the bibliography. Examples of some of the styles are:

- APA (American Psychological Association)[1]
  Mitchell, T. R., & Larson, J. R., Jr. (1987). *People in organizations: An introduction to organizational behavior* (3rd ed.). New York: McGraw-Hill.

- Chicago Manual of Style[2]
  Mitchell, Terence R., and James R. Larson, Jr. *People in Organizations: An Introduction to Organizational Behavior.* 3d ed. New York: McGraw-Hill, 1987.

- MLA (Modern Language Association)[3]
  Mitchell, Terence R., and James R. Larson, Jr. *People in Organizations: An Introduction to Organizational Behavior.* 3rd ed. New York: McGraw-Hill, 1987.

- Science (Scientific Style and Format)[4]
  Mitchell TR, Larson JR, Jr. 1987. People in Organizations: An Introduction to Organizational Behavior. 3d ed. New York: McGraw-Hill.

- Turabian[5]
  Mitchell, Terence R., and James R. Larson, Jr. *People in Organizations: An Introduction to Organizational Behavior.* 3d ed. New York: McGraw-Hill, 1987.

- Style Manual (U.S. Government Style Manual)[6]
  Mitchell, Terence R., and James R. Larson, Jr. *People in*

Organizations: An Introduction to Organizational Behavior. 3rd ed. (New York: McGraw-Hill, 1987).

Each bibliography has a particular focus or arrangement. The most common are:

- Subject: bibliographies gathering together publications or other information packages that are all about a particular subject (e.g., *The New Press Guide to Multicultural Resources for Young Readers*).[7]

- Author: bibliographies of all or some of the works of a particular author and sometimes including sources about the author (e.g., *A Bibliography of Jane Austen*).[8]

- Language: bibliographies of textual entities in which the text is a certain language (e.g., *An Extensive Bibliography of Studies in English, German, and French on Turkish Foreign Policy, 1923–1997*).[9]

- Time period: bibliographies listing all works that came to light in a particular time period (e.g., *British Women Writers, 1700–1850: An Annotated Bibliography of Their Works and Works About Them*).[10]

- Locale: bibliographies listing all information packages created in a particular location. This could be a large locale such as a whole continent, or a smaller locale such as a country, region, state, city, or community (e.g., *Area Bibliography of Japan*).[11] It could also be an institution, such as a bibliography of all the works of the faculty in a particular university.

- Publisher: bibliographies listing all of the products of a particular publisher (e.g., *The Stinehour Press: A Bibliographical Checklist of the First Thirty Years*).[12]

- Form: bibliographies listing information packages that appear in a certain form, format, or genre (e.g., videocassettes, electronic resources, poetry, biographies, etc.). These are virtually always combined with one of the other foci (e.g., *Maps and Mapping of Africa: A Resource Guide*).[13]

Two or more of these foci are often combined in bibliographies. For example, the title above that illustrates "language" is a combination of language, subject, and time period; the one illustrating "time period" is a combination of subject, locale, and time period; and the one illustrating "form" is a combination of form and locale.

Pathfinders

A special kind of bibliography in libraries is truly meant to be a retrieval tool. Reference librarians have created pathfinders for decades, although some creators of electronic pathfinders seem to think the idea originated in electronic form. Pathfinders are subject bibliographies with a special function in the library world. Each pathfinder focuses on the resources available in the defined setting for a user who wishes to pursue research in the specific subject area.

OCLC (Online Computer Library Center) has a facility for creating pathfinders in its Web interface. This has, for the first time, allowed easy sharing of pathfinders among libraries and has facilitated sharing of responsibility for creating pathfinders.

Catalogs

Catalogs provide access to individual items within collections of information packages (e.g., physical entities such as books, videocassettes, and CDs in a library; artists' works in an art museum; Web pages on the Internet; etc.). Each information package is represented by a description of the package that is somewhat longer than a bibliography description. The descriptions are assigned one or more *access points*. Literally, an access point can be almost any word in a record when keyword searching is used. However, the term *access point* is usually applied to a particular name, title, or subject that is listed on the record separately from the description. An access point is constructed in a certain order (e.g., surname followed by forename or forenames), and it is maintained under authority control. *Authority control* is the process of pulling together all the forms of name that apply to a single name; all the variant titles that apply to a single work; and all the synonyms, related terms, broader terms, and narrower terms that apply to a particular subject heading.

The descriptions are constructed according to a standard style selected by a particular community (e.g., *AACR2* for libraries, some archives, and some museums; GILS for some government information; the Dublin Core for Internet information packages; etc.). Several different standards for description are discussed in more detail in Chapter 7.

Purposes of Catalogs

Catalogs have traditionally served two main groups. One group is employees of the institution who need to retrieve information packages or visual images or objects, or who need to retrieve information about those packages. For example, the catalog is used by collection development librarians in their process of discovering what the library already owns or does not own before ordering new acquisitions; another such use is by the employee of a museum who is looking for objects to place in an exhibit.

The most commonly thought-of use for a catalog, though, is use by patrons of the institution who wish to borrow material or make use of it on the premises. If such users have a known work in mind, they may search for it in the catalog by author or title (called *known-item searching*). If the catalog is online, users might also search by keyword if they only remember certain words of the title, for example. If users know they want works of a particular author, they may search under the author's name. If users do not know of a particular work but are searching for something on a particular topic, they may use a subject search or a keyword search of subject headings and/or titles.

In online catalogs keyword searches are useful for helping a person find a record that looks like it might be on the user's topic, and then identifying from that record an authority-controlled subject heading for the topic or a classification notation for the topic. One may then do a subject search for the subject heading or may go to the location of the classification notation in the stacks to determine if there are pertinent works shelved with the one that has been identified. Some catalogs also allow a call number search of a classification notation so that one can see all the works that have been given that classification.

Charles Cutter gave his "objects" of a catalog in 1904, speaking only of library catalogs in which books were represented. These "objects," if broadened to archives, museums, and the like, still seem to represent what catalogs are supposed to do. Cutter said that a catalog should be able:

1. To enable a person to find a book of which either:

    (A) the author
    (B) the title   } is known.
    (C) the subject

2. To show what the library has

    (D) by a given author
    (E) on a given subject
    (F) in a given kind of literature.

3.   To assist in the choice of a book

(G)   as to the edition (bibliographically).
(H)   as to its character (literary or topical).[14]

Another important purpose served by catalogs has traditionally been to act as an inventory of the collection—that is, to provide a record of what is owned. Often a *shelflist* has been used to accomplish this purpose. A shelflist includes one copy of every record in a catalog arranged in the order in which the information packages, objects, and so forth, are arranged on the shelf. Originally, shelflists were literally in the order of items on the shelf, starting a new sequence with each change in format, or change in collection location, or change in size. Later, shelflists often were arranged by classification notation regardless of format or other categorization. This is the way the concept works in online catalogs. The purpose of serving as an inventory is still there, but the mental image of a "shelf list" with arrangement as it is on the shelf is lost.

The shelflist function is very fuzzy when Internet resources are added to a catalog. When Internet resources are added, the institution may have purchased the right to make them accessible to the users, but they are not owned by the institution. With paper serials in a library, the library has always had control of how many years of back issues were kept. With Internet resources, whether right to access has been purchased or not, there is no control over how long the information will be available on the Internet, or whether it will remain at the same URL.

A *union catalog* is a variation of the concept that a catalog represents just the holdings of one institution. A union catalog represents the holdings of more than one institution or collection. A union catalog of a main library and its branches, for example, shows items that may be held in one or more branches in addition to those held in the main library. The location information indicates where an item is held. A union catalog of a consortium of institutions works the same way; location information shows which items are housed in which of the cooperating institutions. The ultimate union catalog is one maintained by a bibliographic network (see description in Chapter 5). The largest of these is OCLC, where each information package has one master record, and associated with the record is a holdings record that shows the holding symbol of each member of the network that has cataloged the package through OCLC or has asked that its symbol be added to the record.

In keeping with the ideals of UBC, the Internet may ultimately serve as a giant union catalog for the world. With the use of the Z39.50 protocol that allows users to search many online catalogs using the commands with which they are familiar, great progress has been made in searching for information not found locally. (Z39.50 is a national standard that defines a protocol that allows one computer to query another computer and transfer search results without the user having to know the search commands of the remote computer. It is described in more detail in Chapter 5.) However, a user now often has to search one catalog after another. As more sophistication develops in adding catalogs to the Internet, there may eventually be a seamless interface among catalogs, so that one can concentrate on the search instead of having first to decide which catalogs to search.

Forms of Catalogs

Catalogs can have different formats from catalog to catalog. The formats discussed here are:

- book

- card

- COM (Computer Output Microform)

- OPAC (Online Public Access Catalog)

Book Catalogs. Book catalogs originally were just handwritten lists. After the invention of printing with moveable type, book catalogs were printed, but not always in a discernible order. Eventually, entries were printed in alphabetical or classified order, but they were very expensive and could not be reproduced and updated often. In the early 1900s book catalogs were almost completely replaced with cards that updated the catalog as soon as they were filed and were relatively inexpensive. Book catalogs had a brief renaissance in the 1960s and 1970s when (1) computers again made it easy and less expensive to make book catalogs; (2) large card catalogs became unwieldy; and (3) rapid growth of new libraries and new branches made it desirable to have multiple copies of catalogs. But in order to keep a book catalog up-to-date, supplements were usually produced, resulting in multiple look-ups for one search. In addition, it was usually three to six months before supplements were produced, meaning that new materials were not represented in the catalog during that time.

Online catalogs have replaced both book and card catalogs in most situations, but book catalogs are still used for catalogs of exhibits, artists' works, subject archives, and so forth. Book catalogs provide a way to make the contents of special collections known to users in many locations. For example, book catalogs of historical societies are popular acquisitions by collectors of genealogical materials. This use, though, may be replaced by availability of such catalogs on the Web. Book catalogs also still exist in some libraries and archives as the only access to older materials.

An advantage of book catalogs over online catalogs and Internet versions of online catalogs has been that book catalogs are compact and portable and can be consulted anywhere they can be carried. (However, with laptop computers and wireless technology, online catalogs become equally accessible.) In addition, scanning a page of book catalog entries is relatively fast, and many people prefer this to scrolling through screen after screen of online responses.

Card Catalogs. Card catalogs were popularized in the United States by Library of Congress (LC) cards, first made available for sale in 1901, and by H. W. Wilson cards, which began production in 1938 in response to the needs of small libraries. (Both have now ceased card production.) Technological advances encouraged further use of the card catalog. First, typewriters made handwritten cards unnecessary. Offset printing was used by LC for its cards. Then photocopying allowed the local creation of whole card sets from one master card. Finally, the advent of computer printing made it possible to have customized cards made either locally or at a distant facility. When created at a distance, the cards were shipped to the receiver in boxes already alphabetized and ready to file.

Because of the influence of LC cards, card catalogs and the order of information on cards in libraries have been standardized for several decades. Users of card catalogs could go from library to library, using catalogs with confidence that they would be able to use distant catalogs with as much ease as their local ones.

Online catalogs have replaced most card catalogs in the United States, but some libraries, archives, museums, and art galleries still have card catalogs, especially small institutions or those where there has been only minimal conversion of data to machine-readable form. In many other countries there are more card catalogs.

COM Catalogs. The creation of Computer Output Microform (COM) catalogs became possible in the 1960s. They are produced on either microfiche or microfilm and require a microform reader in order to be able to use them. They are produced like book catalogs, to some extent. However, because they do not have to be reproduced on paper and be bound, they can be completely reproduced with new additions every three months or so without having to go through the supplement stage.

COM catalogs have been replaced rather quickly by online catalogs. It has been found that users will use microfilm if that is the only way to get the information they need, but most people find the readers hard to use and difficult to read.

OPACs. Online Public Access Catalogs (OPACs) are the predominant form of catalog in the United States and in a number of other countries today. In these catalogs records are stored in computer memory or on CD-ROM discs. The records are displayed only as needed. There is much flexibility in the "look" of the displays. Online catalogs have not yet been standardized, although in two or more institutions that have purchased the same system, the displays look somewhat similar. But without Z39.50, searching an unfamiliar online catalog can be daunting. Writers in the field have called for standardization, so that patrons can move from catalog to catalog or search multiple catalogs from the same location and find records displayed in the same manner.[15]

Arrangements Within Catalogs

The records within catalogs must be arranged in some fashion or they are unusable. In card catalogs, records are arranged by being filed in a certain order. In book and COM catalogs, records are arranged by being printed one after another in a certain order. Records in OPACs are arranged internally within the database either in sequence of order of entry into the system or in random order. So the "arrangement" discussed here applies to the arrangement of the displayed responses to search queries in the case of OPACs.

In general there are three basic arrangements that make sense to users, although there are many variations. Catalog records can be in classified order, in alphabetical order, or in chronological order. Within the basic order, display of records can be further subarranged in one of these same orders, or others.

Classified. Classified catalogs usually have more than one section. In what is considered to be the main section of the catalog, the arrangement or display is in the order of the classification scheme used in that institution. That is, this part is arranged in subject order, where the subject is represented by a classification notation. There can be as many classification notations assigned to a single record as there are subject concepts in the information package. Classified catalogs have the advantage that users can look at records for broader and narrower concepts at the same place they are looking for records on a specific concept. In a way it is similar to browsing in the stacks with a classification notation, except that in the case of the classified catalog, each information package is represented by several notations representing all of its concepts, not just one, as is true of items in the stacks.

As it is nearly impossible for anyone to know all the classification notations relating to a subject, there should be a section of the catalog that lists verbal representations of all topics and gives the notation for that topic. In some situations this function is provided by placing a copy of the classification schedule at the catalog. And, of course, there are users who want to search for authors and/or titles, so there should be another section of the catalog for these. In book, card, or COM catalogs, these subject, author, and title sections are arranged in alphabetical order. In OPACs they are word-searchable and the order of displays varies.

Classified catalogs have traditionally been used in European and other countries where several languages are spoken and represented in the setting. The classified subject section of the catalog can include records for every language represented, several languages being interfiled at the same classification notation. The sections of the catalog that give access to subject terms, authors, and titles can be in the language(s) appropriate to the clientele. The United States has not traditionally felt the need for this approach. Among the reasons the concept is being reconsidered today is that access to catalogs on the Internet is global, and a classified catalog can hold and display records in any language with classification notations that are universal. If indexes to a classified catalog are made in many languages, access can be gained through one of many languages. In addition, it makes browsing and broadening and narrowing of searches easy, which is especially helpful for inexperienced online users.

Alphabetical. Early American catalogs were arranged by broad subject categories in alphabetical order. With a collection consisting of a few books there was little need for elaborate classification or arrangement. As catalogs grew, the broad categories needed to be subdivided, so somewhat narrower categories were created and placed alphabetically within each broad category. For example, if the broad category were domestic animals, the subcategories under it might be cats, cows, dogs, horses, mules, and so forth. These were called "alphabetico-classed" catalogs. As subject categories multiplied, it became more difficult to predict the subject category and where it would be found. It began to make sense to place all subcategories in alphabetical order regardless of class. Charles Cutter was instrumental in the development of what he called the "dictionary" catalog. He recommended alphabetical arrangement with authors, titles, and subjects all interfiled in the same file.

The dictionary card catalog was the standard for the first half of the twentieth century. Later, catalogs in large libraries became complicated to file new cards into because of size. Attempts to break up the large files resulted in "divided" catalogs. They were sometimes divided into two files and sometimes into three files. If there were two files, they were divided so that authors and titles were in one and subjects were in the other. In three files, the division was authors, titles, and subjects. In the author/title/subject arrangement, records for works about a person were often filed in the subject file, while records for works the person wrote were filed in the author file. However, it was considered useful to keep records for works by and about a person together, so sometimes all *names* were placed in one file rather than just authors being placed in that file. The divided catalog was easier and less expensive for the keepers of the catalog, but assumed that users knew the difference among author, title, and subject entries, which was not always the case.

With the development of OPACs in the 1980s the divided catalog was moved online. One usually had to search either by author or by title or by subject. In this case, though, it was seldom possible to retrieve works both by and about a person in the same search. In some ways the sophistication that had been achieved in card catalogs was abandoned. For example, one could not have criticisms of a work displayed with editions of that work, and at first there were no references from unused forms of names and topics to the used forms. Many catalogs still do not allow searches for works both by and about a person, both editions of a work and its criticisms, or other more sophisticated searching, although efforts are being made to improve this situation.

Chronological and other. Displays are not now always in alphabetical order, although searches for *specific* authors or titles generally bring up alphabetical displays. However, subject and keyword search display results are often in chronological order, usually latest first, although when choice of arrangement is given, reverse chronological order (i.e., earliest first) may be offered. Many systems now allow users a choice of the order in which the results are to be displayed. Among the choices offered for an alphabetical display may be whether to arrange by author or by title. Improvements of this sort are gradually being added to online catalogs.

Indexes

Indexes provide access to the analyzed contents of information packages (e.g., articles in a journal, short stories in a collection, papers in a conference proceeding, etc.). Although back-of-the-book indexes also provide access to the analyzed contents of one work, they are not retrieval tools in the sense defined here; they are prepared at the time of publication of the work, not at a later time in an effort to provide bibliographic control. They do, however, aid with retrieval of the information found in the text at hand. Indexes that are retrieval tools give access in a tool separate from the information package being analyzed to smaller works included in that information package. Such indexes often do not have authority control of names, although most publishers of indexes use a thesaurus for selection of terms to stand for subject concepts.

Indexes are not limited to what is available in a local setting, and they do not usually give location information as such. They do give, as part of the surrogate record, the larger work in which the smaller work can be found. It is then necessary for a user of the index to search a catalog for the location of the larger work. If the larger work is not found in the local catalog, the user may search a union catalog or take a request to Interlibrary Loan (ILL).

Indexes can be found in print form or in machine-readable form—either CD-ROM or online. Some print versions are arranged in alphabetical dictionary fashion, with entries for authors, titles, and subjects. (See Figure 2.1.) Others are "divided," having an author/title part separate

Archives

> *See also*
> Local history and records
> Manuscripts

Carr, D. A Community Mind [As generated and maintained by our cultural institutions] bibl f *Public Libr* v41 no5 p284-8 S/O 2002

> . . .

Automation

> *See also*
> Online catalogs
> Retrospective conversion

Brown, A. J. E. and others. When Images Work Faster than Words: The Integration of Content-Based Image Retrieval with the Northumbria Watermark Archive. bibl f diag il *Restaurator* v23 no3 p187-203 2002

Gilliland-Swetland, A. J. Popularizing the finding aid: exploiting EAD to enhance online discovery and retrieval in archival information systems by diverse user groups. (In Ecoded Archival Description on the Internet. Haworth Information Press 2001 p199-225) bibl f tab

Needham, L. The development of the online archive catalogue at the University of Birmingham using CALM 2000. il *Program* v36 no1 p23-9 2002

Fig. 2.1. Sample entry from the printed version of the index *Library Literature & Information Science: 2002.* **(Source:** *Library Literature & Information Science: 2002* **[New York: H. W. Wilson, 2003], p. 27.)**

from the subject index. Both CD-ROM and online indexes have interfaces that dictate how these will be searched and how displays will appear. (See Figures 2.2 and 2.3.) As with OPACs there is no standardization from index to index. Although OPACs at least often have the standardization that comes from using the *Anglo-American Cataloguing Rules,* 2nd ed. *(AACR2),* there is no standard commonly used by the various indexes. The National Information Standards Organization (NISO) tried to update Z39.4–1984, "Basic Criteria for Indexes,"[16] but committees could not come to agreement with the American Society of Indexers, and so Z39.4 was withdrawn in 1996.

Indexes tend to be created by for-profit organizations. Often there is a charge for using the online versions directly. The print versions are sold, usually to libraries, or libraries pay for the right to allow their

In Database: Library Lit&Info Science 12/84-4/03

TITLE: Popularizing the finding aid: exploiting EAD to enhance online discovery and retrieval in archival information systems by diverse user groups
AUTHOR(S): Gilliland-Swetland,-Anne-J
SOURCE: In: Encoded Archival Description on the Internet Haworth Information Press, 2001. p. 199-225
DESCRIPTORS: Archives-Automation; Archives-Cataloging; End-user-searching
DOCUMENT TYPE: Book-Chapter

Fig. 2.2. Short view of Gilliland-Swetland entry from Figure 2.1, as it appears in the online index for *Library Literature & Information Science.*

In Database: Library Lit&Info Science 12/84-4/03

TITLE: Popularizing the finding aid: exploiting EAD to enhance online discovery and retrieval in archival information systems by diverse user groups
AUTHOR(S): Gilliland-Swetland,-Anne-J
SOURCE: In: Encoded Archival Description on the Internet Haworth Information Press, 2001. p. 199-225
PUBLICATION YEAR: 2001
PHYSICAL DESCRIPTION: bibl f tab
ISBN: 0789013975
LANGUAGE OF WORK: English
DESCRIPTORS: Archives-Automation; Archives-Cataloging; End-user-searching
DOCUMENT TYPE: Book-Chapter
UPDATE CODE: 20021105
ACCESSION NUMBER: 200201016100

Fig. 2.3. Long view of Gilliland-Swetland entry from Figure 2.1, as it appears in the online index for *Library Literature & Information Science.*

patrons to use the indexes online without the charge. Some libraries have both print and online access, although there seems to be a trend to continue only with the online versions. In any case the index often is cataloged so that the whole index can be found through the catalog.

Finding Aids

Finding aids are long descriptions of archival collections. A finding aid may also be called an inventory. Archives usually maintain control over collections of archival materials from personal or corporate sources, not over individual pieces. Thus a finding aid describes a collection. Some finding aids are published, and this is increasingly true as archives add finding aids to the Web. (See Figure 2.4.) The finding aid itself is often cataloged; that is, a surrogate record to be available in the institution's catalog is created describing the finding aid and providing name, title, and subject access points for it.

Home | Resources | Services | Information | Organization | Search This Site | Comments

Heinz House Papers

Finding Aid

- Scope and Contents Note

    o Search/Browse the Heinz House Papers

- Arrangement of the Heinz House Papers

- Description of the Heinz House Papers

- Appraisal and Sampling Note

- Appendices

May 2001 -- http://www.library.cmu.edu/Libraries/Heinz/House
Jennie Benford, University/Heinz Archivist, jbenford@andrew.cmu.edu

H. John Heinz III Archives

Carnegie Mellon University Libraries

Fig. 2.4. Introductory page for a finding aid found on the Web at: http://zeeb.library.cmu.edu/Libraries/Heinz/House.

Registers

Registers constitute the primary control tools for museums. A register may also be called an accession log. It functions like a catalog, although it has additional kinds of access points. The process of registration in a museum is much like the process of cataloging in a library. During the process, the registrar will identify the object, the donor, any associations (e.g., having belonged to a particular person), any information needed for insurance purposes, and so forth. An identification number is assigned. The accession record becomes the basis for one or more files that help provide organization of the museum's content.

Search Engines and Directories

Search engines are tools developed for computer systems, particularly the Internet, that find representations of requested words or phrases that can be found in the documents covered by the tool. They were developed for the purpose of searching full text documents for particular words or phrases. They may or may not provide results that are as intellectually satisfactory as the results from other retrieval tools, but users often report satisfaction because they find *something* related to what they were searching for and find it fast. But most users do not know if what they found is authentic, authoritative, or the best that is available on their topic. Searches for known items or for specific names are often somewhat less satisfactory than searches for topical information. Search engines are becoming more sophisticated, but there are still drawbacks such as no distinction among homographs and no connections for synonyms. Google[17] is one of the most sophisticated, both in giving searching assistance (e.g., asking, "Did you really mean to search for . . . ?" in response to a misspelled word) and in display of results.

Some search engines are specifically for searching a particular site, such as the site for an organization such as OCLC. Other search engines are for searching the whole Internet (although only a small percentage of the Internet is actually searched by each one). Each search engine collects a database of records automatically created by a program called a robot, agent, spider, or the like. Such a robot is typically programmed to go onto the Web to retrieve and download copies of certain target Web pages and everything linked to them, everything linked to the links, and so on. The robot's database is what is searched from the search engine's search box. Obviously, not every Web page on the Internet is searched by every search engine—thus, a variety of responses can be had from searching the various engines.

Display of results is usually arranged on a best-match basis. Best-match, or relevance, is calculated in various ways with different weightings given by search engines to such factors as how many search terms are found in each Web page or file; how often each term is found in a page or file; whether the terms are in proximity or dispersed; whether the terms are in metadata, at the top of the document, or buried further down; and how common (or not) a particular search term is. With the development of metadata, search engines have promise of more sophisticated retrieving. In addition, more sophisticated methods of calculating relevance are being developed. For example, Google uses a formula that includes how often a page is linked to by other pages.

Variations from basic search engines include directories and subject gateways. Yahoo!,[18] for example, adds human intervention to the creation of its database. Humans add subject terms and categorize the records into a directory-type structure. Searching can be by "drilling" down through the categories or by keyword. Some are organized according to traditional library classification (e.g., Cyberstacks),[19] but most are created anew by the persons who devise the directory. Comparison of the categories used by different directories will show that the hierarchies can be quite different from directory to directory.

Subject gateways are similar to directories but with a focus on a particular subject area. These are often constructed by academic libraries, sometimes working in groups, or by associations/organizations interested in a subject area and dedicated to providing information on the subject. Examples of the latter are "The Gateway to Educational Materials (GEM)"[20] and the Texas Medical Association's "Internet Gateway to Health Resource Links."[21]

CONCLUSION

A century ago Charles Cutter stated that catalogs should enable people to find books for which titles, authors, or subjects were known; should show what was available in a library by a particular author, on a particular subject, or in a kind of literature; and should assist in the choice of a book by its edition or character. A century later, Cutter's "objects" are still quite appropriate, except that they have been expanded to all kinds of information packages beyond just books in libraries, and to a number of different kinds of retrieval tools beyond catalogs. This chapter has discussed the major retrieval tools used in the organization and retrieval of recorded information. The surrogate records that make up a retrieval tool must be created and encoded, either by humans or programmed robots (programmed by humans). Chapters 6 through 11 address creating records for retrieval tools. But first, in the next chapter, a historical look at the development of organizing processes through a number of centuries serves to give us a perspective on where we are and how far we've come.

NOTES

All URLs accessed June 2003.

1. *Publication Manual of the American Psychological Association,* 4th ed. (Washington, D.C.: American Psychological Association, 1994).

2. *Chicago Manual of Style,* 14th ed. (Chicago: University of Chicago Press, 1993).

3. Walter S. Achtert and Joseph Gibaldi, *The MLA Style Manual* (New York: Modern Language Association of America, 1985).

4. *Scientific Style and Format: The CBE Manual for Authors, Editors, and Publishers,* 6th ed. (Cambridge, England; New York: Cambridge University Press, 1994).

5. Kate L. Turabian, *A Manual for Writers of Term Papers, Theses, and Dissertations,* 6th ed. (Chicago: University of Chicago Press, 1996).

6. U.S. Government Printing Office, *Style Manual* (Washington, D.C.: U.S. Government Printing Office, 1984).

7. Daphne Muse, ed., *The New Press Guide to Multicultural Resources for Young Readers* (New York: New Press; distributed by W. W. Norton, 1997).

8. David Gilson, *A Bibliography of Jane Austen* (Winchester, England: St. Paul's Bibliographies, 1997).

9. Mustafa Aydn and M. Nail Aikan, *An Extensive Bibliography of Studies in English, German, and French on Turkish Foreign Policy, 1923–1997* (Ankara, Turkey: Ministry of Foreign Affairs, Center for Strategic Research, 1997).

10. Barbara J. Horwitz, *British Women Writers, 1700–1850: An Annotated Bibliography of Their Works and Works About Them* (Lanham, Md.: Scarecrow Press, 1997).

11. Ria Koopmans-de Bruijn, *Area Bibliography of Japan* (Lanham, Md.: Scarecrow Press, 1998).

12.   David Farrell, *The Stinehour Press: A Bibliographical Checklist of the First Thirty Years* (Lunenburg, Vt.: Meriden-Stinehour Press, 1988).

13.   John McIlwaine, *Maps and Mapping of Africa: A Resource Guide* (New Providence, N.J.: Zell, 1997).

14.   Charles A. Cutter, *Rules for a Dictionary Catalog*, 4th ed. (Washington, D.C.: Government Printing Office, 1904; reprint, London: The Library Association, 1962), p. 12.

15.   For more about standardization in online systems as well as more about OPACs, see Chapter 5.

16.   *American National Standard for Library and Information Sciences and Related Publishing Practices—Basic Criteria for Indexes, ANSI Z39.4–1984* (New York: American National Standards Institute, 1984).

17.   Google. Available: http://www.google.com/.

18.   Yahoo! Available: http://www.yahoo.com/.

19.   McKiernan, Gerry, "CyberStacks(sm)." Available: http://www.public. iastate.edu/~CYBERSTACKS/homepage.html.

20.   GEM Project Site, "The Gateway to Educational Materials (GEM)." Available: http://www.geminfo.org/.

21.   Texas Medical Association, "Internet Gateway to Health Resource Links." Available: http://www.texmed.org/lis/gth.asp.

SUGGESTED READINGS

Buckland, Michael K. "What is a 'Document'?" *Journal of the American Society for Information Science* 48, no. 9 (September 1997): 804–809. Also available: http://www.sims.berkeley.edu/~buckland/whatdoc.html.

Cleveland, Donald B., and Ana D. Cleveland. *Introduction to Indexing and Abstracting.* 3rd ed. Englewood, Colo.: Libraries Unlimited, 2001. Chapter 1: "Introduction", Chapter 2: "The Nature of Information", Chapter 3: "The Organization of Information", and Chapter 5: "Types of Indexes and Abstracts."

Fox, Michael J., and Peter Wilkerson. *Introduction to Archival Organization and Description: Access to Cultural Heritage.* The Getty Information Institute, 1998. Section entitled "Practice." Available: http://www.schistory.org/getty/index.html

Gilster, Paul. *Digital Literacy.* New York: Wiley, 1997.

Inventories and Registers: A Handbook of Techniques and Examples. Chicago: Society of American Archivists, 1976.

Levy, David M. "Cataloging in the Digital Order." In *Digital Libraries '95: The Second Annual Conference on the Theory and Practice of Digital Libraries, June 11–13, 1995, Austin, Texas.* Available: http://www.csdl.tamu.edu/DL95/papers/levy/levy.html.

Library of Congress. *Manuscript Finding Aids.* Available: http://lcweb.loc.gov/rr/mss/f-aids/mssfa.html.

Matthews, Joseph R. "The Value of Information: The Case of the Library Catalog." *Technical Services Quarterly* 19, no. 2 (2001): 1–16.

"Report of the Working Group on Standards for Archival Description." *American Archivist* 52 (Fall 1989): 440–461.

Rowley, Jennifer, and John Farrow. *Organizing Knowledge: An Introduction to Managing Access to Information.* 3rd ed. Aldershot, England; Burlington, Vt.: Ashgate, 2000. Chapter 11: "The Internet and Its Applications."

Taylor, Arlene G. *Wynar's Introduction to Cataloging and Classification.* 9th ed., with the assistance of David P. Miller. Englewood, Colo.: Libraries Unlimited, 2000. Chapter 1: "Cataloging in Context" and Chapter 19: "Processing Centers, Networking, and Cooperative Programs."

CHAPTER 3

DEVELOPMENT OF THE ORGANIZATION OF RECORDED INFORMATION IN WESTERN CIVILIZATION

It is often said that you can't tell where you're going until you know where you've been. This chapter looks at where we've been and addresses these questions: How did we arrive at this state of organization? What basic principles of organization have been developed over the last several centuries? Practices and ways of organizing that we now take for granted were once thought of for the first time by intelligent and serious scholars, just as we are coming up with innovative ideas for today's organization that will be taken for granted in the next century.

INVENTORIES, BIBLIOGRAPHIES, CATALOGS, AND CODIFICATION

Antiquity

One of the oldest lists of books we know about appears on a Sumerian tablet found at Nippur from about 2000 B.C.E. Sixty-two titles are recorded on this tablet of which twenty-four are titles of currently known literary works. We don't know what purpose the list served. Its use may or

Much of the material in the first half of this chapter is based on Ruth French Strout, "The Development of the Catalog and Cataloging Codes," *Library Quarterly* 26, no. 4 (October 1956): 254–275.

may not have resembled that of a catalog. However, the fact that the Sumerians were indefatigable writers makes it hard to believe that they had no catalogs. They seem to have kept everything: history books, medical prescriptions, love poems, business invoices, schoolchildren's homework assignments, and the first-known letter home from a student who threatens to drop out of school unless his parents fork over more money for a suitable wardrobe.

Through the archaeological discoveries of excavations of ancient civilizations, we know that tablets and other resources were used to inscribe titles of books, but we don't know for what purpose. They might have been ownership tags (e.g., the ones that had the names of the king and queen and a title on each small plaque), or they might have been relics of something like a bibliography or a catalog. There are more remnants of early records from Babylonia than from Egypt, probably due to the fact that Babylonians wrote on clay tablets, while Egyptians wrote on papyrus.

Around 1500 B.C.E. the Hittites evidently saw the need to convey bibliographic information as part of a written work. Their tablets bore colophons that identified the number of the tablet in a series, its title, and often the name of the scribe. (A *colophon* is a set of data at the end of a "document" that gives varying kinds of bibliographic data. It might give information usually found on a title page, and, in items after the invention of printing with moveable type, it gives such information as date of printing, printer, typeface used, etc.)

Around 650 B.C.E. people in the city of Nineveh had developed a library in which they seem to have taken great care to preserve order and authenticity. The "documents" bore elaborate colophons, but there is no evidence of anything like a catalog.

Two of the great libraries of antiquity were in Pergamum and Alexandria—two active centers of Greek civilization. Later writings have referred to *Pinakes* from both libraries. *Pinakes* is plural of *pinax,* a word that means tray or dish. It is thought that such trays had slightly raised edges and that wax could be poured in the middle; when hardened, the wax could be written in with a stylus. If this was indeed the medium, it is no wonder that no remnants have survived. Writers have quoted from the Pinakes of Alexandria, which was created by Callimachus. The work may have been a catalog, or it may have been a bibliography of Greek literature. Callimachus has been given credit as being the first cataloger of whom we have knowledge.[1]

There are a few generalizations about bibliographic practices of the time that can be drawn from quotations of scholars who quoted from Callimachus's work. For example, a few general categories were considered to be a sufficient subject approach. Callimachus's subjects were epic and other nondramatic poetry, drama, law, philosophy, history, oratory, medicine, mathematical science, natural science, and miscellanea. A scholar would go to the general subject and then look for the author being sought. The arrangement of entries under the general subject was sometimes classified, sometimes chronological, and sometimes alphabetical, although the Greeks never arrived at a strictly alphabetical arrangement. They sometimes grouped entries by initial letter, but there are no examples of arrangement by any letter past the first one. This probably indicates that their lists were not nearly as long as ours.

Greek civilization seems to have given us the basis for our Western idea that "main entry" ought to be "the author." This kind of entry has not appeared in any work that has survived from early Eastern civilizations. Even today in Asian countries the traditional entry for a book is its title. One Japanese librarian of my acquaintance once observed that the principle of author entry goes along with democracy, since it rests upon belief in the importance of the individual.

Little information is available about Roman libraries. From sources that mention them, there is evidence that there was some way of finding a designated book when it was requested. This was probably through "fixed location." One story goes that if a nobleman got into an intellectual argument, he would send a servant to the library to retrieve a certain book that would prove his point.

Middle Ages

We know that during the Middle Ages in Europe there were church and monastery libraries. There was no demand for books, and knowledge was not sought in any way that would require the use of catalogs. Through copying by monks, a system was set up by which the monastery became the sole keeper, manufacturer, and finally, lister of books through many centuries.

One of the earliest listings of the holdings of a medieval library was dated in the eighth century. It was written on the final flyleaf of a book and consisted of a list of brief titles with authors added to some of them. It probably served as an inventory record and may have represented the shelf arrangement, although there were no location symbols accompanying the titles. This list was typical of most of the so-called catalogs of the following centuries—the briefest sort of inventories recorded in the most casual places.

From the ninth through the thirteenth centuries, the libraries continued to produce lists that seemed to be inventories. One list, which specified that its purpose was for inventory, stated that the library contained 246 volumes. It would be quite unrealistic to expect libraries of this size to feel any need for catalogs. Even after libraries grew to the size of 600 or 700 volumes, lists were still inventories. Occasionally such a list would use author entries, but in no discernible order. A few listed works contained in each volume, and the number of volumes to a work. (Books into which works were copied were often bound blank pages. Works were copied into them in the order in which the scribe picked them up. Several works could be copied into one bound blank volume, but it might take several bound volumes to copy a very long work.) In a few lists there was a subject arrangement, but it was very broad, often using only two categories: biblical and humanistic. At least one list from the thirteenth century added some unusual descriptions in designating books variously as "useless," "legible," "old," and "good," but we do not know whether they were used as an aid in identification for inventory or to help the reader by pointing out which books could be easily read.

Toward the end of the thirteenth century, someone whose identity is not known started a project that might be considered a milestone in the history of catalogs. This was the compilation of the *Registrum Librorum Angliae,* a union list of holdings of English monastery libraries in which, in a quite modern way, each library was assigned a number for coding purposes. The *Registrum* was never finished. There are evidences of later attempts to compile continuations of it, although no finished version has survived.

European Renaissance

The fourteenth century brought some improvements, and a few lists of this period might be called shelflists. The outstanding list of the fourteenth century is from St. Martin's Priory at Dover, dated 1389. In fact, it may be the first of the lists that could be justly designated a catalog. It is divided into three sections. The first is a listing by call number, a number representing fixed location even to the placing of the individual volume. The second section of the catalog, likewise arranged by call number, gives the contents of each volume, with the paging and opening words for each work included. The third part is a landmark in the development of cataloging: a catalog of analytical entries and an alphabetical listing, but with entries of the usual medieval type—some under author, others under title followed by author, with still other entries beginning with such words as *book, part,* or *codex,* obviously with no importance attached to the entry word. (An analytical entry is an entry made for each of the works in a volume, as opposed to making only one entry for the entire volume.)

College libraries began in the fourteenth century but did not bring any innovations to the development of bibliographic control. The earliest lists from college libraries revert to the primitive inventories of the preceding centuries. This is possibly explained by the fact that college library book collections were small; it was not unusual for a college library at that time to have only one hundred books.

The main new practice from the fifteenth century was the use of references. In one catalog, the references were not separate entries but were appended to a sort of contents note pointing out in what other place in the library a certain item might be found (e.g., "which seek in the 96th volume of theology"). In the catalog of St. Augustine's Abbey, Canterbury, though, references reached the status of separate entries. A typical example is: "The Meditations of Bernard, not here because it is above in the Bible which was given by W. Wylmynton."

In the middle of the fifteenth century came an event that challenged everything about bibliographic control—the invention of printing with moveable type. Suddenly, instead of unique manuscript copies of works, there were identical duplicates of many works. A new breed of people came into being for the task of listing the works available—people we might now call "bibliographers."

Toward the close of the fifteenth century, German bibliographer and librarian Johann Tritheim stands out as having taken an important step in the development of bibliographic control. He not only compiled a bibliography in chronological order, which was unusual enough for his time, but he also appended to this an alphabetical author index. It is difficult to understand why such a simple and useful device had not always been used; yet it took centuries of compiling book lists to reach this degree of accomplishment.

From Inventories to Finding Lists to Collocating Devices

Following the precedent set by Tritheim, bibliographers in the sixteenth century continued to take the lead in making improvements. One of these, Konrad Gesner, published an author bibliography in 1545 and a subject index in 1548, and in the process set a new standard of excellence. He continued to use forenames of authors for entry words, according to the tradition of the time, but he recognized the possible inconvenience of this practice and so he prefixed to his bibliography an alphabetical list of authors in which the names were inverted. In addition, his main listing included references from variant spellings of names to the accepted entry form (e.g., "Thobias, see Tobias"). Gesner included in his work (titled the

Pandectarum) the suggestion that libraries use copies of his bibliographies as their catalogs by inserting call numbers beside entries that represented their holdings, thus providing themselves with both an author and a subject catalog. This proposal, remember, was made in 1548.

In 1595, Andrew Maunsell, an English bookseller, compiled his *Catalog of English Printed Books* and in the preface stated his rules for entry. He advocated the entry of personal names under surnames rather than forenames. He set up the principle of uniform entry for the Bible, which, prior to Maunsell's collocating them, had been entered under whatever the title page said (e.g., Holy Bible, The Word of God, Bible, etc.). He insisted that one should be able to find a book under all three—the author's surname, the subject, and the translator. These were radical and sudden advances in the development of bibliographic control.

By the beginning of the seventeenth century, catalogs were beginning to be looked upon as finding lists rather than inventories. Early in the century Sir Thomas Bodley offered to build up the Oxford University Library, which had been destroyed by fire some fifty years before. Bodley took a great interest in the catalog because he expected that it would be useful in his acquisitions program; he wanted the catalog to tell him if the library already owned a work. He insisted upon a classified catalog with an alphabetical author index arranged by surname, and he also wanted analytical entries.

In 1697 Frederic Rostgaard published a discourse on cataloging in which he called for subject arrangement subdivided at once chronologically and by size of volume. For the preceding century, size of volume had been a traditional way of dividing catalogs. Rostgaard proposed a printed catalog, with the spread of two facing pages divided into four parallel columns, each column to contain books of a certain size, arranged so that books of various sizes that had been published on a certain subject within the same year would come directly opposite each other in parallel columns. He recommended an alphabetical index of subjects and authors to be placed at the end of the catalog, with authors entered by surname. The word order of titles as found on the title page was to be preserved. His final suggestion was that his rules not be followed when it seemed best to arrange things differently.

As the eighteenth century began, bibliographic control seemed to have hit a plateau that did not change for most of the century. Catalogs were sometimes classified and sometimes alphabetical; indexes were considered useful, though by no means necessary; some catalogs were still divided according to the size of books; authors were now always entered under surname and were often arranged chronologically; the wording of the title page had assumed a certain degree of prestige and was now being transcribed literally and without being paraphrased; imprints were included; bound-with notes were used; references were quite common; and some analytical entries were used in most catalogs.

In 1791, following the French Revolution, the new French government sent out instructions for cataloging the collections of the libraries that had been confiscated throughout the country. Here we have the first instance of a national code. Libraries were directed to make card catalogs— apparently the first appearance in history of the card catalog. It was introduced, not because someone thought it would be a convenient form, but because, with wartime shortages, it was a practical way of getting available materials. Confiscated playing cards were to be used for the purpose—aces and deuces were to be reserved for the longest titles. (Playing cards of the time were blank on the back, rather than having pictures. They were also larger than today's cards.) There was no theory or philosophizing in this code. The title page was to be transcribed on the card and the author's surname underlined for the filing word. If there was no author, a keyword in the title was to be underlined. A collation was added that was to include number of volumes, size, a statement of illustration, the material of which the book was made, the kind of type, any missing pages, and a description of the binding if it was outstanding in any way. (This elaborate collation was partly for the purpose of identifying valuable books that the government might offer for sale in order to increase government revenue.) After the cards were filled in and put in order by underlined filing word, they were to be strung together by running a needle and thread through the lower left corners to keep them in order.[2] Here we have a number of procedures that have continued to the present. This code, coming at the end of the eighteenth century, makes a good stepping-stone to the extensive cataloging developments of the nineteenth century.

Period of Codification

The nineteenth century brought a period of much argument over the relative virtues of classified and dictionary catalogs, not only among librarians, but also among readers and scholars in general and even in reports to the House of Commons of Great Britain. Feelings ran very high on the subject, and rather emotional arguments were made: "from the statement that classified catalogs and indexes were not needed because living librarians were better than subject catalogs, to the opinion that any intelligent man who was sufficiently interested in a subject to want to consult material on it could just as well use author entries as subject, for he would, of course, know the names of all the authors who had written in his field."[3]

What was needed was a person who could persuade others of the value of cataloging and subject analysis. That person turned out to be Anthony Panizzi, a lawyer and a political refugee from Italy who was appointed assistant librarian at the British Museum in 1831. When he was appointed Keeper of the Printed Books in 1837, there was much objection. One history book states that it was because "firstly, Panizzi was an Italian by birth, and it was felt that only an Englishman should be in charge of one of our national institutions; secondly, it was said that Panizzi had been seen in the streets of London selling white mice."[4] No further explanation is given. Another writer, though, gives this account: "Meetings were held against the 'Foreigner' and one of the speakers made an open statement that Panizzi had been seen in the streets of London selling white mice: had it been a few years later, possibly the distinctive title of organ-grinder would have been added."[5]

In 1836 a committee of the House of Commons was charged with inquiry into the management and affairs of the British Museum. One of the "affairs" was the state of catalogs and cataloging. During hearings on the topic, witnesses came to testify for and against the catalogs. Many of the witnesses became quite vehement about one or another sort of entry. Panizzi was able again and again to persuade the committee members to accept his views.

Panizzi wrote his views into a cataloging code known as the "91 Rules" and gained official approval for it in 1839, although he had to give up his concept of "corporate main entry" in order to get approval. Panizzi's code shows that we had at last arrived at "modern" cataloging, because he tried to deal with many of the same problems we are still arguing about today.

Halfway through the nineteenth century, cataloging in the United States began to warrant attention. Until this time American cataloging had been generally a century behind European cataloging. For example, of the three catalogs printed at Harvard, one had been divided into three alphabets according to the size of books; all three contained only very brief records; and none provided a subject approach.

In 1850 Charles C. Jewett published a code for the catalog of the Smithsonian Institution. With this code Americans began to have influence in cataloging. Jewett acknowledged his debt to Panizzi and varied in only a few instances from the instructions in the "91 Rules." Jewett is given credit for extending the principle of the corporate author further than Panizzi had. Research now shows that Jewett copied these rules word-for-word from Panizzi's original draft, which had had *more* than ninety-one rules.[6] Panizzi had been forced to drop his rules for entry under corporate author. So what Jewett actually did was to bring the concept of corporate authorship to public attention.

Jewett's philosophy of the purpose of a code was this: "*Uniformity* is, then, imperative; but, among many laborers, can only be secured by the adherence of all to rules embracing, as far as possible, the minutest details of the work."[7] In light of this philosophy, it is interesting to observe that the second edition of Jewett's rulebook contains only thirty-nine rules in fifty-eight pages.

When Charles Cutter published his *Rules for a Printed Dictionary Catalogue* in 1876, he strengthened the concept that catalogs not only should point the way to an individual publication, but should also assemble and organize literary units. That is, they should be collocating devices. This was not an entirely new principle: Maunsell had used the heading "Bible"; Panizzi had strengthened it by introducing corporate and government entries; and Jewett had given further support by use of real names rather than pseudonyms. But it was Cutter who actually stated it as a formal principle.

Cutter was also the first to make rules for subject headings as a way to gain subject access to materials through the catalog. And he was the last to incorporate into one set of rules instructions for the description of items, guidelines for subject headings, and rules for filing entries. At the end of the nineteenth century, each of these areas (i.e., description, subject headings, and filing) took on lives of their own and followed separate paths of development. We will now follow the first two paths separately. (Filing arrangement is discussed in Chapter 12.)

TWENTIETH CENTURY

Description

In the area of description, the twentieth century was an era of codes. The British and the Americans collaborated on a code in 1908. Its importance lies in its being the first international cataloging code, and in the extent of its rapid and widespread adoption and use by all types and sizes of libraries in the two countries.

In the 1920s four prominent American librarians helped with writing the Vatican Code, which was published in Italian in 1931. It was quickly accepted by catalogers in many countries as the best and most complete code in existence, but because it was in Italian, most Americans could not use it.

The British and Americans began cooperative work toward a new edition of the 1908 code in the 1930s, but the outbreak of war ended this cooperation. The American Library Association (ALA) proceeded independently in producing its preliminary second edition in 1941. This code was published in two parts: one for entry and heading, and one for description of books. It was widely attacked on the grounds of complexity and too-extensive enumeration of cases. The most famous attack was that of Andrew Osborn in his article titled "The Crisis in Cataloging."[8] It is one of the classic statements in cataloging theory, and certainly, one of the historical turning points in code development.

In response to all the criticism, the ALA Division of Cataloging and Classification undertook revision of the first part (entry and heading) of the 1941 code. In 1949 the revision was published as the *A.L.A. Cataloging Rules for Author and Title Entries*. The *Rules for Descriptive Cataloging*, published by the Library of Congress (LC), was substituted for the second part (description of books) of the 1941 rules. The ALA portion of the 1949 rules again was criticized as being a continuation of Osborn's "legalistic" characterization. In 1951 ALA commissioned Seymour Lubetzky to do a critical study of cataloging rules. Lubetzky said cataloging should be done according to principles, and he drafted a code based on principles. It was welcomed by progressives, but conservatives began worrying about probable costs of changes.

An International Conference on Cataloging Principles was held in Paris in 1961, at which a draft statement of principles, based on Lubetzky's code, was submitted. The international participants agreed to adopt these principles and to work in their various countries for revised rules that would be in agreement with the accepted principles. These principles, often referred to as the *Paris Principles* (or *IFLA Principles*) are important because, for the first time, there was multinational agreement upon which to base future international developments.

The Americans and the British again cooperated on a new set of cataloging rules, and in 1967 published the *Anglo-American Cataloging Rules* (although it had to be published in separate North American and British versions because of inability to come to agreement on a few points). These rules were based on the Paris Principles, although they deviated in some respects.

In 1974 the International Federation of Library Associations (IFLA) issued the *International Standard Bibliographic Description (ISBD)*, produced as a means for the international communication of bibliographic information. *ISBD*'s objectives were to make records from different sources interchangeable, to facilitate their interpretation against language barriers, and to facilitate the conversion of such records to machine-readable form.

AACR2, the second edition of the *Anglo-American Cataloguing*

Rules, was published in 1978 to incorporate *ISBD,* to bring nonbook materials into the mainstream, to take into account machine processing of bibliographic records, to reconcile the British and American texts, and to conform more closely to the Paris Principles. Four major national libraries (United States, Canada, Great Britain, and Australia) agreed to standard interpretation and implementation of *AACR2,* and many other countries have now adopted it for national use. Revised editions of *AACR2* were published in 1988 and 1998. These were mainly cumulations of changes incurred in the process of "continuous revision." A significant revision of *AACR2* was published in 2002.

Subject Access

Verbal Subject Access

For centuries philosophers worked on classifying knowledge; Callimachus, Plato, Aristotle, and Bacon are among the most famous. Librarians tried to adapt these classifications for books by assigning letters and/ or numbers to the concepts classified by the philosophers. Other than this, there was not much interest in subject access in libraries before Charles Cutter. As already mentioned, Cutter included a section of guidelines for subject headings in his *Rules for a Dictionary Catalog.*

The *A.L.A. List of Subject Headings* was first published in 1885, and the preface stated that it was to be considered an appendix to Cutter's *Rules for a Dictionary Catalog.* It was based on headings found in five major catalogs of the time, including the Boston Athenaeum and the Harvard subject index. A second revised edition was published in 1905 with the statement that "further changes are not to be expected for many years."[9] However, new terminology became necessary rapidly, and interleaved and annotated editions became unwieldy. Many librarians asked for the list of subject headings that were appearing on LC cards, and so in 1914 the first edition of *Subject Headings Used in the Dictionary Catalogues of the Library of Congress* was published. The title was changed to *Library of Congress Subject Headings (LCSH)* in 1975. *LCSH* has appeared in multiple editions in its printed version, with a new edition every year beginning in 1988, but it is changed daily in its online version.

The *Sears List of Subject Headings (Sears)* was first published in 1923 as *List of Subject Headings for Small Libraries.* It was prepared by Minnie Earl Sears in response to demands for a list of subject headings that was more suitable to the needs of the small library than the ALA or the LC lists. Recognizing the need for uniformity, Sears followed the form of the LC subject headings—she eliminated the more detailed ones and simplified some terminology. *Sears* continues to be published for small libraries in print, although it is maintained in electronic format by its publisher.

Classification

Meanwhile, classification had developed at LC from arrangement by size in the early 1800s to arrangement by the eighteen broad categories of the Bacon-d'Alembert system in 1814 when the Library burned. To reestablish it, Thomas Jefferson sold Congress his library, which was classified using forty-four main classes based on his interpretation of the Bacon-d'Alembert system. By the end of the century it was clear that the rapidly growing collection needed more detail in classification.

Melvil Dewey, in 1876, issued anonymously the first edition of his classification. He divided all knowledge into ten main classes, with each of those divided again into ten divisions, and each of those divided into ten sections—giving one thousand categories into which books could be classified. Like its predecessors, it was enumerative in that it listed specific categories one by one. In later editions he added decimals so that the one thousand categories could be divided into ten thousand, then one hundred thousand and so on. He also introduced the first hints of "number building," or "faceting," when he made tables for geographic areas and for forms of material. (*Faceting* comprises small notations that stand for subparts of the whole topic and are strung together to create a complete classification notation. This is discussed further in Chapter 11.) Notations from these tables could then be added in numerous places to show a certain subject category as being relevant to a particular geographic area.

When LC decided it must improve over Jefferson's classification, Dewey Decimal Classification (DDC) was in its fifth edition, and Cutter had begun his own enumerative classification scheme, called the Expansive Classification. This scheme began with letters of the alphabet, expanded with second letters, and then expanded further with numbers. LC representatives talked with Dewey to convince him to allow them to adapt his scheme, but ran afoul of his intransigence. They did not adopt Cutter's classification directly, but created their own scheme based upon his model.

The Universal Decimal Classification (UDC) was developed in 1895 by two Belgian lawyers, Paul Otlet and Henri LaFontaine. UDC was based on the DDC (then in its fifth edition), but was, with Dewey's permission, expanded by the addition of detailed subdivisions and the use of signs to indicate complex subjects. Why Otlet and LaFontaine were able to get Dewey's permission when LC was not is unclear; but it may have been because UDC was not at the outset intended as a library classification, but as a means to organize documents (see more about this below). UDC expanded Dewey's "standard subdivisions" to about a dozen generally applicable "auxiliaries," which could be joined together as needed in the form we now call "faceting."

During the twentieth century faceted classification became of interest because it allows the classifier to express all aspects of an interdisciplinary subject in the same classification notation. The term was first used with this meaning by S. R. Ranganathan in his Colon Classification (called "Colon" because of its use of the punctuation mark "colon" as a major facet indicator) in the early 1930s. As mentioned earlier, Dewey had already provided for some "number building," and Library of Congress Classification (LCC) even included a few such facets (although developed only class by class and not applicable through the entire scheme). Ranganathan introduced the fully faceted approach by means of classification notations constructed entirely from individual facets in a prescribed sequence from the most specific to the most general.

Special Materials

Archives

U.S. developments in bibliographic control of special materials (i.e., archives, museums) have nearly all come since the turn of the twentieth century. European archival practice stemmed from working with public archives (e.g., land grants, laws, etc.). Archival materials were kept because of legal and other administrative value. The concept of *provenance* emerged in France about 1840, and the concept of *original order* came from the Prussians shortly thereafter.[10]

As in libraries, the first archival catalogs were lists and then inventories. In early archival practice in the United States, material was collected for its artifactual value. It was often cataloged at the item level without any concern for provenance or original order. Thus, the context in which the archival record was originally created was lost. This practice lasted in the United States through the mid-1930s, when European ideas began to influence U.S. practice and when the National Archives and the Society of American Archivists were formed. Early cataloging codes in the United States (e.g., Cutter, *AACR*) dealt with cataloging manuscripts, but at the item level. In 1983 publication of *Archives, Personal Papers, and Manuscripts (APPM)* brought the library and archival traditions together. *APPM* is based on *ISBD* and *AACR2*, but also includes archival principles. A special

MARC format was developed (called MARC-AMC). It has now been incorporated with the other special MARC formats in the process of "format integration."

Museums and Art Galleries

As in libraries and archives, museums began first with lists and later expanded to include inventories. Museum documentation is the idea that guides cataloging of art and artifacts. It is a system that provides an indispensable record of information associated with objects for research. Museums are now joining the library and archives communities in codification of descriptive practice. The Internet has spurred this action because of the demand from researchers for access to pictures and textual descriptions of artifacts and art. Although museums and art galleries still do not have standard means for creating surrogate records, libraries with these kinds of collections use *AACR2*'s chapter for cataloging realia and then enter these descriptions into a MARC format.

Subject Access to Special Materials

Subject access to special materials follows the needs of the user communities. For verbal subject access, archivists use *LCSH* and the *Art & Architecture Thesaurus (AAT)*. The museum community has developed specialized lists and thesauri (often called *lexicons*). Museums also use the *AAT*. Archives do not lend themselves to classification. Some collections of art and artifacts are classified, however. Some natural history museums classify specimens of organisms that can be identified to the genus and species level. Two other examples include the American Museum of Natural History, which uses Romer's classification of vertebrae, and art collections with Christian iconographic themes that use ICONCLASS, developed in the Netherlands.

Mechanization of Bibliography

Automation first entered the organization of information picture in the 1870s when the typewriter was introduced into libraries. Typewriters were highly controversial at first because they were so noisy. Many libraries were one-room affairs with the cataloger sitting at a table in the back. Patrons, who had been used to the quiet of the cataloger creating handwritten cards, found the clacking of the typewriter annoying. Some librarians objected, too, because typed cards were not esthetically pleasing compared to cards written in "library hand," a method of writing in which the letters were carefully formed to be completely readable.

The Documentation Movement

The trend to mechanize bibliography began with the Documentation Movement in Europe in the 1890s. The nineteenth century brought the development of professional organizations and the growth of scientific research, both of which created a dramatic increase in the number of published journals. Paul Otlet and Henri LaFontaine spearheaded a movement for bibliographic control in libraries to go beyond books to provide access to parts of books, articles in journals, research documents, brochures, catalogs, patents, government records, archives, photographs, and newspapers. The goal of the Documentation Movement was to capture, record, and provide access to all information in all formats for the improvement of science.

A conference organized by Otlet and LaFontaine was held in Brussels in 1892, with its focus on the creation of Universal Bibliographic Control (UBC). The magnitude of the undertaking necessitated an entirely new body of techniques different from conventional library practice for organization, subject analysis, bibliographic description, and annotation. This quest for new techniques of bibliographic control naturally led to a search for new technology. The concept of documentation was transported to the United States in the 1930s, and in 1937 the American Documentation Institute was formed. In 1938 the International Federation for Documentation was established and was devoted almost exclusively to the promotion of Universal Decimal Classification (UDC). From its inception, UDC was not intended as a library classification, but rather as a means to organize and analyze *documents,* a term then defined to include such things as journal articles, scientific papers, patents, and the like, but not books or journals.

An important technological advance for the documentation field was the development of microphotography by Eastman Kodak in 1928. This was seen as a means of collecting, storing, and accessing vast quantities of information, and it was predicted that microfilm would supplant the conventional book.

World War II had an impact on the mechanization of bibliographic control in two ways. First, it created an immediate scientific information explosion, since the U.S. government's imperative was to "get the bomb first." Scientific research was conducted rapidly and in secrecy, with a critical need for immediate dissemination of research results from lab to lab. This heightened the government's awareness of the need for bibliographic control and brought with it government funding to develop a mechanized process. Second, as the outcome of the war shifted in favor of the Allies, huge quantities of German scientific literature were confiscated. This material needed immediate bibliographic control in order to be useful. Microfilms were made and distributed through a committee attached to the Office of Strategic Service. The distribution was under the direction of Frederick Kilgour. At the same time, the Central Information Division of the Office of Strategic Service was working on the subject analysis of documents using IBM punched card equipment. The war itself was the impetus for many technological advances; some of these advances could now be applied to organizing and accessing the hoards of scientific and technical literature that also were an outgrowth of the war.

In 1945 Vannevar Bush opened the way for a new era in documentation and information science with his article "As We May Think." Bush developed the idea of *memex,* a "device in which an individual stores all . . . books, records and communications, and which is mechanized so that it may be consulted with exceeding speed and flexibility."[11] Using the medium of microfilm (in 1945, remember), Bush described in detail the hypertext-based scholar's workstation of today. Memex was based on the concept of *associative indexing,* similar to human thought process, where items are linked together and any item can immediately lead to the access of other related information. Bush even predicted new forms of encyclopedias where information could be coded and connected to pertinent articles. A man of vision, Bush believed that science should implement the ways in which we produce, store, and consult the record of the human race.

The 1950s and 1960s saw many and varied attempts at mechanization using the current technology. Calvin Mooers coined the phrase "information retrieval" in 1950. He and other information scientists of the day, such as Ralph Shaw and Mortimer Taube, worked on developments such as the "Rapid Selector," designed to provide subject access to microfilm by a method that used holes punched in the sides of the film. Another technique used a knitting-type needle to access subjects on punched cards. Taube was especially concerned with the linguistic problems of documentary analysis and retrieval.

In 1957, *Sputnik,* the first artificial satellite launched into space from Earth, pushed information needs to the forefront of the scientific community once again. There was increased interest in improving access to recorded knowledge in both the government (National Science Foundation, National Library of Medicine, Library of Congress, etc.) and the private sector (IBM, General Electric, Kodak, RAND Corp., etc.). The field of documentation became the field of information science with a great deal of money made available for research and development. The 1960s saw a period of tremendous technological advances in communication and information processing. The computer became established as the means of storing massive amounts of data and providing high-speed access. In 1968 the American Documentation Institute changed its name to the American Society for Information Science (ASIS). By this time the use of machines for the retrieval of information was solidly entrenched in the Information Science community, a community that had developed quite separately from libraries until this point.

Library Automation

In the late 1960s two developments changed the face of bibliographic control forever. At the Library of Congress, Henriette Avram engineered the creation of the MARC format, enabling the machine readability of bibliographic records. And Fred Kilgour started OCLC and was its first director. To the astonishment of all who knew him, he left his position as associate director of the Yale University Library to run the Ohio College Library Center. He had a vision and the ambition to carry it out. With the development of the MARC format, OCLC was able to provide cataloging information via cable and terminal to all its member libraries, which in turn were able to put their original cataloging online for the use of all other members. In 1977 another major network came into being particularly to serve research libraries—the Research Libraries Information Network (RLIN).

CONCLUSION

We see here the coming together of the information science track and the library science track, which had previously developed separately. There seems often to be a very wide gulf between information science and library science (e.g., jokes are cracked about information science being library science for men), but both are interested in and working on the organization of information, as we see in the chapters that follow.

NOTES

All URLs accessed June 2003.

1. For more information about Callimachus's work, see Rudolf Blum, *Kallimachos: The Alexandrian Library and the Origins of Bibliography* (Madison: University of Wisconsin Press, 1991).

2. Joseph Smalley, "The French Cataloging Code of 1791: A Translation," *Library Quarterly* 61, no. 1 (January 1991): 1–14.

3. Ruth French Strout, "The Development of the Catalog and Cataloging Codes," *Library Quarterly* 26, no. 4 (October 1956): 268.

4. Dorothy May Norris, *A History of Cataloging and Cataloging Methods* (London: Grafton, 1939), p. 206.

5. Louis Fagan, *The Life of Sir Anthony Panizzi*, 2nd ed., reprint (New York: Burt Franklin, 1970), p. 134. (Originally published 1880.)

6. Personal communication with Michael Carpenter.

7. Charles Coffin Jewett, *On the Construction of Catalogues of Libraries, and Their Publication by Means of Separate, Stereotyped Titles*, 2nd ed. (Washington, D.C.: Smithsonian Institution, 1853), p. 18.

8. Andrew D. Osborn, "The Crisis in Cataloging," in *Foundations of Cataloging: A Sourcebook*, eds. Michael Carpenter and Elaine Svenonius (Littleton, Colo.: Libraries Unlimited, 1985), pp. 90–103. Originally published in *Library Quarterly* 11, no. 4 (October 1941): 393–411.

9. *A.L.A. List of Subject Headings*, 2nd ed., rev. (Boston: American Library Association Publishing Board, 1905), p. vi.

10. Ernst Posner, "Some Aspects of Archival Development Since the French Revolution," *American Archivist* 3, no. 2 (April 1940): 159–172, especially pp. 167–168.

11. Vannevar Bush, "As We May Think," *Atlantic Monthly* 176 (July 1945): 101–108. Available: http://www.theatlantic.com/unbound/flashbks/computer/bushf.htm. Also available: http://www.ps.uni-sb.de/~duchier/pub/vbush/vbush.shtml.

SUGGESTED READINGS

Baker, Nicholson. "Discards." *New Yorker* 70, no. 7 (4 April 1994): 64–86.

Berner, Richard C. "Historical Development of Archival Theory and Practices in the United States." *Midwestern Archivist* 7, no. 2 (1982): 103–117.

Burke, Frank G. "Archives: Organization and Description." In *World Encyclopedia of Library and Information Services*. 3rd ed. Chicago: American Library Association, 1993, pp. 63–68.

Bush, Vannevar. "As We May Think." *Atlantic Monthly* 176 (July 1945): 101–108. Available: http://www.theatlantic.com/unbound/flashbks/computer/bushf.htm. Also available: http://www.ps.uni-sb.de/~duchier/pub/vbush/vbush.shtml.

Dunkin, Paul S. *Cataloging U.S.A.* Chicago: American Library Association, 1969. Chapter 1: "Mr. Cutter's Catalog" and Chapter 2: "The Prophet and the Law: Codes After Cutter."

Fishbein, Meyer H. "Archives: Records Management and Records Appraisal." In *World Encyclopedia of Library and Information Services*. 3rd ed. Chicago: American Library Association, 1993, pp. 60–63.

Harris, Michael H. *History of Libraries in the Western World.* 4th ed. Metuchen, N.J.: Scarecrow Press, 1995.

Hopkins, Judith. "The 1791 French Cataloging Code and the Origins of the Card Catalog." *Libraries & Culture* 27, no. 4 (Fall 1992): 378–404.

Humbert, de Romans. *Regulations for the Operation of a Medieval Library*. St. Paul: Associates of the James Ford Bell Library, University of Minnesota, 1980.

Jackson, Sidney L. *Libraries and Librarianship in the West: A Brief History.* New York: McGraw-Hill, 1974.

Lancaster, F. W. "Whither Libraries? or Wither Libraries." *College & Research Libraries* 39, no. 5 (September 1978): 345–357; reprinted in *College & Research Libraries* 50, no. 4 (July 1989): 406–419.

Osborn, Andrew D. "The Crisis in Cataloging." In *Foundations of Cataloging: A Sourcebook,* edited by Michael Carpenter and Elaine Svenonius. Littleton, Colo.: Libraries Unlimited, 1985, pp. 90–103. Originally published in *Library Quarterly* 11, no. 4 (October 1941): 393–411.

Reynolds, Dennis. *Library Automation: Issues and Applications.* New York: Bowker, 1985. Chapter 4: "History: The Public Catalog."

Russell, Beth M. "Hidden Wisdom and Unseen Treasure: Revisiting Cataloging in Medieval Libraries." *Cataloging & Classification Quarterly* 26, no. 3 (1998): 21–30.

Smalley, Joseph. "The French Cataloging Code of 1791: A Translation." *Library Quarterly* 61, no. 1 (January 1991): 1–14.

Stoll, Clifford. *Silicon Snake Oil: Second Thoughts on the Information Highway.* New York: Doubleday, 1995, pp. 197–203.

Strout, Ruth French. "The Development of the Catalog and Cataloging Codes." *Library Quarterly* 26, no. 4 (October 1956): 254–275.

Taylor, Arlene G. "Cataloguing." In *World Encyclopedia of Library and Information Services.* 3rd ed. Chicago: American Library Association, 1993, pp. 177–181.

Taylor, Arlene G. *Wynar's Introduction to Cataloging and Classification.* 9th ed., with the assistance of David P. Miller. Englewood, Colo.: Libraries Unlimited, 2000. Chapter 2: "Development of Cataloging Codes."

CHAPTER 4
ENCODING STANDARDS

The problem addressed in this chapter is: How and why do we encode surrogate records (metadata) for machine manipulation? As mentioned at the end of Chapter 2, surrogate records in a bibliographic tool must be encoded for machine manipulation if they are to be placed into an online database. This chapter addresses several ways to encode records: MARC (MAchine-Readable Cataloging) is one standard that has been used for encoding library catalog records for more than three decades (since 1968). SGML (Standard Generalized Markup Language) came into use after 1986 when it became a standard for encoding text. It has been adapted for encoding surrogate records. HTML (HyperText Markup Language, a very simplified application of SGML), XML (eXtensible Markup Language, a subset of SGML), and many SGML/XML applications are widely used on the Web.

In the minds of many in the profession, metadata content and encoding for the content are inextricably entwined. Metadata records can be created by first determining descriptive content and then encoding the content, or one can start with a "shell" comprising the codes and then fill in the contents of each field. In this chapter encoding standards are discussed before covering creation of content. The same content can be encoded with any one of several different encoding standards and some metadata standards include both encoding and content specification. Creation of metadata content is covered in Chapters 6–11.

ENCODING OF CHARACTERS

Before addressing the "higher-level" encoding of records, it may be useful to say a few words about how computers are able to handle the very basic level of the characters that make up content that appears as a record. Each letter of an alphabet, each numeral, each symbol, and each of these in every language that exists has to be represented by a code, because, fundamentally, computers just deal with numbers. They store letters and other characters by assigning a code to each one. An ISO standard, ISO/IEC 10646, *Universal Multiple-Octet Coded Character Set* (UCS) is the first standardized character set with the purpose of including all characters in all written languages of the world (including all mathematical and other symbols). Unicode is an American industry counterpart that is kept compatible with UCS. Unicode is overseen by the Unicode Consortium and was named for its aim to embrace three characteristics: universality, covering all modern written languages; uniqueness, with no duplication of characters even if they appear in more than one language; and uniformity, with each character being the same length in bits.

UCS/Unicode provides a unique 16-bit (or 31-bit) unit of encoding for every character in every modern language.[1] Because many systems operate with 8-bit encoding, there are various ways of combining "octets" to create the characters. UCS defines two multi-octet encodings, UCS–2 and UCS–4. Unicode has developed UCS Transformation Formats (UTF) which use a special signal to indicate the number of octets. The most common of these are UTF–8 and UTF–16.[2]

Before UCS/Unicode, there were a multitude of different encoding systems for the display of characters, such as ASCII and EBCDIC. At this writing information retrieval systems are in the process of implementing UCS/Unicode support in their products. XML, discussed below, adopts UCS as the basis of its character encoding.

ENCODING OF RECORDS (SYNTAX)

Surrogate records are encoded by assigning tags, numbers, letters, or words (i.e., codes) to discrete pieces of information. For example, a personal author name is given the tag "100" in MARC coding; or in an XML markup language, such as the TEI (see discussion below), it is preceded with "<author>" and is followed with "</author>." Such encoding is often referred to in metadata schemas as the "syntax" of the schema.

Surrogate records have to be encoded in order to be able, first, to provide for access to the contents of the surrogate record. Encoding allows for the setting off of each part of the record (called a *field* or an *element*). This enables the creation of searching programs that allow the searching of certain fields. If a user wishes to search only for personal authors, the MARC code 100 and the code 700 identify those fields as personal author fields during the search for a personal author. As noted above, the same result is achieved in XML by labeling the author through <author> </author>.

A second use for encoding is to provide for display. In a similar manner to the searching of only certain fields, computer programs can be written so that each field will display in a certain position according to the wishes of those creating the display. For example, when the TEI pair <author> </author> or the MARC tag 100 is used to identify a name of a person who is the author of an information package, that author's name can be displayed at the top of the record or after the title, and can be displayed with a label or not.

A third use for encoding is to allow integration of many languages and scripts to be displayed and searched in the same file. Institutions that participate in organizing recorded information collect information in many languages and many scripts. Languages that are in the Roman script have always been able to be interfiled, although filing them alphabetically was sometimes a problem. Languages in other scripts had to be "Romanized" in order to interfile them in the paper world. Online, however, if the display of other than Roman scripts is provided for, the coding allows for identification of the fields of the surrogate record regardless of the language knowledge of the human doing the organizing.

A fourth use is for data transmission. Institutions that collect recorded information tend to have their own online systems into which they place encoded surrogate records for the information packages they have collected. When these information packages are duplicates of those found in other institutions' online systems, cooperative arrangements are made to exchange surrogate records so that each institution does not have to create every record for every package from "scratch." Encoding allows such exchange to proceed.

CURRENTLY USED EXAMPLES OF STANDARDS FOR ENCODING RECORDS

Recently a proliferation of encoding standards has erupted. The examples discussed here are:

- MARC (MAchine-Readable Cataloging)

    - *MARC 21* (MARC agreed upon by the United States, Canada, and Great Britain)

    - UNIMARC (UNIversal MARC)

- SGML (Standard Generalized Markup Language)

    - XML (eXtensible Markup Language)

    - DTDs (Document Type Definitions) and XML Schemas

        → TEI (Text Encoding Initiative) DTD

        → HTML (HyperText Markup Language)/XHTML

        → EAD (Encoded Archival Description) DTD

        → MARC DTDs and XML Schemas

        → ONIX (Online Information eXchange) DTD

MARC (MAchine-Readable Cataloging)

The MARC communications format (see Figure 4.1) is used for transmitting data from one system to another. It has a leader, directory, control fields, and variable fields. The leader is somewhat like the leader on a roll of film. It identifies the beginning of a new record and contains a few codes that identify, among other things, the kind of information package that is being described. The record directory contains a series of fixed-length (twelve characters) segments that identify the field tag, length, and starting position of each field in the record. The MARC directory was a major contribution to the information science world. Instead of fixed-length fields only, which was common in databases in the 1960s, the directory allowed variable-length fields, now common in most databases.

Control fields carry alphanumeric data elements. In *MARC 21* these field tags begin with the digit 0. Several of the control fields have subfields that are fixed in length. Control fields are used for such data as fixed-length descriptive data, LC control numbers, and codes for date and time of latest transaction. Some control fields are called fixed fields; one of these (*MARC 21* field 008) is often called *the* "fixed field" and is usually displayed quite differently from other fields. Variable data fields carry alphanumeric data of variable length. These fields often contain traditional

| Leader

| Directory →

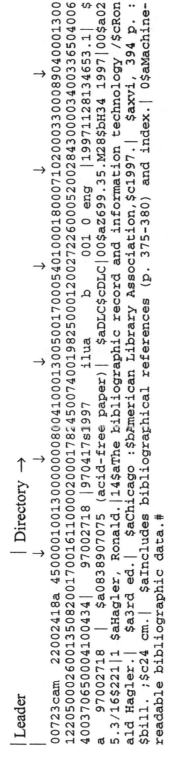

```
00723cam  22002418a 4500010013000000080041000130050017000540100018000071020003300089040001300
122050002600135082001700161100002000017824500740019825000120027226000520028430000340033650040006
40037065000410043418 97002718 |970417s1997    ilua    b    001 0 eng   |199711281346S3.1|  $
a  97002718  |  $a083889070075 (acid-free paper)|  $aDLC$cDLC|00$az699.35.M28$bH34 1997|00$a02
5.3/16$221|1 $aHagler, Ronald.|14$aThe bibliographic record and information technology /$cRon
ald Hagler.|  $a3rd ed.|  $aChicago :$bAmerican Library Association,$c1997.|  $axvi, 394 p. :
$bill. ;$c24 cm.|  $aIncludes bibliographical references (p. 375-380) and index.|  0$aMachine-
readable bibliographic data.#
```

Fig. 4.1. Record in the MARC communications format. Directory is divided into twelve-character segments as shown by the arrows at the top of the record. Directory continues through line two and for the first eighteen characters of line three. In each twelve-character segment the first three characters are the MARC tag for the field represented, the next four characters give the length of the field, and the last five characters give the starting position for that field in the portion of the record that follows the directory.

cataloging data, but may carry additional information as well, such as codes for date/time and place of an event, or a geographic area code.

When records are received in the MARC communications format, each system displays records according to its own programming. OCLC and RLIN put the "fixed field" at the top and use abbreviations to interpret the codes; but they do not use the same abbreviations as each other. LC puts the "fixed field" in the 008 field position, without using abbreviations or separations. Local systems have a "technical services" display that is quite different from network systems' displays. Public catalog displays do not include the "fixed field" at all (except in the few system implementations that allow a MARC view for the OPAC). System displays also vary in such things as spacing before and after subfield codes, placement of indicators, and the like (see Figures 4.2, 4.3, and 4.4).

Control and variable fields have tags, indicators, subfield codes, and field terminators. Tags are three-digit numbers (from 001 to 999) designating the kind of field. The first digit designates a broad grouping. For example, the first digit "1" designates a "main heading field." A convention is followed in which all fields beginning with a certain digit, let's say 6, are identified as a group, in this case designated 6xx. 6xx fields are, in general, subject access fields (e.g., 600 is for a personal name used as subject; 610 is for a corporate name used as subject; 650 is for a topical subject, etc.).

LC Control Number: 97002718

000 00994pam 2200253 a 450
001 706941
005 19971128134653.1
008 970417s1997 ilua b 001 0 eng
010 __ |a 97002718
020 __ |a 0838907075 (acid-free paper)
040 __ |a DLC |c DLC |d DLC
050 00 |a Z699.35.M28 |b H34 1997
082 00 |a 025.3/16 |2 21
100 1_ |a Hagler, Ronald.
245 14 |a The bibliographic record and information technology / |c Ronald Hagler.
250 __ |a 3rd ed.
260 __ |a Chicago : |b American Library Association, |c 1997.
300 __ |a xvi, 394 p. : |b ill. ; |c 24 cm.
504 __ |a Includes bibliographical references (p. 375-380) and index.
650 _0 |a Machine-readable bibliographic data.

Fig. 4.2. Formatted display of the record in Figure 4.1, as displayed in the Library of Congress Online Catalog.

```
     OCLC 36909449
     Books  Rec stat p        Entered 19970417       Replaced 20010523
     > Type a       ELvl          Srce         Audn          Ctrl         Lang  eng
       BLvl m       Form          Conf  0      Biog          MRec         Ctry  ilu
                    Cont  b       Gpub         LitF  0       Indx  1
          Desc a    Ills  a       Fest  0      DtSt  s       Dates 1997,
```

010		97-2718
040		DLC ‡c DLC ‡d UKM ‡d NLC
015		GB97-77064
020		0838907075 (acid-free paper)
020		0888022808 (Canada)
050	00	Z699.35.M28 ‡b H34 1997
055	02	Z699.35*
082	00	025.3/16 ‡2 21
100	1_	Hagler, Ronald.
245	14	The bibliographic record and information technology / ‡c Ronald Hagler.
250		3rd ed.
260		Chicago : ‡b American Library Association, ‡c 1997.
300		xvi, 394 p. : ‡b ill. ; ‡c 24 cm.
504		Includes bibliographical references (p. 375-380) and index.
650	_0	Machine-readable bibliographic data.
650	_6	Données bibliographiques lisibles par machine.

Fig. 4.3. Formatted display of the record in Figure 4.1, as displayed by OCLC.

```
Tag    Ind 1 Ind 2  Field Data
000                 00797cam__2200253_a_4500
001                 1716497
005                 19990522225058.0
008                 970417s1997____ilua_____b____001_0_eng__

010                 ‡a    97002718
020                 ‡a 0838907075 (acid-free paper)
035                 ‡a (lcb)97002718
035                 ‡9 ASB9899C1
040                 ‡a DLC ‡c DLC ‡d DLC
050     0     0     ‡a Z699.35.M28 ‡b H34 1997
082     0     0     ‡a 025.3/16 ‡2 21
100     1           ‡a Hagler, Ronald.
245     1     4     ‡a The bibliographic record and information technology / ‡c Ronald
Hagler.
250                 ‡a 3rd ed.
260                 ‡a Chicago : ‡b American Library Association, ‡c 1997.
300                 ‡a xvi, 394 p. : ‡b ill. ; ‡c 24 cm.
504                 ‡a Includes bibliographical references (p. 375-380) and index.
650           0     ‡a Machine-readable bibliographic data.
999                 ‡a PWBO 05/14/98
948                 ‡a so:vp;ctm:sac
```

Fig. 4.4. Formatted display of the record in Figure 4.1, as displayed in the technical services version of the Voyager (Endeavor) cataloging subsystem at the University of Pittsburgh.

Fields with tags beginning with 7 are 7xx fields, that is, additional access points.

Indicators consist of two positions following a tag. These positions contain coded information interpreting or supplementing the data in the field. They are independent of each other. An example in *MARC 21* is the indicators for the 245 (title) field. The first indicator is supposed to tell whether a title added entry is called for. This is a holdover from card days when an additional card for title was not made when the title was the main entry. In most cases now, it really functions as an indicator of whether a title should be the main entry for the record (0 = yes; 1 = no). The second indicator tells how many characters (counting a blank as one character) should be skipped over to get to the first filing character. For example, for an English title beginning with "the," the second indicator is "4." Some fields do not need indicators, in which case one or more of the indicators may be identified as being "blank."

A subfield code consists of a delimiter and a letter or number that follows the delimiter. It indicates which subfield of a field follows. The purpose of subfield codes is to identify elements in a field that might require separate treatment. The delimiters that begin a subfield code show the "limit" of a particular subfield, using unique characters that indicate the beginning of a particular subfield. The delimiter may be represented differently depending on the system: ‡ or $ or |, for example. The lowercase letter or number that follows the delimiter is a data element identifier. For example, in a 245 field, subfield "a" identifies the title proper, subfield "b" identifies the subtitle or other title information, and subfield "c" identifies a statement of responsibility (e.g., author). The letters and numbers have different meanings from field to field. The following are subfield codes: ‡a, ‡b, ‡2, and so forth. (It should be noted that in some systems, most notably OCLC, the ‡a code of the first element in a field is not shown by the system.)

The field terminator is a special character that follows the last data element in the field. As with the delimiter, the field terminator may be displayed in different ways or it may not be displayed at all. It is necessary that it be there, however, because with variable-length fields, it is essential to be able to tell the computer where one field ends and another begins.

MARC 21

MARC 21 came into being in 2000 as a result of agreement between the United States and Canada to merge their national MARC formats

(USMARC and CAN/MARC), compromising on the differences between them. In 2001 the British Library announced that it would adopt *MARC 21.* The first MARC format was developed at the Library of Congress (LC) in 1968. It was identified simply as MARC until other versions were developed in the 1970s, and was then called LC-MARC. Finally, the name USMARC came to distinguish it from more than twenty other national versions (e.g., CAN/MARC, UKMARC, RUSMARC, DenMARC, etc.).

MARC 21 is based on ANSI standard Z39.2, *American National Standard for Bibliographic Information Interchange* (1971, revised 1985).[3] The international version is ISO 2709:1996, *Information and Documentation—Format for Information Exchange.*[4] The name *MARC 21* is meant to point both to the future (twenty-first century) and to its international character and is considered a continuation of both the U.S. and Canadian formats in one edition. *MARC 21* records may be encoded with either an 8-bit encoding called MARC-8 or with the Unicode UTF–8 encoding rules, using a subset of UCS/Unicode until all systems can accommodate the full UCS/Unicode set of characters.[5]

MARC 21 actually has formats for five types of data. The following formats are currently defined:

- bibliographic format—for encoding bibliographic data in records that are surrogates for information packages (see Figures 4.2–4.3)

- authority format—for encoding authority data collected in authority records created to help control the content of those surrogate record fields that are subject to authority control (see Figures 8.9 and 10.2)

- holdings format—for encoding data elements in holdings records that show the holdings and location data for information packages described in surrogate records

- community information format—for encoding data in records that contain information about events, programs, services, and the like, so that these records can be integrated with bibliographic records

- classification data format—for encoding data elements related to classification numbers, the captions associated with them, their hierarchies, and the subject headings with which they correlate

UNIMARC

UNIMARC (UNIversal MARC)[6] was developed in 1977 as a vehicle for interchange of MARC records between national bibliographic agencies. The most recent version includes updates made in 2000. It conforms to ISO 2709, as does *MARC 21*. UNIMARC calls for use of ISO character set standards, but also allows parties to an exchange to agree on the character set to be used.

The proliferation of national MARC formats necessitated development of UNIMARC. At first it was thought that UNIMARC would act only as a conversion format. In this capacity it requires that each national agency create a translator to change records from UNIMARC to the particular national format and vice versa. When a translator is in place, records can be translated to UNIMARC to be sent to other countries, and records received from other countries can be translated from UNIMARC to the national format. In addition to this use, a few national agencies that did not already have a MARC format have adopted UNIMARC as the standard in their countries. UNIMARC has been adopted by the countries of the European Community in order to produce "unified catalogues."

Differences between UNIMARC and *MARC 21* are immediately apparent upon looking at the list of blocks beginning with 0, 1, 2, etc. For example, the 1xx fields are "coded information" rather than "main entry" fields, and the 2xx block is a descriptive information block in which a title field is designated 200, rather than 245 as in *MARC 21*. Also, the second indicator of the 200 field is blank and therefore does not tell how many characters to skip for an article. UNIMARC also allows for embedded fields (e.g., an authority record number may appear at the beginning of an access point field). It de-emphasizes "main entry" in the 7xx block, where 700 is for "Personal Name–Primary Intellectual Responsibility," but if the concept of main entry does not exist or is not distinguished in a source format, then 701 is used for all personal names.

SGML (Standard Generalized Markup Language)

SGML is a metalanguage—that is, a language for describing markup languages. It is an international standard for document markup and conforms to ISO 8879:1986, *Information Processing—Text and Office Systems—Standard Generalized Markup Language (SGML)*.[7] Unlike the MARC family of encoding languages, it does not contain a predefined set of tags that can be used to markup documents, nor is it a standard template for producing particular types of documents. Instead, it is a set of rules for designing markup languages that describe the structure of a document so that documents may be interchanged across computer platforms (both text and markup are encoded in the same character set, formerly ASCII, but increasingly Unicode). It allows documents to be represented in such a way that text may be separated from structure without using a word processor. "Structure" means that the coding says: this is the title, this is the first chapter, this is a section heading, this is a paragraph, this is a quoted statement, and so on. Or, for surrogate records, the coding may say: this is a title element, this is a creator element, this is a publisher element, this is a subject element. SGML is flexible enough to define an infinite number of markup languages.

SGML defines data in terms of entities (or things or objects), elements, and attributes (or properties). An entity is a "thing" (or information package) to be encoded (e.g., a document, a part of a document, a surrogate record). An element is a particular unit from the text such as a title, a chapter title, a section heading, a paragraph, a publisher name, a classification number, and so forth. An attribute gives particular information about an element (e.g., specifying that the text should be printed in italics, giving the name of the thesaurus from which a subject term has been taken, etc.). The relationships between entities, elements, and attributes can be described using SGML.

SGML prescribes markup that consists of delimiters and tags. Delimiters are defined symbols (e.g., <, >, </, "), and are used to construct tags (e.g., <author> is a tag). Tags usually appear before and after an element in the form: **<tag>element</tag>** (e.g., <author>Edward Gaynor</author>). Attribute values are delimited by "..."or '...' (e.g., <quote lang='spa'>¿Que pasa?</quote>). Tags may be nested. This is similar to MARC subfields. An example of a nested set of tags from TEI (described below) is: **fileDesc> <titleStmt> <title>...</title> <author>...</author></ titleStmt> <publicationStmt>...</publicationStmt> </fileDesc>.**

Because SGML is not itself a markup language, it requires users either to define a Document Type Definition (DTD) at the beginning of a document or to declare a particular external DTD as the one being followed. DTDs are discussed further below.

XML (eXtensible Markup Language)

XML is a subset of SGML. As the Web has grown, HTML (discussed further below) has been criticized because it is too simplistic to provide for many desirable applications. Some thought for a while that full support of SGML on the Web was the answer. However, SGML is fairly complex and has features that make the programming involved complicated and lengthy. Plug-ins were developed to supplement HTML, but they require the user to download the plug-in and install it. The programming language Java seemed promising for enhancement of HTML functionality, but a person has to be able to program to create a Web page with it. XML has been developed as an answer to these problems.

XML (ISO 8879) is touted by its developers as being just as easy to use on the Web as HTML but at the same time being as powerful as SGML.[8] In addition, because XML was developed some years after SGML, it incorporates techniques needed for multimedia files, such as the ability to identify the format used to encode an illustration. It is essentially a version of SGML that can be used on the Web. Its components are the same: entities, elements, and attributes. XML, however, does not require a DTD (although it is recommended). An XML system can assign a default definition for undeclared components of the markup.

DTDs (Document Type Definitions) and XML Schemas

A DTD is an SGML or XML application. A DTD defines, with its own notation, the structure of a particular *type* of document, particularly with markup declarations. It gives advance notice of what names and structures can be used in a particular document type so that all documents that belong to a particular type will be alike. In the XML environment "schemas" have evolved as richer forms of DTDs. Schemas can define content and semantics of documents in addition to structure. An XML schema differs from a DTD in being expressed in XML syntax itself, and in following XML rules. Therefore, a developer does not have to learn another notation, and the software does not have to have a different parser. For example, a DTD for a "memo" might have the following lines:

```
<!DOCTYPE memo [
<!ELEMENT memo (to, from, date, subject?, para+) >
<!ELEMENT to (#PCDATA) >
<!ELEMENT from (#PCDATA) >
... etc.
] >
```

An XML Schema for the same memo would be written in XML and look like XML tagging:

```
<xs:element name="memo">
  <xs:complexType>
    <xs:sequence>
      <xs:element name="from" type="xs:string"/>
      <xs:element name="to" type="xs:string"/>
      etc., ...
    </xs:sequence>
  </xs:complexType>
</xs:element>
```

A schema can also define shared vocabularies with links to the namespaces in which those vocabularies reside, which is not part of a DTD. In any case either a DTD or schema defines:

- all elements that might be part of that particular document type

- element names and whether they are repeatable

- the contents of elements (in a general way, not specifically)

- what kinds of markup can be omitted

- tag attributes and their default values

- names of permissible entities

A DTD or schema may be created for only one document, in which case it may be contained at the beginning of the text, but creating a DTD is time-consuming. It makes more sense to create DTDs or schemas that can be used for many documents. These exist separately from the texts that refer to them. Many DTDs and schemas have been created and are in general use. A few of these are discussed below as examples. They are:

- TEI DTD—for encoding literary texts

- HTML/XHTML—for encoding Web pages

- EAD DTD—for encoding archival finding aids

- MARC DTDs and XML schemas—for encoding *MARC 21* records

- ONIX DTD—for encoding publishers' records

TEI (Text Encoding Initiative) DTD.[9] The TEI DTD was created to overcome the difficulty of the multiple encoding schemes that were being used to encode old, literary, and/or scholarly texts. Once encoded, the documents could not be exchanged easily. TEI makes it possible to make features of a text explicit in a format that allows the processing of that text by different programs running on different machines. The text can be represented exactly as it appears in its original printed form (in the case of encoding text from books). Texts can be exchanged for research purposes (e.g., textual analysis).

TEI can also be used for newly created documents, especially in cases where authors have a particular vision of how the text should look. TEI was originally created for texts in the humanities but is no longer limited to humanities texts. The guidelines provide a framework that can be used to describe many kinds of texts. TEI Lite[10] is a subset of TEI in much the same way as XML is a subset of SGML. TEI Lite may be considered to contain a "core" set of tags from TEI. The structure of the first part of a TEI Header is shown below. For an example of a completed TEI Header, see Figure 4.5.

```
<teiHeader>
  <fileDesc>
    <titleStmt> ... </titleStmt>
    <editionStmt> ... </editionStmt>
    <extent> ... </extent>
    <publicationStmt> ... </publicationStmt>
    <seriesStmt> ... </seriesStmt>
    <notesStmt> ... </notesStmt>
    <sourceDesc> ... </sourceDesc>
  </fileDesc>
  <! -- remainder of TEI Header here -- >
</teiHeader>
```

The modules making up the TEI DTD can be configured for use either as an SGML DTD or an XML DTD.

HTML (HyperText Markup Language)/XHTML.[11,12] The HTML DTD was developed to enable the creation of Web pages. It is a basic markup language that allows almost anyone to be a Web author. It provides for creation of simple structure, enables display of images, and provides for establishing links between documents. Users of an HTML-encoded document can navigate through the text itself if internal links have been made, or can move from one text to another with external links. In HTML 4.01 there are specific provisions for elements that can be used to describe properties of a document (e.g., title, expiration date, a list of keywords, etc.), making it possible to encode metadata (see discussion in Chapter 7). For an example of an HTML-encoded document, see Figure 4.6.

```
<html>
<head>
<title>Finding Aid</title>
</head><teiHeader>

<fileDesc>
<titleStmt>
<title>The Child in the House: An Electronic Edition</title>
<author>Walter Pater</author>
<sponsor><name id="CETH">Center for Electronic Texts in the Humanities (CETH)</name></sponsor>
<respStmt><resp>Digitized, proofed, edited and encoded in TEI SGML by </resp>
<name id="piez">Wendell Piez</name></respStmt>
</titleStmt>
<extent>6200 words in <gi>text</gi>; approximately 41K bytes uncompressed.</extent>
<publicationStmt>
<distributor><address><addrLine><name>Center for Electronic Texts in the
Humanities</name></addrLine><addrLine>169 College Avenue</addrLine>
<addrLine>New Brunswick NJ 08903</addrLine></address></distributor>
<availability><p id="ch0.01">Freely available for non&dash;commercial use when distributed with this header
intact.</p></availability>
<date value="1995">November 1995</date>
</publicationStmt>
<sourceDesc><bibl id="MS"><author>Walter Pater</author><title>Miscellaneous Studies</title>
<edition>Library Edition</edition>
<pubPlace>London</pubPlace>
<publisher>Macmillan and Co.</publisher><date value="1910">1910</date></bibl>
</sourceDesc>
</fileDesc>

<encodingDesc>
<projectDesc><p>This text is prepared as a dual&dash;purpose TEI pilot: to implement the TEI Lite DTD with SoftQuad
Author/Editor and WordPerfect 6.1 SGML edition SGML&dash;aware editors running on a PC platform); and to assess
application of the TEI preparatory to developing documentation for TEI markup procedures.</p></projectDesc>
<tagsDecl><rendition>The TEI tag <gi>sic</gi> appears where a doubtful reading occurs in the Library Edition and may be
rendered with its &lsquo;corr&rsquo; [correction] attribute in square brackets. The <gi>foreign</gi> tag appears for foreign
words printed in Italics in the original text, and can be so rendered.</rendition></tagsDecl>
<refsDecl><p id="ch0.05">The text of &ldquo;The Child in the House&rdquo; is designated with the unique ID
&lsquo;ch&rsquo; to distinguish it from other works of Pater in a Collected Electronic Edition. The paragraphs of this text are
designated with ID attributes, providing unique identifying codes, in the form &lsquo;chX.Y&rsquo;, where X is 0 (for
paragraphs in the header) or 1 (for paragraphs in the text body), and Y is the Arabic number of the paragraph.</p><p
id="ch0.06">Empty <gi>pb</gi> [page break] elements also appear at the beginning of every page occurring in the Library
Edition. The &lsquo;ed&rsquo; attribute is specified as MS (MS designating the volume <title>Miscellaneous Studies</title>in
the Library Edition); the appropriate page number appears as the &lsquo;n&rsquo; attribute, with a code in the form
&lsquo;MS.N&rsquo; appearing as the &lsquo;id&rsquo; attribute. This information is encoded so as to provide external
references to the most commonly available complete print edition of Pater's works, and not strictly for encoding of
cross&dash;references within an electronic edition; for these, the forementioned paragraph coding, or an extension of it, may be
used.</p></refsDecl>
</encodingDesc>

<profileDesc><langUsage><language id="Eng">British English</language>
<language id="Deu">German</language>
<language id="Fra">French</language>
<language id="La">Latin</language></langUsage>
</profileDesc>

</teiHeader>
```

Fig. 4.5. TEI Lite–encoded record. TEI Lite coding is in bold. (This is only the Header of a TEI-encoded document.)

```
<!DOCTYPE HTML PUBLIC "-//W3C//DTD HTML 4.0 Transitional//EN"
    "http://www.w3.org/TR/REC-html40/loose.dtd">
<html>
<head>
<TITLE>Libraries/Heinz/House: Heinz House Papers Finding Aid [Carnegie Mellon Libraries]</TITLE>
</head>

<BODY TEXT="#000000" BGCOLOR="#FFFFFF" LINK="#006600" VLINK="#339933"
ALINK="#990000">
<CENTER>
<FONT SIZE="-1">
<A HREF="/">Home</A> |
<A HREF="/Research/">Resources</A> |
<A HREF="/Services/">Services</A> |
<A HREF="/Info/">Information</A> |
<A HREF="/Libraries/">Organization</A> |
<A HREF="/search">Search This Site</A> |
<A HREF="/comment.html">Comments</A>
</FONT>
</CENTER>
<p>
<hr>
<center><h2>Heinz House Papers</h2></center>
<center><h3>Finding Aid</h3></center>
<br>
<ul>
<li> <a href="Scope.html">Scope and Contents Note</a><p>
<ul><li> <a href="http://heinz1.library.cmu.edu/cgi-bin/claritgw?op-
NewSearch&template=helios">Search/Browse the Heinz House Papers</a></ul><p>
<li> <a href="Arrangement.html">Arrangement of the Heinz House Papers</a><p>
<li> <a href="Description.html">Description of the Heinz House Papers</a><p>
<li> <a href="Appraisal.html">Appraisal and Sampling Note</a><p>
<li> <a href="Appendices.html">Appendices</a></ul>
<p><br>
<hr>


<font SIZE=-1>
May 2001 -- http://www.library.cmu.edu/Libraries/Heinz/House<br>
Jennie Benford, University/Heinz Archivist,
<a href="mailto:jbenford@andrew.cmu.edu">jbenford@andrew.cmu.edu</a>
<p>
<strong>
<a href="http://www.library.cmu.edu/Libraries/Heinz/">H. John Heinz III Archives</a>
<p>
<a href="/">Carnegie Mellon University Libraries</a></font></strong>
</p>
</body>
</html>
```

Fig. 4.6. HTML-encoded document. HTML encoding is in bold. (The display of this record is shown in Figure 2.4 on p. 43.)

XHTML is a reformulation of HTML 4 as an XML application, with three DTDs corresponding to the ones defined by HTML 4. They are:

- XHTML 1.0 Strict—to be used to obtain very clean structural markup that does not include any markup for layout; layout instructions should be handled by using a style sheet

- XHTML 1.0 Transitional—to be used to take advantage of XHTML features including style sheets but making small adjustments so that older browsers which cannot understand style sheets can still read the pages

- XHTML 1.0 Frameset—to be used in creating pages that partition a browser window into two or more frames

A major benefit of migrating to XHTML is in being conformant to XML while still having the content be able to be displayed correctly by older browsers.

EAD (Encoded Archival Description) DTD.[13] The EAD DTD is a scheme for encoding archival and library finding aids—primarily inventories and registers. As with other DTDs, it does not specify intellectual content but defines the encoding designations. The EAD eases the ability to interchange finding aids among institutions and allows users to find out about collections in distant places. For an example of an EAD-encoded document, see Figure 4.7. Version 2002 of the EAD DTD functions both as an SGML DTD and an XML DTD. It conforms to all SGML/XML specifications. "Switches" have been included in the DTD for turning off SGML-only features and turning on XML features.

MARC DTDs and XML Schemas.[14] In the mid-1990s LC's Network Development and MARC Standards Office developed MARC-to-SGML DTDs that were converted to XML DTDs as the technology changed. There are two MARC DTDs: one called "MARC Bibliographic/Holdings/Community Information Record XML DTD" and the second called "MARC Authority/Classification Record XML DTD." The MARC DTDs treat the MARC record as a particular type of document. They define all the elements that can appear in a MARC record and specify how they will be tagged and represented with XML coding. A goal of development of the MARC DTDs was that MARC records should be translatable to XML automatically, and that an XML-encoded MARC record should be easily translated back to a MARC record. One of the features that makes this possible is that each field of an XML-encoded record contains all the tags, indica-

```
<!DOCTYPE EAD PUBLIC "-//Society of American Archivists//DTD ead.dtd (Encoded
Archival Description (EAD))//EN"[
<!ENTITY cutspec Public  "-//University of California, Berkeley::Library//TEXT
(CU union table specifications)//EN"  "cutspec.sgm">
<!ENTITY hdr-cu-s-spcoll PUBLIC  "-//University of California, San
Diego::Mandeville Special Collections Library//TEXT (eadheader: name and
address)//EN"  "hdrcussp.sgm">
<!ENTITY tp-cu-s-spcoll PUBLIC "-//University of California, San
Diego::Mandeville Special Collections Library//TEXT (titlepage: name and
address)//EN"  "tpcussp.sgm">
<!ENTITY ucseal PUBLIC "-//University of California, Berkeley::Library//NONSGML
(University of California seal)//EN"  NDATA GIF>]>

<?Pub Inc>
<ead>
<?Pub Caret>

<eadheader audience="internal"  langencoding="ISO 639" findaidstatus="unverified-full-draft">
<eadid type="SGML catalog">

PUBLIC "-//University of California, San Diego::Mandeville Special Collections
Library//TEXT (US::CU-S::MSS 0401::Arthur Conan Doyle. Sign of the four.)//EN"
"MSS 0401.sgml"
</eadid><filedesc><titlestmt>
<titleproper>Arthur Conan Doyle Sign of the four</titleproper>
</titlestmt>

<publicationstmt>
&hdr-cu-s-spcoll;<date>&copy; 1997</date>
<p>The Regents of the University of California. All rights reserved.</p>
</publicationstmt></filedesc>

<profiledesc>
<creation>Machine-readable finding aid derived from database output.</creation>
<langusage>Description is in <language>English.</language></langusage>
</profiledesc>
</eadheader>

<frontmatter>
<titlepage>
<titleproper>Arthur Conan Doyle Sign of the four, 1890</titleproper>
<num>MSS 0401</num>
<publisher>Mandeville Special Collections Library<lb>GEISEL LIBRARY<lb><extptr
displaytype="present"  entityref="ucseal"><lb>UNIVERSITY OF CALIFORNIA, SAN DIEGO
<lb>La Jolla, CA  92093-0175</publisher>
<p>&copy; 1997 The Regents of the University of California. All rights reserved.</p>
<date>This file last updated: August 1997.</date>
</titlepage>
</frontmatter>

<findaid>
<archdesc language="en"  level="collection"  langmaterial="en">
<did>
<head>DESCRIPTIVE SUMMARY</head>
<unittitle label="Title">Arthur Conan Doyle. Sign of the four.,
<unitdate type="inclusive">1890</unitdate></unittitle>
<unitid label="Collection number">MSS 0401</unitid>

<physdesc label="Extent">0.10 linear feet (1 item (1 leaf) in one folder.)</physdesc>
```

```
<repository label="Repository"><corpname>Mandeville Special Collections Library,
Geisel Library, UC, San Diego</corpname><address><addressline>La Jolla, CA
92093-0175</addressline></address></repository>
<unitloc label="Shelf Location">For current information on the location of these
materials, please consult the Library's online catalog.</unitloc>
</did>
<admininfo>
<head>ADMINISTRATIVE INFORMATION</head>

<prefercite>
<head>Preferred Citation</head>
<p>Arthur Conan Doyle. Sign of the four., MSS 0401.  Mandeville Special
Collections Library, UCSD.</p>
</prefercite>

</admininfo>

<bioghist>
<head>BIOGRAPHY</head>
<p>British novelist and physician.</p>
</bioghist>

<scopecontent>
<head>SCOPE AND CONTENT</head>
<p>The first leaf of the manuscript of the Sherlock Holmes novel, with
holograph corrections and printer's notations.  Glued to backing. </p>
</scopecontent>
</archdesc>
</findaid>
<ref>http://roger.ucsd.edu/search/t?ucsd MSS 401 </ref>
</ead>
```

Fig. 4.7. EAD-encoded finding aid. EAD coding is in bold.

tors, and subfield codes of the MARC field in addition to the contents of the field. (This is not true of the MARCXML Schema, which is briefer.) For an example of an XML-encoded MARC record, see Figure 4.8.

Two XML schemas have been developed by the Library of Congress' Network Development and MARC Standards Office: a MARCXML Schema[15] and MODS (Metadata Object Description Schema).[16] The MARCXML Schema supports XML markup of full *MARC 21* records. MODS is an XML schema that is intended to be able to carry selected data from existing *MARC 21* records as well as to enable the creation of original resource description records. It includes a subset of MARC fields and uses language-based tags rather than numeric ones, in some cases regrouping elements from the *MARC 21* bibliographic format. Because it is a subset, after records have been converted from *MARC 21* to MODS, the MODS records cannot be converted back to *MARC 21* records without loss of data. Version 2.0 was made available early in 2003. Rebecca Guenther has written a description of MODS, along with an explanation of reasons for its devel-

```
    <?xml version="1.0" encoding="UTF-8" ?>
_ <collection xmlns="http://www.loc.gov/MARC21/slim">
_ <record>
  <leader>01142cam 2200301 a 4500</leader>
  <controlfield tag="001">92005291</controlfield>
  <controlfield tag="003">DLC</controlfield>
  <controlfield tag="005">19930521155141.9</controlfield>
  <controlfield tag="008">920219s1993 caua j 000 0 eng</controlfield>
_ <datafield tag="010" ind1="" ind2="">
  <subfield code="a">92005291</subfield>
    </datafield>
_ <datafield tag="020" ind1="" ind2="">
  <subfield code="a">0152038655 :</subfield>
  <subfield code="c">$15.95</subfield>
    </datafield>
_ <datafield tag="040" ind1="" ind2="">
  <subfield code="a">DLC</subfield>
  <subfield code="c">DLC</subfield>
  <subfield code="d">DLC</subfield>
    </datafield>
_ <datafield tag="042" ind1="" ind2="">
  <subfield code="a">lcac</subfield>
    </datafield>
_ <datafield tag="050" ind1="0" ind2="0">
  <subfield code="a">PS3537.A618</subfield>
  <subfield code="b">A88 1993</subfield>
    </datafield>
_ <datafield tag="082" ind1="0" ind2="0">
  <subfield code="a">811/.52</subfield>
  <subfield code="2">20</subfield>
    </datafield>
_ <datafield tag="100" ind1="1" ind2="">
  <subfield code="a">Sandburg, Carl,</subfield>
  <subfield code="d">1878-1967.</subfield>
    </datafield>
_ <datafield tag="245" ind1="1" ind2="0">
  <subfield code="a">Arithmetic /</subfield>
  <subfield code="c">Carl Sandburg ; illustrated as an anamorphic adventure by Ted
    Rand.</subfield>
    </datafield>
_ <datafield tag="250" ind1="" ind2="">
  <subfield code="a">1st ed.</subfield>
    </datafield>
_ <datafield tag="260" ind1="" ind2="">
  <subfield code="a">San Diego :</subfield>
  <subfield code="b">Harcourt Brace Jovanovich,</subfield>
  <subfield code="c">c1993.</subfield>
    </datafield>
_ <datafield tag="300" ind1="" ind2="">
  <subfield code="a">1 v. (unpaged) :</subfield>
  <subfield code="b">ill. (some col.) ;</subfield>
  <subfield code="c">26 cm.</subfield>
    </datafield>
```

```
- <datafield tag="500" ind1="" ind2="">
  <subfield code="a">One Mylar sheet included in pocket.</subfield>
    </datafield>
- <datafield tag="520" ind1="" ind2="">
  <subfield code="a">A poem about numbers and their characteristics. Features
      anamorphic, or distorted, drawings which can be restored to normal by viewing
      from a particular angle or by viewing the image's reflection in the provided Mylar
      cone.</subfield>
    </datafield>
- <datafield tag="650" ind1="" ind2="0">
  <subfield code="a">Arithmetic</subfield>
  <subfield code="x">Juvenile poetry.</subfield>
    </datafield>
- <datafield tag="650" ind1="" ind2="0">
  <subfield code="a">Children's poetry, American.</subfield>
    </datafield>
- <datafield tag="650" ind1="" ind2="1">
  <subfield code="a">Arithmetic</subfield>
  <subfield code="x">Poetry.</subfield>
    </datafield>
- <datafield tag="650" ind1="" ind2="1">
  <subfield code="a">American poetry.</subfield>
    </datafield>
- <datafield tag="650" ind1="" ind2="1">
  <subfield code="a">Visual perception.</subfield>
    </datafield>
- <datafield tag="700" ind1="1" ind2="">
  <subfield code="a">Rand, Ted,</subfield>
  <subfield code="e">ill.</subfield>
    </datafield>
    </record>
    </collection>
```

Fig. 4.8. XML-encoded *MARC 21* record. *MARC 21* tags and content are in bold. (Source: Library of Congress, MARC/XML Web pages, http://www. loc.gov/standards/marcxml//Sandburg/sandburg.xml.)

opment, advantages, features, and prospective uses.[17] Because it has a high compatibility with *MARC 21* records, and because it provides for richer and more structured data than is possible with the Dublin Core (see discussion in Chapter 7), MODS may eventually be preferred by libraries to the Dublin Core as a means of resource description.

The Library of Congress's Network Development and MARC Standards Office has also developed a MARCXML framework[18] that includes many components such as schemas, style sheets, and software tools. The framework is intended to be flexible and extensible to allow users to adapt their work with MARC data in many ways.

ONIX (Online Information eXchange) DTD.[19] ONIX is a standard format that publishers can use to distribute electronic information about their books and other publications. In the online environment it replaces the information found on the jacket cover or container. ONIX covers both content of elements (see discussion in Chapter 7) and encoding. "ONIX Messages" are created by using an XML software application and the ONIX DTD for encoding the data. XML was chosen because it is optimized for data exchange between computers, tags are human-readable, and XML software is inexpensive enough even for smaller publishers. The latest version at this writing is Release 2.0, which adds coverage of e-books and extends coverage of nonbook media. For an example showing part of an ONIX record, see Figure 4.9.

FRAMEWORKS

Each of the encoding standards discussed above is a kind of shell or container. The shell is there waiting for text to be inserted. The text to be inserted may be suggested in the encoding standard, or it may be controlled by another standard. For example, the text in a *MARC 21* record is usually controlled by rules (e.g., *AACR2*) that follow the *International Standard Bibliographic Description (ISBD)* and the Paris Principles and by the conventions of a thesaurus (e.g., *Library of Congress Subject Headings*) and a classification scheme (e.g., *Dewey Decimal Classification*); but there are some *MARC 21* fields for which the rules for content appear in the *MARC 21* standard itself (e.g., the *MARC 21* field 007 gives specific codes for a "fixed field" for certain materials such as microforms or motion pictures).

The container that constitutes the encoding format for one record is just one kind of container. The next level of container holds more than one record and can also provide a means for linking together metadata for different kinds of resources (e.g., metadata for documents that are linked with metadata for the persons and organizations responsible for them and, perhaps, linked with metadata for other documents). Such containers can be called frameworks.

Warwick Framework

The Warwick Framework[20] (named for the location of the conference where it was framed) might be considered to be a container for containers. It is described as a container architecture. As proposed it was to be a mechanism for pulling together distinct packages of metadata that

```
<?xml version="1.0"?>
<!DOCTYPE ONIXMessage SYSTEM "onix-international.dtd">
<ONIXMessage release="1.1">
<FromCompany>B2B Soluciones</FromCompany>
<FromPerson>Horacio Gonzalez horacio.gonzalez@b2bsoluciones.com (5411) 4590-2394</FromPerson>
<ToCompany>EDItEUR</ToCompany>
<ToPerson>David Martin +44 (0)20 8843 8607</ToPerson>
<MessageNumber>1</MessageNumber>
<SentDate>200007311330</SentDate>
<MessageNote>Prueba en Espa&ntilde;ol</MessageNote>
<DefaultLanguageOfText>spa</DefaultLanguageOfText>
<Product>
<RecordReference>95073126091</RecordReference>
<NotificationType>03</NotificationType>
<ISBN>9507312609</ISBN>
<DistinctiveTitle>La resistencia</DistinctiveTitle>
<Contributor>
<PersonName>Ernesto S&aacute;bato</PersonName>
<PersonNameInverted>S&aacute;bato, Ernesto</PersonNameInverted>
<BiographicalNote>ERNESTO SABATO naci&oacute; en Rojas, provincia de Buenos Aires, en 1911. Hizo
cursos de filosof&iacute;a en la Universidad de La Plata, trabaj&oacute; en el Laboratorio Curie y
abandon&oacute; la ciencia en 1945 para dedicarse a la literatura. Ha escrito varios libros de ensayos:
Uno y el universo, Hombres y engranajes, El escritor y sus fantasmas, Apolog&iacute;as y rechazos; tres
novelas: El t&uacute;nel, Sobre h&eacute;roes y tumbas y Abadd&oacute;n el exterminador, y en 1998
sus memorias: Antes del fin. ...
</Contributor>
<NumberOfPages>149</NumberOfPages>
<MainSubject>
<MainSubjectSchemeIdentifier>25</MainSubjectSchemeIdentifier>
<SubjectCode>863A</SubjectCode>
<SubjectHeadingText>Narrativa argentina</SubjectHeadingText>
</MainSubject>
<AudienceCode>01</AudienceCode>
<ImprintName>Seix Barral</ImprintName>
<PublisherName>Planeta</PublisherName>
<CountryOfPublication>AR</CountryOfPublication>
<PublicationDate>200005</PublicationDate>
<CopyrightYear>2000</CopyrightYear>
    ...
<OtherText>
<TextTypeCode>18</TextTypeCode>
<TextFormat>00</TextFormat>
<Text>
"Les pido que nos detengamos a pensar en la grandeza a la que todav&iacute;a podemos aspirar si nos
atrevemos a valorar la vida de otra manera. Nos pido ese coraje que nos sit&uacute;a en la verdadera
dimensi&oacute;n del hombre."
    ...
</Text>
</OtherText>
<OtherText>
<TextTypeCode>23</TextTypeCode>
<TextFormat>00</TextFormat>
```

```
<Text>Extracto del Libro
LA RESISTENCIA
"Hay d&iacute;as en que me levanto con una esperanza demencial, momentos en los que siento que las
posibilidades de una vida m&aacute;s humana est&aacute;n al alcance de nuestras manos. Este es uno
de esos d&iacute;as."
  ...
</Text>
</OtherText>
<OtherText>
<TextTypeCode>07</TextTypeCode>
<TextFormat>00</TextFormat>
<Text> S&aacute;bato present&oacute; su nuevo libro, "La Resistencia"
Ernesto S&aacute;bato present&oacute; ayer su libro "La Resistencia" en un local de una cadena de
disquer&iacute;as ubicado en Santa Fe y Callao. Ante el anuncio de que el escritor estar&iacute;a
all&iacute; firmando libros, a las seis de la tarde empez&oacute; a formarse una fila de unos 300
lectores/fans que peregrinaron con un objetivo: volver a casa con su ejemplar autografiado.
  ...
</Text>
<TextSourceTitle>Diario Clar&iacute;n</TextSourceTitle>
<TextPublicationDate>20000617</TextPublicationDate>
</OtherText>
  ...
<SupplyDetail>
<SupplierName>Planeta</SupplierName>
<AvailabilityCode>IP</AvailabilityCode>
<Price>
<PriceTypeCode>01</PriceTypeCode>
<PriceAmount>15</PriceAmount>
<CurrencyCode>ARP</CurrencyCode>
</Price>
<Price>
<PriceTypeCode>01</PriceTypeCode>
<PriceAmount>15</PriceAmount>
<CurrencyCode>USD</CurrencyCode>
</Price>
</SupplyDetail>
</Product>
</ONIXMessage>
```

Fig. 4.9. Part of an ONIX "message." (Source: Editeur, "ONIX International Version 1.01: Sample ONIX Files." Available: http://www.editeur.org/onixsamples.html.)

are related to the same information package, but that need to be separately controlled (e.g., *AACR2*/MARC record, Dublin Core record, EAD finding aid, all describing the same collection). This was intended to help to avoid having to expand any one encoding container to include every possible piece of information needed by any specialized group of users. Each metadata package could be maintained by its respective community. In this way specific communities could focus on their specific requirements without having to generalize to the broadest scope possible.

Bringing together metadata records into the proposed Warwick Framework was a way to allow for the interchange of data among different communities. It was also intended to allow selective access to certain metadata records while ignoring others. Responsibility for the maintenance and updating of particular metadata records was to remain with their original communities, while the information in them could be shared among all of the communities. The container architecture was to be modular, and encoding of records did not have to be compatible with each other. There were to be three kinds of packages: packages containing actual metadata records, packages containing references to other objects in the infrastructure, and packages that would be the "container" architecture. The latter needed some type of encoding structure; so proposals for both MIME-based and SGML-based implementations were made. It was this process that led to the next step in the evolution of metadata frameworks, the Resource Description Framework (RDF).

RDF (Resource Description Framework)

RDF is a framework for metadata that promotes interoperability.[21] It provides an infrastructure that enables the encoding, exchange, and re-use of metadata in a way that is unambiguous, so that machines can "understand" the semantics of the metadata and therefore can use it in the process called resource discovery. The goal is for much more precision than is possible in a full-text search (full-text searching being the method currently relied upon by most search engines). More precision is possible because RDF identifies the "namespaces" from which it draws its semantics.[22] That is, various information communities may develop DTDs or schemas for the metadata to describe their resources, and they establish a location on the Web (i.e., a namespace) where the DTDs or schemas are maintained or updated. The machine reading the RDF statements can then appropriately interpret the statements by reference to the namespaces.

RDF provides a model that is syntax-independent. The model says that a resource is any object that can be uniquely identified by a Uniform Resource Identifier (URI). Resources have properties, and properties have values. A value can be a string of characters or a number or can be another resource. If a value is another resource, then that resource, in turn, has properties that have values, some of which could be other resources. There is no limit to the number of levels of connections to resources. The collection of properties of a resource is called a description. Figure 4.10 is a simple illustration of the model. In this illustration, a resource, called "Doc-

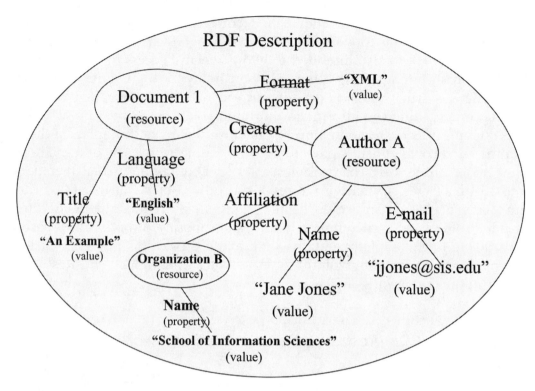

Fig. 4.10. Data model for an RDF description.

ument 1," has properties named Format, Creator, Language, and Title. Each property has a value with the value of the Creator property being another resource called "Author A." This resource has properties named Affiliation, Name, and E-mail. The value of the Affiliation property is yet another resource called "Organization B."

The model, however, must be expressed concretely if it is to be used for the interchange of metadata. W3C has directed that the syntax for RDF be XML. Using XML, an RDF description identifies the fact that it is RDF, identifies the namespace to be used for the property names, and provides the description. Figure 4.11 shows a simple RDF XML-encoded description. In this example the first two lines say that this is XML using RDF for the description container. The next two lines identify the fact that the tags come from both the RDF and Dublin Core namespaces with the locations of those namespaces. The remainder is the description of the resource, followed by the required end tags.

```
<?xml version="1.0"?>
<rdf:RDF
    xmlns:rdf="http://www.w3.org/1999/02/22-rdf-syntax-ns#"
    xmlns:dc="http://purl.org/dc/elements/1.0/">
<rdf:Description rdf:about="http://www.dra.com/SR/rdfarticle.html">
    <dc:creator> Mark Needleman </dc:creator>
    <dc:title> RDF: Resource Description Framework </dc:title>
    <dc:publisher> Serials Review </dc:publisher>
    <dc:format> text/html </dc:format>
    <dc:language> en </dc:language>
</rdf:Description>
</rdf:RDF>
```

Fig. 4.11. Example RDF description using Dublin Core and XML. (Source: Mark H. Needleman, "RDF: The Resource Description Framework," *Serials Review* **27, no. 1 [2001]: 60.)**

METS (Metadata Encoding & Transmission Standard)

Another kind of framework is one that is being developed as an initiative of the Digital Library Federation (DLF) by the Network Development and MARC Standards Office of the Library of Congress. The METS schema[23] is a framework for encoding descriptive, administrative, and structural metadata that describe objects within a digital library, expressed using the XML schema language. METS provides an encoding format for holding metadata aimed at managing, preserving, displaying, and exchanging digital objects. It was created to handle complex, reformatted digital information packages. (A single digitized photograph would not need the structural components provided by METS.) The schema is extensible and modular in its approach.

A METS document comprises five components: descriptive metadata, administrative metadata, file groups, the structural map, and behavior metadata. It may also include a header containing meta-metadata. METS does not define the elements in the administrative and descriptive sections. It allows the repository to choose from a number of extension schemas. For example, the management of the repository might choose to use Dublin Core as their descriptive metadata schema. Both administrative and descriptive metadata can be wrapped into a METS document, or pointers to metadata records held outside the METS document can be included. The file groups list all of the files contained within the digital object. For example, in a digital object that consists of a collection of images accompanied by text, there might be file groups for thumbnail images, for the master images, for TEI encoded text, and for pdf versions. The structural map specifies the ways in which the files fit together to create the digital information package. This map is hierarchically structured and may be presented to the user for navigational purposes. The behavior section describes how the object is to perform. METS, in 2003, is being tested and further developed and has been implemented in a number of institutions.

Semantic Web

The idea of the Semantic Web[24] was first articulated in 1997 by Tim Berners-Lee, the man also given credit for "inventing" the Web itself.[25] The Semantic Web is intended to give a kind of structure to the Web that will allow computers to deal with its content in meaningful ways. It is intended that information will be defined in such a way that its "meaning" or "semantics" can be discernible, shared, and processed by automated tools as well as by people. Berners-Lee and colleagues give an example of a brother and sister needing to coordinate their schedules with a certain kind of physical therapy specialist who is a provider for the right insurance plan so that one of them can take their mother to the specialist. The Semantic Web allows their "agents" (or computer robots) to work together to find the right place at a time one of them has available, all within a few minutes.[26]

Berners-Lee and colleagues state, "For the semantic web to function, computers must have access to structured collections of information and sets of inference rules that they can use to conduct automated reasoning."[27] The components required for this framework include URIs, XML, RDF, and ontologies. URIs provide a way to identify every resource as well as relationships among resources. XML allows creators of Web pages to create their own tags to annotate sections of text or images—that is, to create structure for a document, if not meaning. Meaning comes through RDF with its assertions that resources have properties with values. Because different terms can be used to express the same concept (e.g., "head" can be the beginning of a document, the top of a body, the leader of a group, the top of a nail, etc.), there is a need for documents or files that formally define such terms and their relationships to other terms. In the library and archival fields, authority files have provided control of terms and their relationships for decades. In the artificial intelligence field, ontologies are being constructed to formally define relationships among terms, usually terms in a particular field.[28] Suppose, for example, an RDF statement says that a resource has a "chair" property with a value identified as another resource. Would this mean that the resource is in a museum of furniture?

Or is the resource a person who leads a committee or a department? A human, of course, could tell from the context, but a computer intelligent agent would need assistance. The agent could be referred to an ontology of terms applying to people in an academic environment that might explain the use of "chair" in the concept of "leader of a university department." Ontologies can also assist with the problem of the same thing being given different names in different environments (e.g., "Pittsburgh, PA" being called "<place>" or "<location>" or "<CityState>" in different databases).

Several groups within W3C are working toward realization of the Semantic Web, including an RDF Core Working Group and a Web Ontology Working Group.[29] The reader should be alert to rapidly changing developments in this area.

CONCLUSION

This chapter has discussed some of the ways of encoding surrogate record information to create metadata records and frameworks. An understanding of this coding and how it is accomplished is necessary to an understanding of the systems in place today for the retrieval and display of various kinds of surrogate/metadata records. These systems are discussed in the next chapter. Then there are some separate standards for creation of the text to be included in surrogate/metadata records, and there are some standards that include both prescription of text and encoding in the same standard. These are discussed in Chapters 6 and 7.

NOTES

All URLs accessed June 2003.

1.   Unicode, *Frequently Asked Questions: Basic Questions.* Last updated 27 June 2003. Available: http://www.unicode.org/unicode/faq/basic_q.html.

2.   F. Yergeau, "UTF-8, a Transformation Format of ISO 10646." January 1998. Available: http://www.isi.edu/in-notes/rfc2279.txt; and Olle Järnefors, "A Short Overview of ISO/IEC 10646 and Unicode." Last updated 26 February 1996. Available: http://www.nada.kth.se/i18n/ucs/unicode-iso10646-oview.html.

3.   *American National Standard for Bibliographic Information Interchange: Draft*

(New York: American National Standards Institute, 1984). Revision of ANSI Z39.2–1979.

4. *Information and Documentation—Format for Information Exchange*, 3rd ed. (Geneva, Switzerland: International Organization for Standardization, 1996). ISO 2709:1996(E).

5. "MARC 21 Specifications for Record Structure, Character Sets, and Exchange Media: Character Sets." January 2000. Available: http://www.loc.gov/marc/specifications/speccharintro.html.

6. IFLA Universal Bibliographic Control and International MARC Core Programme (UBCIM), *UNIMARC Manual: Bibliographic Format 1994.* Last updated 1 March 2000. Available: http://www.ifla.org/VI/3/p1996-1/sec-uni.htm.

7. *Information Processing: Text and Office Systems: Standard Generalized Markup Language (SGML)* (Geneva, Switzerland: International Organization for Standardization, 1988). ISO 8879:1986/A1:1988(E).

8. W3C, "XML in 10 Points." Created 27 March 1999; revised 13 November 2001. Available: http://www.w3.org/XML/1999/XML-in-10-points.

9. Text Encoding Initiative. "The TEI Guidelines." 31 March 2002; revised 17 May 2002. Available: http://www.tei-c.org/Guidelines2/index.html.

10. Lou Burnard and C. M. Sperberg-McQueen, *TEI Lite: An Introduction to Text Encoding for Interchange.* June 1995; revised May 2002. Available: http://www.tei-c.org/Lite/.

11. "HyperText Markup Language (HTML) Home Page." Last modified 5 July 2003. Available: http://www.w3.org/MarkUp/.

12. "XHTML™ 1.0: The Extensible HyperText Markup Language (Second Edition): A Reformulation of HTML 4 in XML 1.0. W3C Recommendation." 26 January 2000; revised 1 August 2002. Available: http://www.w3.org/TR/xhtml1/.

13. "Encoded Archival Description (EAD): Official EAD Version 2002 Web Site." Available: http://lcweb.loc.gov/ead/.

14. Library of Congress, Network Development and MARC Standards Office, "MARC in XML." 16 January 2003. Available: http://www.loc.gov/marc/marcxml.html.

15. Library of Congress, Network Development and MARC Standards Of-

fice, "MARCXML: MARC 21 XML Schema: Official Web Site." 10 June 2003. Available: http://www.loc.gov/standards/marcxml/.

16. Library of Congress, Network Development and MARC Standards Office, "MODS: Metadata Object Description Schema: Official Web Site." 6 June 2003. Available: http://www.loc.gov/standards/mods/.

17. Rebecca S. Guenther, "MODS: The Metadata Object Description Schema," *Portal: Libraries and the Academy* 3, no. 1 (2003): 137–150.

18. Library of Congress, Network Development and MARC Standards Office, "MARC XML Architecture." 16 April 2002. Available: http://www.loc.gov/standards/marcxml/marcxml-architecture.html.

19. Editeur, "ONIX for Books." Available: http://www.editeur.org/onix.html.

20. For a discussion of the Warwick Framework, see: Susan S. Lazinger, *Digital Preservation and Metadata: History, Theory, Practice* (Englewood, Colo.: Libraries Unlimited, 2001), pp. 193–195.

21. W3C, "Frequently Asked Questions about RDF." Last updated 27 March 2003. Available: http://www.w3.org/RDF/FAQ.

22. For more on namespaces and semantic interoperability, see Chapter 6.

23. "METS: Metadata Encoding & Transmission Standard: Official Web Site." Available: http://www.loc.gov/standards/mets/.

24. W3C, "Semantic Web." Last updated 30 May 2003. Available: http://www.w3.org/2001/sw/.

25. Tim Berners-Lee, "Realising the Full Potential of the Web." Based on a talk presented at the W3C meeting, London, 3 December 1997. Available: http://www.w3.org/1998/02/Potential.html. A popularized explanation is found in: Tim Berners-Lee, James Hendler, and Ora Lassila, "The Semantic Web," *Scientific American* 284, no. 5 (May 2001): 34–38, 40–43. Also available: http://www.scientificamerican.com/article.cfm?articleID=00048144-10D2-1C70-84A9809EC588EF21&catID=2.

26. Berners-Lee, Hendler, and Lassila, "The Semantic Web."

27. Ibid.

28. For more about ontologies, see Chapter 10.

29. W3C, "Semantic Web Activity Statement." Last updated 12 May 2003. Available: http://www.w3.org/2001/sw/Activity.

SUGGESTED READINGS

Berners-Lee, Tim, James Hendler, and Ora Lassila. "The Semantic Web," *Scientific American* 284, no. 5 (May 2001): 34–38, 40–43. Available: http://www.scientificamerican.com/article.cfm?articleID=00048144-10D2-1C70-84A9809EC588EF21&catID=2.

Bray, Tim. "What is RDF?" January 24, 2001. Available: http://www.xml.com/pub/a/2001/01/24/rdf.html.

Bryan, Martin. "An Introduction to the Extensible Markup Language (XML)." *Bulletin of the American Society for Information Science* 25, no. 1 (October/November 1998): 11–14. Also available: http://www.personal.u-net.com/~sgml/xmlintro.htm.

———. "An Introduction to the Standard Generalized Markup Language (SGML)." The SGML Centre, 1992. Available: http://www.personal.u-net.com/~sgml/sgml.htm.

Burnard, Lou, and C. M. Sperberg-McQueen. *TEI Lite: An Introduction to Text Encoding for Interchange.* June 1995; revised May 2002. Available: http://www.tei-c.org/Lite/.

Caplan, Priscilla. *Metadata Fundamentals for All Librarians.* Chicago: American Library Association, 2003. Chapter 2: "Syntax, Creation, and Storage."

"Encoded Archival Description (EAD): Official EAD Version 2002 Web Site." Available: http://lcweb.loc.gov/ead.

Fritz, Deborah A., and Richard J. Fritz. *MARC 21 for Everyone: A Practical Guide.* Chicago: American Library Association, 2003.

Furrie, Betty. *Understanding MARC Bibliographic: Machine-Readable Cataloging.* 7th ed. Library of Congress, Cataloging Distribution Service, 2003. Available: http://www.loc.gov/marc/umb.

Gaynor, Edward. "From MARC to Markup: SGML and Online Library Systems." *ALCTS Newsletter* 7, no. 2 (1996): A–D. Also available (archival copy): http://xml.coverpages.org/gaynorMARC96.html.

Johnson, Bruce Chr. "XML and MARC: Which Is 'Right'?" *Cataloging & Classification Quarterly* 32, no. 1 (2001): 81–90.

Kelly, Brian. "What is . . . XML?" Last updated 18 May 1998. Available: http://www.ariadne.ac.uk/issue15/what-is/.

Lazinger, Susan S. *Digital Preservation and Metadata: History, Theory, Practice.* Englewood, Colo.: Libraries Unlimited, 2001. Chapter 7: "Standards for Structural Interoperability: Frameworks and Wrapper Technologies."

Library of Congress, Network Development and MARC Standards Office. "MARC in XML." 16 January 2003. Available: http://www.loc.gov/marc/marcxml.html.

"The MARC 21 Formats: Background and Principles." Prepared by MARBI in conjunction with Network Development and MARC Standards Office, Library of Congress. Washington, D.C.: Library of Congress, 1996. Available: http://lcweb.loc.gov/marc/96principl.html.

Miller, Eric. "An Introduction to the Resource Description Framework." *Bulletin of the American Society for Information Science* 25, no. 1 (October/ November 1998): 15–19.

National Center for Supercomputing Applications. "A Beginner's Guide to HTML." Last updated January 24, 2001. Available: http://archive. ncsa.uiuc.edu/General/Internet/WWW/HTMLPrimer.html.

Needleman, Mark H. "RDF: The Resource Description Framework." *Serials Review* 27, no. 1 (December 10, 2001): 58–61.

Taylor, Arlene G. *Wynar's Introduction to Cataloging and Classification.* 9th ed., with the assistance of David P. Miller. Englewood, Colo.: Libraries Unlimited, 2000. Chapter 3: "Introduction to the MARC Formats."

W3C. "Frequently Asked Questions about RDF." Updated 27 March 2003. Available: http://www.w3.org/RDF/FAQ.

———. "RDF Primer: W3C Working Draft 23 January 2003." Available: http://www.w3.org/TR/rdf-primer/.

Yee, Martha M., and Sara Shatford Layne. *Improving Online Public Access Catalogs.* Chicago: American Library Association, 1998. Chapter 3: "The Building Blocks: The Structure of Bibliographic and Authority Records."

CHAPTER 5
SYSTEMS AND SYSTEM DESIGN

This chapter provides an overview of some of the issues involved in organizing information as they relate to systems and system design. The tools described in Chapter 2 require an adequate system design to enable users to find desired information. In order to ensure this discovery, systems must be designed to retrieve and display metadata in useful and logical ways. This chapter looks at the system components available to help organize information, the considerations needed to maintain innovations in system design, and a range of other systems issues.

SYSTEMS

The *Dictionary of Computing* defines the term *system* as "anything we choose to regard (a) as a whole and (b) as comprising a set of related components. . . . In computing the word is freely used to refer to all kinds of combinations of hardware, software, data and other information, procedures, and human activities."[1] Managing systems may involve a single source of data handled through a single type of software, or may involve a more complex mixture of various data sources, pieces of hardware, and software components.

In organizing information, the term *systems* generally refers to what we call an "information system." An information system performs three basic functions: storage (data organization), retrieval (based on queries),

This chapter was edited and new material was added by Daniel N. Joudrey.

and presentation (interface design). Each one of these functions is indispensable, and the operation of each depends on the other two. System design decisions need to take into consideration all three of these functions. Data is stored in a system using a specific format that is suitable for containing the type of information being stored. Quick retrieval is achieved using indexing. A user or another system uses a query language in order to retrieve data stored in the system. Once the data is retrieved, the proper presentation renders the raw data usable. Among the institutions discussed in this book, libraries were the first to automate. Though the question "Why automate?" is rarely asked these days, Larry Milsap reminds us that libraries automated in order to:

- provide access to the complete catalog from multiple locations

- increase and improve access points

- increase and improve search capabilities

- eliminate or reduce inconsistencies and inaccuracies of card catalogs

- reduce the increasing problems and costs of maintaining card catalogs

- deal with pressures and influences for change[2]

With the move to automation came major changes in the ways libraries performed daily tasks and fulfilled their obligations to patrons. Today, the "automation revolution" is a thing of the past, and archives, museums, and other institutions have joined in having their information resources organized in automated information systems. The integration of automation into work processes is assumed. This does not mean, however, that all of the problems of systems and organizing information have been resolved. Information professionals still have much work to do and it is unlikely that all the problems will be completely resolved before new questions come along.

Databases

One of the most basic tools used for organizing information is the database. Databases are organized collections of data. They are the structures that underlie many of our information systems. A database is a set of records, each representing a specific entity, all constructed in the same way (with common attributes), and connected by relationships. The records may contain numeric information, text, or graphic representations.

Records are the basic components of a database. A record comprises data fields or data elements (such as author's name, stock number, employee's date of birth, etc.), which describe chosen attributes of an entity (a book, a product, an employee, or any other entity). A database *can* be in paper format, but it is usually thought of as being machine-readable. Databases become necessary when there is too much information for humans to process and analyze by themselves. An everyday example to help clarify the basic components of a database is a checkbook. Each entity (transaction) has a record (a row in the checkbook). Each entity has attributes, such as a date, a check number, a description of the transaction, a payee, an amount, and the adjusted balance. In each column, there is a field for holding the value of each attribute. The attribute values identify, describe, and explain the entity and may indicate relationships between entities.[3] Of course, most databases are more complex, but this example does contain all elements of the basic structure. It should be noted that a variety of organizational methods may be used to manage the data stored inside a database, and these methods vary from system to system. A key feature of bibliographic databases is the use of indexes created to hold different types of information. For example, separate indexes may be created to track author data, title data, subject data, and the like; the number and types of indexes that are created vary from system to system.

Databases may be categorized based on their structures (i.e., methods of organizing data). Most often, they are divided into hierarchical and relational databases. *Hierarchical* databases use a traditional tree structure as the model for holding information. They consist of one file composed of many records, which in turn are made up of numerous data fields. These databases tend to be rather inflexible and use more space as data is often repeated. In *relational* databases the records may be divided into parts, which are held in various files. These parts are linked to each other to form individual records. Each individual piece of information is stored in only one place, but it may be used in several records. For example, an author's name may be stored in a file for names, but each record for each work of the author is displayed with the author's name in the display.

Databases serve various functions. They may hold administrative data, a collection of images, or raw numerical data. They may contain surrogate records or hold the actual items of interest. They may be repositories of full-text articles or they might keep track of inventory and sales. The functions of databases can be divided into two categories: reference databases and source databases. Reference databases contain links or pointers to information sources held outside of the database, for example, a journal index containing information about the location and contents of articles that are stored elsewhere. Source databases contain the actual information sought, for example, a human resources database containing employee information.

Databases created as information retrieval tools contain surrogate records. The retrieval tools described in Chapter 2 can all be held in computer databases, although bibliographies and finding aids are more likely to be displayed as text. A computer database may be held in computer memory or stored elsewhere, such as on a CD-ROM or a remote server.

Databases underlie almost all the tools we use to organize information. Indexing and abstracting services, book sellers, museums, and libraries, to name a few, all rely on databases to hold the records of their inventories. To librarians, two of the most familiar implementations of databases are Bibliographic Networks and Integrated Library Systems.

Bibliographic Networks

Bibliographic networks have as their main resource a huge database of catalog-type records. Access to the database is available for a price, and members of the network can contribute new records and download existing ones. Databases maintained by bibliographic networks are essentially online union catalogs. Bibliographic networks acquire many machine-readable cataloging records from the Library of Congress and other subscription sources. The databases also include cataloging records contributed by participating libraries. In either case, the records contain two kinds of information: (1) descriptive cataloging and subject/classification data, typically in the *MARC 21* format; and (2) holdings information for libraries that have added specific items to their collections.

Bibliographic networks were organized in the 1970s to support library technical services operations through cooperative cataloging and computer-assisted card production. Although they have steadily expanded their activities, their continued emphasis on cooperative cataloging most clearly distinguishes them from other online information services that provide access to similar surrogate records. The Library of Congress MARC records, for example, are available online through other information services, but these do not offer online entry of original cataloging data, record editing, or other services that specifically support cataloging services.

The three major bibliographic networks discussed here are:

- OCLC—Online Computer Library Center—largest and most comprehensive

- RLIN—Research Libraries Information Network—especially important for special collections

- A-G Canada—serves Canada and a few customers in the northeastern United States

Bibliographic networks differ in their administrative structures and customer bases. OCLC and RLIN operate as nonprofit membership organizations. A-G Canada (formerly ISM/LIS, which grew out of UTLAS at the University of Toronto) operates as a for-profit company. OCLC and A-G Canada are general-purpose bibliographic networks that are available to libraries of all types and sizes. Although RLIN was specifically created to meet the special needs of research institutions, participation is open to other types of libraries. OCLC and RLIN offer services to all libraries all over the world. A-G Canada is found mostly in Canada, with a few customers in northeastern United States. OCLC encourages participation through regional networks that act as its authorized agents.

More than three-fourths of the customers of bibliographic networks are OCLC participants. Customers are libraries and other organizations that may access bibliographic network databases through one or more terminals installed at their own facilities, although more and more customers gain access through the Internet. Although it is typical for organizations to subscribe to a single bibliographic network, some libraries employ one network for current cataloging and another for retrospective conversion, resource sharing, or other activities. Many large libraries are full members of RLIN or OCLC and at the same time are "tape-loading" members of the other. (A tape-loading member sends a magnetic tape containing all records cataloged through the primary network to the other network.)

Bibliographic network databases are specifically designed to automate cataloging. If existing cataloging copy is available, it is displayed in the full MARC format, or in OCLC it can alternatively be displayed in Dublin Core format. A record editor can move, change, delete, or otherwise edit individual field values to meet local cataloging requirements (called *copy* cataloging). If no cataloging copy is available, a cataloger may create a record (called *original* cataloging). To facilitate cataloging decisions and promote consistency, bibliographic networks provide online access to the Library of Congress Name Authority and Subject Authority files. OCLC and RLIN offer online access to these on a search-only basis. A-G Canada creates linkages between a library's cataloging records and their associated authority records so that unauthorized forms are automatically changed to authorized forms or are called to the attention of the cataloger before they can be added to the database. All the networks have Interlibrary Loan (ILL) subsystems, which are an obvious use of a union catalog. A variety of retrospective conversion products are offered as well.

Integrated Library Systems (ILSs)

Integrated Library Systems are more than just online public access catalogs (OPACs). They are fully integrated computer systems that include various modules to perform different functions. Their purpose is to incorporate the functionality of five or six separate database tools into one integrated system, all using the same database. The greatest benefit comes from information-sharing among the various modules, reducing duplication of data and effort. An ILS may have modules to support acquisitions, cataloging, authority control, circulation, serials management, interlibrary loan, public access (the OPAC), course reserves, and system management. These systems may also be known as Integrated Library Management Systems (ILMSs), Library Management Support Systems (LMSSs), or sometimes as Library Housekeeping Systems, particularly in the United Kingdom.

History of the ILS. Before the first ILS appeared on the scene, computers were already being used to organize information. As mentioned in Chapter 2, computers were used in catalog production in the 1960s and 1970s to produce COM and book catalogs. At that time, computers were not the desktop machines we think of today, but were instead large mainframe systems that were run in batch mode. A quick look-up in the computer was not possible; "jobs" (e.g., queries) were sent in batches and often the results were not available until the next day. Record formats were defined locally, as the MARC standard was still in its infancy. It was not until the late 1970s that minicomputers, which could provide some online access to information, began appearing in libraries.[4] In order to have online catalogs, there had to be a convergence of computing power, mass storage, low costs, software that could handle large files, and the files themselves in electronic format.[5]

The first automated library systems were created in the 1970s. Many of these commercially produced products were turnkey systems. A turnkey system is a computer system that includes all the hardware and software necessary for a particular function. Often these products were developed to handle only one specific type of function, such as circulation. Then as more vendors got into the library automation game (increasing competition), additional modules were created to expand system functionality. Numerous systems failed, but by the 1980s, a second generation of online catalogs began to appear with increased search capabilities.[6] In recent years, some vendors have focused on certain types of libraries and have tailored their systems to meet specialized needs. A number of early systems were created as in-house products, but by the end of the twentieth century, most of those systems had been replaced by commercially developed packages. Despite a great show of interest in recent years in open source software (OSS), most libraries do not have the resources to develop and maintain their own systems.[7] The Library of Congress (LC) had been one of the last "holdouts" before it announced in 1999 that it would replace its thirty-year-old in-house computer systems with a commercially produced ILS. A major reason that LC replaced its systems (which consisted of seven separate record systems) was that data in an ILS can be shared among the different modules.

ILS Developments. In the last ten to fifteen years, there have been tremendous improvements in Integrated Library Systems. Many of these developments have centered around the OPAC; others have affected the entire system. Some of the major developments in Integrated Library Systems include: the move to GUI interfaces; widespread implementation of client-server architecture;[8] the use of industry-standard relational databases; support for Unicode to enable the use of multiple scripts and multiple languages; implementation of self-service features; personalized interfaces; enhanced content; and the creation of authentication mechanisms for remote users.[9] In addition, as discussed in Chapter 1, ILSs are developing packages for object management, collection management, license and rights management, linking, and search and discovery. A number of these are using XML, and some systems are experimenting with XML for their traditional modules. For more information about current trends, see the April 1 issue of *Library Journal*, which contains a review of the ILS marketplace each year.

Development of Online Public Access Catalogs (OPACs)

The online public access catalog is probably the most familiar ILS module and is the one that needs the most system design attention, due to its use by people "off the street" who do not have in-depth training in system use. Charles Hildreth states, "The online public access catalog is the first major development that brings the benefits of automation directly to the user as a means of expanded access to library collections and as a means of organizing and presenting bibliographic information for effective self-services."[10] The OPAC has been a focus of system design research for many years. System design issues are examined below after looking at the developmental stages of the OPAC.

OPAC stages are most often described in terms of "generations." The first generation of OPACs appeared in the early 1980s as crude finding lists, often based on circulation system records[11] or based on simple MARC records, perhaps with a circulation, serials, or acquisitions module.[12] Based on card catalogs and early online information retrieval systems, their searching capabilities were limited to author and title searches, using only left-anchored searching (i.e., all searches must be based on the first word or words of a particular text string starting at the left; for example, in left-anchored searching the title "organization of information" must be searched starting with the word "organization" and cannot be found under "information"). The interface was menu-based and fairly primitive. These early systems had no subject access and no reference structures.

First generation OPACs were little more than poor imitations of print retrieval tools. Some systems were programmed to respond to commands in which a "code" (e.g., "a" for author, "t" for title, etc.) was to be followed by an exact string of characters that would be matched against the system's internal index. In some others, derived key searching was supported (i.e., taking parts of names and/or titles to create a search string).[13] In many early systems, the display of results was by the "last in, first out" principle (i.e., the last records entered into the system were those listed first in the display). These first generation systems were highly intolerant of user mistakes. There was little or no browsing and little or no keyword searching, with or without Boolean operators. Access points were limited only to those that were available in the card catalog, that is, left-anchored searches. First generation OPACs were primarily book finding lists and worked best for known-item searching.[14]

With designers learning from the problems of the first generation, the second generation of OPACs in the late 1980s showed major improvements. This generation was marked by significantly improved user interfaces. Keyword searching, with its use of Boolean operators, was introduced, thus increasing the number of access points available for searching. This meant that searches were no longer required to be exact word or phrase, left-anchored searches; words could now be matched, even if they were in the middle of a text string. Also greatly enhancing the searching process were truncation and wildcard support, browsing capabilities (including index term browsing), use of full MARC records, interactive search refinement, and subject access to items. Second-generation OPACs also provided greater manipulation of search results and provided better help systems with more informative error messages[15] (although there is still a lot of work to be done in this area).

Up to the second generation of OPACs, the characteristics distinguishing each generation are fairly clear. As we move beyond the second generation, however, there are differences in how the profession refers to the more recent developments in OPACs. Some consider the systems that are currently in use (WebPACs with GUI interfaces, Z39.50 compliant systems, etc.) to be third-generation OPACs. Others describe the third generation as catalogs that are still in experimental stages.

Hildreth acknowledges the improvements made in catalogs during the 1990s, but refers to these recently improved catalogs as E³ OPACs rather than as third generation. E³ OPACs are so named because they are *enhanced* in functionality and usability, *expanded* in indexing, data records, and collection coverage, and *extended* through linkages and networks, acting as gateways to additional collections. They are marked by an improved, more intuitive graphical user interface (or GUI, the icon-based, point-and-click interface we have come to expect from Macintosh and Windows-based personal computers).

Hildreth describes the upcoming generation of systems as accepting natural language query expressions, where the user can search in his/her own words. They will have automatic term conversion/matching aids (spelling correction, intelligent stemming, synonym tables) and closest, best-match retrieval as opposed to today's systems, which require an exact match for an item to be retrieved as possibly relevant. The next generation will provide ranked retrieval output and relevance feedback methods. Hypertext, related-record searching, and browsing will be common, as will the integration of keywords, controlled vocabulary, and classification-based search approaches. These OPACs will be full-collection access tools with expanded scope and coverage.[16] While vendors are making great progress in today's OPACs, it may still be some time before all of these innovations come to the OPAC marketplace.

SYSTEM DESIGN

In the last thirty years in archives, libraries, museums, and other agencies that collect and organize information there has been a proliferation of systems positions. Among the responsibilities for such a position are managing networking functions, management of databases, dealing with access issues, Web page management, online services support, managing the ILS (in libraries), system design, and a host of other duties. Information technology professionals help to bridge the gaps between the limitations of information systems and the requirements for efficient, helpful organization and display of information through developing better system designs.

Organization of Information and System Design

At times, it can be unclear where the process of organizing information ends and that of system design begins. In a display of surrogate records from a retrieval tool, both aspects come together to present to the user the information sought. This set of results combines features of the organizing process (standard punctuation, forms of headings, etc.) and features of system design (labels, screen layout, etc.) in the presentation of the information. When the information is clear, easily retrieved, and well presented, the user does not notice system design or organizing elements. It is only when there are problems or confusion that these elements are discussed.

In the print world, system design was not separate from the process of creating surrogate records. Panizzi's rules included principles for what information to include in surrogate records and also standards for placing those records into a cohesive catalog. Cutter's rules included record-creation rules that emphasized collocation (i.e., placing those records in logical juxtaposition with each other) and also included a section of filing rules (i.e., Cutter's design for the card catalog). Each edition of rules that has come from the American Library Association has assumed the system design of a card catalog. Standards for the creation of bibliographies and indexes often assume a print format, generally in book form.

Of course, the term *system design* was not used for the process of deciding how print tools would be arranged and laid out. The same people who created surrogate records also controlled the display of those records. They did not think of themselves as system designers. Yet some print tools were and still are quite sophisticated finding and collocation systems. They could be sophisticated because the designers knew the contents of the surrogate records intimately. As the tools became automated though, the task of design was taken on by people who understood computers, but often had little or no knowledge of the contents of the records that would make up the system. System design is a necessity for the retrieval of organized information, whether it is or is not done by the same people who create surrogate records. It can be a design that simply displays, in no particular order, every record that contains a certain keyword. Or it can be a design that displays records in a sophisticated way to show relationships among records and among works, as well as responding to requested search words.

System design research can be divided into two categories: technology-focused research and user-centered research. These two categories are not mutually exclusive. There are overlapping concerns and interconnections between the two (e.g., the system's search functionality and the user's information-seeking behavior have important connections).

Users' needs and search behavior *should* influence the design of the technological systems we use (whether they do or not is another issue). While this book is not an appropriate forum for a treatise on information retrieval and information-seeking behavior, it is helpful to start with the basic underlying assumption that users approach retrieval tools with an information need. How they meet that need is greatly affected by the characteristics of the system they encounter.

Searching Methods

According to Hildreth, there are two methods of searching, *querying* and *browsing*, both of which can be divided further. Querying can be phrase matching or keyword matching.[17] Phrase matching is matching a particular search string to the exact text located in surrogate records in the system (or more precisely, to particular indexes created by the system). This type of query demands that the words of the string be found together in the same order as given in the search query. It does not allow for the terms or strings to be found in various fields (or indexes). Allowing the terms to be scattered is a characteristic of the second type of query. Keyword searching involves matching discrete words to the system's indexes, often using Boolean operators or proximity formulations to combine them. Keywords may be matched against terms that occur in more than one field or index.

Browsing, too, can be divided into two categories. Pre-sequenced, linear browsing allows users to scan lists of terms, headings, or brief titles to find topics or items of interest. This is the more structured approach, using the system's internal organization of the data to guide browsing activities. Hildreth's second type of browsing is nonlinear and multidirectional. This is browsing that is more serendipitous. It is unstructured. It uses or can use hypertext links to navigate between various items and may be more exploratory or seemingly more random.

While querying is great when the users know exactly what they want, browsing in many cases may be a preferable alternative to retrieving hundreds of records in response to a query. For example, if a user is looking for an item by an author with the last name "Shaw," but only has an initial "L." for the forename, a browsing approach will put the searcher into an index of all personal names with the surname Shaw, at the point where the "L" forenames would begin. From that point, the user may scan names either before or after the name entered. If this listing contains, in addition to the name, the entire authoritative heading for the author, including dates and the number of records associated with that name, then the user can more easily determine which name represents the "L. Shaw" sought. A subject browsing option would provide the user with a list of subjects that surround the word that was input as the search. In cases where the user is unsure of what is wanted, or when the user does not know the exact string used in the system to describe what is sought, browsing may provide a more manageable approach to meeting the user's information need.

Retrieval Models

Despite the presence of browsing in retrieval tools, our current systems are oriented toward exact-match queries, in which the exact specifications of the query must be satisfied by the document representation in order to create a match. In order for a system to work fairly well, users must have a good idea of what they are looking for. This is an all-or-nothing approach. It is precise and rigid, purely mechanistic, and the burden is placed on users, not on the system. If there is no exact match, then nothing is retrieved.

However, other models do exist. For example, probabilistic retrieval is based on term weighting (which is based on word frequency). Probabilistic systems return results that match the query to some degree and are displayed in the order of decreasing similarity. Such models have been subjects of research for many years. They represent attempts to find ways around the limitations of exact-match, Boolean-based retrieval. Such retrieval models are not without criticism. They do not take into account information-seeking behaviors such as browsing or exploratory searching, which are not query-based. In the best of all possible systems, a variety of search options and retrieval techniques would be available.

Over the years, many researchers and practitioners have made suggestions for improving online retrieval systems, but the creators of these systems have seemingly not paid attention to many of the suggestions. Evidence of this comes from two articles by Christine Borgman. In 1986 she wrote an article titled "Why Are Online Catalogs Hard to Use?"[18] A decade later she wrote another article, "Why Are Online Catalogs *Still* Hard to Use?"[19] Borgman says that OPACs are still hard to use because their design still does not reflect an understanding of user searching behavior. She suggests that a long-term goal of system designers should be to design intuitive systems that require a minimum of instruction. Instruction has often been touted as the way around inadequate system design, but in this age of remote access, where instruction may not be available, one has to agree with Borgman: "Good training is not a substitute for good system design."[20]

Standardization and Systems

David Thomas mentions that a user's need for standardized description has not been acknowledged in online systems, leading to a loss of familiarity for the user.[21] Standardization was a key feature of the card catalog. Users who were familiar with one catalog could apply the same knowledge and skills to other catalogs they encountered with a minimum of difficulty. Standardization, however, does not happen overnight. It takes time to develop. The lack of standardization today is reminiscent of a century ago, when catalogs contained cards of varying sizes (e.g., 2 by 5 inches, 2 by 10 inches, 3 by 5 inches, etc.) and the information placed on cards lacked a standard order. Standardization came when Melvil Dewey's 7.5-by-12.5-centimeter catalog cabinets won out over other sizes.[22] In the library cataloging community, there have been recent calls for standard interfaces for online catalogs. As Martha Yee states, "The lack of standardization across OPACs can make it difficult for catalogue users to apply their knowledge of one OPAC to searching another OPAC in a different library."[23]

Today there are no real standards, just broad guidelines and suggestions. Due to the competitive nature of vendors in the OPAC marketplace, a standard interface is unlikely to occur anytime soon. Vendors develop new features, and each vendor places different levels of importance on different aspects of its system design. Some have different internal organization schemes; some have different search capabilities. Vendors try to develop the most appealing interface, search features, and modules in order to gain a greater market share. This competition contributes to the lack of standardization in system design, but then again, it may be increasing long-term system innovations and progress. This may be a question of finding the right balance between standardization and market forces. Online indexes, too, have a great deal of variety and little standardization. This is a continuation of a long history of lack of standardization in print indexes. It seems that commercial enterprises have little interest in standardizing.

Some areas in which standardization has been recommended include:

- display
- basic search queries
- treatment of initial articles
- use of Boolean operators, proximity, and truncation
- punctuation.

These are discussed below.

Display

One of the key areas in which the lack of standardization is most apparent is in system displays. Displays can be divided into two categories, the display of sets of retrieved results and the display of metadata in surrogate records, both of which incorporate issues of screen layout and design.

Display of Retrieved Results. The first concern in the display issue is whether the initial search results appear as a list of individual records or as a list of headings displayed first before the actual records are presented for viewing. An example may help clarify the problem here. Some systems, in response to a search for an author with the surname "Benson," display all Bensons in the system grouped by forename initials. One can browse through this list and find the appropriate heading before having lists of works to sift through. Other systems return results that are lists of works related to each Benson without one knowing first how many Bensons there are. One is required to page through the list of both authors *and* titles instead of being able to browse the list of names first.

The second concern in display of results is the order in which results are shown. As mentioned earlier in this chapter, first-generation catalogs often worked on the "last in, first out" principle. As systems matured, they began to display responses to specific searches, such as those for author or title, in alphabetical order sorted by a certain field. In catalogs and indexes, the main entry[24] ("author" in most cases) was usually chosen as the field (or sort key) by which responses would be arranged. However, results of less specific searches, such as keyword, were usually displayed in reverse chronological order, using date of publication or date of record creation or entry. As systems have become more sophisticated, more control of the display has been given to the user. In some systems users can specify a field (mostly from a short, predefined list of options) to be used for arranging the displayed search results. However, such sorting may still present problems. For example, if one chooses to have results sorted by author, then the main entry is displayed in the sorted list, but the main entry may not be the author that a user is interested in (e.g., not the Benson who is a second or later author of an information package).

Display of Records. When dealing with the display of individual records several questions must be addressed. These include: Does the display provide an appropriate amount of information? Which fields should be displayed? What labels should be used? In what order should the information appear? Will patrons be able to view the information on a single screen?

The type of information contained in catalog records is guided by long-established and sometimes elaborate rules. However, in local situations many records may be either longer (e.g., addition of contents notes, reviews, etc.) or shorter (e.g., minimal level records) than the common standard. Information contained in index records is quite variable. Each commercial index has its own standard for inclusion of information in records. Differences may include length of citation, abbreviations, inclusion of abstracts, and precoordinated or postcoordinated controlled vocabulary (or no controlled vocabulary).

In the case of MARC records, some data that a cataloger includes in a record often goes unseen by the public (e.g., many pieces of coded information). In a good system design, coded information could be programmed to be displayed or to be searched in meaningful ways, but neither of these options is universally available. Indexes use their own encoding schemes, perhaps MARC-based or perhaps internally created. They display records in a variety of ways, often allowing the user some control over the types and amount of information they see. Other kinds of metadata are so new that they have no typical way of being displayed.

There are often three levels of display in an online catalog: a one- or two-line version, a brief display, and a full display. Although "full" seldom means that all information in an encoded record is displayed, some systems do allow the display of the entire MARC record, complete with MARC tagging, to the public. The default display, when only one record is retrieved in response to a query or after a user has selected a record to view from a list, is usually the brief view. The amount and kinds of information omitted from a full record to make a brief display differ from system to system. Allyson Carlyle and Traci Timmons surveyed 122 Web-based catalogs and determined that personal author, title, and publication fields are almost always displayed in default single-records, but other fields are displayed less frequently, and the ones that are displayed are treated inconsistently (e.g., title fields sometimes include statements of responsibility, but sometimes do not).[25] Thomas notes that users find only a few fields useful; so there should be guidelines for selecting the most-needed fields for display.[26] Once employed, these guidelines could also help to reduce screen clutter.

The labeling of metadata in records also varies from system to system, and there are differences in the terminology used for labeling. Often, records for serials suffer from labeling problems more than do records for monographs. The holdings information can be confusing for the user even with the most explicit labels available. In addition, the need for labeling metadata at all is being questioned. Labels can be confusing and do not necessarily cover everything in a field. For example, in the MARC format, the 245 field, usually labeled "title," also contains the statement of responsibility (i.e., persons or corporate bodies responsible for the intellectual contents of an information package). If, instead of labeling every field, displays made use of the *ISBD* format (with its standardized punctuation and set order of information), confusing labels could be eliminated.[27] In addition, the *ISBD* format would allow more information about an information package to be displayed on one screen. All new metadata formats are calling for labels, albeit sometimes different ones for the same concept. These have or will have the same problems with labels as do MARC-formatted records and the records displayed in various commercial indexes.

The increase in use of labels has triggered an increase in the use of brief displays. Walt Crawford, Lennie Stovel, and Kathleen Bales found that when *ISBD* format is used, only 30 percent of records need a second screen to display the entire record. With labels, 84 percent of records need a second screen to display the entire record.[28] (This was before WebPACs, in which long records require scrolling rather than moving to a second screen. However, the principle is similar in light of research showing that users tend to look at what they see in a "first view" before scrolling or retrieving a second screen.) Thomas found that users spent no more time reading screens or performing tasks when the records were not labeled than when the records were labeled. He points out that although many assert the need for labels, there is no empirical evidence that labeled displays are superior.[29] One could assume, then, that using nonlabeled displays would cause few or no problems for users, and the need for brief records could be eliminated for more than four-fifths of records. However, labels and brief displays persist.

One difficulty with brief displays is that what is included in them is inconsistent from system to system. Some delete all notes, which can cause confusion, while some keep only the first note. Notes are designed to give information that clarifies data given in earlier areas of the description. Without the notes, users may be misled by the information that is given. In many cases, subject headings are not present. Some brief displays show no statements of responsibility or added entries. If a user has searched for an author or other contributor, the brief display may not mention that person or corporate body, especially when the statement of responsibility is not included in the title area. This may cause confusion if the user does not understand that the label "author" is only used for the first-named person or body responsible for the item. How many users understand that? One cannot approach a new system expecting that the metadata presented in the display will be the same as in the last system used.

Display Guidelines. These different approaches to both types of displays (i.e., display of retrieved results and display of records) have led some to work toward guidelines for standardizing displays. A task force of the International Federation of Library Associations and Institutions (IFLA) in 1999 issued guidelines to assist libraries in designing or redesigning their OPACs. The guidelines consist of thirty-seven principles based on the objectives of the catalog and the types of searches users conduct.

> The guidelines recommend a standard set of display defaults, defined as features that should be provided for users who have not selected other options, including users who want to begin searching right away without much instruction. . . . The goal for the display defaults recommended is ease of use, defined as the provision of as much power as possible with as little training as possible. If such defaults were widely implemented, users would benefit by being able to transfer catalogue use skills acquired in one library to many other libraries.[30]

The efforts of the IFLA task force and many researchers have been focused on the users' need for powerful, but easy-to-use search tools. While this goal is noble, nothing guarantees that system vendors will comply with any of the suggestions and guidelines. Whether or not the 1999 IFLA guidelines, or the body of OPAC display research, have made an impact, has yet to be seen.

Basic Search Queries

When approaching a new retrieval tool users must determine in which ways they can search. Author, title, keyword, and subject (or descriptor) searches are usually found in current retrieval tools. OPACs also often allow call number searches. In some systems, the user may be offered searches that are less common, such as name/title combination searches or journal title searches. While some search types may be fairly typical among systems, the ways in which systems are indexed are anything but consistent. To illustrate, consider some of the following questions that might arise as a user begins a search. Are all authors (primary and secondary; personal and corporate) included in the same author index? How are authors searched? If keyword searching is available, which fields are searched? Can the system be searched by form or genre? How can I find works by *and* about an author? These are only a few of the questions a user might ask when beginning a new search. Due to the lack of standardization, the answers will vary from system to system.

Users may or may not be able to choose whether an author search is interpreted by the system as an exact match, browse, or keyword search. Users may not understand there are differences among these searches. For efficiency, a user must know how the system will search a particular string. If a search for "Smith, William" is entered, will the system search for that word string exactly, no more and no less (i.e., an exact match search)? Will it search for any entry beginning with that exact word string (i.e., a browse search)? Will it search any author-related field that contains both the words "William" and "Smith" (e.g., "Barney, William Smith" or "William, Jonathan Smith"; i.e., a keyword search)? If a user wishes to see a record for a particular William Smith, whose middle names and/or dates are not remembered, then an exact match or a keyword match probably is not satisfactory. Browsing is the only efficient solution.

The results of keyword searching are determined by the fields that are searched in the system. Some systems have generic keyword searches that search almost every field of a record (or rather, a general keyword index). In others, choices can be made as to the type of keyword search desired. There may be separate buttons or pull-down menus so users can specify the types of keyword searches they want. The fields to be included in different types of keyword searches vary from system to system. For example, some subject keyword searches search subject heading/descriptor fields *and* title fields, while others search subject heading/descriptor fields only. Note fields also may contain subject-laden terminology, but they are almost never included by system designers as fields to be searched by subject keyword searches.

Form/genre searching is relatively new and it is hoped that users will find this concept easy to understand. If users are interested in autobiographies or in specialized dictionaries, it is helpful for them to include the form or genre in the search. Few systems, so far, allow searching by form/genre, but as more metadata incorporates the concept, the need for this type of search increases. In certain fields, such as visual materials, searches by form/genre are almost indispensable.

Over the years, it has become apparent that not all users understand the differences among searching by author, title, or subject. This was discovered when card catalogs changed from the strict dictionary form to the divided catalog form. Users were especially confused by looking for persons as authors in an "author catalog" versus looking for works *about* those same persons in a "subject catalog." The problem was alleviated in some card catalogs by placing all works by and about persons in a "name catalog." Very few online systems have allowed this solution, however. Users have to know that to find works about a person, one has to do a subject search, but to find works by a person, one has to do an author search. Or they may search by keyword, but the results list is then a mixture of works by and about the person that is less than satisfactory.

Other searching considerations include choosing the collection or the library branch to search and/or choosing types of search limits (e.g., language, date, etc.) allowed by the system. These are handled differently from system to system.

Initial Articles

Another example of the lack of consistency among systems is the handling of initial articles (*a, an, the,* and their equivalents). In many systems, there are instructions to omit initial articles when entering a search string. Users tend to follow this advice *if* the instruction is noticeable and if it can be seen from the search box. If a search still includes the initial article, one of the following may result:

- System returns a message that the user received no hits, and no other information is included at all.

- System provides the user with a message to remove the initial article and try again.

- System treats an initial article differently depending on whether it is a keyword, browse, or exact word search.

- System simply eliminates the article, without notifying the user, and performs the search.

The last possibility in the bulleted list may be good for some searches, but there are, of course, times when the article (or what *appears* to be an article—a foreign word, perhaps) is needed for the search to be successful (e.g., a book titled *A is for Apple*).

Truncation, Boolean Operators, and Proximity

Other examples of the lack of standardization are found in the manner in which systems handle truncation, Boolean operators, and proximity. Users need to know if there is automatic right-truncation and, if not, which truncation symbol is to be used. Automatic right-hand truncation happens when a user inputs a search word or string, and the system returns everything that begins with that word or string. For example, a search for "Smith, Will" retrieves not only records for the name "Will Smith" but also records with the heading "Smith, Will Abraham" and "Smith, William." If right-hand truncation is not automatic, a symbol must be used to indicate that right-hand truncation is desired in a search. The symbol may be a pound sign (#) or an asterisk (*) or a dollar sign ($) or any other of a number of characters. For example, a search for "catalog#" could result in retrievals of the following terms: catalog, catalogs, catalogue, catalogues, cataloger, cataloguer, cataloging, cataloguing, and so forth.

Use of Boolean searching is far from consistent among systems. Most allow more than one word per command or search, but the ways in which multiple terms are treated can vary considerably. If default Boolean is used, the default may be AND or it may be OR. Most online catalogs, for example, treat a search with multiple terms as if the operator AND has been inserted between them. That is, all terms in the search must be present in a record for that record to be retrieved. Many search engines, though, treat such a search as if OR has been inserted between terms. That is, each record retrieved contains at least one of the terms, but not necessarily all the terms.

When Boolean operators are expressly inserted, a user must know the order in which operations are carried out. For example, in a search for "catalogs OR indexes AND libraries," most systems execute the operators from left to right (i.e., records with either the term "catalogs" or the term "indexes" combined with the word "libraries"). Some online retrieval systems, however, may search for records with the term "catalogs" OR records containing both "indexes" and "libraries." The best possible solution would be to use parentheses to ensure that the execution will be carried out as desired: "(catalogs OR indexes) AND libraries"; although this may be beyond the knowledge of many users.

Users also need to know if proximity formulations are supported, and if so, how specific the formulations are. Proximity formulations are often used in indexes and some search engines, but less often in library catalogs. The degree of sophistication in formulation may range from a simple NEAR or ADJ (adjacent) to an indication of the distance allowed to appear between terms (e.g., within two words).

Punctuation

Punctuation can be a source of great confusion for users. When approaching a new system, there are a number of questions that need to be asked. They include: Do subject heading searches use hyphens between subdivisions? Are quotation marks used to indicate exact phrases? Are diacritical marks used and understood? (For example, are the accent marks necessary in "résumé," and if, so how are they to be entered?) Must all punctuation marks be stripped, and if not, which ones can be used and which ones must be deleted? Are there filing rules based on punctuation that will thwart a user's ability to find desired results?

Removing punctuation from a string of text in order to provide better potential for matches is called "normalization." Normalization is intended to allow better matching because users are not always precise in the placement of such marks as diacritics and commas. However, depending upon the algorithm used for normalization, results may be different from system to system.

A telling example of how the lack of standardization can affect users comes from an article by J. H. Bowman, who looked at how the ampersand (&) and the hyphen (-) are treated in various online catalogs.[31] Bowman found that the symbols were treated quite differently in various systems. The hyphen affected searching and the system's indexing in at least six different ways. In some systems, it was treated like a space. In others, it was treated as if it were a null character (i.e., nothing there, not even a space, thereby bringing the two pieces of the hyphenated word together into one word). Some systems treated it as both a null character and as a space (which meant the terms were indexed at least twice). Some viewed the hyphen simply as a hyphen, while one used the hyphen as a Boolean NOT (i.e., the hyphen as a minus sign). In one system, the hyphen invalidated the search altogether. In addition, Bowman found that the hyphen was sometimes processed differently in keyword searches than it was in phrase matching queries. The ampersand, too, had a variety of treatments. It was seen as an ampersand, as a Boolean AND equivalent, as a search string terminator, and as a null character. Besides the obvious effects that these different treatments have on arrangement of results lists (and on the frustration levels of users scrolling through long lists of results), they can also have an impact on meta-searching.

Meta-Searching and Z39.50

Meta-searching is the ability to search and retrieve results from more than one source of information while using only a single, common interface. It features an all-inclusive overlay (one-search box) to multiple systems, which may include catalogs, indexes, databases, and other electronic resources. This is a developing technology and the vocabulary has not, as of yet, been standardized. The meta-searching interface may be referred to as: a common-user interface, an integrated interface, a standardized interface, or simply as a meta-database. Wendi Arant and Leila Payne give the following three conceptual models for meta-searching:

- a single interface that masks multiple databases and platforms

- a single, monster database with all sorts of data

- some combination of the two[32]

While it appears that users may indeed desire this type of searching as a
means of streamlining the research process, there are some downsides to
consider. Meta-searching functionality is limited to the level of the "lowest
common denominator." That is, if very sophisticated searching is available
in one system but not the other, then the searching that can be done from
the more sophisticated system can only be in terms of the searching allow-
able in the other system. In addition, precision may be greatly reduced
because authority control of names and subject terms may or may not be
implemented in all systems, and the types of controlled vocabulary may
differ completely.

Steps toward resolving problems in meta-searching may come
from the Z39.50 protocol. This communication protocol is a national standard developed by the National Information Standards Organization
(NISO). Z39.50 (the number assigned to the first version of this standard)
began as an attempt to get diverse library systems to communicate and share
bibliographic information. The protocol establishes how one computer (the
client) can query another computer (the server) and transfer search results
from one to the other.

The Z39.50 protocol comprises three components: an abstract
model of information retrieval activities, a language consisting of syntax and
semantics for information retrieval, and a prescription for encoding search
queries and results retrieval for transmission over a network.[33] The abstract
information retrieval model, not tied to any specific design, allows it to
interact with many information retrieval systems. Its fundamental components are the query, the database, records, results sets, and retrieval records.
The standard's language allows the abstract conceptual model to be shared
and understood among diverse systems. The creators of Z39.50 developed
standard semantics to express queries. Attribute sets are used to define the
types of qualifiers available for a search term. The combination of attribute
types and values provides the way to express specifically the semantic intention of the query and to communicate what is expected of the server.

In simple terms, using the Z39.50 protocol, one system translates
a set of local commands into a set of universal commands that are then
sent to another computer. The second system translates the universal commands into equivalent commands for the second system. The results are
then returned to the first computer in the same fashion. If two institutions

both have Z39.50 installed, OPAC users in one institution can search the catalog of the other institution using the commands of the local system with the results display looking like the display used in the local system. At this point, the implementation of Z39.50 limits the searching of various catalogs to the lowest common denominator. The sophisticated programming of one system cannot be passed through Z39.50 to the other system.

In addition to attribute sets, the Z39.50 protocol uses profiles to ensure interoperability:

> Profiles in Z39.50 tend to be used in order to gather particular suites of attributes, record syntaxes, and other factors together in order to meet the needs of a particular community, whether that be subject, area, or application based. Profiles span a wide range of task areas, including a profile for the geospatial community, one for government information, one for the cultural heritage sector, and others. These profiles are often developed within the community with a requirement for them.[34]

Individual communities may create more than one profile. For example, there are several library application profiles. One of the most recognized is the Bath profile *(The Bath Profile: An International Z39.50 Specification for Library Applications and Resource Discovery)*, currently in draft form for its second release.[35]

While Z39.50 has proven to be a useful protocol, the developers' and implementers' groups are exploring ways to ensure the protocol's continued relevance. An initiative referred to as ZING *(Z39.50 International: Next Generation)* is attempting to make the intellectual and semantic content of Z39.50 more broadly available and more attractive to those who need to implement or use it. The contributors to this initiative hope to lower barriers to implementation, but at the same time, preserve the intellectual contributions that Z39.50 has accumulated in the last two decades.[36]

User-Centered System Design

Christine Borgman stated that one of the reasons that online catalogs were hard to use was that the designers did not take into account users' needs. Anna Schulze states, "Most information professionals would agree that user-centered design makes an important contribution to high quality information systems. However, there is no general agreement about how to define the term 'user-centered design' or how to best implement user-centered design strategies in the development of systems and services."[37] She goes on to say that user-centered design, depending on the situation, may refer to enhancing system performance to deliver better results, designing for particular users since one size does not fit all, or understanding the user through continual user input into the design process. The three keys to user-centered design are observation and analysis of users at work, assistance from relevant aspects of design theory, and iterative testing with users.[38] These are processes that are incorporated into information architecture (see discussion in Chapter 1), which has so far been associated with designing Web sites. In discussing the lack of specific named roles for those who practice the process of information architecture, Andrew Dillon says that "conducting user-centered design does require specific skills and does involve methods and practices that shape designs in desirable ways. Information Architecture just happens to be a much better term for user-centered design and the creation of usable information spaces."[39]

Universal Design

A specific type of user-centered design is the idea of universal design. Sharon Farb states, "the goal of universal design is to accommodate the widest spectrum of users, which in turn increases commercial success."[40] Without attention to universal design, systems present multiple barriers to people with disabilities. For example, GUI interfaces, multicolumn layout, and Web sites with frames may not be readable by users of speech and Braille devices; the computer mouse may not be operable for people with visual or certain orthopedic difficulties; audio cues cannot be heard by people with hearing loss; screen colors may obscure text for people with color blindness and for others with visual impairment; blinking cursors may be detrimental to people with epilepsy; and workstations may be inaccessible to people in wheelchairs. Farb advocates implementing universal design from the outset of a system design project to create products usable by all individuals, some of whom may encounter barriers in accessing information with the current level of technology implemented in many information systems.[41]

Multiple Languages/Scripts

User-centered design is also needed to assist people whose native languages and writing scripts vary from the ones used by the majority of users. Much material is available, particularly in research institutions, in multiple languages and scripts. Ever since library catalogers stopped handwriting catalog cards, there has been a problem producing records in such non-Roman languages as Greek, Arabic, Hebrew, Japanese, Chinese, Korean, Russian, and others. Romanization was developed as a way to write the metadata in Roman characters and be able to interfile the records with those in English and other Roman-alphabet languages. However, a majority of native speakers of non-Roman languages have found it difficult or impossible to read the Romanized records or to search for what they need. As a result, extensive non-Roman language collections have been underutilized.

For at least two decades, records created in the bibliographic networks have included vernacular characters or scripts (first for Chinese, Japanese, and Korean, and gradually adding others) along with the Romanized data, but systems have not been able to display the vernacular to the public. With development of a universal character set—the Unicode standard—systems now have the ability to display records in many vernaculars.[42] Each character in every modern written language is represented with a 16-bit unit of encoding with no duplication. Commercially available information systems are in the process of adding this coding. Users also need interfaces to be developed so that they can search in the vernacular in addition to seeing vernacular displays of records.

Other Aids for Users

Many recommendations for improving system design to benefit users have been made over the years. One of particular importance to users is that of spelling correction. It has been proposed that spell-check programs should be incorporated into the search process. Many systems now include normalization of search strings, which eliminates the need for users to input punctuation. However, research has shown that users often make spelling errors. When users receive no results due to misspelled search words, they may walk away thinking the retrieval tool does not contain the information they were seeking. Some systems are beginning to assist with this. For example, Google asks a user who uses "excercise" in a search if "exercise" was really meant (although on the Web, there are many "hits" using the misspelled word "excercise"). Other systems, such as those used in the airline industry, use sound-based codes so that names that sound alike but are spelled differently can be found easily. It has been suggested that such codes could be incorporated into information retrieval system design, along with dictionaries of alternative (e.g., American/British) spellings.

There have also been suggestions that making more use of MARC coding could improve systems. For example, the "fixed field" (MARC field 008) of a MARC record has coded information that is used in some systems to limit searches. Type-of-record codes (e.g., indicating sound recordings, serials, visual materials, etc.) are already used in a number of systems. In addition, the fixed field gives information as to whether the information package being represented contains an index or bibliographical information, whether it is fiction or a biography, what the predominant language is, in which country it was published, its date of publication, and other such coded data. For example, a searcher might wish to find everything written by a prolific author that is not fiction. Good system design should be able to accommodate such a search. In addition to use of the fixed field, use of certain other MARC fields and subfields could enhance a system. For example, subfield codes in subject fields could be used to make indexes of geographic areas or form/genre terms. The 043 field, which contains encoded geographic information concerning the place covered by the content of the information package, and the 045 field, its chronological equivalent, could also be used effectively.

Other recommendations to improve system design for users have addressed some of the following issues:

- In many systems, there are too few error messages, which are needed to help users understand their mistakes.

- Sometimes terminology used in error messages is not defined.

- Help screens are not always clear.

- Often the help system does not explain how to start or to refine a search

- When users retrieve no hits or too many hits, instructions are needed to guide the user in how to increase or reduce results.

- *Stopword* lists (lists of words that are so common that they are of no use when searching) differ from system to system. They differ in application (e.g., stopwords that apply only at the beginning of a search string vs. stopwords that apply anywhere in the search string) and in which terms are used as stopwords (e.g., "committee" is a stopword in one system, but not another).

Authority-Control Integration

Authority control is a mechanism for creating consistency in on-line systems and for allowing greater precision and better recall in searching.[43] Precision is enhanced by the use of "authorized" forms of names, while recall is improved by the system of references created. In order for authority control to be successful, authority work must be consistent and thorough. In an integrated system, authority records are linked to bibliographic records to ensure collocation of records that all relate to the same name, uniform title, or subject heading. These linkages may be one-to-one (e.g., an author who is associated with one information package), or they may be one-to-many (e.g., a single author who has written several titles), or they may be many-to-one (e.g., linking more than one author to a single information package). In subject headings, it is less common to find a one-to-one relationship as there are often many works on the same topic. For a graphic representation of the relationship between bibliographic and authority records, see Figure 5.1. The figure shows the many-to-one and

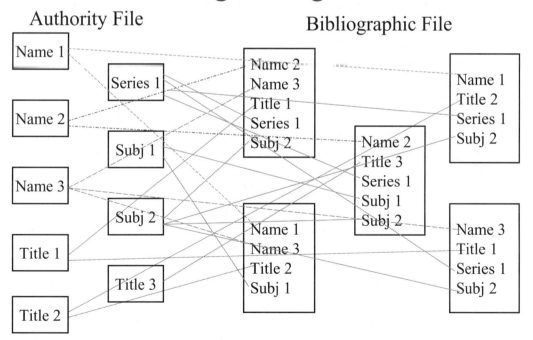

Fig. 5.1. Schematic representation of Authority File/Bibliographic File linkage.

one-to-many relationships between authority records and bibliographic records.

The way this system linkage works, in simple terms, is this: Each name and subject access point (and some of the title access points) in a bibliographic record has an authority record. Each authority record may be linked to as many bibliographic records as are appropriate, and each bibliographic record may be linked to as many authority records as are appropriate. In the schematic representation in Figure 5.1, there are lines from the authority records in the first two columns to the associated names, titles, or subjects in the records in the two right columns. In a system design there would be what are called "pointers" (e.g., the record number could be used as a pointer) in each authority record to each bibliographic record that uses the name, title, or subject in that record. There would also be pointers in each bibliographic record back to the several authority records that represent all the names, titles, and subjects for that record. The result is that if a user searches for, say, an unused term, the authority record presents a reference to the used term. Then when the user requests records for the used term, all the bibliographic records using that term are displayed. Going in the other direction, if a user has found a bibliographic record that looks promising and wants more on that subject, the link from the subject back to the subject authority record allows the system to pick up from that record the pointers to all the bibliographic records that use that subject.

Because authority work on names and controlled subject vocabulary is expensive, time-consuming, human-based work, keyword searching is often touted as being a sufficient method for retrieving information packages. However, research has shown that keyword searching may result in false drops (i.e., irrelevant retrievals) because the word retrieved has a different meaning from the intended meaning and also may result in loss of recall because synonyms or near-synonyms were not retrieved with the word sought. Users need to know, when searching, whether or not there are authority-controlled names and titles and controlled vocabulary, because, if not, users will have to think of all synonyms, related terms, and different forms of a name on their own.

Related to the need to know whether there are authority-controlled names and subject terms, users need to know whether subject relationships are available to help them to browse a subject area, to broaden or narrow searches, and to look at related topics. In the area of subject searching there have been suggestions that keyword searches be matched against both free text terms and controlled vocabulary, and that system additions be made to assist users in taking advantage of the power of controlled vocabulary. For example, the development of ways to show subject relationships in such indexes as MEDLINE could be incorporated into other retrieval tools. Tree structures, in which broader and narrower terms are shown in hierarchical relationships, have been shown to be quite useful and effective. Another example comes from commercial indexes, which often provide the ability to "explode a search." This allows a user to take advantage of the relationships among terms that are built into a controlled vocabulary. An exploded search is one in which the vocabulary term chosen is searched along with all of its narrower terms. Some systems search only the first level of narrower terms, while others search for narrower terms several levels further down in the hierarchy.

Another improvement to subject access might be to enhance subject terms with classification captions and terminology. Experimental systems have shown the viability of this approach. A notable one is the Cheshire II system created by Ray Larson and others.[44] In this system, words from the classification schedules that match the classification notation on the surrogate record are brought together with subject headings, with subject-related title words and subject-related terms from other parts of a surrogate record to create "subject clusters." Searching a cluster allows more accurate system responses than does searching each heading one by one.

CONCLUSION

This chapter has discussed systems and system design as they relate to the organization of information. In the days of paper indexes and card catalogs, organizers were also the designers of the systems. Perhaps a goal today would be for organizers and system designers to become so conversant in each other's languages and knowledge that each could step into the other's position with ease. Sophisticated design is wasted if the metadata that the system presents is inadequate, and sophisticated metadata is wasted if the system design is lacking.

Information organizers have provided guidelines and suggestions for interface design and for the display of results and records. Researchers and practitioners have long aimed at resolving some of the problems that users encounter in retrieval systems. There are large bodies of research on information-seeking behavior, user needs, the importance of subject access, and various retrieval methods. Some of the problems we see today could be eliminated if vendors would accept the guidelines and suggestions created by information organizations, professionals, and researchers.

After forty years of using automated systems in organizing information, it is unfortunate that we must continue to ask the question: "Why are systems still hard to use?" There are ways to institute standard features in all systems so that users can develop a lasting familiarity with retrieval tools, but that will not detract from the ability of vendors to create innovative and competitive products for the marketplace. In order for users to get the most benefit from the information tools available, organizers and system designers must work closely together. While there has been much progress in system design and in the communication between organizers and designers, there is still a long way to go.

NOTES

All URLs accessed June 2003.

1. *A Dictionary of Computing,* 4th ed. (Oxford; New York: Oxford University Press, 1996), pp. 489–490.

2. Larry Milsap, "A History of the Online Catalog in North America," in *Technical Services Management, 1965–1990: A Quarter Century of Change, A Look to the Future: A Festschrift for Kathryn Luther Henderson,* eds. Linda C. Smith and Ruth C. Carter (Binghamton, N.Y.: Haworth Press, 1996), pp. 79–91.

3. M. Jay Norton, "Knowledge Discovery in Databases," *Library Trends* 48, no. 1 (Summer 1999): 9–21.

4. Lucy A. Tedd, "OPACs through the Ages," *Library Review* 43, no. 4 (1994): 27–37.

5. Milsap, "A History of the Online Catalog," p. 79.

6. Ibid., pp. 85–86.

7. Marshall Breeding, "The Open Source ILS: Still only a Distant Possibility," *Information Technology and Libraries* 21, no. 1 (March 2002): 16–18.

8. Some vendors still offer standalone systems, but the number of vendors offering such systems is decreasing.

9. John Akeroyd and Andrew Cox, "Integrated Library Management Systems: Overview," *Vine,* no. 115 (2000): 3–10.

10. Charles R. Hildreth, "Online Catalog Design Models: Are We Moving in the Right Direction? A Report Submitted to Council on Library Resources August, 1995." Available: http://phoenix.liu.edu/~hildreth/clr-opac.html.

11. Akeroyd and Cox, "Integrated Library Management Systems," p. 3.

12. Mary K. Bolin, "Catalog Design, Catalog Maintenance, Catalog Governance," *Library Collections, Acquisitions, & Technical Services* 24 (2000): 53–63.

13. An example is a title search for *Gone with the Wind.* In OCLC, the derived search would be gon,wi,th,w. This is based on the prescribed "formula" for title searching of 3,2,2,1. That means the first three letters of the first non-stopword in the title, followed by the first two letters of the second word (whether stopword or not), and so on.

14. Tedd, "OPACs through the Ages," p. 28.

15. Hildreth, "Online Catalog Design Models."

16. Ibid.

17. Ibid.

18. Christine L. Borgman, "Why Are Online Catalogs Hard to Use? Lessons Learned from Information Retrieval Studies," *Journal of the American Society for Information Science* 37, no. 6 (June 1986): 387–400.

19. Christine L. Borgman, "Why Are Online Catalogs *Still* Hard to Use?" *Journal of the American Society for Information Science* 47, no. 7 (July 1996): 493–503.

20. Ibid., p. 501.

21. David Thomas, "The Effect of Interface Design on Item Selection in an Online Catalog," *Library Resources & Technical Services* 45, no. 1 (January 2001): 20–45.

22. This was reinforced by the Library of Congress selling its cataloging on "3 x 5" cards. The size of the Library of Congress cards actually was, and continued to be, 7.5 cm x 12.5 cm, but the United States did not change to the metric system as Dewey believed was imminent. The size was just under 3 in. x 5 in., and the cards came to be called "3 x 5" cards.

23. Martha M. Yee, "Guidelines for OPAC displays," in *From Catalog to Gateway: Briefings from the CFFC,* paper no. 14, *ALCTS Newsletter Online* 10, no. 6 (December 1999). Available: http://www.pitt.edu/~agtaylor/ala/papers/YeeOPACGuidelines.pdf.

24. For more information on main entry, see Chapter 7.

25. Allyson Carlyle and Traci Timmons, "Default Record Displays in Web-Based Catalogs," *Library Quarterly* 72, no. 2 (April 2002): 179–204.

26.   Thomas, "The Effect of Interface Design," pp. 42–44.

27.   For more information on *ISBD*, see Chapter 7.

28.   Walt Crawford, Lennie Stovel, and Kathleen Bales, *Bibliographic Displays in the Online Catalog* (White Plains, N.Y.: Knowledge Industry Publications, 1986), pp. 165–171.

29.   Thomas, "The Effect of Interface Design," p. 32.

30.   Yee, "Guidelines for OPAC displays."

31.   J. H. Bowman, "The Catalog as Barrier to Retrieval—Part 1: Hyphens and Ampersands in Titles," *Cataloging & Classification Quarterly* 29, no. 4 (2000): 39–60.

32.   Wendi Arant and Leila Payne, "The Common User Interface in Academic Libraries: Myth or Reality?" *Library Hi Tech* 19, no. 1 (2001): 63–76.

33.   William E. Moen, "Resource Discovery Using Z39.50: Promise and Reality," in *Proceedings of the Bicentennial Conference on Bibliographic Control for the New Millennium, November 15–17, 2000* (Washington, D.C.: Library of Congress Cataloging Distribution Service, 2001). Also available: http://lcweb. loc.gov/catdir/bibcontrol/moen_paper.html.

34.   Paul Miller, "Z39.50 for All," *Ariadne* 21 (20 September 1999). Available: http://www.ariadne.ac.uk/issue21/z3950/.

35.   *The Bath Profile: An International Z39.50 Specification for Library Applications and Resource Discovery.* Release 2, Draft 1—February 2002. Available: http://www.nlc-bnc.ca/bath/bp-release2-1stdraft.htm.

36.   Library of Congress, *ZING, Z39.50 International: Next Generation.* Last updated 2 January 2003. Available: http://www.loc.gov/z3950/agency/ zing/zing-home.html.

37.   Anna Noakes Schulze, "User-Centered Design for Information Professionals," *Journal of Education for Library and Information Science* 42, no. 2 (Spring 2001): 116.

38.   Ibid.

39.   Andrew Dillon, "Information Architecture in JASIST: Just Where Did We Come From?" *Journal of the American Society for Information Science and Technology* 53, no. 10 (2002): 822. Also available: http://www.gslis.utexas. edu/~adillon/publications/jasisintro.pdf.

40.   Sharon Farb, "Universal Design and the Americans with Disabilities

Act: Not all Systems Are Created Equal—How System Design Can Expand Information Access," in *From Catalog to Gateway: Briefings from the CFFC*, paper no. 16, *ALCTS Newsletter Online* 11, no. 1 (Spring 2000). Available: http://www.pitt.edu/~agtaylor/ala/papers/FarbUniversalDesign.pdf.

41. Ibid.

42. Unicode Home Page. (Unicode Standard 4.0 [2003] and earlier versions are available here.) Available: http://www.unicode.org/. For more about Unicode, see Chapter 4.

43. For more information on authority control, see Chapter 8.

44. Ray R. Larson, Jerome McDonough, Paul O'Leary, and Lucy Kuntz, "Cheshire II: Designing a Next-Generation Online Catalog," *Journal of the American Society for Information Science* 47, no. 7 (July 1996): 555–567.

SUGGESTED READINGS

Akeroyd, John, and Andrew Cox. "Integrated Library Management Systems: Overview." *Vine* 115 (2000): 3–10.

Bates, Marcia J. "The Design of Browsing and Berrypicking Techniques for the Online Search Interface." *Online Review* 13, no. 5 (October 1989): 407–424.

Beheshti, Jamshid. "The Evolving OPAC." *Cataloging & Classification Quarterly* 24, no. 1/2 (1997): 163–185.

Borgman, Christine L. "Why Are Online Catalogs *Still* Hard to Use?" *Journal of the American Society for Information Science* 47, no. 7 (July 1996): 493–503.

Carlyle, Allyson. "Fulfilling the Second Objective in the Online Catalog: Schemes for Organizing Author and Work Records into Usable Displays." *Library Resources & Technical Services* 41, no. 2 (April 1997): 79–100.

Dixson, Larry E. "Z39.50 and Its Use in Library Systems (Part One)." In *From Catalog to Gateway: Briefings from the CFFC*, paper no. 3. *ALCTS Newsletter* 5, no. 6 (1994): A–D.

———. "Z39.50 and Its Use in Library Systems (Part Two)." In *From Catalog to Gateway: Briefings from the CFFC*, paper no. 4. *ALCTS Newsletter* 6, no. 1 (1995): A–D.

Drabenstott, Karen M., and Marjorie S. Weller. "Failure Analysis of Subject

Searches in a Test of a New Design for Subject Access to Online Catalogs." *Journal of the American Society for Information Science* 47, no. 7 (July 1996): 519–537.

Farb, Sharon. "Universal Design and the Americans with Disabilities Act: Not All Systems Are Created Equal—How Systems Design Can Expand Information Access." In *From Catalog to Gateway: Briefings from the CFFC*, paper no. 16. *ALCTS Newsletter Online* 11, no. 1 (Spring 2000). Available: http://www.pitt.edu/~agtaylor/ala/papers/FarbUniversalDesign.pdf.

Fidel, Raya, and Michael Crandall. "The AACR2 as a Design Schema for Bibliographic Databases." *Library Quarterly* 58, no. 2 (April 1988): 123–142.

Hagler, Ronald. *The Bibliographic Record and Information Technology.* 3rd ed. Chicago: American Library Association, 1997. Chapter 4: "File Structure and Access Strategy."

Hearst, Marti A. "Interfaces for Searching the Web." *Scientific American* 276, no. 3 (March 1997): 68–72. Also available: http://www.hackvan.com/pub/stig/articles/trusted-systems/0397hearst.html.

Hildreth, Charles R. "The Use and Understanding of Keyword Searching in a University Online Catalog." *Information Technology and Libraries* 16, no. 2 (June 1997): 52–62.

Jacsó, Péter, and F. W. Lancaster. *Build Your Own Database.* Chicago: American Library Association, 1999. Chapter 1: "What is a Database?", Chapter 2: "Database Content", and Chapter 3: "Quality and Usability Factors."

Larson, Ray R. "Classification Clustering, Probabilistic Information Retrieval, and the Online Catalog." *Library Quarterly* 6, no. 2 (April 1991): 133–173.

Larson, Ray R., Jerome McDonough, Paul O'Leary, and Lucy Kuntz. "Cheshire II: Designing a Next-Generation Online Catalog." *Journal of the American Society for Information Science* 47, no. 7 (July 1996): 555–567.

Library of Congress. *Gateway to Library Catalogs: Z39.50.* 9 June 2003. Available: http://lcweb.loc.gov/z3950/gateway.html.

Meghabghab, Dania Bilal. *Automating Media Centers and Small Libraries:*

A Microcomputer-Based Approach. Englewood, Colo.: Libraries Unlimited, 1997. Chapter 9: "Future OPACs."

Miller, Paul. "Z39.50 for All." *Ariadne* 21 (20 September 1999). Available: http://www.ariadne.ac.uk/issue21/z3950/.

Moen, William E. "Resource Discovery Using Z39.50: Promise and Reality." In *Proceedings of the Bicentennial Conference on Bibliographic Control for the New Millennium, November 15–17, 2000.* Washington, D.C.: Library of Congress Cataloging Distribution Service, 2001, pp. 185–206. Also available: http://lcweb.loc.gov/catdir/bibcontrol/moen_paper.html.

Olson, Hope A., and John J. Boll. *Subject Analysis in Online Catalogs.* 2nd ed. Englewood, Colo.: Libraries Unlimited, 2001. Chapter 10: "User-System Interfaces" and Chapter 11: "Evaluation of Subject Retrieval in Online Catalogs."

Schulze, Anna Noakes. "User-Centered Design for Information Professionals." *Journal of Education for Library and Information Science* 42, no. 2 (Spring 2001): 116–122.

Taylor, Arlene G. *Wynar's Introduction to Cataloging and Classification.* 9th ed., with the assistance of David P. Miller. Englewood, Colo.: Libraries Unlimited, 2000. Chapter 19: "Processing Centers, Networking, and Cooperative Programs" and Chapter 20: Catalog Management.

Wool, Gregory J. "Bibliographical Metadata; or, We Need a Client-Server Cataloging Code!" In *Finding Common Ground: Creating the Library of the Future without Diminishing the Library of the Past,* edited by Cheryl LaGuardia and Barbara S. Mitchell. New York: Neal-Schuman, 1998, pp. 398–401.

Yee, Martha M. "Guidelines for OPAC Displays." In *From Catalog to Gateway: Briefings from the CFFC,* paper no. 14. *ALCTS Newsletter Online,* 10, no. 6 (December 1999). Available: http://www.pitt.edu/~agtaylor/ala/papers/YeeOPACGuidelines.pdf.

Yee, Martha M. and Sara Shatford Layne. *Improving Online Public Access Catalogs.* Chicago: American Library Association, 1998. Chapter 1: "Objectives of the Catalog" and Chapter 2: "Interfaces."

CHAPTER 6
METADATA

$\mathcal{M}$*etadata* is often described as "data about data."[1] This definition assumes that an information package (a Web page, an MP3 audio file, a book, etc.) is data. Therefore, a description of the attributes and contents of that information package (or MP3, etc.) would be data about data. This definition represents the very broadest level of the concept. In this context it has even been suggested that movie reviews are a form of metadata. In a cursory survey of terminology usage, numerous definitions can be found, ranging from the aforementioned "data about data" to more complex, lengthier definitions. What they all have in common is the notion that metadata is structured information that describes the attributes of information packages for the purposes of identification, discovery, and sometimes management. The term has come into use because of concern that some kind of standardized representation is needed for Internet resources if we are ever to be able to discover the most useful and reliable information available for our information needs (a process called resource discovery).

FOLDOC: Free On-Line Dictionary of Computing defines metadata as "definitional data that provides information about or documentation of other data managed within an application or environment. . . . Meta-data may include descriptive information about the context, quality and condition, or characteristics of the data."[2] This definition implies that metadata includes not only descriptive information such as that found in traditional retrieval tools, but also information necessary for the management, use, and preservation of the information package (e.g., data about where the pack-

The first draft of this chapter was originally written by Daniel N. Joudrey.

139

age is located, how it is displayed, its ownership and relationships, its quality and condition, etc.).

Even among information professionals, metadata concepts can appear complex and confusing. This is due in part to the multifaceted nature of the topic. It is also due to the overly broad, pervasive "data about data" definition. With that as a primary description, it is no wonder that many refer to any number of interrelated concepts as "metadata." It is also important to remember that the term "metadata" may mean different things to different communities. When a librarian, familiar with Dublin Core (a general purpose, user-friendly schema), speaks of metadata, she or he has a different notion of the concept than someone working with FGDC geospatial metadata (a highly detailed, more complex approach).[3]

Metadata systems can be classified into three levels of complexity. The first level is the simple format, in which the metadata is really no more than some unstructured data found in the resource itself. This is reflected by the search engine approach to organizing the Web that uses automated indexing techniques. The second level is the structured format. This includes formal metadata element sets that have been created for the general user. This level of metadata may have a basic template for metadata creation and does not require professional-level description. The Dublin Core reflects this level of complexity. The third level of complexity is the rich format. Libraries, archives, and museums tend to use systems in this category. Information professionals use these formats to create comprehensive, more detailed descriptions. They are more complex in nature and may combine metadata elements with encoding and content standards. Examples of rich formats are found in bibliographic records that are created using MARC and *AACR2* and in archival records created using the EAD.

People can mean many different things when they refer to "metadata." Discussions of the topic may be about any of the following or any combination of the following conceptual components: the information package and its attributes, content standards (rules for describing the package), metadata schemas, metadata elements, metadata records, and encoding formats. While we may discuss these as distinct conceptual components, in practice it is not so clearly divided. The concepts are so intertwined that efforts to separate them often result in confusion. An example to illustrate this can be found in the MARC format. While many consider MARC to be only an encoding format, others refer to it as a metadata schema. MARC exhibits properties of both, and on close examination it even acts as a content standard by dictating the contents and formats of certain data elements, especially the fixed fields. So it is not surprising that there is some confusion about metadata.

THE BASICS OF METADATA

Metadata may be divided into three broad types: *administrative metadata, structural metadata,* and *descriptive metadata.*[4] These three categories are somewhat fluid, however. They are not necessarily the only ways to describe metadata types. Some authors may include four categories of metadata, while others might include seven. Because there is no formal metadata taxonomy, what one author might refer to as "use metadata," another author might call "structural metadata" or "administrative metadata." The three categories chosen here seem to reflect the most common usage today. All of the additional types of metadata are included as subtypes, mostly under administrative metadata. In this text, administrative metadata includes metadata for object management, rights management, maintenance and preservation, and meta-metadata.

Metadata can describe information packages at various levels of *granularity.* It can be created for individual information packages, for pieces of those information packages, or for entire collections of information packages. In other words, a single photograph found on a Web site might be described with metadata. Alternatively, the Web page on which the picture is found could be the object of description, or an entire Web site containing several Web pages and pictures might be described in the metadata record.

Different communities might describe information on any or all of these levels of granularity, depending on the information package, the community's approach to organizing information, and the needs of their users. Traditionally organized into units larger than a single item, archival materials are described at a less granular level than are library materials or museum objects. Digital libraries may combine or alternate between collection-level and item-level descriptions, based on the nature of a particular collection, the size of the collection, and the users of the collection. In other words, a digital library might describe individual objects (e.g., a digitized map), individual collections (e.g., a digitized collection of 1,200 maps), or both.

The information package represented by the metadata may also be at various levels of intellectual expression. The metadata might describe a *work,* an *expression* of that work, a *manifestation* of the expression, or an individual *item* representing the manifestation. These categories are from the *Functional Requirements for Bibliographic Records,*[5] published by the International Federation of Library Associations and Institutions (IFLA), and are described further in the next chapter.

Metadata can be a header to a digital document, it can be "wrapped" in a digital object's packaging (e.g., descriptive metadata inside a METS object), or it can be a record that is separate from the resource that it describes. Metadata records that are separate can be collected into a single database, or they can be collected in a file such as an XML file, or they can be distributed among a variety of locations. As mentioned in Chapter 4, on encoding standards, metadata records are often in the form of encoded, separate records that describe and substitute for information packages. These records are held in retrieval tools to allow users to browse or search for the records instead of trying to navigate through each individual item in the collection. Because metadata generally includes encoding, the term is rarely applied to records found in paper tools.

METADATA SCHEMAS

In order for it to be used to its full potential, metadata cannot be unstructured descriptions of resources; it must be standardized and controlled. Without formal rules, metadata description is no better than keyword access. The basic units of metadata are the schema and the element. Metadata elements are the individual categories or fields that hold the individual pieces of description of an information package. Typical metadata elements include title, creator, creation date, subject identification, and the like. Metadata schemas are sets of elements designed to meet the needs of particular communities. While some schemas are general in nature, most are created for specific types of information. Schemas have been designed to handle government information, geospatial information, visual resources, and many other types of information packages. As a result, schemas can vary greatly. They vary in the number of data elements, in the use of mandatory and repeatable elements, in encoding, and in the use of controlled vocabularies, among other things. While most schemas focus on descriptive elements to support resource discovery, some contain elements to support administrative and structural purposes. With the various needs of different communities, it is not possible to create a perfect, one-size-fits-all metadata schema.

According to Sherry Vellucci, there are three characteristics found in all metadata schemas. They are: (1) structure, (2) syntax, and (3) semantics.[6] *Structure* refers to the data model or architecture used to hold the metadata and the way metadata statements are expressed. (Structure here is referring to the structure of the metadata. It should not be confused with the "structural metadata" described later in this chapter, which refers to the structure of the resource being described.) Two examples of such models are RDF and METS, described in Chapter 4. *Syntax* refers to the encoding of the metadata. This may be the MARC format for bibliographic records or an XML or SGML DTD for other types of metadata. *Semantics* refers to meaning, specifically the meaning of the various data elements. Semantics help metadata creators understand, for example, what "coverage" or "modification date" means in a given schema.

The semantics of a metadata schema do not dictate the content placed into the elements. This is the province of content standards (or content rules) and controlled vocabularies. Content standards determine such things as how the date will be formatted within the metadata elements. For example, it might specify that all dates will be entered using the YYYY-MM-DD format. Controlled vocabularies refer to lists of words in which certain terms are chosen as preferred and their synonyms act as pointers to the preferred terms, thereby limiting the range of values that can be entered into a field. Controlled vocabularies are often used in object-type and in subject-related data elements. If such rules and systems did not exist, information retrieval effectiveness could be compromised.

METADATA CHARACTERISTICS

In order for metadata to be as useful as possible in meeting the diverse needs of information users, there are some special characteristics of the electronic environment that require attention. They are: interoperability, flexibility, and extensibility.[7] *Interoperability* refers to the ability of various systems to interact with each other no matter the hardware or software being used. Interoperability helps minimize the loss of information due to technological differences. Interoperability can be further divided into semantic, syntactic, and structural interoperability. *Semantic interoperability* refers to ways in which diverse metadata schemas express meaning in their elements. In other words, does the element "author" in one schema mean the same thing as "creator" in another schema? *Structural interoperability* refers to how metadata records are expressed. Is the metadata statement understandable by other systems? *Syntactic interoperability* refers to the ability to exchange and use metadata from other systems. Syntactic interoperability requires a common language or encoding format.

Flexibility refers to the ability of "metadata creators to include as much or as little detail as desired in the metadata record, with or without adherence to any specific cataloging rules or authoritative lists."[8] *Extensibility* refers to the ability to use additional metadata elements and *qualifiers* as needed to meet the specific needs of various communities. Qualifiers help to sharpen the focus of an element or might prescribe a specific vocabulary to be used in that element. An example of extensibility can be found in the education community. In order to meet their specific needs, a standard element set was extended by adding new elements such as grade-level and audience. There is a note of caution about extensibility, however. As extensibility increases, interoperability tends to decrease. This is because as the schema moves further away from its original design (with additional elements or qualifiers), it is less understandable to other systems. This is a trade-off that needs to be considered carefully before being implemented.

METADATA AND CATALOGING

Some definitions of metadata refer exclusively to electronic materials, but the term is not necessarily restricted to digital objects and Web resources only. Many authors like to point out that the library profession has been creating metadata for millennia. Even the earliest Sumerian lists contained metadata in some form. Some authors equate creating metadata for electronic resources with the cataloging of books. Some consider cataloging to be a subset of activities under the broader concept of metadata creation.

Parallels between the two processes certainly exist. The basic objectives of metadata creation and cataloging (providing a description of and access to items) are alike. The processes used to create the descriptions are also similar. Both focus on attributes that allow users to identify information packages and to select the packages that most closely meet their needs. Electronic and analog materials share many characteristics. Both generally have titles, creators, creation dates, subject matter, and publication sources of some sort. There are enough similarities between the two activities to see that a relationship exists between creation of metadata and cataloging.

While there are parallels, differences are also claimed. Some feel the dissimilarities are too great to equate metadata with cataloging. Stefan Gradmann states that the differences lie in who creates the metadata (non-professionals), why it is created (resource discovery, not just description), the process (more efficiently produced), and materials to be covered (electronic resources).[9] It is puzzling that these are presented as distinctions. For at least three decades, much cataloging has been done by people called "paraprofessionals." The ideal of having authors create their own metadata is not coming to pass, and it is also being discovered that lack of consistency in metadata creation is a problem in resource discovery, the second difference listed. But cataloging has always been about resource discovery. That is why there has been such an emphasis on access points for names and subjects with a concentration on authority control for these. Classification has provided yet another way for users to discover resources by finding them beside other materials on the same subject. With respect to the third difference, "process," the processes of cataloging have become more efficient with the advent of computers. Finally, the conventions of cataloging have been expanded to apply to electronic resources, as seen in the latest version of the *Anglo-American Cataloguing Rules.*[10] In many ways it appears that metadata creation is a reinvention and/or extension of cataloging.

Most of the objections raised to the comparison tend to focus on certain characteristics of electronic resources. Electronic resources have particular differences that must be considered. These differences are important to acknowledge, even though they do not negate the relationship between cataloging and metadata creation. The first of these is more a perceived difference than a real one. It is the degree to which there is difficulty in determining what is an information package. There has always been some difficulty in deciding what is a "catalogable unit," but the world in which cataloging is done has had centuries to develop standards and practices. For the most part one physical item has been equated with one bibliographic record. However, there have remained the problems of when to provide just one record for multiple items (e.g., serials, multivolume sets) or when to provide multiple records for one item (e.g., anthologies of short stories, articles in journals). Now we have the same problem for digital resources. What is a describable unit on the Web or in a digital library? Do we create metadata for a single Web page or for the entire site that contains it? Do we describe a digital image or a collection of digital images? This returns us to the granularity issues mentioned earlier. In addition, with a digital object, what exactly is being described? Should the metadata describe the digital image only? Should it describe both the digitized photo and the original analog photograph? Should that be one record or two?

An obvious difference is that remote-access electronic resources have no physical carriers, unlike books, maps, or compact discs. A key feature of bibliographic cataloging is the physical description (e.g., 280 p. ; ill.; 26cm. *or* 1 videocassette (15 min.) : sd., col. ; ¾ in.). Except, perhaps, for the indications of illustrative matter, this is unnecessary for a Web site.

Another distinction between electronic and analog resources relates to the concept of edition. For some electronic resources, like commercial software, it is obvious when a new edition or version has been released. But for others, like Web sites, it is not so obvious. Web sites can be ephemeral and/or unstable. Some Web sites simply disappear without a trace. Others can (and do) change often. While some sites may have relatively stable content, others are updated frequently. Unlike most tangible information packages (where updated information necessitates a new physical carrier), an updated Web site can be difficult to detect. This is complicated by the fact that the old site is generally gone for good. If a Web page is slightly altered, does that make it a new edition? Probably not, but at what point does a new edition emerge? At what point is new metadata required? When changes occur, it is not always obvious whether the metadata for that Web site should also change.

Location information also differs. When metadata records and information packages are both encoded and accessible online, the encoded nature of the metadata records allows users to locate and access an information package almost simultaneously. Therefore, special attention must be paid to location/access metadata for electronic resources. URLs are far more likely to change than are call numbers in an average library.

The last major difference between analog and electronic resources that we will discuss is that found in their structure. Compared to the structure of an analog resource, the structure of a digital object can be very complex. For example, a digitized book requires more and different types of metadata than does a book upon the shelf. For the most part the physical book requires mostly descriptive data, such as title, author, publisher, subject, with some administrative information in addition. The digital object, however, requires extensive structural metadata in order for the object to be displayed and to function properly. This is in addition to descriptive metadata about the digitized resource, descriptive metadata about its original analog equivalent (if such exists), and administrative metadata as well.

OBJECTIVES OF AN INFORMATION SYSTEM

One of the primary purposes of creating metadata is to help users find information packages that they might need. It is helpful then, when creating metadata, to look at the objectives that users may have when approaching an information retrieval system, so that their goals and needs may be met. The following list of tasks comes from IFLA's *Functional Requirements for Bibliographic Records*.[11] These objectives include:

- **Find**—Users approach retrieval systems to search for information packages that meet certain criteria. They may wish to find all articles published by *Cataloging & Classification Quarterly* in 1999, all books written by Ranganathan, or all video recordings of Puccini operas held by the Carnegie Library of Pittsburgh.

- **Identify**—The metadata records found in retrieval tools help users to identify entities. This may involve distinguishing between similar information packages or identifying an item that corresponds to a citation in a bibliography.

- **Select**—Systems help users to select information packages that are appropriate for their needs. This may involve such characteristics as language, edition, or system requirements.

- **Obtain**—Users approach systems in order to acquire or gain access to information packages.

In addition to these four objectives, Elaine Svenonius adds a fifth objective—**navigate**. This objective takes into account the information-seeking behavior of some users who cannot articulate their information needs, but use the structure of the information system to help them find the information they are seeking.[12] In order to meet the needs of users, as well as the needs of information professionals, metadata should be created with these objectives in mind.

TYPES OF METADATA

As mentioned above, there are three broad categories of metadata: administrative, structural, and descriptive. Until recently, most metadata discussions focused on descriptive metadata only. It is only within recent years that administrative and structural metadata needs have been recognized, or at least acknowledged, as "metadata issues."

Administrative Metadata

Who decides what an object is called? Where is it held? Who decides when it needs to be updated or transformed? How are these processes accomplished? How did the object come into this collection? Was it digitized in-house, by an outside vendor, or was it born digital? These are questions that can be answered by administrative metadata.

Administrative metadata is created for the purposes of management, decision making, and record keeping. It provides information about the storage requirements and migration processes of digital objects. Administrative metadata assists with monitoring, reproducing, digitizing, and backing up digital information packages. It includes information such as:

- acquisition information (e.g., how and when the information package was created, modified, and/or acquired; administrative information about analog source from which a digital object was derived)

- ownership, rights, permission, reproduction information (e.g., what rights the organization has to use the material; what reproductions exist and their current status)

- legal access requirements (e.g., who may use the material and for what purposes)

- location information (e.g., URL; call number)

- use information (e.g., use and user tracking; content re-use; exhibition records)

- use management (e.g., what materials are used, when, in what form, by whom)

- preservation information

  - integrity information (e.g., checksums)

  - documentation of physical condition

  - documentation of actions taken to preserve (e.g., refreshing data; migrating data; conservation or repair of physical artifacts)

Some administrative metadata elements can be generated automatically (as can structural metadata elements). Unlike structural and descriptive metadata, administrative metadata elements can be repository-specific. They might focus on local requirements, such as who makes decisions about these information packages.

Administrative metadata may be described as having several subtypes. These include: preservation metadata, access and rights metadata, and meta-metadata. Each of these is discussed in turn.

Preservation Metadata

Technology changes rapidly. Data files from just a few years ago—our WordStar documents and VisiCalc spreadsheets—are now old and no longer functional. They have been lost because there were no plans to keep the data usable and no real understanding of how fast things change. With this in mind, we must consider how much more we are willing to lose. Will the Word documents and Access databases we create today be usable in 200 years? What about 20 years? Or 10 years, even? If we are going to save this information from oblivion, we must consider a number of questions. Should we preserve the look and feel of the software, or are we concerned with content only? Do we need a standards library? One hundred years from now, will users still know what a *.jpg* or a *.tiff* is? Without documentation, will they be decipherable? When we preserve an information package, how do we determine which version of that package needs to be preserved? In other words, how do we determine the best edition?

These questions are preservation metadata concerns. In recent years, OCLC and the Research Libraries Group, the National Library of Australia, and the CEDARS project in the UK have all initiated preservation metadata initiatives.[13] Preservation metadata is the information needed to ensure the long-term storage and usability of digital content. It includes information about the processes used in preserving the digital content, including reformatting, migration, emulation, conservation or repair, file integrity, representation, provenance, and decision making data. Typical preservation metadata elements might include: structural type, file description, size, properties, software and hardware environments, source information, object history, transformation history, context information, digital signatures, and checksums.

Rights and Access Metadata

Who can access an information package and for what purposes? Who can make copies? Who owns the material? Are there different categories of information objects in the collection? Are there different categories of users who can access different combinations of those objects?

Rights and access metadata is information about who has access to information packages, who may use them, and for what purposes. It deals with issues of creators' intellectual property rights and the legal agreements allowing users to access this information. In rights and access metadata, information about parties, contents, and transactions can be found. These are issues currently being examined. The <indecs> project is the most widely known model for rights metadata.[14] It focuses on e-commerce applications. Typical rights metadata elements might include: access categories, identifiers, copyright statements, terms and conditions, periods of availability, usage information, and payment options.

Meta-Metadata

If metadata is data about data, then meta-metadata is data about the data about data. Not only can metadata track administrative data about the information package, it can also track information about the metadata. Ensuring authenticity of the metadata and tracking internal processes are some of the uses of meta-metadata. While some meta-metadata resides within some descriptive records (e.g., the record creation information and modification dates in a MARC record), other meta-metadata must be tracked in other ways. In 1999, Renato Iannella and Debbie Campbell proposed to the Dublin Core Metadata Initiative (DCMI) *The A-Core: Metadata About Content Metadata*.[15] "A-Core" stood for Administrative Core and seemed to be a core set of administrative metadata. DCMI preferred a tool for users of metadata to manage metadata, and so the proposal was revised in 2002 by Hytte Hansen and Leif Andresen as *AC-Administrative Components*.[16] AC focuses on elements that describe attributes of the metadata record, track changes and updates, and provide information for the interchange of records. It is currently out for comments at this writing.

Structural Metadata

If an information organization received a digital object, one that it had no part in creating, could the object be opened? Would it be known what the object was? Would it be known what it does? Would the requirements for presenting the object be understood? If the digital object were a complex, multi-file entity, would it be known how the pieces fit together? Without structural metadata, probably not.

Structural metadata is that which refers to the "makeup" or structure of the file, dataset, or other information package that is being described. It is the technical information that is needed to ensure that a digital information package functions properly. It refers to how related files are bound together and how the object can be displayed and disseminated on a variety of systems. It deals with what an object is, what it does, and how it works. Sometimes, structural metadata is referred to as technical metadata, display metadata, or use metadata. It includes the following kinds of information:

- hardware and software documentation

- technical information (e.g., file size, bit-length, format, presentation rules, sequencing information, running time, structural maps, file compression information)

- version control (e.g., what versions exist and the status of the information resource being described; alternate digital formats, such as HTML or PDF for text, and GIF or JPG for images)

- data to identify a version of an image and to define what is needed to view it

- digitization information (e.g., compression ratios; scaling ratios)

- data related to creation of the digital image (e.g., date of scan, resolution)

- authentication and security data (e.g., encryption keys, password methods)

- associated search protocols (e.g., Z39.50, common indexing protocol, CGI form interface)

Some structural metadata elements can be found in the headers of some file types, but others must be collected manually, or new processes must be developed to capture this metadata at low cost. At this time, the technological and financial resources needed to collect complete structural metadata and to take full advantage of that metadata are not yet here. In some metadata schemas, structural metadata is not well represented in the data elements. In others, it may be unnecessary or inappropriate. For example, with a single textual document in a word processing format, extensive structural data is not necessary. Once the information package becomes more complex, however, more structural metadata becomes necessary.

Implementations of Structural Metadata

The use of structural metadata is not new, but the terminology used to describe it is. An early, successful implementation of structural information is the page-turner model. A page-turner is used for materials with contents that must be ordered in a definite sequence. It provides structure for the contents to be displayed and for the user to navigate through the information package as one normally pages through a book. The page-turner may allow the user to navigate through the resource on more than one level, that is, at a chapter level and at a page level. The page-turner uses structural metadata to bind together individual images of pages to form a complete object (again, this may be on the level of the e-book, a volume of a set, or a chapter). It also may use the structural metadata to associate a text file with each of those individual pages, so that the intellectual content of the page image is searchable. Structural metadata can also associate these images with thumbnail images of the pages, images of greater or lesser resolution, HTML- or XML-formatted pages associated with the Web interface (though this may be done on-the-fly), or some other file.

Descriptive Metadata

Descriptive metadata is that which describes the identifying characteristics of an information package along with analyzing its intellectual contents. It includes the following kinds of information:

- data that identifies an information package (e.g., title; author; date of creation or publication; information regarding the analog source from which a digital object is derived)

- intellectual organization data (e.g., authority control; collocation with related works, names, subjects, etc.; identification of relationships among entities)

- intellectual access data (e.g., subject headings; classification; categorization)

The next two chapters cover descriptive metadata in depth.

MANAGEMENT TOOLS

As metadata applications have become more common and more schemas flourish, tools and systems have been developed to help deal with this proliferation of information. Some of these tools and systems are application profiles, metadata registries, crosswalks, harvesting projects, and templates for metadata creation.

Application Profiles

As stated earlier, there is no "one-size-fits-all" schema. Different schemas have been developed for different purposes, different communities, and different materials. All of these schemas have different strengths and weaknesses. When looking for a metadata schema to meet the needs of a particular institution, a community, or a particular project, it is sometimes discovered that parts of different already-existing schemas would work well if they could be put together. A mechanism to allow metadata implementers to use various elements from different schemas is the *application profile.*

An application profile, according to Rachel Heery and Manjula Patel, is a type of schema unto itself. Application profiles are schemas that consist of data elements drawn from one or more *namespaces.* A namespace is a collection of element type and attribute names. It is the authoritative place for information about the names stored there. For example, the Dublin Core Element Set has a namespace at http://www.dublincore.org. The elements selected for the application profile can be a subset of the elements from one schema, or they can be elements from two or more schemas, combined together. An application profile is a way to declare which elements from which namespaces are used in a particular application or project.[17] An example is one proposed by the Dublin Core Education Working Group for describing educational resources.[18] It proposes two new domain-specific elements ("audience" and "standards") to be recognized in a "dc-ed" namespace and also proposes endorsements of three data elements from the IEEE Learning Object Metadata (LOM) namespace. The latter three elements are InteractivityType, InteractivityLevel, and Typical-LearningTime.

Application profiles have several characteristics that distinguish them from metadata schemas. They may draw on one or more existing namespaces. They may introduce no new data elements. If an implementer introduces new elements, then it is no longer an application profile but becomes a new schema, and the implementer must take responsibility for declaring and maintaining that schema. Application profiles may specify what values are permitted in certain elements. For example, they can specify a particular controlled vocabulary. Finally, they can refine the definitions of elements, but only to make them semantically narrower or more specific.

Metadata Registries

Another tool helpful to the metadata creator is the metadata registry. A registry is a database used to organize, store, manage, and share metadata schemas. Registries provide information about metadata schemas, elements, profiles, definitions, and relationships, using a standard structure as outlined in ISO/IEC 11179–3:2003, "Information Technology–Metadata Registries (MDR)—Part 3: Registry Metamodel and Basic Attributes."[19] They are used to exchange information and clarify meaning and usage. They can help prevent duplication of effort if another institution is interested in creating a schema with many of the same elements. In the future registries may be a source of machine-understandable information about schemas to support activities and agents on the Web. Registries are one of the tools that help to improve interoperability among schemas. An example is the Dublin Core Metadata Registry.[20]

Crosswalks

Crosswalks, too, are tools used to achieve interoperability, specifically semantic interoperability. Without that golden, one-size-fits-all schema, crosswalks are needed so that users and creators understand equivalence relationships among metadata elements in different schemas. Crosswalks are needed so that we can see, for example, that the 700 field in a MARC record is roughly equivalent to the Contributor field in a Dublin Core record. According to Margaret St. Pierre and William LaPlant, "A crosswalk is a specification for mapping one metadata standard to another. Crosswalks provide the ability to make the contents of elements defined in one metadata standard available to communities using related metadata standards."[21] They go on to observe that creation and maintenance of a crosswalk is difficult and susceptible to error. One needs expertise in each standard included in the crosswalk. But because each standard is developed by experts in a particular field with inherent specialized terminology, persons with expertise in several standards are rare. A key difficulty in creating and maintaining crosswalks is the element-mapping process. The mapping might not be too difficult if the schemas

- are relatively simple,

- are for the same types of materials or discipline, or

- have many overlapping concepts.

It is more complex when the mapping

- is cross-domain,

- is between schemas of different levels of complexity, or

- is between schemas with great semantic differences.

Generally, the more metadata schemas that are included in the crosswalk, the more difficult it is to do the mapping.

It is important to remember that the conversion process, via crosswalks, from one schema to another lacks precision. Few metadata crosswalks provide round-trip conversion with no loss of data. Some data is lost in one direction or the other (or both). However, until technology develops that allows machines to understand the meaning of various metadata elements, crosswalks are the best tools we have for semantic interoperability. An example of a crosswalk is *Dublin Core Metadata Element Set Mapping to MODS Version 2.0.*[22] It is a typical example of a situation where just one element of one scheme (in this case Dublin Core) is equivalent to more than one element in the other scheme (in this case MODS). Suggestions are given as to which default MODS element may need to be used when converting a record from Dublin Core to MODS. A number of other crosswalks are listed by Michael Day in *Metadata: Mapping Between Metadata Formats.*[23]

Harvesting Tools and Templates

Other current tools in use include harvesting technologies, which involve automated processes that go out on the Web to "harvest" metadata at a minimal level of complexity. This information is stored and retrieved as needed. In addition, metadata creation tools, software, and metadata templates are among the tools available to improve productivity and consistency. Some of these are commercial products, while others, such as a number of Dublin Core templates,[24] can be found on the World Wide Web free of charge. Templates and harvesting often are used together—that is, an option in completing a template may be to begin by harvesting data from the Web site to be described.

CONCLUSION

This chapter has provided a simple introduction to metadata issues. While many see the topic as simply traditional library cataloging, there are some extensions required for metadata. The complexity, amount, and variety of information required to organize electronic resources may be greater than those for traditional resources. It is important to remember, though, that the ultimate purpose for both cataloging and metadata creation is to allow users to navigate information systems to find, identify, select, and obtain the information packages they need. In addition, it is important that we are careful in the terminology we use in discussing metadata. Although the conceptual components discussed above are highly intertwined, it can be helpful to try to specify the type of information we are referring to when we use the term "metadata." One person's metadata may be another person's content standard.

NOTES

All URLs accessed June 2003.

1. In a Google search performed in October 2002, forty out of the first fifty sites listed "data about data" or some slight variation as a definition of metadata. A common variation being seen is now "structured data about data."

2. *FOLDOC: Free On-line Dictionary of Computing.* Available: http://wombat. doc.ic.ac.uk/foldoc. The definition is for "meta-data," which, FOLDOC says, is not to be confused with "metadata," a term coined by Jack E. Myers, who used the term in a brochure for a product, and registered it as a U.S. trademark.

3. More on these two metadata schemas appears in the next chapter.

4. These categories of metadata are described in detail later in this chapter and in the next.

5. International Federation of Library Associations and Institutions, IFLA Study Group, *Functional Requirements for Bibliographic Records (FRBR)* (München: Saur, 1998). Available: http://www.ifla.org/VII/s13/frbr/frbr.pdf or http://www.ifla.org/VII/s13/frbr/frbr.htm.

6. Sherry L. Vellucci, "Metadata and Authority Control," *Library Resources & Technical Services* 44, no. 1 (2000): 33–43.

7. Ibid., pp. 36–37.

8. Ibid., p. 36.

9. Stefan Gradmann, "Cataloging vs. Metadata: Old Wine in New Bottles?" *International Cataloguing and Bibliographic Control* 28, no. 4 (1999): 88–90.

10. *Anglo-American Cataloguing Rules, Second Edition, 2002 Revision* (Ottawa: Canadian Library Association; Chicago: American Library Association, 2002).

11. International Federation of Library Associations and Institutions, IFLA Study Group, *FRBR.*

12. Elaine Svenonius, *The Intellectual Foundation of Information Organization* (Cambridge, Mass.: MIT Press, 2000).

13. OCLC/RLG Preservation Metadata Working Group [Home page]. Available: http://www.oclc.org/research/pmwg/; National Library of Australia, *Preservation Activities.* Available: http://www.nla.gov.au/preserve/; *Cedars: CURL Exemplars in Digital Archives.* Available: http://www.leeds.ac.uk/cedars/index.htm.

14. Godfrey Rust and Mark Bide, *The <indecs> Metadata Framework: Principles, Model and Data Dictionary.* June 2000. Available: http://www.indecs.org/pdf/framework.pdf.

15. Renato Iannella and Debbie Campbell, *The A-Core: Metadata About Content Metadata.* 30 June 1999. Available: http://metadata.net/admin/draft-iannella-admin-01.txt.

16. Jytte Hansen and Leif Andresen, *AC-Administrative Components: Dublin Core DCMI Administrative Metadata: A Proposal to Be Discussed in the DCMI Administrative Metadata Working Group.* 7 October 2002. Available: http://www.dublincore.org/groups/admin/proposal-20021007.shtml.

17. Rachel Heery and Manjula Patel, "Application Profiles: Mixing and Matching Metadata Schemes," *Ariadne* 25 (24 September 2000). Available: http://www.ariadne.ac.uk/issue25/app-profiles/intro.html.

18. Jon Mason and Stuart Sutton, *Education Working Group: Draft Proposal.* Date issued: 5 October 2000. Available: http://dublincore.org/documents/education-namespace/.

19. Available for purchase: http://www.iso.ch/iso/en/.

20. Dublin Core Metadata Registry. Available: http://www.dublincore.org/dcregistry/index.html, with an explanation of its use at http://www.dublincore.org/dcregistry/helpServlet.

21. Margaret St. Pierre and William P. LaPlant, *Issues in Crosswalking Content Metadata Standards,* released 15 October 1998. Available: http://www.niso.org/press/whitepapers/crsswalk.html.

22. Library of Congress, Network Development and MARC Standards Office, *Dublin Core Metadata Element Set Mapping to MODS Version 2.0,* 31 March 2003. Available: http://www.loc.gov/standards/mods/dcsimple-mods.html.

23. Michael Day, *Metadata: Mapping Between Metadata Formats,* last updated 22 May 2002. Available: http://www.ukoln.ac.uk/metadata/interoperability.

24. These can be found through the Dublin Core Metadata Initiative Web site. Available: http://dublincore.org/.

SUGGESTED READINGS

Caplan, Priscilla. *Metadata Fundamentals for All Librarians*. Chicago: American Library Association, 2003. Chapter 16: "Administrative Metadata", Chapter 17: "Structural Metadata", and Chapter 18: "Rights Metadata."

Gilliland-Swetland, Anne J. "Setting the Stage." In *Introduction to Metadata: Pathways to Digital Information*. Version 2.0, edited by Murtha Baca 2000. Available: http://www.getty.edu/research/institute/standards/intrometa data/2_articles/index.html.

Hodge, Gail. *Metadata Made Simpler*. Bethesda, Md.: National Information Standards Organization, 2001. Available: http://www.niso.org/news/ Metadata_Simpler.pdf.

Hudgins, Jean, Grace Agnew, and Elizabeth Brown. *Getting Mileage out of Metadata: Applications for the Library*. Chicago: American Library Association, 1999.

International Federation of Library Associations and Institutions. *Digital Libraries: Metadata Resources*. Latest revision 3 February 2003. Available: http://www.ifla.org/II/metadata.htm.

Jones, Wayne, Judith R. Ahronheim, and Josephine Crawford, eds. *Cataloging the Web: Metadata, AACR, and MARC 21*. (ALCTS Papers on Library Technical Services and Collections, no. 10.) Lanham, Md.: Scarecrow Press, 2002.

Lazinger, Susan S. *Digital Preservation and Metadata: History, Theory, Practice*. Englewood, Colo.: Libraries Unlimited, 2001. Chapter 1: "Why Is Digital Preservation an Issue?" and Chapter 2: "What Electronic Data Should Be Preserved?"

"Metadata Standards, Crosswalks, and Standard Organizations." In *Cataloger's Toolbox* (Memorial University of Newfoundland Libraries). Last updated 19 June 2003. Available: http://staff.library.mun.ca/staff/tool box/standards.htm.

"The Value of Metadata." Last updated 8 July 2003. Available: http://www. fgdc.gov/publications/documents/metadata/metabroc.html.

Vellucci, Sherry L. "Metadata and Authority Control." *Library Resources & Technical Services* 44, no. 1 (January 2000): 33–43.

CHAPTER 7

METADATA: DESCRIPTION

Loosely speaking, there are three parts to creating metadata for an information package: (1) encoding (i.e., providing the syntax of the metadata), (2) providing a description of the information package along with other information necessary for management, preservation, and structure of the package, and (3) providing for access to this description. Encoding was discussed in Chapter 4, and the preceding chapter gave a general introduction to providing metadata. This chapter discusses description, and the next four chapters discuss access.

Bibliographic record is the name that has been applied to the description of tangible information packages (e.g., books, sound recordings) for many years. Even though it has been applied to records created for motion pictures, sound recordings, computer files, and the like, the word *bibliographic* has continued to have a stigma arising from *biblio-*, meaning "book." At times the term "surrogate record" has been used instead. A surrogate stands in place of someone or something else. The term can be used for records representing any kind of information package in any kind of information retrieval system. In this and following chapters, "surrogate record" is used to mean the description and access content of a metadata record.

Some definitions are in order before discussing the creation of surrogate records. A *surrogate record* is a presentation of the characteristics of an information package. The characteristics include both descriptive data and access points. The record stands in place of (i.e., is a surrogate for) the information package in information retrieval systems such as catalogs, indexes, bibliographies, and search engines. An *information package* is an instance of recorded information (e.g., book, article, videocassette, Web document or set of "pages," sound recording, electronic journal, etc.). *Descriptive data* is data derived from an information package and used to describe it, such as its title, its associated names, its edition or version, its date of publication, its extent, and notes identifying pertinent features. In metadata records a particular piece of descriptive data may be referred to as the *content* or *value* assigned to an *element*. An *access point* is any term (word, heading, etc.) in a surrogate record that is used to retrieve that record. Access points are often singled out from the descriptive data and are placed under authority control (see discussion in Chapter 8).

A file of surrogate records serves as a filter to keep a user from having to search through myriad irrelevant full texts. Surrogate records must be distinctive enough that no record can be confused with the record for any other information package. A surrogate record's most important function is to assist the user in evaluating the possibility that the information package it represents will be useful and contains information that the user wishes to explore further. Surrogate record descriptions are most helpful when they are predictable in both form and content. Adherence to standards ensures such predictability. Some of the existing standards are discussed below.

UNITS TO BE DESCRIBED

First, it is necessary to decide what is to be described. Traditions have been established in the library world as to what constitutes a "catalogable unit" when dealing with tangible packages. The principle, greatly simplified, has been that one physical package is a catalogable unit with the caveat that packages that follow one another in succession and have the same title also may be a single unit. For example, this book is a single catalogable unit. Volume 1 of *The Works of Shakespeare in Two Volumes* is probably not a catalogable unit; but volumes 1 and 2 together are considered to be a single unit. Packages that come in a set with the same overarching title (although each can also have its own title) also may be called a unit. For example, *Great Books of the Western World* is a set where each volume has its own, often famous, author and title. It might be cataloged as a single unit with multiple volumes, or each volume might be cataloged as a unit.

Electronic resources have thrown this tradition into chaos. It can be very difficult to determine what is a "package" in the electronic environment. It could be a university's home page and everything linked to it, for example, or it could be the grading policy of one department. It is going to take more time to sort this through; it may be that, given the ease of access to Web pages now, a surrogate record can be created for any piece of information that someone determines needs metadata access.

Finite vs. Continuing Resources

One of the ways of determining the unit to be described has been to divide the world of information packages into two groups: (1) those that are complete or which have a predetermined conclusion and (2) those that are ongoing—that is, those which will have additions made to them without a predetermined end in sight. For many years these were called "monographs" and "serials," and distinguishing between them has plagued libraries for decades. The monograph vs. serial distinction has been used to set up working departments in most large academic libraries. In some cases technical services units have been divided so that cataloging and acquisitions departments handle monographs, while serials departments handle serials. Other technical services units have been divided into acquisitions and cataloging, but with each of those departments being further divided into serials and monographs sections.

A new concept in the 2002 revision of *AACR2R* is "continuing resource," defined as "a bibliographic resource that is issued over time with no predetermined conclusion. Continuing resources include serials and ongoing integrating resources."[1] An "integrating resource" is defined as "a bibliographic resource that is added to or changed by means of updates that do not remain discrete and are integrated into the whole."[2] This expresses the nature of many Web resources (e.g., online scholarly journals that store articles in a single cumulating database, along with continually changing Web sites of all kinds) and has the added advantage of including traditional looseleaf print publications, which were in limbo in the past division of "monograph vs. serial."

Most ILSs (Integrated Library Systems) have separate modules for serials management. "Serial" was defined in *AACR2R* prior to the 2002 revisions as: "A publication in any medium issued in successive parts bearing numeric or chronological designations and intended to be continued indefinitely."[3] This was quite limiting, and the reality is that most ILS serial modules are designed to handle anything that needs to be received and checked in over a period of time. This can include multiple-volume sets, unnumbered series, and looseleaf updates, none of which were included in *AACR2R*'s previous definition of "serial." The current definition is a bit better: "a continuing resource issued in a succession of discrete parts, usually bearing numbering, that has no predetermined conclusion."[4] However, this still does not encompass the whole range of ongoing resources, resulting in the need for the new concepts of continuing resources and integrating resources.

FRBR's Entities

Another problem in determining the unit to be described, also an issue for decades, is whether organizers should describe a "work" or an "item." This problem was the source of debates between Seymour Lubetzky and Michael Gorman before the adoption of *AACR2*, which came down firmly on the side of describing the "item," whereas Lubetzky believed that *AACR1* had described the "work." IFLA took on the challenge of identifying whether to describe works or items, and issued its report as *Functional Requirements for Bibliographic Records (FRBR)*—1998.[5] It offers the four concepts of *work, expression, manifestation,* and *item.*

The top level, "work," is the one that essentially exists only in the mind of the creator. It is the distinct intellectual or artistic creation, an abstract entity with no single material object one can point to. It is recognized through individual *expressions* of the work. Examples of "works" include Shakespeare's *Romeo and Juliet;* Mozart's *The Magic Flute;* Michelangelo's *David.*

The second level, "expression," is where the work can actually be seen or heard or felt. There can be more than one expression of a single work. An expression is the realization of a work in alphanumeric, musical, or choreographic notation; sound; image; object; movement; among others; or a combination of such forms. For example, for a work of Franz Schubert, expressions can be the composer's score, or a performance by the Amadeus Quartet, or a performance by the Cleveland Quartet. For a newspaper, expressions might be a paper version, a Web version, or a translated version in Spanish. For Michelangelo's *David,* expressions might be the original sculpture in its museum, copies of the sculpture elsewhere, photographs of the sculpture, or digital representations on the Web.

The third level, "manifestation," is a way of giving a name to any one of the formats in which one of the expressions of a work can be found. It is the situation in which exact contents are reproduced to look the same, even though the format is different. In our newspaper example, suppose we are talking about *The New York Times.* A particular issue of the paper could have manifestations as print-on-paper format, as microfilm format, or as reproduction on CD-ROM. Another example might be for the expression of a school's grading policy. It might have manifestations as an HTML text document, a word-processed file version, a PDF version, or a printout of one of these versions.

The fourth level, "item," is the one used to define a single exemplar of a manifestation and is normally the same as the manifestation itself. Exemplars usually are identical to each other, but can be different in interesting ways. For example, there might be a damaged copy, a copy autographed by the author, or a copy bound by a library's rebinding department.

The unit that is usually chosen to be described is the *manifestation*, although in the case of something like a rare book, the *item* will be described specifically. Efforts are being made to answer the question of whether *works* and/or *expressions* can also be described in metadata records. It is hypothesized that such descriptions could be invaluable aids in retrieval of particular resources sought by users. They could also produce such practical results as allowing a user to place a hold on a work at the expression level if there is no reason to need a particular manifestation (e.g., the British edition is as useful to the patron as the American edition).

CREATION OF SURROGATE RECORDS

Once the unit to be described has been determined, a surrogate record is created by selecting important pieces of information (e.g., title, author, date, etc.) from the information package, determining certain characteristics about the package (e.g., size, terms of availability), and then placing those pieces of information in a certain order, usually dictated by a set of rules or conventions for description. These rules or conventions (i.e., *content standards*) are created by different communities to fill the needs of those communities for descriptions of the information packages for which they are responsible. Content standards serve as style manuals for metadata, providing elements to be included, providing definitions of each element, and sometimes providing rules for exactly what information to include in a description, for the structure of that information, and occasionally for its punctuation and order.

Several of today's metadata schemas are outgrowths of rules that were known as bibliographic schemas or "cataloging rules." Such rules were essentially content standards, first for the content of records in print retrieval tools, and later for records to be entered into online retrieval tools. As online retrieval tools came into being, separate standards for the encoding of surrogate records were developed to be used to create "complete" online records. The conceptual pieces necessary for online records are, then, (1) elements (identification of which pieces of information are to be included), (2) content (which may be prescribed with exact format or may be just loosely described in the standard), and (3) syntax (expressed as an encoding format or a markup language). A standard may dictate defined elements only (e.g., Dublin Core), content only (e.g., *AACR2R*), or syntax only (e.g., XML DTDs). Some metadata standards have been created that combine the conceptual pieces in different ways. TEI Headers, for example, specify what elements are required, dictate the content and form of those elements, and specify the SGML/XML syntax.

An information package's properties may be described using community-specific or schema-associated rules. Discussed here are several examples of metadata from different communities. The emphasis in this chapter is on the content component of each schema discussed, including the elements required by each for description of information packages. Examples of surrogate record creation tools to be discussed are:

- Bibliographic and General Metadata Schemas

  - *ISBD (International Standard Bibliographic Description)*

  - *AACR2R (Anglo-American Cataloguing Rules, Second Edition, 2002 revision)*

  - Dublin Core (DC)

  - MODS (Metadata Object Description Schema)

- Domain-Specific Metadata Schemas

  - *ISAD(G) (General International Standard Archival Description)*

  - *APPM (Archives, Personal Papers, and Manuscripts)*

  - EAD (Encoded Archival Description)

  - TEI (Text Encoding Initiative) Headers

  - GILS (Government Information Locator Service)

  - FGDC (Federal Geographic Data Committee) *Content Standard for Digital Geospatial Metadata (CSDGM)*

  - VRA (Visual Resources Association) Core Categories for Visual Resources

  - CIMI XML Schema for SPECTRUM

  - ONIX (Online Information eXchange)

- Other Surrogate Record Types
  - Index records
  - On-the-fly records

Bibliographic and General Metadata Schemas

Content standards in the library field were developed long before encoding standards and continue to exist as separate standards. Examples of such content standards to be discussed here are ISBD and *AACR2R*. As the need for metadata for other communities, especially for electronic resources in those communities, became apparent in the mid-1990s, the Dublin Core was conceived and developed as a general-purpose schema. And MODS is the most recently developed general-purpose schema.

ISBD (International Standard Bibliographic Description)

The *International Standard Bibliographic Description*[6] was designed in the early 1970s to facilitate the international exchange of cataloging records by standardizing the elements to be used in the description, assigning an order to these elements, and specifying a system of symbols to be used in punctuating the elements. Actually, there are several *ISBD*s based upon format of the information package to be described.[7] The one discussed here is *ISBD(G)*, where the "G" stands for "General." There are also separate *ISBD*s for monographs, rare (antiquarian) materials, serials, continuing resources, cartographic materials, electronic resources, non-book materials, and printed music.

When the *ISBD* was adopted as an international standard, it was expected that national cataloging agencies would incorporate it into their national cataloging rules. It has been incorporated into several, including the *Anglo-American Cataloguing Rules, Second Edition, 2002 Revision (AACR2R)*, which is discussed in more detail below.

ISBD requires that an information package be totally identified by the description, independent of any access points. It contains eight areas:

- Area 1—Title and statement of responsibility
- Area 2—Edition
- Area 3—Material (or type of publication) specific details
- Area 4—Publication, distribution, etc.

- Area 5—Physical description

- Area 6—Series

- Area 7—Notes

- Area 8—Standard number and terms of availability

Each area contains more than one element. Area 1 contains the title (called the title proper) assigned to the information package by persons responsible for its existence. There may be more than one title (e.g., same title in two languages, subtitle, etc.), and there may be other information necessary to the understanding of the title (e.g., information about the place and date of a conference, etc.). The "statement of responsibility" element of Area 1 contains the names of persons or corporate bodies that are responsible for intellectual content of information packages, but not those responsible for presentation and packaging. For example, the name of the artist performing on a music CD would be included here, but not the name of the company that produced the CD.

Area 2 contains a statement about the version of the information package represented in the surrogate record being created. It might be a new edition of a work, a new version of a software package, or a version of a work that is put out for a particular geographic area (e.g., the city edition of a newspaper that serves a region). Area 2 also may contain a statement of responsibility, this one relating only to the package being described (e.g., a person who has worked on the edition in hand but did not work on earlier editions).

Area 3 contains data that is particularly important to a particular type of work. For example, in describing serials, it is important to identify the date and the volume number of the first issue of the serial. An important point is that Area 3 is used only for some types of works, and this is determined by a specific implementation of *ISBD* in a particular national code.

Area 4 contains the name of the entity (e.g., publisher, institution, manufacturer, etc.) that is responsible for the presentation and packaging of the information package, along with its geographic location. There may be more than one such name and/or location. An important, broadly applicable element in this area is the date of public appearance of the package.

Area 5 contains a physical description of an information package that is in tangible form. The physical description includes the extent of the item given in terms of what kind of item it is (e.g., 2 disks, 365 p., 4 videocassettes, etc.), the dimensions of the item (often height, but also sometimes width, diameter, etc.), and other physical details such as information about illustrations or about material from which an object is made. This area, in general, is not meant for description of remote electronic resources, although some kinds of "other" details, such as information about illustrations and whether or not they are in color could be important descriptive information about some electronic resources.

Area 6 contains the title of any series of which the information package is part. A series is a group of separate works that are related in subject or form and/or are published by the same entity (e.g., Library Science Text Series). There may also be information other than the series title. A series title can have the same kinds of additional title information as does the title proper in Area 1. Series may have statements of responsibility that relate only to the series. If the series has an ISSN (International Standard Serial Number), it may appear in Area 6.

Area 7 contains notes relating to the information package being described. Notes may, to name a few, describe the nature, scope, or artistic form of the work; give the language of the text; identify the source of the title if there is no chief source of information; or explain relationships of this work to others. This is the most free-form of the areas.

Area 8 contains a number that is accepted as an international standard—at the moment only the ISBN (International Standard Book Number) or the ISSN. The area also contains information about the terms of availability of the information package (e.g., it is free to members but others must pay, or it is unavailable to the public for a certain number of years, etc.).

There are two things especially to remember when using *ISBD* for creation of surrogate records. First, *ISBD* punctuation is prescribed, and it precedes and predicts the data element that comes next. For example, a space-slash-space in Area 1 says that the statement of responsibility is coming next. Second, the order of data is prescribed. For example, in Area 1 the prescription for content and punctuation is: **title [GMD] : subtitle / 1st statement of responsibility ; 2nd statement of responsibility**. It can be seen that the prescribed punctuation is both preceded and followed by a space.

Finally, we should say a few words about the formats that *ISBD* records take. In the *ISBD* standard each area is to be set off from the next area by a period-space-dash-space or by the starting of a new line or paragraph. British practice in creating printed catalogs has been to have the areas follow one after another; but American practice has been to create cards and other printed catalogs by having Areas 1, 5, and 7 each begin a new "paragraph," and if there is more than one note in Area 7, each note begins a new "paragraph." (Figures 7.1 through 7.3 are formatted using American practice.) In *AACR2,* both British and American formats are accepted. In most instances, at this time, format is a moot point, because the data created using rules based on *ISBD* are placed into MARC records. Displays that are based on these records seldom use the "card" format. They are much more likely to have labels (e.g., "TITLE:" for Area 1).

Anglo-American Cataloguing Rules, Second Edition, 2002 Revision (AACR2R)

The descriptive part of *Anglo-American Cataloguing Rules, Second Edition, 2002 Revision*[8] is based on *ISBD*. (The access part of *AACR2R* is based on the Paris Principles; see discussion in Chapter 8.) After a general descriptive chapter in *AACR2R*, other descriptive chapters cover different kinds of materials or patterns of publication:

- books, pamphlets, printed sheets—chapter 2

- cartographic materials—chapter 3

- manuscripts (including manuscript collections)—chapter 4

- music—chapter 5

- sound recordings—chapter 6

- motion pictures and videorecordings—chapter 7

- graphic materials—chapter 8

- electronic resources—chapter 9

- three-dimensional artifacts and realia—chapter 10

- microforms—chapter 11

- continuing resources—chapter 12

Rules are numbered so that the numbers of the *ISBD* areas follow the chapter number. Here is an example of *ISBD* areas as rules in chapter 5 of *AACR2R*:

- rule 5.1—Title and statement of responsibility area

- rule 5.2—Edition area

- rule 5.3—Material specific details area

- rule 5.4—Publication, distribution, etc., area

- etc.

An example of the same rule in more than one chapter is:

- rule 1.1B—general title proper

- rule 2.1B—book title proper

- rule 3.1B—map title proper

- rule 4.1B—manuscript title proper

- etc.

Each chapter prescribes a "chief source of information" from which much of the information is to be taken. For example, the chief source of information for a book is its title page. The chief source is preferred when the elements vary on or in various parts of the same information package (e.g., if the title on the sound recording label is different from that on the container, then the one on the label is preferred).

A GMD (general material designation) in Area 1 (title and statement of responsibility area) indicates the class of item being described (e.g., art original, electronic resource, motion picture, text, etc.). In this example: **American women artists [slide] : the twentieth century**, "[slide]" is the GMD. In practice there are some classes of items that are not given a GMD in accord with the practice of the Library of Congress (LC). For example, [map], [text], and [music] are in *AACR2R*'s GMD list but are not used by LC. This kind of information is given in the *LCRIs* (*Library of Congress Rule Interpretations*). Implementation of *AACR2R* in the United States is dominated by the Library of Congress, and anyone using this set of rules should also consult the decisions about how catalogers at LC interpret and apply *AACR2R*, as found in the *LCRIs*.

In *AACR2R*, Area 3 [material (or type of publication) specific details] is used only for maps, printed music, computer files, and serials. Some examples of the wording that may be used in Area 3 for each of the four types of information packages are:

- map: **Scale 1:24,000 ; Polyconic proj.**

- printed music: **Score and set of parts**

- electronic resource: **Electronic programs (2 files : 250, 800 statements)**

- serial: **Vol. 1, no. 1 (Jan. 1997)-**

AACR2R itself prescribes three levels of description that are considered to conform to "standard." The first level includes the minimum elements required to meet the standard. It is most likely to be used in small libraries, but LC catalogs serials at this level "enhanced," which means that a few additional elements have been prescribed by LC. The second level is the level used by LC for most cataloging. The third level includes every possible element set out in the rules. It is used only in cataloging such things as rare items. See Figures 7.1, 7.2, and 7.3. (These figures are shown in *ISBD* format.)

There is one additional interpretation of *AACR2R* that should be mentioned. The Program for Cooperative Cataloging (PCC), which operates out of LC but is a cooperative group of catalogers from many places, has defined a set of Core Records (slightly different for different types of materials).[9] The Core Records present the minimal standard for what to include in a nationally acceptable *AACR2R* record. The description part of the Core Record calls for complete description in Areas 1 through 6 and 8 and for some of the notes in Area 7. It is a "minimal" standard because it prescribes much less in the access points arena.

An additional source of description rules based on *ISBD* is *The Concise AACR2, 1998 Revision* by Michael Gorman.[10] It cannot be called a

Wireless personal communications / edited by Theodore S. Rappaport.—Kluwer Academic Publishers, 1997.

xii, 225 p. – (The Kluwer international series in engineering and computer science ; SECS 242).

"Papers in this book were originally presented at the 7th Virginia Tech/MPRG Symposium on Wireless Personal Communications held June 11-13, [1997], in Blacksburg, Virginia."

Includes bibliographical references and index.
ISBN: 0-7923-8017-7

Fig. 7.1. *AACR2* **first-level description.**

Wireless personal communications : improving capacity, services, and reliability / edited by Theodore S. Rappaport. -- Boston : Kluwer Academic Publishers, 1997.

xii, 225 p. : ill. ; 24 cm. -- (The Kluwer international series in engineering and computer science ; SECS 424).

"Papers in this book were originally presented at the 7th Virginia Tech/MPRG Symposium on Wireless Personal Communications held June 11-13, [1997], in Blacksburg, Virginia."

Includes bibliographical references and index.
ISBN: 0-7923-8017-7

Fig. 7.2. *AACR2* **second-level description.**

The works of the late Right Honorable Joseph Addison, Esq. : with a complete index. -- Birmingham : printed by John Baskerville, for J. and R. Tonson ... London, 1761.

4 v. : ill., port. ; 30 cm. (4to).

Vol. 1: xxv, [3], 537, [5], 415-525 (i.e. 415-537), [5] p., [4] leaves of plates; v. 2: [8], 538, [14] p.; v. 3: 579, [13] p.; v. 4: 555, [13] p. Last leaves of v. 2 and 4 blank. Page 537 of last numbered section of v. 1 misnumbered 525.

References: Gaskell, P. J. Baskerville 17.

Contents: v. 1. Preface. Poems on several occasions. Rosamond. An essay on Virgil's Georgics. Cato. The drummer, or, The haunted house. Poemata. Dialogues upon the usefulness of ancient medals -- v. 2. Remarks on several parts of Italy, &c. The Tatler. The Spectator, no. 1-89 -- v. 3. The Spectator, no. 90-505 -- v. 4. The Spectator, no. 507-600. The guardian. The Lover. The present state of the war, and the necessity of an augmentation, considered. The Whig-examiner. The Free-holder. Of the Christian religion.

LC copy: In v. 1 leaves Zzzz2-3 incorrectly bound before Zzz1. Vol. 2 lacks the blank at the end.

Fig. 7.3. *AACR2* third-level description. (Source: *Bibliographic Description of Rare Books* [Washington, D.C.: Office for Descriptive Cataloging Policy Processing Services, Library of Congress, 1981], p. 55.)

"standard" because it is a work of personal authorship and has not been adopted as official by any group. However, it is based strongly on *AACR2R* and provides a way of applying much of *ISBD* without complicated rules or esoteric examples.

The Dublin Core (DC)

The Dublin Core[11] (shortened form of Dublin Core Metadata Element Set—named for its first workshop, held in 1995 in Dublin, Ohio) was created in order to have an internationally agreed-upon set of elements that could be "filled in" by the creator of any electronic document. Participants in the workshops and conferences that have developed DC are experts from many different fields (e.g., publishers, computer specialists, librarians, software producers, text-markup experts, etc.). Therefore, it is a cross-domain standard and can be the basis for metadata for any type of resource in any field. It has been approved as NISO Standard Z39.85–2001,[12] and ISO approval is being sought. It is used internationally and a number of application profiles have been developed for specific domain applications that use the basic DC as the starting point.

The Dublin Core Metadata Initiative (DCMI) oversees the development of implementations of the standard. DC has been implemented through the use of HTML for a number of years. Templates have been developed that anyone can use to fill in the DC elements.[13] Such templates can be filled in and previewed, and then HTML-formatted data can be returned to the user's screen to be copied and pasted into a document header. More recently it has been implemented using XML. A document giving guidelines for implementing Dublin Core in XML can be found at the DCMI Web site.[14] Development work on a DC standard for using RDF/ XML has been in process since 1999.

The DC Element Set consists of fifteen elements that can be divided into three groups:[15]

- Elements related to the content of the resource

    - Title—the name of the resource (information package)

    - Subject—the topic(s) of the content of the resource; use of controlled vocabularies and formal classification schemes is encouraged

    - Description—a textual statement of the content of the resource; could be an abstract, a table of contents, or free-text account

    - Source—information about an original resource from which this one is derived in whole or in part; it is recommended that best practice is to use a string or number from a formal identification system to identify the referenced resource

    - Language—an indication of the language of the intellectual content (text) of the resource; recommended best practice is to use the language tags defined in RFC 3066[16]

    - Relation—a reference to a related resource along with its relationship to the present source, such as a work that the described resource is a version of, is based on, or is referenced by; as with Source, recommended best practice is to use a string or number from a formal identification system to identify the referenced resource

    - Coverage—an identification of spatial location (i.e., a physical region), temporal period (note that this element is for the subject, and the Date element below is for the date of creation of the resource), or jurisdiction (e.g., a named administrative entity);

both spatial and temporal characteristics should be taken from a controlled list, or geographic area should be spelled out, and date should be in a standard form such as YYYY-MM-DD

- Elements related to the resource when viewed as intellectual property

  - Creator—the name of the person or organization primarily responsible for creating the intellectual content of the resource (e.g., author, artist, composer, etc.)

  - Publisher—the name of the entity responsible for making the resource available (e.g., publishing house, university or one of its departments, other corporate body, etc.)

  - Contributor—the name of a person or organization that has made significant intellectual contributions to the content of the resource, but ones that are secondary to the name in the Creator element (e.g., editor, illustrator, etc.)

  - Rights—a statement, link, or identifier that gives information about rights held in and over the resource (e.g., whether use is restricted until a certain time, time at which the resource will be removed from display, etc.)

- Elements related mainly to the issue of resource-as-an-instance

  - Date—the date of an event in the lifecycle of the resource (such as its creation or availability date or date of revision); it is recommended that ISO 8601 (Date and Time Formats) be used, especially YYYY-MM-DD as the form for a date[17]

  - Resource Type—a designation of the nature or genre of the content of the resource (e.g., home page, poem, technical report, dictionary, etc.); recommended best practice is to select a value from a controlled vocabulary such as the DCMI Type Vocabulary[18]

- Format—a designation of the physical or digital manifestation of the resource, such as the software, hardware, etc., required to use the resource; recommended best practice is to select a value from a controlled vocabulary

- Identifier—a string or number that uniquely identifies the resource (e.g., URI, URL, DOI, or ISBN)

From the above elements, Creator, Contributor, and Subject are access point elements, covered in Chapters 8, 10, and 11.

General principles for DC, when it was established, were: (1) the core set can be extended with further elements needed by a particular community; (2) all elements are optional; (3) all elements are repeatable; and (4) any element may be modified by a qualifier or qualifiers. The form of the content of each element is not prescribed. See Figure 7.4 for an example DC record.

For a time there were two camps among the DCMI community, each with strong advocates. The Minimalist camp wanted just the fifteen elements with no qualifiers. The Qualifiers camp insisted that subelements are both useful and necessary. In a sense, both have won. The NISO standard is just the basic elements, but qualifiers are accepted parts of the implementations. There are two kinds of qualifiers now used. "Type" qualifiers explain what kind of information is included in the element. "Scheme" qualifiers explain what scheme has been used to provide the content of the element. For example, the use of "type" qualifiers is illustrated by the following HTML statements (as implemented in OCLC's WorldCat):

- meta name="DC.Creator.namePersonal" [designation of Creator element as being a personal name]

- meta name="DC.Format.extent" [designation of Format element as giving the extent of the item]

- meta name="DC.Publisher.place" [designation of Publisher element as giving the location of the publisher]

Examples of the use of "scheme" qualifiers:

- meta name="DC.Identifier" scheme="ISBN" [designation of Identifier element as using the International Standard Book Number scheme]

- meta name="DC.Subject.class" scheme="LCC" [designa-

Title	TPOT, technical processing online tools
Title.alternative	TPOT
Title.alternative	Technical processing online tools
Identifier.URI	http://tpot.ucsd.edu/
Type.AACR2-gmd	[electronic resource].
Type.Note	Web site primarily in HTML format
Contributor.namePersonal	Janczyn, George J.
Contributor.nameCorporate	UCSD Libraries.
Coverage.spatial.MARC21-gac	n-us-ca
Creator.namePersonal	
Date.issued.MARC21-Date	1994-9999
Description.note	Title from home page (viewed Jan. 19, 1999).
Description.note	Produced and managed by George J. Janczyn.
Description.note	"Serving the technical services departments of the UCSD Libraries since January 1994."
Description	Presents Technical Processing Online Tools (TPOT), serving the Library Technical Services departments of the University of California at San Diego. Provides links to TPOT news and information and to information about cataloging, acquisitions, special collections, training resources, and Innopac. Also offers access to a search utility and to information about the Library of Congress, the Online Computer Library Center (OCLC), the Internet, and Melvyl.
Format.IMT	
Language.ISO639-2	eng
Publisher	University of California, San Diego,
Publisher.place	[La Jolla, Calif. :
Relation.requires	Mode of access: Internet via World Wide Web.
Rights	
Source.URI	
Subject.class.DDC	021.65
Subject.class.DDC	025.02
Subject.class.DDC	025.3
Subject.nameCorporate.LCSH	UCSD Libraries.
Subject.topical.LCSH	Technical services (Libraries)
Subject.topical.LCSH	Cataloging.
Subject.topical	Library information networks.

Fig. 7.4. Dublin Core record. (Source: OCLC WorldCat as viewed in Connexion, record number 33959367.)

tion of Subject element as being of the classification type
using the Library of Congress Classification scheme]

- meta name="DC.Subject.topical" scheme="LCSH" [des-
ignation of Subject element as being of the topical type
using the Library of Congress Subject Heading scheme]

Several groups have applications of the Dublin Core. Among
these, as noted already, is OCLC with an implementation in its database,
WorldCat. Catalogers using this system can view and download records encoded with MARC or encoded with an HTML or XML/RDF implementation of DC. A number of application profiles based on DC are in existence.
An example is the "DC-Library Application Profile."[19] It is made up of the
fifteen DC elements plus an additional three elements from other namespaces: Audience, Edition, and Location.

MODS (Metadata Object Description Schema)

MODS was discussed in Chapter 4 as an encoding standard. It is
actually a hybrid metadata schema that incorporates both encoding rules
and a set of named elements. It was developed by the Library of Congress'
Network Development and MARC Standards Office in consultation with
other experts. MODS provides an alternative "between a very simple metadata format with a minimum of fields and no or little substructure (for
example, Dublin Core) and a very detailed format with many data elements
having various structural complexities such as MARC21."[20] It is richer than
Dublin Core but simpler than the MARC format. Its development as an
XML standard means that its language-based tags can be understood by any
English-speaking person; although as with all language-based tagging, international use by non-English readers is problematic.

Decisions on which elements of MARC to place into MODS included decisions to combine some MARC elements into a single element
and to drop others altogether. In addition some MARC elements recur in
more than one element as subelements, which are defined in MODS as
XML complex types. For example, "name," "identifier," and "titleInfo" can
be used as both elements and subelements with the same definition for
each. "Name," for example, can be the primary name associated with the
resource, or it can be a name associated with a related information package.[21]

MODS has twenty top-level elements and forty-seven subelements.
(Subelements used under more than one top-level element are counted
only once.) The top-level elements are:

titleInfo	abstract	targetAudience
name	tableofContents	cartographics
typeOfResource	note	accessConditions
genre	subject	extension
publicationInfo	classification	recordInfo
physicalDescription	relatedItem	location
language	identifier	

An example of subelements follows, showing the subelements under "publicationInfo":

placeCode	dateCaptured
place	edition
publisher	issuance (continuing, monographic)
dateIssued	frequency
dateCreated	

MODS was made available officially in June 2002, and experimentation has proceeded since then. For example, the Library of Congress's MINERVA (Mapping the Internet: Electronic Resources Virtual Archive) Project[22] is being expanded with the collaboration of the Internet Archive, SUNY, and the University of Washington.[23] Contractors are assisting with collecting and archiving Web sites focused on particular themes, and metadata is being created for these using MODS. The MODS records can be converted to MARC to be added to the Library of Congress' online catalog. (See Figure 7.5.)

Domain-Specific Metadata Schemas

Many metadata schemas have been developed by different communities to be used in specific situations for specialized resources. They support description that allows for details needed by users searching for resources in a particular domain. Only a few are given here as examples.

ISAD(G) (General International Standard Archival Description)

The *ISAD(G)*[24] standard gives guidance for archival description. Like *ISBD*, it is intended that it be used with national standards or as a basis to develop national standards. It is designed to facilitate the creation of archival descriptions that "identify and explain the context and content of

```
- <mods:mods xmlns:mods="http://www.loc.gov/mods/">
  - <mods:titleInfo>
      <mods:title>Campbell County, Wyoming /</mods:title>
    </mods:titleInfo>
  - <mods:name type="corporate">
      <mods:namePart>Campbell County Chamber of
         Commerce</mods:namePart>
    </mods:name>
    <mods:typeOfResource>cartographic</mods:typeOfResource>
    <mods:genre authority="marc">map</mods:genre>
  - <mods:originInfo>
    - <mods:place>
        <mods:code authority="marc">wyu</mods:code>
        <mods:text>[Gillette, Wyo.]</mods:text>
      </mods:place>
      <mods:publisher>Campbell County Chamber of
         Commerce</mods:publisher>
      <mods:dateIssued>[1982?]</mods:dateIssued>
      <mods:dateIssued encoding="marc">1982</mods:dateIssued>
      <mods:issuance>monographic</mods:issuance>
    </mods:originInfo>
    <mods:language authority="iso639-2b">eng</mods:language>
  - <mods:physicalDescription>
      <mods:extent>1 map ; 33 x 15 cm.</mods:extent>
    </mods:physicalDescription>
    <mods:note type="statement of responsibility">this map reproduced by
       Campbell County Chamber of Commerce.</mods:note>
    <mods:note>In lower right corner: Kintzels-Casper.</mods:note>
  - <mods:subject>
    - <mods:cartographics>
        <mods:scale>Scale [ca. 1:510,000].</mods:scale>
      </mods:cartographics>
    </mods:subject>
  - <mods:subject authority="lcsh">
      <mods:geographic>Campbell County (Wyo.)</mods:geographic>
      <mods:topic>Maps</mods:topic>
    </mods:subject>
    <mods:classification authority="lcc">G4263.C3 1982
      .C3</mods:classification>
    <mods:identifier type="lccn">83691515</mods:identifier>
  - <mods:recordInfo>
      <mods:recordContentSource>DLC</mods:recordContentSource>
      <mods:recordCreationDate
        encoding="marc">830222</mods:recordCreationDate>
      <mods:recordChangeDate
        encoding="iso8601">19830426000000.0</mods:recordChangeDate
        >
      <mods:recordIdentifier>5466714</mods:recordIdentifier>
    </mods:recordInfo>
  </mods:mods>
```

Fig. 7.5. MODS record. (Source: Library of Congress, MARC/XML Web pages.)

archival material in order to promote its accessibility."[25] Although much information is acquired and recorded at every stage of the management of archival resources, the *ISAD* rules are for description of materials starting at the point that it has been decided to preserve and control them. The rules in the standard do not explain how to describe special materials such as sound recordings, maps, etc. Manuals that already exist for such materials are expected to be consulted as needed.

There are twenty-six elements identified in *ISAD*. Each has rules that include the name of the element, a statement of the purpose of the element in a description, the rules that apply to the element, and examples, if possible. The elements are organized into seven areas of descriptive information:

- Identity Statement Area—includes information essential to identify the unit being described

- Context Area—includes information about the origin and custody of the unit being described

- Content and Structure Area—includes information about the subject matter and the arrangement of the unit being described

- Condition of Access and Use Area—includes information about the availability of the unit being described

- Allied Materials Area—includes information about other information packages that have an important relationship to the unit being described

- Note Area—includes information that cannot be accommodated into any of the other areas

- Description Control Area—includes information about the preparation of the archival description (e.g., by whom, when, how, when revised, etc.)

Only a few of the elements are considered essential for international exchange of descriptive information:

- Reference code—code made up of standardized country code, repository code, and local repository specific numbers

- Title—concise title conveying authorship, subject matter, and form of material

- Creator—originator of a particular collection

- Date(s)—dates of creation or subject matter, depending upon the nature of the unit being described

- Extent of the unit of description—statement of the bulk, quantity, or size

- Level of description—statement of the grouping being described (e.g., fonds or subfonds; series, subseries, file, or item)

The standard does not dictate the encoding that is to be used, although there has been much cooperation with the development of the EAD DTD (see below).

Archival APPM (Archives, Personal Papers, and Manuscripts) *Records*

The *APPM*[26] is a standard for the description of archival materials that has been accepted by most of the archival community. It is based on *AACR2R*. It indicates that when cataloging archival collections, the finding aid is considered to be the chief source of information. *APPM* follows the structure of *ISBD*. Archival materials usually do not have official titles, so the cataloger must assign one. Guidelines are given for creating cataloger-supplied titles. Archival materials are those that are not published. If a collection is published, the published version is no longer archival material. Archival materials do not have "series" as defined in the library community; archival "series" are another concept entirely. In archival collections a series is a logical group of files, books, correspondence, or other such set. The concept is discussed further in Chapter 12.

EAD (Encoded Archival Description)

The *EAD Version 2002*,[27] discussed as an SGML/XML DTD in Chapter 4, was created specifically to encode finding aids. Its "Design Principles" state: "EAD is a data structure and not a data content standard. It does not prescribe how one formulates the data that appears in any given data element—that is the role of external national or international data content standards."[28] Guidelines for finding aids are already in existence (e.g., *ISAD(G)* discussed above), so the EAD does not need to contain prescriptions for content. However, it has a header that is based heavily on the TEI Header (see below). The header is meta-metadata, that is, metadata about the metadata in the rest of the EAD record. The content placed in the EAD Header is based on the rules in the *APPM*. In many instances archival collections have been cataloged using *APPM*/MARC instead of, or in addition to, finding aids being created. The EAD Header resembles such a catalog record.

TEI (Text Encoding Initiative) Headers

As discussed in Chapter 4, TEI was originally an SGML DTD (and is now also available as an XML DTD) that was created in order to provide a way of encoding old, literary, and/or scholarly texts so that encoded versions could be exchanged easily. It is suggested in guidelines that one needs to customize TEI to get the best from it. A specific popular customization that is used by a core constituency is *TEI Lite*.[29] This is the version used in this discussion.

A part of TEI is a TEI Header, created so that there would be metadata as part of the text file. The guidelines suggest the possibility of "independent headers" and give a separate set of guidelines to govern independent TEI Headers. These stand alone from the text itself and can be used as surrogate records in retrieval tools.[30]

One strong motivation for the creation of a standard for a TEI Header was to provide a source of information for cataloging. TEI folk collaborated with library catalogers for the "file description" part of the TEI Header. They wanted the mapping from TEI to a catalog record and vice versa to be as simple as possible. The standard for a TEI Header[31] calls for many of the same elements as does *ISBD;* therefore the content greatly resembles *ISBD* and *AACR2* content.

The TEI Header has four sections, only one of which is required. The four sections are file description, encoding description, profile description, and revision description. The file description is required and contains a bibliographic description of the text. It includes, for example, the title; author(s); publication information; and the source description, which is a description of the original source from which the electronic text was derived. The encoding description explains what rules or editorial decisions were used in transcribing the text (e.g., how quotations and spelling variations were treated). The profile description has information characterizing various descriptive aspects of a text and contains what *AACR2R* calls added access points (e.g., name[s] other than author[s]). It also contains language information, subject terminology, and classification notation(s). The revision description contains a record of every change that has been made to the text, including when each change was made and by whom.

Form of the content to go into the fields of the header is not dictated in the guidelines for TEI Headers. However, the guidelines for the independent TEI Header have mandatory and recommended elements and recommend the use of structured information rather than unstructured information. This means that one should use a standard such as *AACR2R* or *ISBD* when filling in the TEI Header elements. For some elements the recommendation is for unstructured free text, especially for those parts that are not governed by *AACR2R* or *ISBD*. For an example of a TEI Header, refer back to Figure 4.5 (p. 83).

GILS (Government [or Global] Information Locator Service) Records

GILS[32] came about because in 1994 Congress passed the Paperwork Reduction Act, and the Office of Management and Budget directed all U.S. federal agencies to create and make available to the public metadata on their information holdings. GILS was intended to require all federal agencies to provide the records, called "locators," for all their information resources. Some agencies have created only one brief record that describes all their information as a whole. Others, though, have records for either groups of resources or individual resources. The latter is illustrated by government libraries that are able to describe their resources as a whole and then link to their catalogs, which contain individual records for most of the resources.

The GILS metadata format is complex in order to allow for any level from brief to detailed. It is described in the GILS Web site "About" document as being "a kind of souped-up version of your trusty library catalog record."[33] Annex E of the *Application Profile for the Government Information Locator Service (GILS)*[34] presents twenty-eight core elements, while the *Guidelines for the Preparation of GILS Core Entries*[35] and the list provided by GPO Access[36] present twenty-two core elements. In all cases several of the elements have subelements. The mandatory core elements are:

- Title—element intended to convey significant information to allow users to make initial decisions on likely relevance

- Originator—identifies the originating agency, as listed in the U.S. Government Manual where applicable

- Abstract—narrative description of the information package

- Purpose—description of the function of the information package and why it is offered

- Agency Program—identifies the program or mission supported by the information resource

- Availability—grouping of subelements that together describe how the resource is made available

  - Distributor—several subfields giving information about the distributor, such as name, address, telephone number, hours of service, and the like

  - Order Process—explains how to obtain the information package from the distributor

- Sources of Data—identifies the provider(s) of data, such as whether it is generated by the agency or is received from outside the agency

- Access Constraints—describes any constraints that limit the public's ability to consult the information package described

- Use Constraints—describes any constraints or legal issues for using information from the information package (e.g., copyright, restrictions on right to reproduce, preparation of derivative works, etc.)

- Point of Contact—several subfields give information about the organization (or person) to contact regarding further information about the information resource

- Schedule Number—an identifier associated with the information resource for records management purposes

- Control Identifier—a unique number created by the originating agency that distinguishes the record from all other GILS records

- Record Source—the name of the organization that has created the GILS record (as opposed to the creator of the information resource)

- Date of Last Modification—the date of the last modification of the GILS record (may be the date the record was created if it has not been further modified)

There are also nonmandatory elements for such things as Controlled Vocabulary, Spatial Reference, Time Period of Content, and Cross Reference. The format does not prescribe the content that should go into most of the Core Elements fields, but a few fields do specify content and form. For example, the date is to be expressed as YYYYMMDD, names of agencies are to be in the form found in the U.S. Government Manual and are to be strictly controlled, and state names in addresses are to use the two-character mail abbreviation. Definitions of the fields and examples of usage of the fields are given in the aforementioned "Guidelines" document.[37] GILS was influenced by both MARC and the Z39.50 standard for sending and retrieving search results. The "GILS Profile"[38] calls for participants to have Z39.50-compliant servers. (See discussion of Z39.50 in Chapter 5.)

As already mentioned, there is very little prescribed content for what is to be described in a record. The "item" being described may include one document, an entire database, or anything in between. The GILS format may be used to describe not only paper resources and databases, but also people, events, meetings, artifacts, and the like—anyone or anything that is considered by an agency to be an information resource.

The U.S. Government Printing Office (GPO) maintains a GILS database that provides access to GILS records from many agencies.[39] Examples of GILS records may be viewed at this site. Encoding is in HTML; however, the GILS site includes under the topic "important areas under development" a document entitled "XML Encoding Rules (XER)."

FGDC (Federal Geographic Data Committee) Content Standard for Digital Geospatial Metadata

The title of this standard is *Content Standard for Digital Geospatial Metadata*,[40] but it has become familiarly known as the FGDC metadata standard. Like GILS it was mandated in 1994 with the directive that each agency should document all new geospatial data it collects or produces. The standard aims to provide a common set of terminology and definitions for metadata about digital geospatial data.

The FGDC standard consists of identification and definitions of elements; it does not dictate content layout or an encoding scheme, although it does provide "information about the values that are to be provided for the data elements."[41] Like the standards already discussed, it provides a way for users to learn what resources are available, whether the resources will meet their specific needs, where to find the data, and how to access the data. Version 2 of the standard was published in mid-1998. It has the following sections:

- identification information
- data quality information
- spatial data organization information
- spatial reference information
- entity and attribute information
- distribution information
- metadata reference information
- citation information
- time period information
- contact information

Within each of the sections, elements are listed. For example, within the section "Metadata Reference Information" the elements listed begin with: (1) date, (2) review date, (3) future review date, (4) contact, (5) standard name, (6) standard version, and so forth. Nearly all elements specify that they are "free text."

Like the standards already discussed, this one has application profiles that extend the base standard by adding elements to meet specific requirements. An example FGDC-endorsed profile of the CSDGM is the *Metadata Profile for Shoreline Data*.[42] Also, like other standards, encoding using XML is recommended. The FGDC has an XML DTD for encoding FGDC metadata.[43]

Finally, it should be mentioned that there has been activity attempting to harmonize the FGDC Metadata Standard with ISO Metadata Standard 19115 for geographic information. At this writing, agreement has not been reached.[44]

VRA (Visual Resources Association) Core Categories for Visual Resources

According to the VRA Core Categories[45] Web site, the core categories "are designed to facilitate the sharing of information among visual resources collections about *works* and *images*." Version 3.0 of the Core Categories was released in 2002. This version includes the names of the categories, each followed by a definition, information about qualifiers, recommendations for use of controlled vocabularies or standardized lists, and mapping to the previous version of the VRA Core Categories and the Dublin Core. Format of content is not prescribed. There are seventeen basic categories:

- Record Type—identifies the record as being for a work (the physical or created object) or for an image (the visual surrogate of objects)

- Type—identifies the specific type of work or image being described (use of *Art & Architecture Thesaurus [AAT]*[46] terms recommended)

- Title—the identifying phrase (may be qualified as variant, translation, series, or larger entity)

- Measurements—identifies the size, shape, scale, dimensions, format, or storage configuration (may be qualified as dimensions, format, or resolution)

- Material—identifies the "substance" that composes a work; often the material(s) used for the work, e.g., paper and ink, or bronze (may be qualified as medium or support; use of *AAT* terms recommended)

- Technique—identifies the processes, techniques, or methods used in making the work (use of *AAT* terms recommended)

- Creator—identifies the names of entities that have contributed to the design, creation, or production of the work or image (may be qualified as role, attribution, personal name, or corporate name; use of authority files recommended)

- Date—identifies date(s) associated with appearance of the work or image (may be qualified as creation, design, beginning, completion, alteration, or restoration dates; use of standard date presentations recommended)

- Location—identifies geographic location and/or a specific site location (may be qualified as current site, former site, creation site, discovery site, current repository, or former repository; use of controlled terms recommended)

- ID Number—identifies unique identifiers assigned to the work or image (may be qualified as current repository, former repository, current accession, or former accession)

- Style/Period—identifies a defined style, time period, group, movement, etc., characteristics of which appear in the work or image (may be qualified as style, period, group, school, dynasty, movement; use of *AAT* terms recommended)

- Culture—identifies a culture, people, or country that a work or image originates from or has been associated with (use of controlled terms recommended)

- Subject—terms that describe the work or image and that represent what it depicts or expresses (use of controlled terms recommended)

- Relation—identifies a related work and the relationship that exists (may be qualified as identity or type)

- Description—note about the work or image that may include comments, description, interpretation, and any other information not recorded in other categories

- Source—identifies the source of the information recorded in other categories

- Rights—identifies copyright information, intellectual property statements, or other information needed for rights management

The creators of the VRA Core Categories claim this is "a single universally applicable element set." They encourage arrangement of elements in local applications into sequences that reflect their needs, but seem not to encourage application profiles. Guidelines for description using the VRA Core are included in *Cataloguing Cultural Objects: A Guide to Describing Cultural Works and Their Images.*[47] According to this guide's description, it "provides guidelines for selecting, ordering, and formatting data used to populate catalog records. [It] is designed to promote good descriptive cataloging, shared documentation, and enhanced end-user access." The authors believe that adherence to standard rules will improve management of content and will increase access to cultural heritage information.

The VRA Core Categories site does not recommend any particular encoding standards. However, a link to a MARC mapping done by an individual is included at the VRA Web site.[48]

CIMI XML Schema for SPECTRUM

Museum objects have characteristics that differ from information packages in many other environments, and these affect the description in the surrogate record. First, like most collections of archival materials, museum objects are unique—each specimen is different. Even if the museum object is one of two identical pieces of furniture, let's say, it will have a different provenance, and it will have scratches in different places. Specimens in natural history museums, however, are often more alike because each one is an example of a particular species and is not very different from museum to museum, although the information about source will be different. Another difference is that the identification of objects is often unknown at the time of acquisition. Specimens brought in from an archaeological dig, for example, may have to be researched in order to be identified. In addition, information about an object often changes over time as new evidence becomes available. And there is the possibility that the object may be a forgery or otherwise be mistakenly identified.

Museums that are parts of libraries use chapter 10 of *AACR2R*, "Three-Dimensional Artefacts and Realia." For all museums, CIDOC (Committee on International Documentation) of the International Council of Museums (ICOM) represents about sixty countries and is working on standards to create and present museum information on the Internet. A standard that has been widely accepted in many countries is *SPECTRUM*,[49] a standard for describing museum objects produced by a British organization known as "mda" (lower case letters purposely used as the organization's name, which was formerly the Museum Documentation Association). *SPECTRUM* actually includes much more than just the description of museum objects.[50] It includes twenty possible procedures in a museum documentation system, such as object entry, location and movement control, acquisition, cataloging, loans in, and loans out. It also offers advice on legal and management issues.

The Consortium for the Interchange of Museum Information (CIMI) has developed an XML Schema[51] for the description of museum objects. It is based on SPECTRUM. The CIMI XML Schema enables museums "to encode rich descriptive information relating to museum objects, including associated information about people, places and events surrounding the history of museum objects, as well as information about their management and use within museums."[52]

ONIX International

The publishing world has been developing standards that can be used for description of publications by their publishers. ONIX (ONline Information eXchange) International,[53] now available in Release 2.0, was discussed in the encoding standards chapter as an XML DTD. It includes a data dictionary that defines the content of the elements that are encoded for computer display using the ONIX encoding standard. The elements allow a publisher to present online the information that was previously contained on book jackets and in publishing brochures and catalogs—information such as synopses, quotations from reviews, author biographies, intended audience, and so on. As mentioned in Chapter 4, ONIX uses XML to transmit ONIX messages. A mapping to MARC[54] allows consideration of using ONIX data in library catalogs. There are also experimental projects for linking from MARC records in catalogs to ONIX data held in XML-encoded databases.

Other Surrogate Record Types

Index Records

At the moment there is no official standard for the descriptive content of index records. An ANSI standard Z39.4–1984, subtitled "Basic Criteria for Indexes,"[55] has no mention of the data to be included in the description of an item. The National Information Standards Organization (NISO) tried to update this standard, but committees could not come to agreement with the American Society of Indexers, and so Z39.4 was withdrawn in 1996. NISO has issued a technical report TR-02, *Guidelines for Indexes and Related Information Retrieval Devices,* by James Anderson.[56] There is a separate standard for bibliographic references, Z39.29,[57] that guides the content to be included in entries in bibliographies.

Creators of indexes have their own standards for information to be included in an index record. Agencies like H. W. Wilson that publish several different indexes in different subject areas have some consistency from index to index. Electronic index records tend to include more information than do paper versions. As in OPACs, electronic index records tend to have labels, which are not included in paper versions. (For an example of a labeled index record, refer back to Figure 2.3, p. 42.)

On-the-Fly Records

On-the-fly records are those created electronically for immediate use; they will be changed either momentarily or within a matter of weeks. In some catalogs that have Web interfaces, the MARC records are converted to HTML-encoded records on-the-fly. That is, when a user puts in a search, a listing of authors, titles, and/or dates is returned to the screen. If the user then clicks on number 4 in the list, the MARC record is quickly put through the HTML converter that has been written for that catalog so that it can be displayed on the screen. These records have much of the same descriptive content as is found in the MARC records from which they are derived.

Another kind of on-the-fly record is that produced by search engines. The information that is included in the results display depends upon what has been stored in the search engine's database after collection by the engine's robot. Search engine surrogate records all include a hyperlinked URL. The rest of the record may consist of only the title of a document, or may give the first several lines of the document. Other pieces of information sometimes included are: a description taken from metadata at the head of the Web page (although the vast majority of Web pages still do not contain such metadata), the size of the page or file, a relevance ranking calculated by the search engine, and/or a date (often the date the page or file was loaded into its server). The search engine Google gives a phrase from the contents of the page or file that includes the word or words the user put into the search. (The search engine Yahoo! has records that are created by humans and do not qualify as on-the-fly records.) On-the-fly search engine surrogate records may or may not be helpful in the evaluation of whether or not the information package they represent will be useful to the user. If the information package has a title and the title is indicative of content, then the on-the-fly record is more useful than the record with no title. It is often necessary to look at the information package itself in order to learn what it is about and why it was retrieved in response to the search (see Figure 7.6).

ENVIRONMENTAL INFLUENCES IN DESCRIPTIVE METADATA CREATION

From the preceding descriptions one can see that the creation of surrogate records is somewhat dependent upon the community for which the records are being created. Some communities have long-standing standards. The library community's standard has the longest tradition, being

AltaVista found 17,887 results

About Abortion and the Early Church: Michael Gorman - essay - summary - review
087784397X 0838903258 isbn 0838933076 ...
About **Michael Gorman** - , Where can i find informations about Abortion ... Rules Literature
Michael Gorman- Video Technology and **Libraries** Lita Guides No 1 **Michael Gorman**-
Video Technology and ...
www.new-books.net/57170_michaelgorman.html • Refreshed in past 48 hours • Related Pages

Mike Gorman: Bell's Path the the Telephone–Home Page
Alexander Graham Bell's Path to the Telephone Home Page Introduction **Michael E. Gorman**
Technology, Culture Communications, SEAS University of Virginia To organize and depict, in
abbreviated form ...
jefferson.village.virginia.edu/albell/introduction.html • Related Pages
More pages from jefferson.village.virginia.edu

diglib: Fwd: Michael Gorman at BCLA
... Next][Date Index][Thread Index] diglib: Fwd: **Michael Gorman** at BCLA To:
diglib@lists.uoregon.edu ... mac@SLC.BC.CA> >Organization: Special **Libraries**
Cataloguing, Inc. >Original-recipient: rfc822 ...
www.uoregon.edu/~jqj/diglib/archive/msg00243.html

Keynote Speaker: Michael Gorman
... and the Values of **Libraries**" **Michael Gorman** is Dean of **Library** ... s 2001 Highsmith
award for the best book on **librarianship**. **Michael Gorman** is a fellow of the [British]
Library Association ...
www.nevadalibraries.org/Conference01/Pro.../thkeynote.html • Related Pages

Michael John Gorman
HOME PROJECTS TEACHING PUBLICATIONS **Michael** John **Gorman** Lecturer, Program
in Science, Technology and ... Stanford Humanities Laboratory Stanford **Library** Catalogue
Kircher correspondence project ...
www.stanford.edu/~mgorman • Related Pages
More pages from www.stanford.edu

**Fig. 7.6. Typical on-the-fly records in which it is often not possible to
be certain whether the concept(s) or person sought is actually in the
resource that is represented by the record. In this example the fourth
item clearly represents the librarian Michael Gorman. The third item
probably represents the same person, although the data given are less
clear. (Source: http://www.altavista.com search for "Michael Gorman
librar*" on June 30, 2003.)**

based upon principles that have been developing for centuries. Other communities have recognized the library's long experience and have patterned
their guidelines for creation of surrogate records after the *ISBD* standard.
The creators of TEI Headers, the Dublin Core, VRA Core Categories, and

others have included librarians, along with other people with organizing experience in their planning committees.

CONCLUSION

This chapter has addressed the descriptive part of metadata, which we have called surrogate records. In discussion of the value of surrogate records, it was mentioned that surrogate record descriptions are most helpful when they are predictable in both form and content. The first standards to prescribe form of content were *ISBD, AACR2R,* and *APPM. ISBD* came to its prescription after years of experience with variant practices that brought an understanding of the value of predictability. *AACR2R* and, in turn *APPM,* then followed *ISBD.* The remaining standards discussed, developed more recently, most in the last decade or so, rarely prescribe form of content, although they may prescribe and define elements. Perhaps experience with the large quantities of metadata records that have existed in the library and archival communities will soon lead the newer creators of metadata to reevaluate their need for prescribed content. The next chapter addresses access and authority control, which is accepted as a necessity in the library and archival communities, and is highly recommended in the visual resources community, but has barely been considered in the other communities.

NOTES

All URLs accessed June 2003.

1.   *Anglo-American Cataloguing Rules, Second Edition, 2002 Revision (AACR2R)* (Ottawa: Canadian Library Association; Chicago: American Library Association, 2002), p. D-2. [This work is referred to as *AACR2R* in this chapter unless specific quotations and/or specific pages from the 2002 print version are being cited. In the Anglo-American cataloging community, the work is still *AACR2R* even though additions and changes are regularly issued.]

2.   Ibid., p. D-4.

3.   *Anglo-American Cataloguing Rules, Second Edition, 1998 Revision* (Ottawa: Canadian Library Association; Chicago: American Library Association, 1998), p. 622.

4.   *AACR2R2002*, p. D-7.

5.   International Federation of Library Associations and Institutions, IFLA Study Group, *Functional Requirements for Bibliographic Records (FRBR)* (München: Saur, 1998). Also available: http://www.ifla.org/VII/s13/frbr/frbr.pdf or http://www.ifla.org/VII/s13/frbr/frbr.htm.

6.   *ISBD(G): General International Standard Bibliographic Description.* Annotated text prepared by the ISBD Review Committee Working Group, set up by the IFLA Committee on Cataloguing (New York: K. G. Saur, 1992). Available: http://www.ifla.org/VII/s13/pubs/isbdg.htm.

7.   *Family of ISBDs (as of January 2003).* Available: http://www.ifla.org/VI/3/nd1/isbdlist.htm.

8.   *AACR2R* (see note 1 above).

9.   Program for Cooperative Cataloging, *Introduction to the Program for Cooperative Cataloging BIBCO Core Record Standard.* Available: http://lcweb.loc.gov/catdir/pcc/bibco/coreintro.html; *Chart of PCC BIBCO Core Record Standards.* Available: http://www.loc.gov/catdir/pcc/bibco/core2002.html.

10.   Michael Gorman, *The Concise AACR2: 1998 Revision* (Chicago: American Library Association, 1999).

11.   *Dublin Core Metadata Initiative.* Available: http://dublincore.org/.

12.   *The Dublin Core Metadata Element Set,* ANSI/NISO Z39.85–2001 (Bethesda, MD: NISO Press, 2001). Available: http://www.niso.org/standards/resources/Z39-85.pdf.

13.   One such template is the Nordic Metadata Project's *Dublin Core Metadata Template.* Available: http://www.lub.lu.se/cgi-bin/nmdc.pl.

14.   Andy Powell and Pete Johnston, *Guidelines for Implementing Dublin Core in XML.* DCMI Proposed Recommendation, 2002. Available: http://dublincore.org/documents/2002/12/02/dc-xml-guidelines/.

15.   *Dublin Core Metadata Element Set, Version 1.1: Reference Description.* Date issued: 4 February 2003. Available: http://dublincore.org/documents/2003/02/04/dces/.

16.   *Tags for the Identification of Languages, Internet RFC 3066.* Available: http://www.ietf.org/rfc/rfc3066.txt.

17.   *Date and Time Formats, W3C Note.* Available: http://www.w3.org/TR/NOTE-datetime.

18.   *DCMI Type Vocabulary.* DCMI Recommendation, 11 July 2000. Available: http://dublincore.org/documents/dcmi-type-vocabulary/.

19.   Rebecca Guenther, *DC-Library Application Profile (DC-Lib)*. Available: http://dublincore.org/documents/2002/09/24/library-application-profile/.

20.   Rebecca S. Guenther, "MODS: The Metadata Object Description Schema," *Portal: Libraries and the Academy* 3, no. 1 (2003): 139.

21.   Ibid., p. 140.

22.   Library of Congress, "MINERVA: Mapping the Internet Electronic Resources Virtual Archive." Available: http://www.loc.gov/minerva/minerva.html.

23.   Guenther, "MODS," p. 148.

24.   *ISAD(G): General International Standard Archival Description*. Adopted by the Committee on Descriptive Standards, Stockholm, Sweden, 19–22 September 1999, 2nd ed. (Ottawa: International Council on Archives, 2000). Also available: http://www.ica.org/bibliocds/isad_g_2e.pdf.

25.   Ibid., p. 7.

26.   Steven L. Hensen, comp., *Archives, Personal Papers, and Manuscripts: A Cataloging Manual for Archival Repositories, Historical Societies, and Manuscript Libraries*, 2nd ed. (Chicago: Society of American Archivists, 1989).

27.   *Encoded Archival Description (EAD): Official EAD Version 2002 Web Site*. Available: http://lcweb.loc.gov/ead/.

28.   *Design Principles for Enhancements to EAD*, December 2002. Available: http://www.loc.gov/ead/eaddesgn.html.

29.   *TEI Lite*. Available: http://www.tei-c.org/Lite/.

30.   *Text Encoding Initiative (TEI) Independent Headers*. Available: http://www.ukoln.ac.uk/metadata/desire/overview/rev_21.htm.

31.   Lou Burnard, *Text Encoding Initiative: 20, The Electronic Title Page*, 1995. Available: http://www.tei-c.org/Lite/U5-header.html.

32.   *Global Information Locator Service (GILS)*. Available: http://www.gils.net/index.html. One of the roots of GILS was in the Global Change Research Program, which was focused on a need for long-term access to environmental information. That program chose to employ the "GILS Profile," created for the Government Information Locator Service. In the FAQ at the Global Information Locator Service site is the statement: "From the perspectives of standards and technology, the Global Information Lo-

cator Service is no different than the Government Information Locator Service."

33. *GILS: About—A Powerful, New Way to Find Information.* Last modified 22 June 2003. Available: http://www.gils.net/about.html.

34. *Application Profile for the Government Information Locator Service (GILS),* Version 2, 1997. Available: http://www.usgs.gov/gils/prof_v2.html.

35. *Guidelines for the Preparation of GILS Core Entries.* Last modified 19 March 2002. Available: http://www.dtic.mil/gils/documents/naradoc/.

36. *Making Your Agency's GILS Records Available Online via GPO Access: List of GILS Fields and Their Definitions.* Available: http://www.access.gpo.gov/su_docs/gils/desc.html.

37. *Guidelines for the Preparation of GILS Core Entries.* Available: http://www.dtic.mil/gils/documents/naradoc/.

38. *Application Profile for the Government Information Locator Service (GILS),* Version 2, 1997. Available: http://www.usgs.gov/gils/prof_v2.html.

39. U.S. Government Printing Office, Superintendent of Documents, *GPO Access: Government Information Locator Service.* Available: http://www.access.gpo.gov/su_docs/gils/index.html.

40. *Content Standard for Digital Geospatial Metadata,* Version 2. Available: http://www.fgdc.gov/metadata/contstan.html.

41. Ibid.

42. *Metadata Profile for Shoreline Data.* Available: http://www.fgdc.gov/standards/status/sub5_6.html.

43. *FGDC Metadata DTD 3.0.2 20020205.* Available: http://www.fgdc.gov/metadata/fgdc-std-001-1998.dtd.

44. *FGDC/ISO Metadata Standard Harmonization.* Last updated 28 September 2000. Available: http://www.fgdc.gov/metadata/whatsnew/fgdciso.html.

45. Visual Resources Association, Data Standards Committee, *VRA Core Categories, Version 3.0.* Last updated 20 September 2002. Available: http://www.vraweb.org/vracore3.htm.

46. *Art & Architecture Thesaurus,* 2nd ed. (New York: Oxford University Press, 1994). Also The Getty Information Institute, *The Art & Architecture Thesaurus Browser.* Available: http://www.getty.edu/research/tools/vocabulary/.

47.   Murtha Baca, Patricia Harpring, Elisa Lanzi, Linda McRae, and Ann Whiteside, *Cataloguing Cultural Objects: A Guide to Describing Cultural Works and Their Images* (Bronx, N.Y.: Visual Resources Association, 2003). Available: http://www.vraweb.org/CCOweb/index.html.

48.   Sherman Clarke, *VRA Core 3.0 Mapping to MARC 21 (Bibliographic Format)*. Last updated 5 November 2001. Available: http://php.indiana.edu/~fryp/marcmap.html.

49.   *SPECTRUM: The UK Museum Documentation Standard*, compiled and ed. by Alice Grant, 2nd ed., rev. and ed. by Jeff Cowton (Cambridge, Eng.: Museum Documentation Association, 1997).

50.   "SPECTRUM: The UK Museum Documentation Standard." Last modified 12 May 2003. Available: http://www.mda.org.uk/spectrum.htm.

51.   *CIMI XML Schema for SPECTRUM*. Last updated 24 October 2002. Available: http://www.cimi.org/wg/xml_spectrum/index.html.

52.   Ibid.

53.   ONIX Product Information Standards. Available: http://www.editeur.org/onix.html.

54.   *ONIX to MARC 21 Mapping*, Network Development and MARC Standards Office, Library of Congress, December 2000. Available: http://lcweb.loc.gov/marc/onix2marc.html.

55.   *American National Standard for Library and Information Sciences and Related Publishing Practices—Basic Criteria for Indexes, ANSI Z39.4–1984* (New York: American National Standards Institute, 1984).

56.   James D. Anderson, *Guidelines for Indexes and Related Information Retrieval Devices* (Bethesda, Md.: NISO Press, 1997).

57.   *Documentation—Bibliographic References—Content, Form and Structure,* ISO 690, 2nd ed. (Geneva, Switzerland: International Organization for Standardization, 1987).

SUGGESTED READINGS

ALA/ALCTS/CCS Committee on Cataloging: Description and Access. Task Force on Metadata and the Cataloging Rules. *Metadata and the Cataloging Rules.* Last modified 3 April 1998. Available: http://www.libraries.psu.edu/tas/jca/ccda/tf-tei2.html.

Application Profile for the Government Information Locator Service (GILS), Version 2, 1997. Available: http://www.usgs.gov/gils/prof_v2.html.

Baca, Murtha. "A Picture Is Worth a Thousand Words: Metadata for Art Objects and Their Visual Surrogates." In *Cataloging the Web: Metadata, AACR, and MARC 21*, edited by Wayne Jones, et al. Lanham, Md.: Scarecrow Press, 2002, pp. 131–138.

Baca, Murtha, Patricia Harpring, Elisa Lanzi, Linda McRae, and Ann Whiteside. *Cataloguing Cultural Objects: A Guide to Describing Cultural Works and Their Images*. Bronx, N.Y.: Visual Resources Association, 2003. Available: http://www.vraweb.org/CCOweb/index.html.

Caplan, Priscilla. *Metadata Fundamentals for All Librarians*. Chicago: American Library Association, 2003. Part II: "Metadata Schemes."

CIMI XML Schema for SPECTRUM. Last modified 24 October 2002. Available: http://www.cimi.org/wg/xml_spectrum/index.html.

Content Standard for Digital Geospatial Metadata (CSDGM). Version 2. Last updated 21 March 2003. Available: http://www.fgdc.gov/metadata/contstan.html.

Dublin Core Metadata Initiative. Available: http://dublincore.org/.

Encoded Archival Description (EAD): Official EAD Version 2002 Web Site. Available: http://lcweb.loc.gov/ead/.

Fox, Michael J., and Peter Wilkerson. *Introduction to Archival Organization and Description: Access to Cultural Heritage*. The Getty Information Institute, 1998. Section entitled "Standards." Available: http://www.schistory.org/getty/index.html.

Global Information Locator Service (GILS). Available: http://www.gils.net/index.html.

Gorman, Michael. *The Concise AACR2, 1998 Revision*. Chicago: American Library Association, 1999.

Guenther, Rebecca S. "MODS: The Metadata Object Description Schema." *Portal: Libraries and the Academy* 3, no. 1 (2003): 137–150.

Hsieh-Yee, Ingrid. *Organizing Audiovisual and Electronic Resources for Access: A Cataloging Guide*. Englewood, Colo.: Libraries Unlimited, 2000.

International Federation of Library Associations and Institutions. *Digital Libraries: Metadata Resources.* Last updated 3 February 2003. Available: http://www.ifla.org/II/metadata.htm. (This is a bibliography with hyperlinks to the articles that are available on the Internet.)

Intner, Sheila S., and Jean Weihs. *Standard Cataloging for School and Public Libraries.* 3rd ed. Englewood, Colo.: Libraries Unlimited, 2001. Chapter 4: "Description."

ISBD(G): General International Standard Bibliographic Description. Annotated text prepared by the ISBD Review Committee Working Group, set up by the IFLA Committee on Cataloguing. New York: K. G. Saur, 1992. Available: http://www.ifla.org/VII/s13/pubs/isbdg.htm.

Lazinger, Susan S. *Digital Preservation and Metadata: History, Theory, Practice.* Englewood, Colo.: Libraries Unlimited, 2001. Chapter 6: "Models for Syntactic and Semantic Interoperability: Metalanguages and Metadata Formats."

Miller, Fredric M. *Arranging and Describing Archives and Manuscripts.* Chicago: Society of American Archivists, 1990, pp. 109–118.

Milstead, Jessica, and Susan Feldman. "Metadata: Cataloging by Any Other Name . . ." *Online* (January 1999). Available: http://www.onlinemag. net/OL1999/milstead1.html.

————. "Metadata Projects and Standards." *Online* (January 1999). Available: http://www.onlinemag.net/OL1999/milstead1.html#projects.

Program for Cooperative Cataloging. *Introduction to the Program for Cooperative Cataloging BIBCO Core Record Standards.* Available: http://lcweb.loc. gov/catdir/pcc/bibco/coreintro.html.

Rogers, JoAnn V., and Jerry D. Saye. *Nonprint Cataloging for Multimedia Collections.* 2nd ed. Littleton, Colo.: Libraries Unlimited, 1987. Chapter 1: "Bibliographic Control of Nonprint."

Svenonius, Elaine. *The Intellectual Foundation of Information Organization.* Cambridge, Mass.: The MIT Press, 2000. Chapter 7: "Document Languages."

Taylor, Arlene G. *Wynar's Introduction to Cataloging and Classification.* 9th ed., with the assistance of David P. Miller. Englewood, Colo.: Libraries Unlimited, 2000. Chapter 4: "Description."

Tillett, Barbara B. "Problems and Solutions in Cataloging Electronic Resources." *International Cataloguing and Bibliographic Control* 29, no. 1 (January/March 2000): 14–15.

"User Guidelines for Dublin Core Creation." Version 1.0. Created 29 May 1997. Last updated 11 November 1999. Available: http://www.sics.se/preben/DC/DC_guide.html.

Vellucci, Sherry L. "Options for Organizing Electronic Resources: The Coexistence of Metadata." *Bulletin of the American Society for Information Science* 24, no. 1 (October/November 1997): 14–17.

Visual Resources Association Data Standards Committee. *VRA Core Categories, Version 3.0.* Last updated 20 February 2002. Available: http://www.vraweb.org/vracore3.htm.

Wool, Gregory J. "Bibliographical Metadata; or, We Need A Client-Server Cataloging Code!" In *Finding Common Ground: Creating the Library of the Future without Diminishing the Library of the Past,* edited by Cheryl LaGuardia and Barbara A. Mitchell. New York: Neal-Schuman, 1998, pp. 398–401.

———. "A Meditation on Metadata." *The Serials Librarian* 33, no. 1/2 (1998): 167–178.

CHAPTER 8

METADATA: ACCESS AND AUTHORITY CONTROL

The issues addressed in this chapter are expressed in the following questions: How are resources (including information packages, surrogate records, names, concepts, etc.) made available to users? How do access points affect collocation? How does authority control affect collocation? How can persons or entities with the same name be distinguished from each other? How can variant names that represent the same entity be brought together? How can all expressions and manifestations of the same work be brought together? How can identification of relationships among entities be used to assist users in finding what they need?

NEED FOR ATTENTION TO ACCESS

In most online systems keyword searching is available. If a user knows exactly what words or names have been used in a description, then keyword searching is successful. But users who do not know exact words or names have to guess. This is sometimes successful and sometimes not. Most words in the English language have more than one meaning, and most meanings have more than one word (discussed further in Chapter 10). Many research studies have shown that different users do not think of the same word(s) to express a concept; authors do not necessarily use the same word(s) to write about a concept; authors do not necessarily retain the same name or same form of name throughout their writing careers; corporate bodies do not necessarily use the same name or form of name in their documents, nor are they known by the same form of name by everyone; and titles of works that are reproduced are not always the same in the original and the reproduction. For all of these reasons and more, the library and the archival worlds came to the realization many years ago that bibliographic records need access points (one of which is often designated as the "main" or "primary" one), and these access points need to be expressed consistently from record to record when several different records use the same word or name as an access point.

The rest of the metadata world has also begun to see a need for access points either with consistent form from record to record or with links to resources that identify a person, corporate body, concept, and so forth, uniquely. Much energy in the 1990s was spent on determining what descriptive information is needed for particular forms of information packages, and on how these descriptions can be encoded for display. As metadata accumulates to the massive numbers that library catalogs have been dealing with, the need for attention to problems of access becomes more apparent. Among the more recent communities to address this need has been the art community. The Getty Art Museum has created a set of controlled vocabulary tools[1] including one for terminology in the fields of art and architecture, one for artist names (including biographical information as well as variations in names), and one for geographic names (including vernacular and historical names, coordinates, and place types). The VRA (Visual Resources Association) Core Categories for Visual Resources[2] calls for use of controlled vocabulary for several of the categories, including use of authority files for names.

Another project is being conducted by the Dublin Core community, which has recognized the need for "agent" records to complement and be linked to metadata records for information packages. The term "agent" is being used to refer to creators, contributors, and publishers. The DCMI Agents Working Group[3] is working toward a standard that would have a core set of elements to be used for creating agent descriptions, would describe qualifiers to assist in identifying relationships between agents and related information packages, and would provide a way to link between DC metadata descriptions and agent descriptions. The work, begun in 1998, is still in very slow progress at this writing.

Although the archival community has recognized the need for control of access points for a very long time, it has been relatively recently that they have created standards that provide consistency within the archival community. In 1996 the International Council on Archives published the *International Standard Archival Authority Record for Corporate Bodies, Persons and Families (ISAAR[CPF])*.[4] There is now an ongoing initiative called Encoded Archival Context (EAC). EAC, like EAD (described in the preceding chapter), uses XML for encoding; but while EAD describes archival collections, EAC describes creators. EAC records do more than just control all the different forms of name used by a person or corporate body. According to Daniel Pitti, they also describe "their essential functions, activities, and characteristics, and the dates and places they were active."[5] Pitti goes on to explain that creator descriptions facilitate interpretation of archival records in addition to facilitating access. Understanding the lives and work of people and groups who created the archival collections is essential to understanding the archival records that are the byproducts of those lives and activities.

People working on the concept of the Semantic Web (described in Chapter 4) also have been working on the idea of creating "entity" metadata for people and corporate bodies so that these can be linked with metadata for the information packages with which they are associated. In the language of the Semantic Web, resources (including everything from documents to people to corporate bodies to schemas) have properties and properties have values. In this vision every resource has a unique identifier (e.g., URI) that can lead to the entity metadata that exists for the resource. The value of the property of "creator" can be the URI for a person. If this "access point," then, is attached to every resource related to the same creator, there will be collocation, regardless of form of name used by a person in a particular document.

NEED FOR ATTENTION TO BIBLIOGRAPHIC RELATIONSHIPS

Few information packages exist in total isolation. The majority have various kinds of relationships to other resources. An information package may have a creator who has also created other information packages. It may have the same publisher or be in the same series as other items. It may originate in an institution where a research project has produced multiple reports concerning the same research data. It may be a manifestation of the same work as another package but in a different format or medium. It may have intellectual content that is the same or similar to that of another resource, or it may be an adaptation. It may be a commentary on another work. It may be a supplement to something else or follow it in a sequential manner. It may be a part of a larger work, or conversely, it may be an entity that contains a number of smaller works within it. It may be a performance of a work that also appears in written form.

Successful document retrieval relies on having such relationships identified, at least implicitly, and retrieval is improved when such relationships are made explicit. Information retrieval systems carry the notion that a user interested in one item may very well be interested in others that are related to it. When relationships are merely described (e.g., mentioned in a note)—or not even described—the user is left with chance as the means for discerning related information packages that may be useful. Access points can make relationships explicit. Library cataloging has provided rules for such access points at least since Lubetzky identified principles upon which the Paris Principles were based. However, research to formally identify and categorize relationships began only in the 1980s. Barbara Tillett researched and presented a taxonomy of bibliographic relationships:[6]

- Equivalence relationships—found in exact copies of the same manifestation of a work; include copies, issues, facsimiles, reprints, photocopies, microforms, audiotapes of sound recordings on disc (if same content), and other such reproductions

- Derivative relationships—found in modifications based on particular manifestations; include editions, revisions, adaptations, changes of genre (e.g., dramatization of a novel), new works based on style or thematic content of other works, and the like

- Descriptive relationships—found in description, criticism, evaluation, or review of a work; include book reviews, annotated editions, commentaries, critiques, and the like

- Whole-part relationships—found in a component part of a larger work or in the relationship between a work and each of its various parts; include selections from anthologies or collections, articles from journals, maps in atlases, series that have independent works within them, and the like

- Accompanying relationships—found in bibliographic manifestations that are created for the purpose of complementing particular works; they can complement equally, or one work can be the principal or predominant item; include text with supplements (e.g., teacher's manual for a textbook), software manuals or help programs, concordances, indexes, parts of a kit, and the like

- Sequential relationships—found in bibliographic manifestations that continue or precede other manifestations;

include successive titles of a serial, sequels and prequels of a movie, parts in a numbered series, and the like

- Shared characteristic relationships—found in any works that coincidentally share characteristics in common, such as common authors, titles, subjects, language, country of publication, and the like

Following upon Tillet's research, other researchers have used empirical research to refine definitions and further delineate ways in which such relationships could be explicitly linked in retrieval tools.[7] For example, Richard Smiraglia presented the following taxonomy of the second of Tillet's relationships, derivative relationships:[8]

- Simultaneous derivations—works published in two editions nearly simultaneously, such as a British edition and a North American edition of the same work; may have different titles, different sizes, or other differing characteristics

- Successive derivations—works revised one or more times and issued anew with statements indicating revision, as well as manifestations issued successively that may not have revision statements

- Translations—manifestations of a work presented in languages other than the original

- Amplifications—original works that have added to them such things as illustrations, musical settings, commentaries

- Extractions—manifestations of works in smaller forms such as abridgments, condensations, excerpts

- Adaptations—manifestations that modify original works, such as simplifications, screenplays, librettos, arrangements of musical works, and the like

- Performances—sound or visual recordings of works, each of which may differ in such things as tone, amplification, interpretation, and the like

Making such relationships explicit requires formalized rules for creating what Elaine Svenonius calls a "work language," requiring a "work ID" and, possibly, such connecting devices as references.[9] This, of course, requires a consistent definition of "work," which has eluded organizers and researchers until recently.[10] The *Anglo-American Cataloguing Rules (AACR)* has provided a work language for many years, although somewhat flawed and inconsistent because of the problems with definitions. It has also had difficulty with conceptualization of function for things such as references vs. added entries. The *AACR* work ID in most cases is an author-title combination, but in cases where author is not easily determined or is diffuse, the work ID is title. Both kinds of ID require qualifiers to be added to make relationships explicit, and references are required to bring together variant forms of names of authors and titles.

An attempt by the International Federation of Library Associations and Institutions (IFLA) to formalize the definition of *work* and the direct relationships to it of *expression, manifestation,* and *item* (i.e., as defined in *Functional Requirements for Bibliographic Records [FRBR]*) was discussed in Chapter 7. Research continues on ways to use the *FRBR* hierarchy for logical display of works and their relationships in online catalogs.[11]

The application of *AACR2* in satisfying both the need for attention to access and the need for attention to bibliographic relationships is discussed in the following sections.

CHOICE OF ACCESS POINTS

As mentioned in the preceding chapter, the creation of metadata in a broad sense requires description of the information package, attention to access points for the description, and encoding of the entire surrogate record content. Encoding was discussed in Chapter 4, and the preceding two chapters addressed description. The next step after description is the selection of access points chosen for the purpose of being able to provide access to surrogate records in such a way that names, titles, and subjects are both collocated and differentiated. In this section we discuss choice of access points, selecting one of them as the "main" or "primary" one. This is followed by a section discussing the process of performing authority work on the access points in order to provide predictable and collocated access. The access points addressed in this chapter are the ones for names and titles. Authority control for subject access points is discussed in Chapters 9 and 10.

The principles that underlie *AACR2* are based upon the Paris Principles, which were accepted internationally at the International Conference on Cataloguing Principles,[12] held in Paris in 1961. Names, titles, and name/title combinations are the candidates for access points. *AACR2* calls for access points for persons, corporate bodies, geographic names, and titles, as well as combinations of names and titles. Some specific access points called for by *AACR2* include collaborators, editors and compilers, corporate bodies, titles (including titles of series), related works, and sometimes translators and illustrators. However, these are fairly book-oriented, reflecting the origins of *AACR2*. In fact many access points are for performers, choreographers, programmers, and cartographers, among many others.

Primary Access Point

According to the Paris Principles, one of the access points is selected to be the primary access point. The Paris Principles call this the "main entry" and say that it must be a "full entry." Full entry comes from the days of print catalogs. With print catalogs (i.e., card, book, and COM catalogs) it is necessary to place as many copies of the same surrogate record into the catalog as there are access points. Let us say that a record has the following access points: Author, Joint author, Corporate body, Subject 1, Subject 2, Title, Series title. In such a case there would need to be seven instances of the same surrogate record in the catalog—one filed alphabetically in each of the places where the Author, Joint author, and so forth, would appear (see Figure 8.1). The access point is at the top or head of the copy of the surrogate record in each instance.

Returning to the concept of full entry, in the days of handwritten catalog entries, and later in book catalogs especially, it was often necessary to save time and space by having only one copy of the surrogate record created as a full entry (i.e., containing a complete set of all elements of the record as provided by the cataloger). The rest of the entries were abbreviated. The Paris Principles stated that the place where the full entry should be filed is the alphabetical location of the primary access point or main entry. Soon it became customary to refer to the full entry as the main entry.

Use of "main entry" to mean both "full entry" and "primary access point" causes great confusion today. Print catalogs have long since given up the practice of having one full entry and several abbreviated copies of each surrogate record. Instead, as the technology of photocopying and then computer-printed cards became commonplace, every entry became a duplicate of the full entry. The difference among the copies was that each copy had as its top line (called the "heading") one of the chosen access points.

The concept of full entry is definitely not applicable in Online Public Access Catalogs (OPACs). In an OPAC there is only one copy of the complete metadata record. In response to a particular user request, that copy is displayed on the screen. In this situation "main entry" can refer only to *the access point* that is the main or primary one. In much of the literature

```
JC178   Paine, Thomas, 1737-1809.
.B7         Common sense, by Thomas Paine.
1976    Cutchogue, N.Y., Buccaneer Books, c1976.
            129 p., ill., 22 cm.

            "Epistle to Quakers": p. 117-129.


  1. United States--Politics and Government--
1775-1783.  2. Monarchy.  I. Paine, Thomas.
Epistle to Quakers.  II. Epistle to Quakers.
III. Title
```

```
            Epistle to Quakers.

JC178   Paine, Thomas, 1737-1809.
.B7         Common sense. Buccaneer Books, c1976.
1976
            129 p.
```

Fig. 8.1. The top card is the "main entry card" and is also what one might call the "full entry." The "main entry" (or primary access point) for this record is "Paine, Thomas, 1737–1809." The bottom card is an abbreviated version of the main entry card with one of the added entries typed at the top of the card. This example would require that six cards be filed into the card catalog—one full entry at the alphabetical position for the main entry, and one brief version for each of the five added entries.

that calls for doing away with the main entry, the argument is that we no longer have a system where one copy of a record has all the information. Others understand the current meaning of main entry as the primary access point, but some in this second group also argue against the concept. Others argue forcefully for keeping the main entry concept.

Main Entry Controversy

Controversy over main entry (in the sense of primary access point) is more than two decades old. In 1978 Seymour Lubetzky and Michael Gorman disagreed quite publicly at a conference on the emergence of *AACR2*.[13] *AACR2*'s introduction included the observation that the concept of main entry might have outlived its time. However, there had not been enough time to research the idea, and so the concept was included in *AACR2*. It stated that a library that wished to could choose access points without designating one as the main one. Lubetzky, whose principles underlie the Paris Principles, argued that this was a step backward instead of forward. Gorman believed that the time had come to make the distinction only when necessary to cite one work on the record for another work, a situation which he guessed would happen "less than 1 percent" of the time.[14] Research, however, has shown this estimate to be quite low. Richard Smiraglia found that approximately 50 percent of a sample of works had "derivative" relationships.[15] As explained earlier, derivative relationships exist when one work is derived from another (e.g., editions, translations, adaptations, performances, etc.).

Controversy raged again on the discussion list for the International Conference on *AACR*[16] in the fall of 1997. Martha Yee, a former student of Lubetzky, took up his cause in defense of the main entry. Some contributors suggested that system design can accomplish the same objectives.[17] Among the recommendations from the conference, however, none mentioned main entry.

A recent development is the decision by the Joint Steering Committee for Revision of *AACR* to create a new edition of *AACR* (being informally called "AACR3").[18] One part of the plan for AACR3 is a thorough revision of *AACR2*, chapter 21, "Choice of Access Points." Among the planned revisions of this chapter is a restatement of the rules for choice of entry in terms of the relationships among the entities of *work, expression, manifestation,* and *item* that are presented in the *Functional Requirements for Bibliographic Records*.[19] The reader should watch this rapidly developing work.

Justification for Main Entry

In Chapter 2, Cutter's "objects" of a catalog were quoted. Paraphrased, they are:

- to enable a person to find a book when author, title, or subject is known

- to show what the library has by a given author, on a given subject, or in a given kind of literature

- to assist in the choice of a book as to its edition or as to its character

In many ways main entry is a device for carrying out Cutter's objectives. Reasons given for a need for the main entry include the following:

- to provide a standard citation form to

  - show relationships between works and among expressions and manifestations of a work

  - identify works about other works

  - identify works contained in larger works

- to provide subarrangement under subjects (and as a corollary, to provide a way to subarrange items under classification number)

  - shows prolific authors in a field

  - brings together manifestations of a work

- to provide for collocation of all manifestations of a work, even though the work may be published with different titles (e.g., translations), or editions of a work may be written by different authors

- to assure a judgment of "most important" and most predictable access point in situations where reduction of cataloging time has been mandated (especially where number of required access points has been reduced, as in the Core Record)

Let us briefly discuss each of these justifications for main entry.

Citation. First, choice of a main entry is necessary every time someone cites a work in a document or lists it in a bibliography. That is, there is only going to be one entry for the work being cited, and the citer has to put something first: the first author, the editor, the title, or other choice. Thus the concept of main entry is put into practice with great frequency, but people usually do not recognize that every time they create a bibliography entry they choose a primary access point. Style manuals give suggestions for this choice, but the style manuals differ from each other, so predictability is lost.

Within a surrogate record it is often necessary to refer to another work on the record for the work that is being described. This happens, for example, when one is describing a work that is based on another work (e.g., a screenplay based on a novel), when one work is a version of another work (e.g., a new edition of a work where the new edition is written by a new author), or other such cases (see Figure 8.2). In these cases it is important to refer to the related work in a note in the surrogate record for the work being described. In addition to the note, an access point is constructed that places the main entry and title of the work being cited in controlled form with the main entry in the leading position.

A second kind of instance that requires reference to another work is when the intellectual content of the work for which a surrogate record is being made has as its subject another work (e.g., a criticism of a literary work). In this case one of the subject headings on the surrogate record is the main entry and title of the work that is being discussed (see Figure 8.3).

A third instance occurs when the work being described is part of a larger work (e.g., a volume in a series or set; a work published with one or two other works; see Figure 8.4) or the work being described contains a smaller work within it (e.g., a critique and analysis of a musical composition contains the composition; a work contains one or more previously published works in addition to the main one being described; etc.; see Figure 8.5).

Subarrangement. The second justification for main entry is for sorting search results. If main entries have been chosen, then the results of a subject search can be displayed in the order of the primary access point, which, in a large percentage of cases, is the name of the author or first-named author. This allows searchers to determine the authors who write most in a particular field so that those authors' names can be searched in other retrieval tools. Main entry arrangement under subject headings also serves to collocate editions of works on the same subject.

Collocation. Main entry also provides a way to collocate (i.e., bring together) all derivations of the same work. If there are several manifestations of a work—a translation, an illustrated version, a microform copy, an audio version, and so on—choosing the same main entry for them means that in most retrieval tools they will be displayed together. Of course it is helpful, when all do not have the same title, to have a "uniform title" so that the manifestations will not only be displayed under the same main entry, but will also be displayed together among all the entries under that main entry (see Figure 8.6).

Collocation is an important outcome of the practice of choosing primary access points. Main entry has proved to be, so far, the only way to collocate all manifestations of a work, including instances when manifesta-

Visual Materials	Rec Stat c	Entered 19950511	Replaced 20020712		
Type g	ELvl 7	Srce	Audn	Ctrl	Lang eng
BLvl m	Form	GPub	Time ---	MRec	Ctry xxu
Desc a	TMat m	Tech l	DtSt s	Dates 1994,	

007		m ‡b r ‡d c ‡e b ‡f a ‡g a ‡h f ‡i s
010		95-506926
040		DLC ‡e amim ‡c DLC ‡d OCLCQ
017		PA742-443 ‡b U.S. Copyright Office
043		n-us-ny
050	00	CGC 1381-1386 (ref print)
245	00	Nobody's fool / ‡c a Scott Rudin/Cinehous production ; directed and written by Robert Benton ; produced by Scott Rudin and Arlene Donovan.
257		U.S.
260		United States : ‡b Paramount Pictures : ‡b Capella International, ‡c 1994.
300		12 reels of 12 on 6 (ca. 9950 ft.) : ‡b sd., col. ; ‡c 35 mm. ref print.
500		Paramount Pictures Corporation. DCR 1994; PUB 11Oct94; REG 7Feb95; PA742-443.
508		Associate producer, Scott Ferguson ; music, Howard Shore.
511	1_	Paul Newman, Jessica Tandy, Gene Saks, Bruce Willis, Melanie Griffith, Dylan Walsh, Pruitt Taylor Vince, Josef Sommer, Alexander Goodwin.
520		In this affectionate story of small town life in upstate New York, Sully, a fitfully employed 60-year-old construction worker, is a cheerful curmudgeon who seems to have missed all his chances and made nothing of his life. However, it becomes apparent that Sully, despite his best efforts to be a n'er-do-well, is an important and beloved member of his family and his community. He is, as he says, somebody's father, somebody's grandfather, somebody's friend.
500		Part of summary from Variety, 12-12-94.
500		**From the novel by Richard Russo.**
500		Sources used: Variety, 12-12-94.
650	_0	Fathers and sons ‡v Drama.
650	_0	Family ‡v Drama.
650	_0	City and town life ‡z New York (State) ‡v Drama.
655	_7	Features. ‡2 mim
655	_7	Adaptations. ‡2 mim
700	1_	Benton, Robert, ‡e direction, ‡e writing.
700	1_	Newman, Paul, ‡d 1925- ‡e cast.
700	1_	Tandy, Jessica, ‡e cast.
700	1_	Saks, Gene, ‡d 1921- ‡e cast.
700	1_	Willis, Bruce, ‡d 1955- ‡e cast.
700	1_	Griffith, Melanie, ‡d 1957- ‡e cast.
700	**1_**	**Russo, Richard, ‡d 1949- ‡t Nobody's fool.**
710	2_	Copyright Collection (Library of Congress) ‡5 DLC

Fig. 8.2. Metadata record for a work based on another work with an access point constructed using the main entry and the title of the original work. (Source: OCLC Connexion, WorldCat, record number 32544834.)

Books	Rec Stat	a		Entered	19950601		Replaced	19951101			
Type	a	**ELvl**		**Srce**		**Audn**		**Ctrl**		**Lang**	eng
BLvl	m	**Form**		**Conf**	0	**Biog**		**MRec**		**Ctry**	nju
		Cont	b	**GPub**		**LitF**	0	**Indx**	0		
Desc	a	**Ills**	a	**Fest**	0	**DtSt**	s	**Dates**	1995,		

010		95-68761
040		DLC ‡c DLC
020		0878917527
050	00	PS3537.A426 ‡b C3285 1995
082	00	813/.54 ‡2 20
100	1_	Holzman, Robert S.
245	10	J.D. Salinger's The catcher in the rye / ‡c text by Robert S. Holzman, Gary L. Perkins ; illustrations by Karen Pica.
246	18	Catcher in the rye
260		Piscataway, N.J. : ‡b Research & Education Association, ‡c c1995.
300		v, 113, [1] p. : ‡b ill. ; ‡c 21 cm.
440	_0	MAXnotes
504		Includes bibliographical references (p. [114]).
600	10	**Salinger, J. D. ‡q (Jerome David), ‡d 1919- ‡t Catcher in the rye ‡x Examinations ‡x Study guides.**
700	1_	Perkins, Gary L.

Fig. 8.3. Metadata record for a work that is about another work. The record contains a subject heading that consists of the main entry and the title of the work that is the subject of the work represented by this record. (Source: OCLC Connexion, WorldCat, record number 33406432.)

tions have different titles and editions have different authors. A number of people on the discussion list for the international *AACR2* conference[20] indicated that technology could accomplish this function. As work proceeds on coordinating AACR3 with *FRBR,* there is potential for system design to take advantage of new ways for identifying works and their expressions and manifestations in being able to provide collocated access to those works. Until this or something like it is determined, implemented, and made the norm for catalog display, main entry is still the best way we have to provide collocation.

Judgment of Most Important. Finally, when times are tough and full surrogate records cannot be made, and when brief records have to be created for some information packages, choice of a main entry ensures that at least the "most important" and most predictable access point will be created. The Program for Cooperative Cataloging (PCC) Core Record, mentioned in the preceding chapter, calls for the main entry and perhaps

Books	Rec Stat	c	Entered	19950605	Replaced	20020525				
Type	a	ELvl		Srce	d	Audn		Ctrl		Lang	eng
BLvl	m	Form		Conf	0	Biog		MRec		Ctry	nyu
		Cont		GPub		LitF	1	Indx	0		
Desc	a	Ills		Fest	0	DtSt	s	Dates	1995,		

010		95-77866
040		MdHyP ‡c DLC ‡d FIT ‡d OCL ‡d OCLCQ
020		0679441018 : ‡c $25.00
042		lccopycat
050	00	PS3568.I265 ‡b M46 1995
082	00	813/.54 ‡2 20
100	1_	Rice, Anne, ‡d 1941-
245	**10**	**Memnoch the Devil / ‡c Anne Rice.**
250		1st ed.
260		New York : ‡b Knopf, ‡c 1995.
300		353 p. ; ‡c 25 cm.
490	1_	The vampire chronicles ; ‡v [5th bk.]
520		A vampire is offered work by both God and the Devil. He is Lestat, a man of action who just bumped off a billionaire for smuggling cocaine. The job interviews yield quite a bit of information on his prospective employers, including why God expelled the Devil from Paradise at the time of the Creation. It appears the Devil was against God's scheme to make suffering a regular part of life.
650	_0	Vampires ‡v Fiction.
650	_0	Lestat (Fictitious character) ‡v Fiction.
655	_7	Horror tales. ‡2 gsafd
800	**1_**	**Rice, Anne, ‡d 1941- ‡t Vampire chronicles ; ‡v 5th bk.**

Fig. 8.4. Metadata record for a work that is part of a larger work. Anne Rice's *Memnoch the Devil* is the fifth book in her series called *Vampire Chronicles*. The added entry consisting of main entry and title of the series allows collocation of the series with the author's individual titles. (Source: OCLC Connexion, WorldCat, record number 32683203.)

one other name or title access point to be made and brought under authority control. The choice of added entries depends upon the judgment of the cataloger/indexer and/or the policy of the institution in which the catalog/index is being created.

AACR2 *Principles for Choosing Main Entry*

AACR2 is made up of many rules that seem unfathomable to the uninitiated. However, they are based upon principles that can be laid out in much the same order as the rules themselves. First, most works are cre-

Books	Rec Stat	c	Entered	19970307	Replaced	20020801			
Type	a	ELvl	I	Srce	d	Audn		Ctrl		Lang	eng
BLvl	m	Form		Conf	0	Biog		MRec		Ctry	nyu
		Cont		GPub		LitF	0	Indx	0		
Desc	a	Ills		Fest	0	DtSt	s	Dates	1835,		

040		NJL ‡c NJL ‡d OCLCQ
092		211.5 ‡b P14
100	1_	Paine, Thomas, ‡d 1737-1809.
245	14	The theological works of Thomas Paine : ‡b the most complete edition ever published.
260		New York : ‡b George H. Evans, ‡c 1835.
300		xiv, [7]-384 p. ; ‡c 22 cm.
500		"The age of reason": p. [7]-159.
501		With: Miscellaneous letters and essays on various subjects / by Thomas Paine. Granville, Middletown, N.J. : G.H. Evans, 1844, and 2 other works.
650	_0	Deism.
650	_0	Rationalism.
700	12	Paine, Thomas, ‡d 1737-1809. ‡t Age of reason.
740	02	Age of reason.

Fig. 8.5. Metadata record for a work that contains a smaller work within it. The work being described contains four works of Thomas Paine. One is considered to be a major work and is given an added entry consisting of the main entry and the title (line 13). (Source: OCLC Connexion, WorldCat, record number 36504265.)

ated by a single individual, in which case main entry is the name of the person (or a surrogate for the name, e.g., pseudonym). If the author is unknown and also is unidentified in any way, then main entry is the title. (*Note:* "Unidentified in any way" means that there is not even a phrase such as "Author of Little Nell" as a statement of responsibility.) Other works are works of multiple responsibility, which can be synchronous or asynchronous.[21]

Principles for Choosing Main Entry—Synchronous Responsibility. When responsibility is synchronous, it means that all persons or bodies made the *same kind* of contribution, in which case main entry is the principal responsible party, if one is identified. Under *AACR2*, if no responsible party is identified as the principal one, the first of two or three equally represented responsible parties is chosen as the main entry. If there are more than three responsible parties, and no one party is identified as having principal responsibility, the main entry is the title. The title is also chosen if the work is accepted as sacred scripture by a religious group.

Books   **Rec Stat** c   **Entered** 19980317   **Replaced** 20030109

Type a	**ELvl** I	**Srce** d	**Audn**	**Ctrl**	**Lang** spa
BLvl m	**Form**	**Conf** 0	**Biog**	**MRec**	**Ctry** sp
	Cont b	**GPub**	**LitF** 0	**Indx** 0	
Desc a	**Ills**	**Fest** 0	**DtSt** s	**Dates** 1997,	

040		ZQP ‡c ZQP ‡d NVC ‡d OCLCQ
020		8440670508 : ‡c $14.95
041	1_	spa ‡h eng
090		PR2794.R7 ‡b F3x 1997
100	1_	**Shakespeare, William, ‡d 1564-1616.**
240	10	**Romeo and Juliet. ‡l Spanish**
245	10	**Romeo y Julieta /** ‡c William Shakespeare ; [traducción: Jaime Navarra Farré].
250		1. ed.
260		Barcelona, España : ‡b Ediciones B, S.A./Grupo Zeta, ‡c c1997.
300		167 p. ; ‡c 18 cm.
440	_0	VIB ; ‡v 193/8
500		Translation of: Romeo and Juliet.
504		Includes bibliographical references (p. 161-167).
600	10	Shakespeare, William, ‡d 1564-1616 ‡x Translations into Spanish.
650	_0	English drama (Tragedy) ‡y Early modern and Elizabethan, 1500-1600 ‡x Translations into Spanish.
650	_0	Married people ‡z Italy ‡z Verona ‡v Drama.
650	_0	Family ‡z Italy ‡z Verona ‡v Drama.
655	_7	Tragedies. ‡2 gsafd
700	12	Shakespeare, William, ‡d 1564-1616. ‡t Romeo and Juliet. ‡l Spanish.
700	1_	Navarra Farré, Jaime.

Books   **Rec Stat** n   **Entered** 19951128   **Replaced** 19951128

Type a	**ELvl** I	**Srce** d	**Audn**	**Ctrl**	**Lang** eng
BLvl m	**Form**	**Conf** 0	**Biog**	**MRec**	**Ctry** cou
	Cont	**GPub**	**LitF** 0	**Indx** 0	
Desc a	**Ills**	**Fest** 0	**DtSt** s	**Dates** 1994,	

040		IBA ‡c IBA
090		PR2831.A2 ‡b B4
100	1_	**Shakespeare, William, ‡d 1564-1616.**
240	10	**Romeo and Juliet**
245	14	**The tragedy of Romeo and Juliet /** ‡c by William Shakespeare. Edited by Richard and Joan Bell.
260		Boulder, CO : ‡b Armado and Moth, ‡c 1994.
300		96 p. ; ‡c 22 cm. + ‡e director's script (96 p. ; 28 cm.)
500		Title on cover: "Mr. William Shakespeares The Tragedie of Romeo and Ivliet. Published according to the True Originall Copies."
500		Actor's script and director's script include preface, notes, and glossary.
700	1_	Bell, Richard. ‡4 edt
700	1_	Bell, Joan. ‡4 edt

Fig. 8.6. Two metadata records showing two derivations of a work: one that is a Spanish translation, and one with the original, but out-of-favor title. Each has a main entry and uniform title that allows the works to be collocated despite the different titles. (Source: OCLC Connexion, WorldCat, record numbers 38735799 and 33812768.)

The practice of making access points for only three responsible parties is a questionable one in today's information environment and is currently being examined for possible change by the various bodies responsible for *AACR2R*.[22] More and more information packages are being created jointly by four or more persons, and research supported by large grants of money is often written up by four or more persons. In an information environment where space is not an issue, as it was in card catalog days when the so-called Rule of Three was institutionalized, the practice should be rethought.

The main reason given by rule makers for not changing the practice has been the perceived cost of providing authority control for so many more names. However, this cost should be weighed against the cost to users of either not being able to find a name they seek or not being able to sort through hundreds of similar names. Anyone who has tried to find a particular name on the Web knows the difficulty that is involved in finding anything in a noncontrolled environment. In addition, the problem is exacerbated by the rules for description in *AACR2*, which limit the listing of creators in the description to just the first one listed when there are more than three names. That is, if there are three names, all are listed, but if there are four or more names, only the first one is listed. So even if keyword searching might be successful, it cannot find what is not even listed.

The Rule of Three may finally be overturned in the next edition of *AACR*. The document outlining changes that will be included in *AACR3* states that the recommendation to reconsider the Rule of Three was a trigger toward deciding to do a thorough revision of the chapter having to do with choice of access points.[23]

Principles for Choosing Main Entry—Asynchronous Responsibility. When responsibility is asynchronous, it means that the responsible parties have made *different kinds* of contributions to the existence of the work. Basically, there are three kinds of asynchronous responsibility: (1) responsibility has varied over time, resulting in modifications of works (e.g., work of original author is revised or rewritten by a later author); (2) responsibility has varied during the creation of a completely new work (e.g., artist and writer); or (3) the work emanates from a corporate body, but is written by a person or persons.

When responsibility has varied over time, the main entry is the original author unless it is clear that a later author has greater responsibility. For example, translations are works in which the work originally written by one person is put into another language by another person. Some revisions are works in which the work of an original person may have updates and additional comments written by another person. In the case of repub-

lication of a work, the original work may be intact but with a new introduction and extensive comments written by another person. In all these
cases *AACR2* principle calls for entry under the original author.

On the other hand, there are situations in which a later author
has greater responsibility. For example, in an adaptation, the idea contained in the work is that of the original author but all the words of this
particular version are those of a new author (e.g., Shakespeare's plays completely rewritten as stories for children). Also, some revisions have so much
updating and change that they are really the work of the new author. In
these and cases like them, main entry should be the later author.

When responsibility has varied during the creation of a new work,
main entry is the party deemed to have made the most important contribution. For example, many works are the result of the work of an artist and
a writer. One criterion is whether the work was a collaboration. If so, it
should be entered under the one named first, unless the other is given
prominence by wording or layout. However, in a work that gathers together
works of the artist, if the writer has added only short captions for the works,
the artist would be the primary access point. On the other hand, if the work
was first completed by the writer and then had illustrations added by the
artist, the writer is clearly the one with primary responsibility.

Another example of a situation where responsibility varies during
the creation of a new work is the report of an interview or exchange. If the
work is written up as a report, all in the words of the interviewer (or perhaps
with a few quotations), then the principal responsibility is that of the interviewer. If the work is presented in the exact words of the interviewed per-
son(s), however, that person (or the first-named person) is chosen as the
main entry.

When responsibility involves a corporate body, both the Paris
Principles and *AACR2* list situations when corporate body is to be main
entry (*AACR2*'s list is longer), and in the remainder of cases the main entry
is to be a person or the title. Main entry, according to the Paris Principles,
should be a corporate body when the work is the expression of the corporate thought or activity of the body (e.g., official reports, rules and regulations, manifestos, etc.) or when the wording of the title and the nature
of the work imply that the corporate body is collectively responsible for the
content (e.g., serials whose titles consist of a generic term like *Bulletin* preceded or followed by a corporate body name, if they include some account
of the activities of the body).

The concept of "corporate author" has been a matter of international controversy. Some traditions have declared that corporate bodies
cannot be "authors." When a new edition of *AACR* was being discussed in
the late 1970s, a compromise solution was agreed upon. Its essence was that

even though a corporate body is not in a real sense an author, there are times when a corporate body is so tied to a document (e.g., an annual report) that the body must be chosen as the main entry. Main entry, according to *AACR2,* should be the corporate body, if the work falls into one of six categories:

- administrative nature
- some legal, governmental, or religious works
- collective thought of the body
- collective activity of a conference
- collective activity of a performing group (that goes beyond mere performance)
- cartographic materials emanating from a corporate body[24]

Title Main Entry. Some instances when title is main entry have been mentioned in the preceding discussion, but it is useful to have all of these listed together. The main entry should be title when:

- a work is truly anonymous (*Note:* This does not include works that use a phrase for an author.)
- a work has more than three responsible parties and none is singled out as having had primary responsibility
- a work that compiles the work of several authors has been produced under editorial direction
- a work has a corporate body involved, but the rules for corporate body main entry require title main entry instead
- a work is accepted as sacred scripture by a religious body

Serials usually are entered under title as main entry as a result of these rules. Serials and other works with title main entry present a special challenge when there are changes in the title. *AACR2* calls for new surrogate records to be made when a serial title change is *major* versus when the change is *minor.* A major change is one occurring in the first five words (not an initial article) in the title or a change in the name of a corporate body that is part of a title. (Minor changes in the first five words, such as a change in a preposition or an abbreviation of a word, are exceptions to this rule.) In order to collocate the records for works that have had major title changes, uniform titles are used (see discussion of uniform titles below).

Additional Access Points

In all the cases just discussed, every responsible party and title that has been considered to be a candidate for primary access point should be an access point, if not the primary one. In the cataloging world these nonprimary access points are also called "added entries." When access points are made for every responsible party, it is not necessary for a user to have to guess which one has been chosen to be the primary access point or even to understand what main entry is all about. The usefulness of choosing a primary access point is to be able to display results of searches in a logical and collocated fashion, not to require a user to understand it. The fact that our systems do not provide such displays is a criticism of system design.

AUTHORITY CONTROL

The process called authority control was named that because it was thought necessary to determine an "authorized" form for every entity known by variant forms. Thus, for example, the English form of Confucius has been determined by the Library of Congress to be the authoritative form, and the names given to this person in many other languages, including his Chinese name for himself, have been relegated to positions of "unauthorized" forms.

As the world of information becomes more global, a need has been felt to recognize that many different language forms can be "correct" forms for access purposes. In addition, the concepts of "authority" and "control" in a culture with an emphasis on individualism are not readily welcomed, and the words have negative connotations for many people. Efforts were made by the author and others a few years ago to begin using "access control" instead of "authority control." But "access control" has come to mean an operating system feature that controls the access that certain categories of users have to files and to functions. (It has also come into use in some airports to name the function of determining who may enter a country.) We have not found a better term. Thinking in terms of global or international access allows the possibility for authority records to contain all variant forms for an entity, without designating one as the "right" one. In such a circumstance one of the variants could be designated as the default for display, but a good system would allow the user to bypass the default if desired. In any case, a search for any one of the variants for an entity should retrieve all metadata records associated with the entity.

All access points (whether main or added entries) need to be under authority control so that:

- persons or entities with the same name can be distinguished from each other,

- all names used by/for a person, body, or place, and/or all manifestations of a name of a person, body, or place will be brought together,

- all differing titles of the same work can be brought together.

In other words, like the need for main entry, the need for authority control is for collocation—for bringing together everything related to a person, corporate body, place, or work, regardless of what name has been used for the person, corporate body, place, or work. One has only to look at some Web sites that do not have authority control to see that there is value in collocation of forms of name. For example, a search for "Gorman, Michael" at Amazon.com in April 2003 resulted in the following first five out of sixty-four results:

1. *Practical Algorithms for Image Analysis* by Michael Seul [coauthors for this are Lawrence O'Gorman and Michael J. Sammon, but this information is not available on the initial screen]

2. *Cruciformity: Paul's Narrative Spirituality of the Cross* by Michael J. Gorman

3. *The Concise Aacr2: 1998 Revision* by Michael Gorman [the acronym for AACR really had only the first "A" capitalized]

4. *Evangelical Dictionary of Christian Education* by Michael J. Anthony

5. *The Enduring Library* by Michael Gorman

One can see that two of the first five are for the librarian, Michael Gorman, but we know that there are a number of titles by this same person that might be among the remaining fifty-nine items. In addition, two of the first five retrievals are not even for someone named Michael Gorman. A search for "Gorman, Michael" in the catalog of the University of Pittsburgh the same day yielded:

#	Titles	Headings
1	2	Gorman, Michael
2	1	Gorman, Michael, 1897–
3	33	Gorman, Michael, 1941–
4	2	Gorman, Michael, 1944–
5	1	Gorman, Michael, 1952–
6	2	Gorman, Michael E., 1952–
7	3	Gorman, Michael M.

One may not know from this list which is the librarian, but once it is determined to be number 3, then all titles relating to that person are found together, and it is not necessary to look at any of the other entries.

The entries from the catalog shown above are called "headings." Current practice dictates the establishment of a heading for each name or title that is intended to be an access point. The term *heading* comes from print catalog days, as already mentioned, when each access point was printed at the top of the copy of the surrogate record and was called the heading for the record (see Figure 8.7). In the online world "heading" has come to mean the exact string of characters of the authorized form of the access point as it appears in the authority record. It no longer appears at the head of a record, although sometimes it is at the head of a list of records in a catalog display (see Figure 8.8).

Again, the library world has had authority control for the longest time, and therefore its principles are given below as an example. *AACR2* does not have a section for authority control, per se, but its chapters 22–25, on form of heading for personal, geographic, and corporate names, and uniform titles, explain how headings are constructed and brought together with references from other names and forms of name representing the same entity. In the plan for AACR3 mentioned above, these chapters

```
          Calorie guide to brand names and
                basic foods

641.10 Krause, Barbara.
Kra        Calorie guide to brand names and basic
           foods / by Barbara Krause. -- New York :
           Penguin Books, 1996. -- 262 p. -- ISBN
           0-451-18524-2

              1. Calories (Food).  2. Food--Caloric
           content--Tables.  I. Title.
```

Fig. 8.7. Catalog card showing the title placed at the top of the record as the "heading" for the card.

#	Title <	Full Title	Date	Library System
☐ 1	Cataloging and classification.	Cataloging and classification, by Maurice F. Tauber. Subject headings, by Carlyle J. Frarey.	1960	ULS: Pittsburgh Campus
	Click on title for more information.			
☐ 2	Cataloging and classification.	Cataloging and classification, by Maurice F. Tauber. Subject headings, by Carlyle J. Frarey.	1960	Health Sciences Library System
	Location: Falk Library - Storage	Call Number: Z695 T222 1960	Status: Not Checked Out	
☐ 3	Cataloging and classification.	Introduction to cataloging and classification; a teaching guide with illustrations of major principles for descriptive cataloging and classification, by Bohdan S. Wynar and Earl Tannenbaum with the assistance of Carol Christensen.	1966	ULS: Pittsburgh Campus
	Click on title for more information.			
☐ 4	Cataloging and classification.	Manheimer's Cataloging and classification : a workbook / Jerry D. Saye ; with Desretta V. McAllister-Harper.	1991	ULS: Pittsburgh Campus
	Location: Information Sciences Library (316 Information Sciences Bldg)	Call Number: Z693 S384 1991	Status: Not Checked Out	
☐ 5	Cataloging and classification : a workbook /	Cataloging and classification a workbook / Martha L. Manheimer.	1980	ULS: Pittsburgh Campus
	Click on title for more information.			
☐ 6	Cataloging and classification : a workbook /	Cataloging and classification - a workbook / Martha L. Manheimer.	1975	ULS: Pittsburgh Campus
	Click on title for more information.			
☐ 7	Cataloging and classification : an introduction /	Cataloging and classification : an introduction / Lois Mai Chan.	1994	ULS: Bradford Campus
	Location: Bradford Campus Library - 2nd Floor - Circulating	Call Number: Z 693.5 .U6 C48 1994	Status: Not Checked Out	

Fig. 8.8. Screen from PITTCat, the online catalog at the University of Pittsburgh, showing "headings" in the left-hand box under the word "Title."

will become the core of a new "Part III" that will contain explicit instructions on creating authority records.[25]

In the process of authority control, even though there may be a desire to provide more global access by not designating one of the variants as the authorized one, it is still necessary to go through the process of creating a heading in particular locales so that one form can be designated for default display for cases where a user does not wish to designate a preference. The following section discusses the principles involved in heading creation for names and titles. Headings for subject concepts are discussed in Chapter 10.

Headings for Access Points

Headings are maintained in authority files, which are collections of authority records. Each authority record identifies the form of name or title that has been selected as "authoritative" according to the rules. It lists many of the variant forms of name or variant forms of title that belong with the authorized form. It identifies sources of information about the variant forms of name or title or about the person or body or work represented by the name or title (see Figure 8.9).

In the process of creating headings for *names* one must make at least one of three choices, and often must make all three: (1) choice of which name to use, (2) choice of which form of that name to use, (3) choice of format. In the third choice there are two subchoices: (a) choice of entry word; (b) choice of what additions need to be made to the name to distinguish it from same or similar names.

In the process of creating headings for *titles,* it is necessary to: (1) choose which title will be used, and (2) decide upon the arrangement of the title and whether it is to be followed by distinguishing factors such as language and date. Principles for making these decisions are presented in the following subsections.

Principles for Choice of Personal Name

Choice of which name to use is required in cases where a person has used different names, not including differently shortened forms of one part of a name. The first principle is to use the latest name of a person if the person's name has been changed. Examples:

- Chris Wallace changed to Notorious B.I.G.—use Notorious B.I.G.

Rec stat	c	Entered 19810716		Replaced 20000204164435.0			
Type	z	Upd status	a	Enc lvl	n	Source	
Roman	l	Ref status	a	Mod rec		Name use	a
Govt agn	l	Auth status	a	Subj	a	Subj use	a
Series	n	Auth/ref	a	Geo subd	n	Ser use	b
Ser num	n	Name	a	Subdiv tp	n	Rules	c

010		n 81073496 ‡z n 82138607
040		DLC ‡c DLC ‡d DLC
100	0_	**Diana, ‡c Princess of Wales, ‡d 1961-**
400	1_	Spencer, Diana Frances, ‡c Lady, ‡d 1961-
400	0_	Di, ‡c Lady, ‡d 1961-
400	0_	Dayānā, ‡c Princess of Wales, ‡d 1961-
670		Dunlop, J. Charles and Diana, a royal romance, c1981 (subj.) ‡b p. 6, etc. (Lady Diana Frances Spencer; b. July 1, 1961)
670		Leete-Hodge, L. The Country Life book of the royal wedding, 1981: ‡b table of contents (Diana, Princess of Wales)
670		Carretier, M.-P. Lady Di chez elle, c1987.
670		The Washington post, Aug. 31, 1997 ‡b (Diana d. Aug. 31, 1997 from a fatal car accident)
670		al-Mūsād qatala Dayānā ... 1998- : ‡b v. 1, t.p. (Dayānā)

Fig. 8.9. An authority record showing the "authoritative" heading for Princess Diana (in bold) and three variant forms of her name (in 400 fields). (Source: OCLC Connexion, Authorities, record number 618798.)

- Sarah Ferguson married and became the Duchess of York—use Duchess of York, that is, "York, Sarah Mountbatten-Windsor, Duchess of"

The second principle is to use the predominant name of a person who is known by more than one name. (A nickname is considered to be a different name, not a shortened form of the same name.) Examples:

- Bill Clinton is also known as William Jefferson Clinton—use Bill Clinton

- Mildred Zaharias was known in pro golf as Babe Zaharias—use Babe Zaharias

The third principle is for persons who use pseudonyms. One should use the pseudonym if only one pseudonym is always used with all works. However, if the same writer used different names for separate bibliographic identities, one should use each of the names and create a separate authority record for each bibliographic identity. Different bibliographic identities are represented if a person has used one name for one kind of work and has used another name for another kind of work. Examples:

- Carolyn Heilbrun writes literary criticism using her own name but uses the pseudonym Amanda Cross for her mystery novels—use both names

- Charles Dodgson wrote serious mathematical works using his own name but used the pseudonym Lewis Carroll for his children's stories—use both names

However, if the writer is "contemporary" and uses more than one pseudonym or a real name and one or more pseudonyms, one should use each one for the works that are created using that name. Examples:

- Molly Keane and M. J. Farrell are the same person but the names are used with separate works—use both names

- Evan Hunter, Ed McBain, Hunt Collins, and Richard Marsten are the same person—use all four names

Principles for Form of Personal Name

Once the *name* has been chosen, one then determines which *form* of that name will be used. There may be variants in fullness, language, and spelling. Any of these may be affected by country of residence or activity. The overriding principle is that the form of name used by a person in his or her country of residence or activity is the form that is to be used.

When variant fullnesses have been used by a person, one should use the form most commonly found. For example, one should choose C. S. Lewis over Clive Staples Lewis. If no form predominates, one should choose the latest form. If in doubt, one should use fullest form. However, the form used in the person's country of residence or activity takes precedence. Even though the English-speaking world produces Hans Christian Andersen's works using the full form of name, during his lifetime in his country he preferred H. C. Andersen; so that is the form that should be chosen for the heading.

When there are variants in language one should use the form used by the person in his or her own country of residence or activity. Variants in spelling call for using the new spelling if there has been an official change in orthography. Otherwise, the predominant spelling should be used. Variants in transliteration of names written in a nonroman script are either romanized according to an adopted table, or if well-known, a predominant English form may be used. For example, the Arabic name Qaddafi, can also be transliterated Gadhafi, Kaddafi, Qadhafi, Kadhafi, Gadafi, among others. The predominant spelling seems to be Qaddafi.

Principles for Entry Word and Remaining Structure of Personal Name

The structure of a personal name in an access-controlled record is usually the family name (or surname), followed by forenames, and often followed by dates of birth and/or death. In cases where a person does not have a family name or surname, the entry word is the person's first forename. A good rule of thumb is to use as entry word the part of the name that would be entered first in a telephone book in the person's country of residence or activity.[26] For example, in Brazil the entry word is the last name of a compound surname; in Argentina the entry word is the first name of a compound surname; in Iceland the entry word is the given name (forename) because the last names of persons in Iceland are patronymics, not family names (i.e., a person's last name is the given name of one's parent [often father, but sometimes mother] with either "son" or "dottir" attached to it). If a person has a known preference for the entry word to be used, then the person's preference takes precedence (e.g., a person with an unhyphenated compound surname in English that would ordinarily be entered under the last part may prefer entry under the first part).

Persons with only given names include royalty, persons of religious vocations, pop stars, and the like. In some cases the name consists only of one name followed by distinguishing additions; or, as in the case of royalty, there may be several names. When there is only one name (e.g., Aristotle), that name is the entry word, but there will likely be distinguishing additions.

In order to distinguish an author from others with the same name, additions may be made. The most common ones are birth and/or death dates and full forenames added in parentheses. For example, the name of H. C. Andersen would be followed by full forenames and dates: Andersen, H. C. (Hans Christian), 1805–1875. The Library of Congress has as its policy to add birth and/or death dates and full forenames when they are known at the time of creating the heading for the name, even if there is not yet a conflict with an identical name.

Principles for Choice of Corporate Name

Corporate names differ from personal names in that a corporate name change may signal what is really a new corporate body. And corporate bodies can merge with another body, split into two or more bodies, or absorb another body, among other changes. The rules for choice of corporate names in *AACR2* reflect practice more than they do principle. According to the rules, one is to create a new heading and a separate authority record for each name change. This eliminates the necessity of determining whether a name change signals a new body with a new purpose or is simply a name change, perhaps for political or other such reasons. Then each heading is to be used as the access point on surrogate records for information packages that were created during the time the body had that name.

Each authority record contains a connection to the preceding name of the body or bodies and to the following name. For example, the American Documentation Institute once had the name "Science Service. Documentation Division," and in 1937 the American Documentation Institute changed its name to American Society for Information Science. A properly constructed catalog would have references from each of the second two names to its preceding one and also references from each of the first two names to the name following it (see Figure 8.10). Practice once included the entire history of name changes of a corporate body in one record, but the great amount of work involved dictated an abandonment of the practice in the United States.

Publications of corporate bodies often have more than one form of the body's name on the same information package. There can be an abbreviation, an acronym, a shortened form, or a popular name in addition to the official name. If a variant is not an official name change, one is to use the predominant name. For example, the conventional name Westminster Abbey would be chosen over the official name Collegiate Church of St. Peter in Westminster. If the name is for an international body, and the name is in more than one language, *AACR2* calls for choosing the English form if there is one. It is hoped that with the move to international authority control a new principle would be to choose the name in whichever language is best for the users of the catalog, which is the principle stated in the Paris Principles.

Science Service. Documentation Division

search also under later name

American Documentation Institute

American Documentation Institute

search also under earlier name

Science Service. Documentation Division

American Documentation Institute

search also under later name

American Society for Information Science

American Society for Information Science

search also under earlier name

American Documentation Institute

Fig. 8.10. References necessary in order to connect three names of an organization.

Principles for Entry Word and Form of Heading for Corporate Names

In creating a heading for a corporate body, the general principle is to use the most common form of the name written in direct order as it appears on publications of the body. However, if the body is a government, religious, or other subordinate body, the principle is that the heading for the subordinate body is its own name if that name is distinctive and can stand alone; otherwise, the body's name is added as a subheading to the name of the higher body (e.g., in the heading "American Library Association. Cataloging and Classification Section," the name of the section cannot stand alone; it must be identified by the body in which it is a section). For many government bodies this means that the first word of the heading is the name of the jurisdiction, which is usually the geographic name of the area governed (e.g., "United States. Federal Bureau of Investigation"). Under *AACR2* jurisdiction, names are all in English, if there is an English form, but according to the Paris Principles, geographic names for governments are to be in the language suitable to the users of the catalog.

Principles for Choice of Uniform Title

Uniform titles are created when works have more than one manifestation and need to have title resolution. For example, if a work that has one title is made available in a different form, especially if it has a different title, there needs to be a way to bring these two manifestations together in the retrieval tool (e.g., the film *Gettysburg* based on the novel *The Killer Angels* by Michael Shaara). Uniform titles have been used for many years in the creation of bibliographic records for music. It has taken much longer for them to be accepted as useful in other situations, although the Library of Congress has long used uniform titles to subarrange and collocate the large number of records that fall under a famous prolific author such as Shakespeare or Mark Twain.

Use of the principle of uniform title requires an understanding of what constitutes a work. As mentioned earlier, a number of individuals have done research in this area,[27] and IFLA has created *FRBR*.[28] Research is proceeding on implementing *FRBR*. But the rules in *AACR2* reflect some inconsistency of interpretation.

The general principle is that if manifestations of a work appear under various titles, one must be chosen, and the original title in the original language is to be preferred unless another title in the same language has become better known. In the case of simultaneous publication of different titles, the choice should be the title of the edition published in the home country of the responsible party. With publication on the Web it remains to be seen how the issue of variant titles will play out. One likely situation that will need a uniform title-type solution will be the case of translated works with translated titles that are different from the original titles.

Uniform titles also serve to differentiate identical titles of different works, especially when title is the principal access point. For example, different serials often have identical titles (e.g., *The Times* is a popular newspaper title that needs to be differentiated by city).

Principles for Arrangement of Uniform Titles

Basically, the words of a uniform title are in direct order as they appear on at least one manifestation of a work. In the United States initial articles are omitted because in the *MARC 21* fields where uniform title is placed in a subfield "t" (e.g., 6xx and 7xx fields) following the main entry, there is no allowance for skipping over initial articles in the process of arranging uniform titles for display. Thus, for a criticism written about Dickens's *The Pickwick Papers,* the uniform title in the 600 field, $t subfield, would be *Pickwick Papers* so that it would be displayed with other titles beginning with "P" rather than those beginning with "T."

There are three main cases where additions to uniform titles may be needed: (1) for conflict resolution, (2) for language identification, and (3) to show parts of a work. An example of conflict resolution is: "Scarlet letter (Choreographic work : Graham)." This is clearly not the famous novel *The Scarlet Letter.* An example of language identification is: "Nome della rosa. English." This would bring the English translation, *The Name of the Rose,* together with its Italian original. An example of a uniform title showing a part of a work is: "Paradise lost. Book 4."

Music uniform titles can be made for all these reasons, and in addition, they are used to organize the works of composers. Such works often do not have distinctive titles, and the same work often has a variety of titles (e.g., Beethoven's Fifth Symphony may be titled Beethoven's Fifth, Symphony no. 5, or The Fifth Symphony, to name only a few). Uniform titles provide a way to organize collections of concertos, quartets, symphonies, and the like (e.g., Mozart, Wolfgang Amadeus, 1756–1791. Concertos, flute, harp, orchestra, K. 299, C major).

Uniform titles are also used for some types of collections in *AACR2.* The theory behind this is dubious, but it seems to be necessary for the purpose of displaying all works of a particular kind together if their titles proper are not distinctive. Thus the record for a work called "Selected works of William Shakespeare" would display with the record for the title "Some works of Shakespeare," if both had the uniform title "Selections." Some uniform titles used in this way are: "Works," "Laws, etc.," and "Novels" (see Figure 8.11).

International Authority Control

Work is proceeding toward international authority control. We do not yet know exactly how this will happen. New structures always come incrementally, and at the beginning of such a process it is not usually possible to make the mental leap to envision the eventual construct. One possibility is that all forms of name could be accumulated on one authority record, with none chosen as *the* one that must be used. Each form would be identified by language. If there were several variant forms in one language, one of them would be designated as preferred for that language. A default display could be whichever form is most appropriate for users in a particular setting. A search for any one of the forms would retrieve records related to the entity represented by the record. A difficulty with this scenario is the immense size of records that would be produced for many

Books	Rec Stat	c		Entered	19961204		Replaced	20020618		
Type	a	**ELvl**	I	**Srce**	d	**Audn**		**Ctrl**		**Lang** eng
BLvl	m	**Form**		**Conf**	0	**Biog**		**MRec**		**Ctry** nyu
		Cont		**GPub**		**LitF**	1	**Indx**	0	
Desc	a	**Ills**		**Fest**	0	**DtSt**	s	**Dates**	1885,	

040		NOC ‡c NOC ‡d OCL ‡d OCLCQ
090		PR4652 ‡b 1885
100	1_	**Eliot, George, ‡d 1819-1880.**
240	10	**Novels. ‡k Selections**
245	10	**Adam Bede ; ‡b Silas Marner, the weaver of Raveloe ; Impressions of Theophrastus Such / ‡c by George Eliot.**
246	3_	Adam Bede ; Silas Marner, the weaver of Raveloe ; Impressions of Theophrastus Such
250		[Library ed.].
260		New York : ‡b J.B. Alden, ‡c 1885.
300		484, 167, 148 p. ; ‡c 21 cm.
700	12	Eliot, George, ‡d 1819-1880. ‡t Silas Marner.
700	12	Eliot, George, ‡d 1819-1880. ‡t Theophrastus Such.
740	02	Silas Marner.
740	02	Impressions of Theophrastus Such.

Books	Rec Stat	c		Entered	19940825		Replaced	20000801		
Type	a	**ELvl**		**Srce**		**Audn**		**Ctrl**		**Lang** eng
BLvl	m	**Form**		**Conf**	0	**Biog**		**MRec**		**Ctry** nyu
		Cont		**GPub**		**LitF**	1	**Indx**	0	
Desc	a	**Ills**		**Fest**	0	**DtSt**	s	**Dates**	1995,	

010		94-24675
040		DLC ‡c DLC ‡d OCL
020		0517122235
043		e-uk-en
050	00	PR4652 ‡b 1995
082	00	823/.8 ‡2 20
100	1_	**Eliot, George, ‡d 1819-1880.**
240	10	**Novels. ‡k Selections**
245	10	**George Eliot, selected works.**
260		New York : ‡b Gramercy Books ; ‡a Avenel, N.J. : ‡b Distributed by Random House Value Pub., ‡c 1995.
300		xii, 820 p. ; ‡c 24 cm.
505	0_	**Silas Marner -- The lifted veil -- Brother Jacob -- Middlemarch.**
651	_0	England ‡x Social life and customs ‡y 19th century ‡v Fiction.
740	01	Selected works.

Fig. 8.11. Two metadata records for two works that pull together different groupings of George Eliot's novels. The uniform title "Novels. Selections" allows these two works to be displayed together under the main entry "Eliot, George." (Source: OCLC Connexion, WorldCat, record numbers 36033332 and 31134215.)

names. Authority records already can have multiple forms of name even in one language; addition of multiple forms in each of multiple languages could result in very large records, indeed (see Figure 8.12).

Instead of one large international authority file, several models for a Virtual International Authority File (VIAF) have been suggested by Barbara Tillet.[29] Current test projects use a distributed model. National bibliographic agencies have independent authority files that can be searched using a standard protocol like Z39.50. When a record for a name or title is not found in the local file, the system uses Z39.50 to search other national authority files, and if the name or title is found, the record can be imported to the local file. Another model would be that of a union authority file to which participants could contribute as they wished. This model has the limitations of lengthy records described above and would also lend itself to less consistent information unless there were strict standards and checks. A variation of the union file model is a "virtual" union authority file. Records would remain in the national files but would be linked to a centralized server that would harvest metadata from the national files. Records for the same entity would be linked at the central server and refreshed regularly. Maintenance of records would continue to be done in the separate files. Projects to test these models are under way.

International authority control requires standards, and there are several that may be used to good advantage. In the international library community, IFLA has issued *Guidelines for Authority Records and References,* now in its second edition.[30] The Z39.50 protocol makes it possible to retrieve and display authority records on the Internet. This enables the sharing of authority records for the same entities in different languages, and forms of heading in any particular language can be verified by experts in that language. The Working Group on Transnational Exchange of Authority Data (a group that is part of IFLA) has looked at the possibility of an International Standard Authority Data Number (ISADN). At this writing the ISADN is on hold while the group considers other models. The OAI (Open Archive Initiative) also shows promise.[31] OAI promotes a protocol (Open Archives Initiative Protocol for Metadata Harvesting, or OAI-PMH) that defines a mechanism for harvesting XML-formatted metadata. It is intentionally simple with the intent of being easier and less costly to implement than Z39.50.

CONCLUSION

This chapter has discussed the creation of name and title access points for surrogate records. The massive amounts of data dealt with in

Rec stat c	Entered 19800501	Replaced 20021127134340.0	
Type z	**Upd status** a	**Enc lvl** n	**Source**
Roman |	**Ref status** a	**Mod rec**	**Name use** a
Govt agn |	**Auth status** a	**Subj** a	**Subj use** a
Series n	**Auth/ref** a	**Geo subd** n	**Ser use** b
Ser num n	**Name** a	**Subdiv tp** n	**Rules** c

010		n 80050515
040		DLC ‡c DLC ‡d DLC ‡d NIC ‡d DLC
100	0_	Confucius
400	0_	Konfuzius
400	0_	K'oeng Foe-tse
400	0_	Kung-foo-tsze
400	0_	Kung-Kew
400	0_	Kong-Fou-Tze
400	1_	K'ung, Ch'iu
400	0_	Kwan-Foo-Tze
400	0_	Kung-tse
400	0_	Konfut ̄s ̃ius
400	0_	Konfut ̄s ̃ï
400	1_	K'ung, Fu-tzu
400	0_	K'ung Fu-tzu
400	0_	Kongja
400	0_	Khong Tju
400	0_	Kōshi
400	0_	K'ung-tzu
400	0_	Kung Fu
400	0_	Kungfutse
400	0_	Confucio
400	0_	Kongzi
400	0_	Konfut ̄s ̃ï
670		Jakobs, P. M. Kritik an Lin Piao und Konfuzius, c1983: ‡b t.p. (Konfuzius)
670		Konfut ̄s ̃ï, 1993: ‡b t.p. verso (551-479 B.C.)
670		His Gespräche (Lun yü), 1910: ‡b t.p. (Kungfutse)
670		Gómez Farías, A. Confucio y Marfin Fierro, c1986.
670		Konfut ̄s ̃ï, 2001.

Fig. 8.12. Authority record for a name that has variants in each of several languages. (Source: OCLC Connexion, Authorities, record number 432385.)

libraries and archives have led to the development of the concept of authority control. Searchers for information need to be able to find works related to specific persons, corporate bodies, places, or other works. As the number of names and titles increases to a critical number, the ability to find specific names and titles and sort them out from similar and identical ones becomes very difficult without authority control. This is likely to be the next step for metadata. The building of the Semantic Web can be enhanced by linking authority files with biographical dictionaries, telephone directories, and official Web sites for named entities, as well as with the information packages created by those entities.

Most information packages have a subject content. It is often the subject content that is sought by users of retrieval tools. The next three chapters address the myriad ways of providing access to subject content.

NOTES

All URLs accessed June 2003.

1. The Getty, "Vocabulary Databases." Available: http://www.getty.edu/research/tools/vocabulary/.

2. Visual Resources Association Data Standards Committee, *VRA Core Categories, Version 3.0.* Last modified 20 February 2002. Available: http://www.vraweb.org/vracore3.htm.

3. DCMI Agents Working Group [Home page]. Last updated 1 November 2002. Available: http://www.dublincore.org/groups/agents/.

4. International Council on Archives, *ISAAR(CPF) International Standard Archival Authority Record for Corporate Bodies, Persons, and Families* (Ottawa: Secretariat of the ICA Ad Hoc Commission on Descriptive Standards, 1996). Available: http://www.ica.org/biblio/cds/isaar_eng.html.

5. Daniel V. Pitti, "Creator Description: Encoded Archival Context," in the proceedings of *International Conference [on] Authority Control: Definition and International Experiences*, Florence, Italy, 12–23 February 2003. Available: http://www.unifi.it/universita/biblioteche/ac/relazioni/pitti_eng.pdf.

6. Barbara B. Tillett, "A Taxonomy of Bibliographic Relationships," *Library Resources and Technial Services* 30, no. 2 (April 1991): 156.

7. For more in-depth treatments of bibliographic relationships, see: Elaine Svenonius, *The Intellectual Foundation of Information Organization* (Cambridge,

Mass.: The MIT Press, 2001), pp. 98–106; and Richard P. Smiraglia, *The Nature of "A Work": Implications for the Organization of Knowledge* (Lanham, Md.: Scarecrow Press, 2001), pp. 35–52.

8.   Smiraglia, *The Nature of "A Work,"* p. 42.

9.   Svenonius, *The Intellectual Foundation of Information Organization*, pp. 95–97.

10.   Martha M. Yee, "What Is a work?" [four-part series published in *Cataloging & Classification Quarterly* 19, nos. 1–2 (1994), and 20, nos. 1–2 (1995)]; Smiraglia, *The Nature of "A Work"*; International Federation of Library Associations and Institutions, IFLA Study Group, *Functional Requirements for Bibliographic Records (FRBR)* (München: Saur, 1998). Available: http://www.ifla.org/VII/s13/frbr/frbr.pdf or http://www.ifla.org/VII/s13/frbr/frbr.htm.

11.   For example, see the *FRBR* Web site of the OCLC Office of Research: "OCLC Research Activities and IFLA's *Functional Requirements for Bibliographic Records.*" OCLC, 2002. Available: http://www.oclc.org/research/projects/frbr/.

12.   A. H. Chaplin and Dorothy Anderson, eds. *Report/International Conference on Cataloguing Principles, Paris, 9th–18th October 1961* (London: IFLA International Office for UBC, 1981).

13.   Doris Hargrett Clack, ed., *The Making of a Code: The Issues Underlying AACR2* (Chicago: American Library Association, 1980).

14.   Michael Gorman, "AACR2: Main Themes," in Clack, *The Making of a Code*, p. 46.

15.   Richard P. Smiraglia, "Authority Control and the Extent of Derivative Bibliographic Relationships" (Ph.D. diss., University of Chicago, 1992).

16.   Joint Steering Committee for Revision of Anglo-American Cataloguing Rules, "Discussion List Archives," in *International Conference on the Principles and Future Development of AACR.* Last updated 11 February 2003. Available: http://www.nlc-bnc.ca/jsc/intlconf.html.

17.   See Chapter 5 for more about system design.

18.   ALA/ALCTS/CCS, Committee on Cataloging: Description and Access, *The Future of AACR.* Last updated April 2003. Available: http://www.libraries.psu.edu/tas/jca/ccda/future1.html.

19. International Federation of Library Associations and Institutions, IFLA Study Group, *Functional Requirements*. (See earlier discussion of *FRBR* in Chapter 7.)

20. Joint Steering Committee for Revision of Anglo-American Cataloguing Rules, "Discussion List Archives."

21. See also Wesley Simonton and Marilyn Jones McClaskey, *AACR2 and the Catalog: Theory, Structure, Changes* (Littleton, Colo.: Libraries Unlimited, 1981).

22. ALA/ALCTS/CCS, Committee on Cataloging: Description and Access, *Task Force on the Rule of Three: Report.* Available: http://www.libraries.psu.edu/tas/jca/ccda/tf-r3a.html.

23. ALA/ALCTS/CCS, Committee on Cataloging: Description and Access, *The Future of AACR.*

24. *Anglo-American Cataloguing Rules, Second Edition, 2002 Revision (AACR2R)* (Ottawa: Canadian Library Association; Chicago: American Library Association, 2002), pp. 313–314.

25. ALA/ALCTS/CCS, Committee on Cataloging: Description and Access, *The Future of AACR.*

26. In *AACR2*, p. 391, a footnote says that the authoritative alphabetic lists are to be lists of the "who's who" type, *not* telephone directories or similar compilations. However, given the ease of access to telephone directories, but not to more formal sources, for most catalogers, and given the similarity of result, this author can see no reason why *AACR2* maintains this restriction.

27. Smiraglia, *The Nature of "A Work."*

28. International Federation of Library Associations and Institutions, IFLA Study Group, *Functional Requirements.*

29. Barbara Tillett, "Authority Control: State of the Art and New Perspectives," in the proceedings of *International Conference [on] Authority Control: Definition and International Experiences*, Florence, Italy, 12–23 February 2003. Available: http://www.unifi.it/universita/biblioteche/ac/relazioni/tillett_eng.pdf.

30. International Federation of Library Associations and Institutions, *Guidelines for Authority Records and References*, 2nd ed. (München: K. G. Saur, 2001).

31. Open Archives Initiative [home page]. Available: http://www.openarchives.org/.

SUGGESTED READINGS

Barnhart, Linda. "Access Control Records: Prospects and Challenges." In *Authority Control in the 21st Century: An Invitational Conference: Proceedings*, sponsored by OCLC, March 31–April 1, 1996. Available: http://www.oclc.org/oclc/man/authconf/barnhart.htm.

Chan, Lois Mai. *Cataloging and Classification: An Introduction*. New York: McGraw-Hill, 1994. Chapter 4: "Choice of Access Points" (especially pp. 107–112) and Chapter 5: "Name Authority Control and Forms of Headings and Uniform Titles" (especially pp. 123–127).

The Getty. "Vocabulary Databases." Available: http://www.getty.edu/research/tools/vocabulary/.

Hagler, Ronald. *The Bibliographic Record and Information Technology*. 3rd ed. Chicago: American Library Association, 1997. Chapter 3: "Access Points" and Chapter 6: "Controlled-Vocabulary Name Access Points."

Holm, Liv Aasa. "Authority Control in an International Context in the New Environment." *International Cataloguing and Bibliographic Control* 28, no. 1 (January/March 1999): 11–12.

Hsieh-Yee, Ingrid. *Organizing Audiovisual and Electronic Resources for Access: A Cataloging Guide*. Englewood, Colo.: Libraries Unlimited, 2000.

Intner, Sheila S., and Jean Weihs. *Standard Cataloging for School and Public Libraries*. 3rd ed. Englewood, Colo.: Libraries Unlimited, 2001. Chapter 5: "Access."

Pitti, Daniel V. "Creator Description: Encoded Archival Context." In the proceedings of *International Conference [on] Authority Control: Definition and International Experiences*, Florence, Italy, 12–23 February 2003. Available: http://www.unifi.it/universita/biblioteche/ac/relazioni/pitti_eng.pdf.

Roe, Kathleen. "Enhanced Authority Control: Is It Time?" *Archivaria* 35 (Spring 1993): 119–129.

Smiraglia, Richard P. *The Nature of "A Work": Implications for the Organization of Knowledge*. Lanham, Md.: Scarecrow Press, 2001, pp. 35–52.

Svenonius, Elaine. *The Intellectual Foundation of Information Organization*. Cambridge, Mass.: The MIT Press, 2000. Chapter 3: "Bibliographic entities" and Chapter 6: "Work Languages."

Taylor, Arlene G. "Authority Control: Where It's Been and Where It's Going." In *Authority Control: Why It Matters.* Conference held at College of the Holy Cross, Worcester, MA, sponsored by the NELINET Cataloging and Technical Services Advisory Committee, November 1, 1999. Available: http://www.nelinet.net/conf/cts/cts99/taylor.htm.

————. *Wynar's Introduction to Cataloging and Classification.* 9th ed. with the assistance of David P. Miller. Englewood, Colo.: Libraries Unlimited, 2000. Chapter 6: "Choice of Access Points", Chapter 7: "Form of Headings for Names and Titles", and Chapter 18: "Authority Control."

Tillett, Barbara B. "Authority Control: State of the Art and New Perspectives." In the proceedings of *International Conference [on] Authority Control: Definition and International Experiences*, Florence, Italy, 12–23 February 2003. Available: http://www.unifi.it/universita/biblioteche/ac/relazioni/tillett_eng.pdf.

————. "Bibliographic Relationships." In *Relationships in the Organization of Knowledge*, edited by Carole A. Bean and Rebecca Green. Dordrecht: Kluwer Academic Publishers, 2001, pp. 9–35.

Vellucci, Sherry L. "Metadata and Authority Control." *Library Resources & Technical Services* 44, no. 1 (January 2000): 33–43.

Wilson, Patrick. "The Catalog as Access Mechanism: Background and Concepts." In *Foundations of Cataloging: A Sourcebook*, edited by Michael Carpenter and Elaine Svenonius. Littleton, Colo.: Libraries Unlimited, 1985, pp. 253–268.

CHAPTER 9
SUBJECT ANALYSIS

At an institute at OCLC in the late 1990s there was unanimous agreement among faculty and participants that access to electronic resources requires controlled vocabulary and classification.[1] Given the more recent attention to ontologies and taxonomies in relation to the Semantic Web, it appears that people still desire a controlled approach to subject access. So far, controlled vocabulary and classification cannot be assigned automatically with a satisfactory degree of accuracy. It is still necessary for humans to determine concepts that need controlled vocabulary terms assigned to them. The need for humans to do conceptual analysis is great; yet many persons who are currently working to apply index terms from a controlled vocabulary have only had instruction in assigning terminology from a particular list, and not instruction in the process of determining "aboutness."

Among the reasons for the failure of automated determination of aboutness is that a computer can determine what words are used in a document but cannot determine meaning; and it cannot even determine words for a nontextual item. A number of writers have pointed out that aboutness is not just in the words used but is highly dependent upon who is using a document and for what purpose. F. W. Lancaster goes so far as to say that the same item can be indexed differently in different information centers and that it *should* be indexed differently if the intended users are interested in the item for different reasons.[2]

Several questions are addressed in this chapter. They include: Why is the process of determining "aboutness" not simple and straightforward? What is the process for determining subject content? How is subject content determined for nontextual materials? How are concepts translated into index terms and classification notations?

PURPOSE OF SUBJECT ANALYSIS

Subject analysis is the part of creating metadata that deals with the conceptual analysis of an information package to determine what it is about and then using that "aboutness" to create controlled vocabulary terms and classification notations. In going through this process, the information organizer accomplishes the following purposes:

- Provides meaningful subject access to information packages through a retrieval tool.

- Provides for collocation of information packages of a like nature.

- Provides a logical location for similar information packages.

- Saves users' time.

If we look at Cutter's "objects" once again, we see that he considered subject access to be an important function of a catalog. Not only did he want a user to be able to find a known work on a certain subject, but he wanted a user to be able to find all the works that the library could offer on a particular subject.

CHALLENGES IN CONCEPTUAL ANALYSIS

Subject analysis deals with, first, the conceptual analysis of an information package. *Conceptual analysis* is the determination of what the intellectual content of an item is "about" and/or determining what an item "is." Second, subject analysis deals with translating the conceptual analysis into the conceptual framework of the classification or subject heading system being used by the cataloger, indexer, or classifier. This means that if one is using the Dewey Decimal Classification (DDC), for example, one must place the concept in a hierarchy starting with one of DDC's top ten categories. Or if one is using *Library of Congress Subject Headings (LCSH)*, one must conceptualize a sentence concerning what the information package is "about," and then make note (physically or mentally) of terms from the sentence that need to be searched in *LCSH* to choose the controlled vocabulary terms to express the concept. Following these conceptual steps, the framework must be translated into the specific classificatory symbols or specific terminology used in the classification or controlled vocabulary system. That is, at this step, one would assign terms from a controlled vocabulary such as *LCSH* or would assign classification notation(s) from a classification schedule such as DDC.

D. W. Langridge, too, views the subject analysis process as a series of discrete activities.[3] He stresses that the conceptual analysis must be independent of any particular classification scheme or controlled vocabulary and that the analysis should be written down so as to avoid muddled notions of aboutness.[4] In addition to examining the various parts of the text, he states that the subject analyzer must keep in mind three basic questions in order to determine the aboutness of an information package.

- What is it?

- What is it for?

- What is it about?[5]

The first question is answered by the fundamental forms (or categories) of knowledge—Is it history? Is it science? Is it philosophy? Langridge identifies twelve distinct forms of knowledge: philosophy, natural science, technology, human science, social practice, history, moral knowledge, religion, art, criticism, personal experience, and prolegomena (logic, mathematics, grammar—the foundations of knowledge). Looking at the disciplines may answer the second question. Is this for a veterinarian? Is it for a zoologist? Is it for a farmer? Langridge sees disciplines as ever-evolving areas of interest or specialization falling under the twelve forms of knowledge. The third question is answered by the topics. Topics are everyday phenomena that we perceive. Langridge understands they are not specific to any one form of knowledge or discipline. Langridge, in his approach to subject analysis, also includes examining the nature of the text (bibliographic structures and mediums) and the nature of the thought (issues of point of view, type of writing, audience, and intellectual level).

Determining what an information package is about can be difficult. Patrick Wilson has discussed the difficulty imposed upon us starting with Cutter, whose second function of a catalog, in part, was that it should show what a library has on a given subject. Wilson has suggested that part of the problem is that we take Cutter's statement to mean that there is an obvious subject in every information package and that we should be able to identify it as *the* subject. In fact a subject can have many facets and there may not be just one thing to mention in response to the question: "What is it about?"[6]

Although some information packages seem to have an easily determined subject, it may not really be so easy. A work titled *History of Sociology* is about the discipline of sociology; but it is more specifically about sociology from a historical perspective while not being about the discipline of history. This distinction has a certain subtlety that is learned through education in our present-day Western tradition. It is possible that in another place and time, history would be considered to be the major subject of anything historical, regardless of the specific topic.

Cultural Differences

An understanding of the place of one's culture as well as one's education in determining subject matter is also important. George Lakoff has written about the research of Brent Berlin and Paul Kay on the understanding of color depending upon one's language. They found that there are eleven basic color categories in English, but in some other languages there are fewer basic color categories. In languages that have only two basic color terms, the terms are the equivalent of *black* and *white,* or *cool* and *warm.* The effects upon subject analysis of growing up in different cultures with different languages, then, means that persons from different places cannot perceive reality in exactly the same way.[7]

Another example is provided by Langridge. He comments upon the unconscious effect that must occur in the mind of a person used to the arrangement of the library in the People's University of China, where all knowledge is divided into three groups: theory of knowledge, knowledge of the class struggle, and knowledge of the productive struggle.[8] Although Western cultural differences are perhaps not so different as those between Western and non-Western, different indexers can expect to see things differently depending upon such things as educational background and cultural upbringing.

Differences in Methods Used

Wilson has described some of the methods that people use to come to their own understanding of what a work is about.[9] Wilson did not name these methods himself. The names used here have been supplied by the author. The first might be called the *purposive method.* One tries to determine what the author's aim or purpose is. If the creator of the information package gives a statement of purpose, then we can presume to know what the work is "about." But some creators give no such statement, and others seem to aim at several things at once.

Wilson's second method of deciding what a work is about might be called the *figure-ground method*. Using this method, one tries to determine a central figure that stands out from the background of the rest of the information package. However, what stands out depends on the observer of the package as well as on its creator. What catches one's interest is not necessarily the same from person to person, and may not even be the same for the same person a few weeks later.

Wilson's third method is the *objective method* (the method, by the way, used in most attempts to have computers do conceptual analysis). One tries to be objective by counting references to various items to determine which one vastly outnumbers the others. Unfortunately, an item constantly referred to might be a background item (e.g., Germany in a work about World War II). It is also possible that the concept that is central to the "aboutness" might not ever be expressed concretely. Wilson gives the example of a work being about a person's political career, but those words are never used in the work. Lourdes Collantes found that when people were asked to read abstracts and then write down subject words or phrases that they believed conveyed the meaning in the abstracts, 8 percent of the readers used words that did not appear anywhere in the abstract.[10]

The last of Wilson's methods is that of *appealing to unity or to rules of selection and rejection*. When using this method, one tries to determine what holds the work together, what cohesiveness there is, and what has been said (selection) and not said (rejection). Again, the observer of the information package has to be objective and also has to know quite a lot about the subject in order to know what was rejected. There may be several ways in which the work can appear to be unified; and creators do not always reach the ideal of a completely unified presentation.

As this discussion indicates, there seems to be no one correct way to determine "aboutness." One can use any or all of these methods, but the different methods will not necessarily lead to the same result. If they give the same result, as they often could, it would appear that *the* subject has been identified. However, a single person might arrive at three or four different subjects using the different methods, and several persons might arrive at different results using the same method.

Consistency

Evidence of the difficulty in determining "aboutness" consistently is found in a number of studies in which people have been asked to give terminology they would use to search for specific items. For example, in a 1954 study by Oliver Lilley, 340 students looked at six books and suggested an average of sixty-two different terms for each book.[11] In the 1992 study already mentioned, Collantes found "an average of 25.6 [topical] names per object or concept."[12] Please note that *this is not a failure of controlled vocabulary.* It is a failure of individuals to determine the same "aboutness" in a document or to come up with the same natural language in cases where the same "aboutness" has been determined. There is evidence that catalogers using the same controlled vocabulary and the same rules for it will produce consistent subject headings, as long as they have the same conceptual analysis to draw upon.[13]

Langridge does not agree that there may be a variety of possible answers to the question "What is it about?" He believes that inconsistencies are the result of confusing this question with the question "What is it for?"[14] Even if one cannot agree with his assessment that determining "What is it about?" is no problem, his "What is it for?" question provides a valuable insight. For example, Richard W. Unger's *The Art of Medieval Technology: Images of Noah the Shipbuilder*[15] appears at first glance to be about Noah and the Ark. However, upon examination of the author's purpose, the table of contents, and the captions with the illustrations, one learns that the work is really about changes in the techniques used in shipbuilding in the Middle Ages. Artists' depictions of Noah building the Ark changed as the techniques changed through the centuries.

Another example is found in the title *History of Sociology,* mentioned earlier. In our culture we treat its aboutness as sociology, treated from the perspective of history. The topic of a resource titled *Introduction to Sociology* is also sociology, but these two resources would look very different. A user looking for one of these treatments probably would not be happy with the other. Answering the "What is it for?" question helps to separate these two treatments.

Nontextual Information

Determination of topics of nontextual information packages is even less clear-cut than for textual resources. Several levels of conceptual analysis may be attempted. Barnett has listed three levels:

1. identification of a concept or combination of concepts representing topical coverage,

2. pre-iconographic or generic identification and enumeration of objects and scenes represented,

3. identification of interpretive thematic or iconographic signif-
    icance associated with objects and scenes depicted.[16]

With art works it is perhaps easiest to enumerate objects and
scenes represented. It may also be possible to identify a subject concept
(e.g., a depiction of a battle scene) and to determine from a work's title a
specific instance of the concept (e.g., the Battle of Gettysburg). With musical works it is much harder to identify concepts or to enumerate what is
represented. If one wants true conceptual analysis of nontextual information packages, such analysis usually must be at the interpretive thematic
level. It is fairly easy to describe how objects look, but identification of
interpretive thematic or iconographic significance for any nontextual information packages requires special study and training.

SUBJECT ANALYSIS PROCESS

A first step in conceptual analysis is to examine the parts of the
information package that stand out.[17] In many instances this information
will be found in the information packages themselves, but in other instances
it will be found in accompanying materials (e.g., user manuals, containers,
inserts from CD-ROM cases, labels, etc.). There are also outside sources
such as publishers' announcements.

Somewhat different techniques have to be used for information
packages that contain text versus information packages that contain nontextual information. Concentrating first on the information packages that
contain text, the following parts should be considered:

- title and subtitle
  A title can be helpful in giving an immediate impres-
  sion of the topic of a document, but a title can also be
  misleading. The title of the Web page *Proceedings of the
  OCLC Internet Cataloging Colloquium*[18] is quite straightforward. On the other hand, the title *A Compendium of
  Tiddlywinks Perversions*[19] is not so clear, and is not assisted by its other title information, *Alleghany Airlines
  Book Club Presents.* Another example is *What the Thunder
  Said,*[20] which turns out to be a Web site devoted to the
  life and works of T. S. Eliot.

- table of contents
  A list of contents can help clarify the topic and identify
  subtopics. A list of contents can be especially helpful

for items that are collections of articles, papers, and the like, by different authors. The table of contents for the *Proceedings of the OCLC Internet Cataloging Colloquium*[21] shows the variety of specific topics covered as well as different levels of specificity (see Figure 9.1).

- introduction, or equivalent
  An introduction often is an aid in determining the author's plan or objective and may serve to indicate an author's point of view. The introduction to *JGarden: The Japanese Garden Database,*[22] for example, explains that this is not just descriptions of the gardens, but draws upon literature, paintings, images, and the like, to provide information "on the history, construction, materiality, people, language, patterns, and processes by which these gardens were constructed."

- index terms, words, or phrases that are printed in typeface different from the rest; hyperlinks; abstract if provided; and others
  These elements provide confirmation or contradiction of impressions gained from examination of the title, table of contents, introduction, and the like. A back-of-the-book index can show what topics are given the most attention by showing the number of pages devoted to each.

- illustrations, diagrams, tables, captions
  Illustrations and their captions are particularly important in assessing the subjects in fields such as art, where, in many cases, illustrations make up the vast majority of the content and therefore must be examined in order to determine "aboutness." The captions for illustrations are often quite descriptive of subject content.

For nontextual information, one has to examine the object, picture, or other representation, itself. Some such information packages are manufactured and include accompanying materials such as boxes with text, instruction sheets, labels, and the like. Electronic nontangible information packages that are basically pictures or other forms of artistic work quite often have captions that explain something about them in text form. For

Proceedings of the OCLC Internet Cataloging Colloquium

San Antonio, Texas
January 19, 1996

Introduction

Field Reports

- The "Ambivalent" Library, Mark Watson, University of Oregon
- Does It Really Matter?: The Choice of Format, Order of Note Fields, and Specifics of 856, Jackie Shieh, University of Virginia Library
- Access Information on the Internet: A Feasibility Study of MARC Formats and AACR2, Amanda Xu, MIT Libraries

Position Papers

- Using Library Classification Schemes for Internet Resources, Diane Vizine-Goetz, OCLC
- Cyberstacks, Gerry McKiernan, Iowa State University
- The Traditional Library and the National Information Infrastructure, Vianne T. Sha, Timothy B. Patrick, Thomas R. Kochtanek, University of Missouri-Columbia
- Access to Networked Documents. Catalogs? Search Engines? Both? Arlene G. Taylor and Patrice Clemson, University of Pittsburgh
- Catalogers and the Creation of Metadata Systems : A Collaborative Vision at the University of Michigan, Kevin Butterfield, University of Michigan
- Modifying Cataloging Practice and OCLC Infrastructure for Effective Organization of Internet Resources, Ingrid Hsieh-Yee, Catholic University of America

ISBN 1-55653-219-9

Fig. 9.1. Web page table of contents for the proceedings of a conference in which the papers are about many different subtopics of the main theme. (Source: http://www.oclc.org/oclc/man/colloq/toc.htm.)

individual works or objects with no accompanying text, however, one must examine the items themselves, and translating ideas into words can be difficult.

Exhaustivity

As one examines documents for subject content, one must have a clear idea about the level of exhaustivity that is required. Exhaustivity is the number of concepts that will be considered in the conceptual framework of the system. The number of concepts any given agency's catalogers/indexers will assign often is guided by local policy. A. G. Brown identifies two basic degrees of exhaustivity: depth indexing and summarization.[23] Depth indexing aims to extract all the main concepts dealt with in an information resource, recognizing many subtopics and subthemes. Summarization identifies only a dominant, overall subject of the item, recognizing only concepts embodied in the main theme.

In library cataloging, subject analysis has traditionally been carried out at the summarization level, reserving depth indexing for other enterprises such as periodical indexes. That is, in the cataloging of books and serials in libraries, the cataloger generally has attempted to find the one overall subject concept that encompasses the whole item. Depth indexing has traditionally been reserved for parts of items (e.g., articles in journals, chapters in books) and has usually been done by commercial indexing enterprises. In the case of an electronic serial such as the *Journal of Statistics Education*,[24] the subject at the summarization level can be no more in depth than "education about statistics," even though the subjects of individual articles are much more specific. There is no reason, however, that "whole items" cannot be indexed more exhaustively. At the summarization level, *Proceedings of the OCLC Internet Cataloging Colloquium* would be about cataloging of Internet resources (see again Figure 9.1). A look at the table of contents, however, shows that depth indexing at another level would allow indexing of various concepts involved in the cataloging of Internet resources, such as classification of the Internet, metadata, search engines, and the like.

It should be pointed out that many books have extensive back-of-the-book indexes, and this has been one of the justifications for subject indexing at the summarization level. That is, there is a difference in degree between "document retrieval" and "information retrieval" (see Figure 9.2). Summarization allows for document retrieval, after which many users use a document's internal index (which, in electronic resource terms, may mean the word search capability) to retrieve the relevant information they need

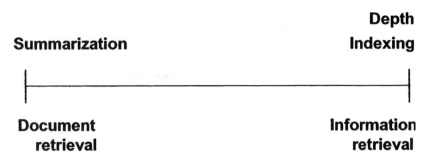

Fig. 9.2. Illustration of the concept that summarization leads to document retrieval and depth indexing leads to information retrieval. The line moves gradually from summarization to depth indexing, and it is possible to have a subject analysis system that is halfway between the two extremes.

from the document. Depth indexing, however, allows retrieval at a much more specific level, even to the retrieval of sections or paragraphs in a document.

Exhaustivity affects both precision and recall in retrieval. Precision is the measurement of how many of the documents retrieved are relevant. Recall is the measurement of how many of the relevant documents in a system are actually retrieved. Depth indexing is likely to increase precision because more specific terminology is used. Summarization is likely to increase recall because the search terms are broader and more sweeping in their application of terminology.

The summarization approach is very useful in retrieving tangible resources (e.g., CD-ROMs, videocassettes, print journals, etc.). As we do more and more indexing of intangible electronic resources (e.g., Web sites), we will have to think carefully about summarization versus depth indexing. Search engines do the ultimate "depth indexing." Often, the occurrence of a word anywhere in a Web site means the Web site will be retrieved by a search on that word, whether or not the word reflects any topic covered in the information package. However, because this approach is based on appearance of words, rather than on the words having the meaning sought, it increases recall while greatly decreasing precision.

In addition to deciding the level of indexing, we face the problem of deciding what is an analyzable unit.[25] Traditionally, as already stated, whole items have been analyzable units in libraries, collections have been analyzable units in archives, and articles in journals have been analyzable units for commercial indexing enterprises (along with individual poems, stories, or essays published in collections). On the Internet there is so far no definition for an analyzable unit. Should it be the whole electronic journal; individual issues of that journal; the whole Web site (i.e., a "home" page along with all links located and controlled at that site); or individual pieces of a Web site? Once we've decided that, we have to rethink whether our users need summarization-level subject headings or depth indexing vocabulary for the analyzable unit.

Identification of Concepts

Different types of concepts can be used as subjects of information packages. The types discussed in this section are:

- topics
- names
  - persons
  - corporate bodies
  - geographic areas
  - other named entities (e.g., buildings, architectural sites, etc.)
- time periods
- form

Topics Used as Subject Concepts

Most people think of topical terms when asked to identify the subject for which they seek information. Topics can be concrete or abstract concepts. A topic represents a principle object of attention in a text or a nontextual composition, or it can represent a theme running through an information package.

Names Used as Subject Concepts

In the process of determining what a document is about, it may be found that the topic, or one aspect of the topic, is a person, a corporate body, a geographic area, or some other named entity.

Persons. An individual person is the topic of a Web site or other resource that is biographical or that covers aspects of a person's career (e.g., the aforementioned site dedicated to T. S. Eliot). Such a work is also, in a sense, about one representative of a group of persons (e.g., literary writers). The Library of Congress in applying the *Library of Congress Subject Headings (LCSH),* for example, has the policy of making a subject heading for the group, as well as for the person, on the assumption that if an information seeker wants to learn about, let's say, "literary writers," then a site about one such person may be of use.

Corporate bodies. A corporate body may be the topic of an information package about an entity such as an oil company or a library. There are also entities whose names resemble corporate body names, but they are not the same. A corporate body is an organization or group of persons who are identified by a name and who act as an entity. Sometimes such bodies have the same name as the building they work in. This is often true of churches, for example, and one then has to be certain whether the building or the corporate group is the topic of the work.

Geographic names. Geographic names can take different roles in the determination of subject content. In some cases a document may actually be about a specific place, as, for example, something about the history and growth of Pittsburgh, Pennsylvania. However, much of the time, the geographic area provides a context for the topical content of the work, as in a work about the projects and life of architect Julia Morgan, who did virtually all of her work in California. Falling between these extremes is the case where the geographic area is the topic of the topic. An example is the exhibition catalog *"A Sweet Foretaste of Heaven": Artists in the White Mountains, 1830–1930.*[26] The exhibition consisted of landscape paintings of the White Mountains of New Hampshire.

Other named entities. Some named entities resemble both corporate names and geographic names, but are neither. Such entities as named buildings, cemeteries, bridges, and archaeological sites fall into this category. An example is the archaeological site name Megiddo (Extinct city).

Chronological Elements as Subject Concepts

The time period can be an important aspect of the subject content of information packages. Time periods limit the coverage of the topic and therefore dictate content in subtle ways. For example, information packages about computer access to information in the 1970s will not be likely to include information about the World Wide Web or about SGML.

Time can be expressed in a number of ways. Named periods (e.g.,

World War II) and styles (e.g., Renaissance) often act as surrogates to chronology. These are of particular importance in the fields of art, architecture, music, and literature, but they have not been particularly well handled by controlled vocabularies or by the MARC format. Only specific dates or date ranges are usually treated separately. Named periods and styles generally have been treated as topical information.

The Concept of Form as Subject

The final step in the conceptual analysis process is the identification of the form of the information package being analyzed or of important parts of that information package. *Form* is not strictly a subject feature. According to Langridge:

> There remain a number of very important characteristics requiring identification which have always been treated as part of the process of subject analysis. I shall refer to these as formal characteristics to distinguish them from the real subject features. Though none of these formal elements alters the subject of a document, some of them can make a considerable difference to its treatment or presentation.[27]

Form is a concept that has been associated with subject analysis from the inception of the idea that books could be entered in catalogs and placed on shelves according to the category they belonged to. Early categories included such forms as encyclopedias, biographies, and histories, as well as subjects such as chemistry and religion. Later, as subject headings evolved to mean what an item is about instead of a category to which the book belonged, the idea of form remained as part of the subject analysis process. Because it was often difficult to separate the ideas of "aboutness" from "form," as in the case of "history," which seems to incorporate elements of both, the concept of form has only recently begun to be treated differently in surrogate records.

In an effort to aid in the process of separating the concept of form from the concept of subject, the Subject Analysis Committee of the American Library Association (ALA) devised a definition for form. The definition was officially approved by appropriate ALA bodies in January 1993:

Form data are those terms and phrases that designate specific kinds or genres of materials. Materials designated with these terms or phrases may be determined by an examination of:

> their physical character (e.g., videocassettes, photographs, maps, broadsides)

> the particular type of data that they contain (e.g., bibliographies, questionnaires, statistics)

> the arrangement of information within them (e.g., diaries, outlines, indexes)

> the style, technique, purpose, or intended audience (e.g., drama, romances, cartoons, commercials, popular works) or a combination of the above (e.g., scores)

A single term may be modified by other terms, in which case the whole phrase is considered to be form data (e.g., aerial photographs, French dictionaries, conversation and phrase books, wind ensemble suites, telephone directories, vellum bound books, science fiction).[28]

Separating form from subject has become increasingly important as the organizing world has become more attuned to organizing information that is not in textual form. Identification of form in the area of music has always been very important and has been accommodated in the past by treating it as subject. Now more information seekers are looking for other kinds of information forms (e.g., chalk drawings, digital maps, sculpture reproductions, etc.). By separating form from subject, it is possible to take advantage of system design that allows searching for forms of information. More recent metadata schemas have categories separate from "subject" that are defined specifically for this concept (e.g., "Resource type" and "Format" in the Dublin Core; "Type" and "Material" in the VRA Core Categories).

TRANSLATING CONCEPTS INTO INDEX TERMS

Answering a series of questions, either formally or informally, can help one go through the subject analysis process quickly. A sample set of questions and an example is found in the book's appendix.

Once the conceptual analysis is complete, the concepts identified must be translated into the controlled vocabulary being used. Finishing a sentence that begins, "This information package is about . . . ," can be helpful. Then terms from that sentence can be identified for searching in the controlled vocabulary. Specific rules for using controlled vocabularies are found in their introductions, as well as, in some cases, manuals that accompany them.

TRANSLATING CONCEPTS INTO CLASSIFICATION NOTATIONS

In order to translate a conceptual analysis into classification notations, it is necessary to understand the hierarchy or the facets of the classification scheme that is to be used. If a hierarchical scheme is used, it is helpful to determine the discipline into which the concept falls. For example, a history of a country is probably considered to fall within the "history" discipline, while a history of chemistry is thought to fall within the broad area of science in a discipline for "chemistry." Creating a hierarchical string for discipline, subdiscipline, topic within discipline, accompanied by concepts of treatment, place, time, and form is helpful in translating a conceptual analysis into a hierarchical classification. Using a faceted classification is much like choosing subject terms from a controlled vocabulary that precoordinates several terms into a subject heading string. Notations for separate facets must be found in the classification and then must be put together according to the rules for the scheme.

CONCLUSION

This chapter has discussed the process of subject analysis that precedes the use of specific tools for assigning controlled vocabulary and classification notations. Before being able to make the best use of the specific tools, however, it is helpful to understand controlled vocabularies and classification schemes in general. The following two chapters address these issues.

NOTES

All URLs accessed July 2003.

1. OCLC Institute, "Knowledge Access Management: Tools and Concepts

for Next Generation Catalogers," institute held 17–19 November 1997, Dublin, Ohio. (Observations of author, who was in attendance.)

2. F. W. Lancaster, *Indexing and Abstracting in Theory and Practice*, 3rd ed. (Champaign, Ill.: University of Illinois, Graduate School of Library and Information Science, 2003), p. 9.

3. D. W. Langridge, *Subject Analysis: Principles and Procedures* (London: Bowker-Saur, 1989), pp. 73–98, 136.

4. Ibid., p. 57.

5. Ibid., pp. 8–10.

6. Patrick Wilson, "Subjects and the Sense of Position," in *Two Kinds of Power: An Essay on Bibliographical Control* (Berkeley: University of California Press, 1968), pp. 69–92. Also reprinted in *Theory of Subject Analysis: A Sourcebook*, eds. Lois Mai Chan, Phyllis A. Richmond, and Elaine Svenonius (Littleton, Colo.: Libraries Unlimited, 1985), pp. 309–320.

7. George Lakoff, *Women, Fire, and Dangerous Things: What Categories Reveal About the Mind* (Chicago: University of Chicago Press, 1987), pp. 24–26.

8. Langridge, *Subject Analysis*, p. 4.

9. Wilson, "Subjects and the Sense of Position," pp. 78–88.

10. Lourdes Y. Collantes, "Agreement in Naming Objects and Concepts for Information Retrieval" (Ph.D. diss., Rutgers University, 1992), p. 154.

11. Oliver L. Lilley, "Evaluation of the Subject Catalog: Criticisms and a Proposal," *American Documentation* 5, no. 2 (1954): 41–60.

12. Collantes, "Agreement in Naming Objects," p. 154.

13. For example: Regene C. Ross, Chair, Task Force on Copy Cataloging, *Report of the Task Force on Copy Cataloging*, May 12, 1993, cited by Thomas Mann, in "'Cataloging Must Change!' and Indexer Consistency Studies: Misreading the Evidence at Our Peril," *Cataloging & Classification Quarterly* 23, nos. 3/4 (1997): 37–38.

14. Langridge, *Subject Analysis*, p. 9.

15. Richard W. Unger, *The Art of Medieval Technology: Images of Noah the Shipbuilder* (New Brunswick, N.J.: Rutgers University Press, 1991).

16. Patricia J. Barnett, "Indexing with the *AAT*," in *Guide to Indexing and Cataloging with the Art & Architecture Thesaurus*, eds. Toni Petersen and Patricia J. Barnett (New York: Oxford University Press, 1994), pp. 33–40.

17.   Some of this section appeared in an earlier form in Arlene G. Taylor, "Books and Other Bibliographic Materials," in *Guide to Indexing and Cataloging with the Art & Architecture Thesaurus*, eds. Toni Petersen and Patricia J. Barnett (New York: Oxford University Press, 1994), pp. 101–119.

18.   Available: http://www.oclc.org/oclc/man/colloq/toc.htm.

19.   Available: http://www.tiddlywinks.org/how_to_play/rules/english/alle ghany/.

20.   Available: http://www.camdenfamily.com/thunder/.

21.   Available: http://www.oclc.org/oclc/man/colloq/toc.htm.

22.   Available: http://www.jgarden.org/default.asp.

23.   A. G. Brown, in collaboration with D. W. Langridge and J. Mills, *An Introduction to Subject Indexing*, 2nd ed. (London: Bingley, 1982), frames 48, 51.

24.   Available: http://www.amstat.org/publications/jse/.

25.   For more about what units are to be analyzed, see Chapter 7.

26.   *"A Sweet Foretaste of Heaven": Artists in the White Mountains, 1830–1930*, with essays by Robert L. McGrath and Barbara J. MacAdam (Hanover, N.H.: Hood Museum of Art, 1988).

27.   Langridge, *Subject Analysis*, p. 45.

28.   American Library Association, Association for Library Collections and Technical Services, Subject Analysis Committee, *Definition of Form Data*, January 1993. Available: http://www.pitt.edu/~agtaylor/ala/form-def.htm.

SUGGESTED READINGS

Bates, Marcia J. "Subject Access in Online Catalogs: A Design Model." *Journal of the American Society for Information Science* 37, no. 6 (1986): 357–376.

Cleveland, Donald B., and Ana D. Cleveland. *Introduction to Indexing and Abstracting*. 3rd ed. Englewood, Colo.: Libraries Unlimited, 2001. Chapter 4: "Vocabulary Control", Chapter 6: "The Indexing Process", and Chapter 7: "The Abstracting Process."

Dooley, Jackie M. "Subject Indexing in Context." *American Archivist* 55, no. 2 (Spring 1992): 344–354.

Lakoff, George. *Women, Fire, and Dangerous Things: What Categories Reveal about the Mind.* Chicago: University of Chicago Press, 1987. Part I: "Categories and Cognitive Models."

Lancaster, F. W. *Indexing and Abstracting in Theory and Practice.* 3rd ed. Champaign: University of Illinois, Graduate School of Library and Information Science, 2003. Chapter 2: "Indexing Principles" and Chapter 7: "Abstracts: Types and Functions."

————. *Vocabulary Control For Information Retrieval.* 2nd ed. Arlington, Va.: Information Resources Press, 1986. Chapter 1: "Why Vocabulary Control?"

Langridge, D. W. *Subject Analysis: Principles and Procedures.* London: Bowker-Saur, 1989. Chapter 5: "Summarization", Chapter 6: "Summarizing in Practice", and Appendix 2: "The Forms of Knowledge."

Pettee, Julia. "The Subject Approach to Books and the Development of the Dictionary Catalog." In *Theory of Subject Analysis: A Sourcebook,* edited by Lois Mai Chan, Phyllis A. Richmond, and Elaine Svenonius. Littleton, Colo.: Libraries Unlimited, 1985, pp. 94–98.

Taylor, Arlene G. "On the Subject of Subjects." *Journal of Academic Librarianship* 21, no. 6 (November 1995): 484–491.

————. *Wynar's Introduction to Cataloging and Classification.* 9th ed., with the assistance of David P. Miller. Englewood, Colo.: Libraries Unlimited, 2000. Chapter 8: "Subject Arrangement of Library Materials."

Weinberg, Bella Hass. "Exhaustivity of Indexes: Books, Journals, and Electronic Full Text." *Key Words* 7, no. 5 (September/October 1999): 1, 6–19.

Wellish, Hans H. "Aboutness and Selection of Topics." *Key Words* 4, no. 2 (March/April 1996): 7–9.

Wilson, Patrick. *Two Kinds of Power: An Essay on Bibliographical Control.* Berkeley: University of California Press, 1968. Chapter 5: "Subjects and the Sense of Position." Reprinted in *Theory of Subject Analysis: A Sourcebook,* edited by Lois Mai Chan, Phyllis A. Richmond, and Elaine Svenonius. Littleton, Colo.: Libraries Unlimited, 1985, pp. 309–320.

CHAPTER 10

SYSTEMS FOR VOCABULARY CONTROL

Subject approaches in the electronic age have become a major way of finding information. Search engines have tried to fill the void on the Internet, yet users become frustrated with the thousands of "hits" from keyword searches. With the massive increase in availability of recorded information it becomes more and more evident that keyword searching alone will not suffice. Virtually every word in the English language has more than one meaning or sense, and many of those senses have more than one nuance; many words can be used as nouns, verbs, adjectives, or adverbs. Search systems that purport to allow the user to use "natural language" cannot yet successfully distinguish among meanings or parts of speech in very large general systems, although progress has been made in narrow subject areas.

In addition, there is evidence that people writing about the same concepts often do not use the same words to express them, and people searching for the same concept do not think of the same words to search for it. Many of the myriad studies of "interindexer consistency" have asked participants to think up words in their heads, not to take vocabulary from a list; therefore, although these studies have been used by some authors to "prove" that subject indexing is worth very little because indexers are "inconsistent," what the studies really show is that people do not think of the same terms to express the same concept. Thomas Mann has given an excellent analysis of some interindexer consistency studies that support these observations.[1] The clear implication is that controlled vocabulary is needed to reconcile all the various possible words that can be used to express a concept and to differentiate among all the possible meanings that can be attached to certain words.

Several questions are addressed in this chapter. They include: How is subject content expressed verbally in surrogate/metadata records? How should an indexing vocabulary be structured? Is a controlled indexing vocabulary necessary or can Natural Language Processing (NLP) be used instead? How do ontologies assist in finding subject content? How is keyword searching used for finding subject content?

CONTROLLED VOCABULARY CHALLENGES

In the process of creating a controlled vocabulary there are certain verbal difficulties that must be dealt with. An understanding of these problems can enhance one's ability to use a particular existing controlled vocabulary.

Specific vs. General Terms

The level of specificity must be decided at the outset of establishing a controlled vocabulary. Various lists may have different thresholds for how specific the terminology will be. "Cats" is not as specific as "Cat breeds." "Cat breeds" is not as specific as "Siamese cats." "Siamese cats" is not as specific as "Bluepoint Siamese cats." In *Library of Congress Subject Headings (LCSH),* for example, the most specific term is "Siamese cats"; in *Sears List of Subject Headings (Sears)* the most specific term is "Cats," although an instruction is given that, if needed, a term for a specific breed of cat may be created.

To some extent the decision on this matter is a function of the type of users who are intended to use the list, and upon the nature of the information packages that are to be assigned terms from the list. If the collection has mainly general kinds of information, then "Cats" is probably sufficient, even to cover a few more specific items. If the users are children likely to be looking for general kinds of information, then again "Cats" is probably sufficient as the most specific level.

Synonymous Concepts

The English language rarely has absolutely true synonyms—that is, situations where two words mean the same thing and have no variations in nuance. However, there are multitudes of synonymous words and phrases that mean so close to the same thing that they can be interchanged for each other. As stated by Hans Wellish, "Authors have, therefore, great freedom in the choice of terms and may use several words for the same concept, which may be admirable from the point of view of style, but would be disastrous when transferred unchanged to an index."[2] These are the terms that make keyword searching so tricky and frustrating.

In the creation of a controlled vocabulary it is necessary to identify all the synonymous terms that should be brought together under one term. Do "attire," "dress," and "clothing" mean the same thing? If not exactly the same, or if they have different nuances, are the differences important enough to warrant separate vocabulary terms for them? Determination should take into account which term is best known to the intended user; but with regional, national, and international differences in English-language usage, a decision may have to be arbitrary.

Word Form for One-Word Terms

Words in English often have more than one form that can mean the same thing (e.g., "clothing" and "clothes"). Also, language evolves, and as it does, a concept has a tendency to be expressed first as two words, then as a hyphenated word, then as one word (e.g., "on line," "on-line," "online"). Sometimes all three forms appear in use at the same time. British and American spellings give us another case of word form difference (e.g., "catalogue" and "catalog"). Prefixes to a word can create a word with a different meaning, but in some cases, where the meaning is opposite, it would not make sense to use both terms in the controlled vocabulary because one of the concepts can never be discussed without the other (e.g., "armament" and "disarmament"; "equality" and "inequality").

A major word form difference is singular versus plural. There is no rule on which form to use. Most of the time the plural will have the broadest coverage (e.g., "videocassettes" rather than "videocassette"); but at times the singular is broader (e.g., "apple" can apply to both the fruit and the tree; "apples" refers only to the fruit). Sometimes the singular and the plural forms of a word have different meanings (e.g., in *LCSH* "art" refers specifically to visual art; "arts" refers to various subdisciplines including visual arts, literature, and the performing arts).

Sequence and Form for Multiword Terms and Phrases

In some controlled vocabularies there are terms and phrases made up of two or more words. Some of these are modified nouns (e.g., "Environmental education"); others are phrases with conjunctions or prepositions (e.g., "Information theory in biology"); and a third group has qualifiers added in parentheses (see discussion below). A problem in constructing such terminology in a controlled way is being consistent in the order and form of the individual words used. For example, "Energy conservation" and "Conservation of energy resources" mean the same thing. The first phrase places the concept with other headings beginning with the word "energy"; the second phrase puts the concept with other things having to do with conservation. If the list creates such phrases, it must be certain to have references from every possible construction of the phrase—referring from them to the construction that was chosen.

Some controlled vocabularies (notably *LCSH*) present some multiword terms and phrases in inverted order (e.g., "Education, Bilingual"; "Asylum, Right of"). Much of this was done in the past in order to collocate a group of headings on a broad concept with subconcepts arranged alphabetically below it. Thus, instead of "Bilingual education" being found in "B" and "Higher education" being found in "H," both were found in "E" as "Education, Bilingual" and "Education, Higher."

Research has shown that few searchers think of such phrases in inverted order, but look for them in direct order. In *LCSH* few new inverted forms are being established, but already-established ones still exist. One therefore finds inconsistencies such as "Moral education" and "Medical education" juxtaposed with "Education, Humanistic" and "Education, Greek."

Homographs and Homophones

Homographs are words that look the same but have very different meanings. "Mercury" can be a liquid metal, a planet, a car, or a Roman god; "bridge" can be a game, a structure spanning a chasm, or a dental device. In a controlled vocabulary there must be some way to differentiate among the various meanings. Two common ways are either to use qualifiers (see discussion below) or to choose a synonym for the homograph to use as the preferred term.

Homographs may or may not be pronounced the same (e.g., "mare" pronounced as one syllable with a silent *e* is a mature female horse; "mare" pronounced as two syllables is a large, dark area on the moon [possibly derived from the Italian *mare,* meaning "sea"]). Traditionally, the fact of different pronunciation did not matter in controlled vocabulary, because the vocabulary was treated visually.

Homophones, which are words that are spelled differently but pronounced the same, have also been ignored in controlled vocabularies in a visual world (e.g., moat and mote, fowl and foul). Because what appears on computer screens is now quite regularly read aloud electronically to people with visual impairments, we need to give attention to pronunciations of homographs and to distinguishing among homophones.

Qualification of Terms

One of the ways of dealing with homographs is to add a qualifier to one or more of the meanings. For example:

Mercury (Planet)
Mercury (Roman deity)

Qualifiers are also used to differentiate usages of a word in different settings. For example:

Adultery (Aztec law)
Adultery (Jewish law)
Adultery (Yanzi law)

Qualifiers can also be used to help identify the context of unfamiliar words. For example:

Yanzi (African people)

Abbreviations and Acronyms

Traditionally, abbreviations and acronyms have either been spelled out, or not, depending upon the intended users of the controlled vocabulary and their expected knowledge. With a move to more global retrieval needs one cannot assume a certain population. Under these circumstances it would probably be best to assume that abbreviations and acronyms should be spelled out. A few, however, have global recognition. An example is AIDS, the acronym for Acquired Immune Deficiency Syndrome (although in Spanish the acronym is SIDA, so in a global index even this acronym might need to be spelled out).

Popular vs. Technical Terms

When a concept can be represented by both technical and popular terminology, the creator of a controlled vocabulary must decide which will be used. For example, *Medical Subject Headings (MeSH)* uses "Neoplasms" where *LCSH* uses "Cancer." If the list is intended to be used for information packages that will be used by a specialized audience only, then specialized terminology is justified. However, in a global information world, one can no longer be certain of a particular audience. Perhaps this is another area where the kind of authority control discussed in Chapter 8 should be put into use. With international authority control, technical terms and their equivalent popular terms could reside on the same record which could be activated by a search on any of the equivalent terms. This is, in fact, the approach used in many ontologies (see discussion below).

Subdivision of Terms

Subdivisions are used in controlled vocabularies that precoordinate terms (see discussion below). Among the uses of subdivisions are:

- to separate by form/genre (e.g., Chemistry—Dictionaries)

- to show treatment of only a part of the larger subject (e.g., Merchant marine—Officers)

- to show special aspects of the larger subject (e.g., Merchant marine—Watch duty)

- to show geographical or chronological limitations (e.g., Black theater—Pennsylvania—19th century)

PRECOORDINATION VS. POSTCOORDINATION

Index terms can be assigned either in a precoordinated fashion (i.e., the indexer constructs subject strings with main terms followed by subdivisions), or in a fashion that requires the searcher of the system to coordinate the terms (i.e., postcoordination). When terms are precoordinated in the controlled vocabulary or are precoordinated by the cataloger or indexer, some concepts, subconcepts, place names, time periods, and form concepts are put together in subject strings. This does not mean that *all* concepts used for indexing a particular item will be placed in the same subject string. That happens only when the subject analysis system attempts to have each subject heading be coextensive with the subject of an item (see discussion of coextensivity and PRECIS below). In most precoordinated systems in use today, there are several precoordinated strings per surrogate record.

With the use of most controlled vocabularies, some postcoordination must still be done by the searcher, even if the cataloger or indexer has already done some precoordination. It is a matter of degree. *LCSH,* for example, has no precoordinated terminology for the concept "dancers and musicians." It is up to the user who wants a work covering this concept to look up "dancers" and "musicians" separately and then determine which metadata records have both terms in their controlled vocabulary sections. In true postcoordinated systems, each concept is entered discretely, without any stringing together of subconcepts, place names, time periods, or form. Searchers must combine terms using Boolean techniques. Keyword searching is the ultimate in postcoordinate indexing.

Postcoordination is sometimes confused with depth indexing, but these are different concepts. Although it is often the case that the numerous terms that result from depth indexing are entered into a postcoordinate system with discrete terms, there is nothing to keep a depth indexer from stringing together concepts with subconcepts or modifiers to make more meaningful precoordinated index terms.

GENERAL PRINCIPLES FOR CREATING CONTROLLED VOCABULARIES

There are some principles that apply in general to creating controlled vocabularies. These are to be distinguished from principles that come into play when applying particular vocabulary terms. The general principles discussed here for creating vocabularies are specificity, literary warrant, and direct entry.

Specificity

Specificity is the level of subject analysis that is addressed by a particular controlled vocabulary. For example, *LCSH* has greater specificity in its established headings than does *Sears.* This is evident in the greater depth of subdivisions that are established under main headings by *LCSH,* and is made physically obvious by the relative size of the printed volumes. Subject heading lists and thesauri that are created for specific subject fields, such as MeSH (Medical Subject Headings) for the field of medicine, are even more specific in the headings created for their specific field than is *LCSH.*

Literary Warrant

Controlled vocabulary tends to be created using the principle of *literary warrant*. This means that terminology is added to a subject heading list or thesaurus when a new concept shows up in the information packages that need organizing and therefore needs to have specific terminology assigned to it. Usually, no attempt is made to add new terminology to a list until it is needed for use in surrogate/metadata records.

Direct Entry

Another principle is that of *direct entry,* which is the entry of a concept under the term that names it, rather than treating that concept as a subdivision of a broader concept. For example, in *LCSH* there is currently a preference for a modified term to express a concept (e.g., Railroad stations) over the use of a broader term subdivided by a narrower term (e.g., Railroads—Stations).

GENERAL PRINCIPLES FOR APPLYING CONTROLLED VOCABULARY TERMS

Once a vocabulary has been created and then has been chosen for use in a particular institution or situation, there are some general principles to be followed in applying that vocabulary. The ones discussed here are specific entry, the number of terms to be assigned, and what to do when the concept is not covered in the particular vocabulary being used.

Specific Entry

The principle of *specific entry* is that a concept should be assigned a term from the thesaurus that is the most specific term for the concept that is available in the controlled vocabulary. An information package about "musicians" should be entered under "musicians," not under "performing artists," or if it is about "flutists," and if that term is in the vocabulary, then the entry should be "flutists," not "musicians." However, if the vocabulary does not get as specific as "flutists," or does not allow creation of such terms for specific categories of musicians, then the principle of specific entry calls for using "musicians" as the most specific entry for that vocabulary. Specific entry allows an experienced user to know when to stop searching for an appropriate controlled vocabulary term. One does not have to keep trying broader terms unless no information is found under the most specific terms.

It should be noted that the concept of specific entry is not the same as the concept of *coextensive entry*. At least one system for subject analysis, the PREserved Context Indexing System (PRECIS), attempts to make subject headings coextensive with the concepts covered in the document analyzed. That is, the subject heading will cover all, but no more than, the concepts or topics covered in the information package. In order to have coextensive coverage using *LCSH,* for example, an information package about crocheting of potholders requires *two* specific entries: one for "crocheting" and another for "potholders." There is no one specific term to cover these two concepts together. In order to have just *one* heading that is coextensive with the subject of such a resource, the heading would have to be "crocheting potholders," or "potholders—crocheting," but these phrases are not available in *LCSH.*

It once was true that "specific entry" could be treated in a relative way. In a small collection there might be only one or two items about "musicians," while there might be several items about "performing artists" that include "musicians" as one type of performing artist; for that collection, there might be a decision that "performing artists" would be the most specific heading used. Now that we are all essentially contributing to a global union catalog, however, we must follow the principle of specific entry in order for searching to be effective.[3] And, if we could break out of tradition and make references from specific terms to broader ones, then "too specific" would not have to be a concern.

Number of Terms Assigned

There should be *no arbitrary limit on the number* of terms or descriptors assigned. If the conceptual analysis has been done at the summarization level, then the number of terms given should be the number that is needed to express that summary. Likewise, if the conceptual analysis has been depth analysis, the number of terms necessary to cover all of the concepts should be allowed.

Concept Not in Controlled Vocabulary

If a *concept is not present in the controlled vocabulary,* it should be represented temporarily by a more general concept. The new concept should be proposed as a new addition to the subject list or thesaurus (e.g., use "Artificial intelligence" until a new heading for "Machine discovery" is established).

INDEX TERMS FOR NAMES

Although the names for many topical concepts are controlled by the controlled vocabulary list itself, proper names are generally controlled by a separate authority file. For example, the Library of Congress (LC) maintains a name authority file, called the NAF (Name Authority File), for names of persons, corporate bodies, geographic names of political entities, and titles of works.[4] Geographic names that are not political entities and other names such as names of archaeological sites are also controlled by LC, but as subject headings rather than as names. The art world has a Union List of Artist Names (ULAN)[5] and a list of geographic names (The Getty Thesaurus of Geographic Names)[6] maintained by the Getty.

CONTROLLED VOCABULARIES

Controlled vocabularies fall broadly into three categories: (1) subject heading lists, (2) thesauri, and (3) ontologies. All three have certain similarities, but they are also different.

First, we compare subject heading lists with thesauri. Subject heading lists have been created largely in library communities; thesauri have been created largely in indexing communities. Both attempt to provide subject access to information packages by providing terminology that can be consistent rather than uncontrolled and unpredictable. Both choose preferred terms and make references from nonused terms. Both provide hierarchies so that terms are presented in relation to their broader terms, narrower terms, and related terms.

There are certain differences that are worth noting:

- Thesauri are made up of single terms and bound terms representing single concepts (usually called *descriptors*). Bound terms occur when some concepts can only be represented by two or more words (e.g., "Type A Personality": the words "type," "A," and "personality" cannot be separated as meaningful components; the entire phrase is necessary for expressing the concept). Subject heading lists have phrases and other precoordinated terms in addition to single terms.

- Thesauri are more strictly hierarchical. Because they are made up of single terms, each term usually has only one broader term. The rules in the *NISO Guidelines for the Construction, Format, and Management of Monolingual Thesauri*[7] that have to do with identifying broader, narrower, and related terms are much easier to follow when working with a single-term system than when working with a phrase system.

- Thesauri are narrow in scope. They are usually made up of terms from one specific subject area. Subject heading lists tend to be more general in scope, covering a broad subject area or, indeed, the entire scope of knowledge.

- Thesauri are more likely to be multilingual. Again, because single terms are used, equivalents in other languages are easier to find and maintain.

Ontologies are similar to both subject heading lists and thesauri in bringing together all the variant ways of expressing a concept and in showing the relationships of a concept to broader, narrower, and related concepts. They are different in that they do not select one term to be a preferred term with synonymous terms being called "nonused" terms.

In the field of philosophy the term ontology has a long and respectable history meaning a systematic account of existence. More recently the term came to be used for the categories of things that may exist in a particular domain and to refer to the knowledge shared by persons working in a particular domain. At some point in the last decade the word was adopted by the information science community to designate the building blocks that are used to help computers and humans share knowledge. Elin Jacob argues that an ontology "constitutes a controlled vocabulary . . . only . . . if the standard concept of a controlled vocabulary is redefined."[8] This author sees no problem with the expansion of the definition of controlled vocabulary to include the kind of control that brings together concepts and shows relationships among them without designating one term as "the authorized one." This is the same kind of redefinition that is taking place with authority control of names (discussed in Chapter 8).

Mechanics of Controlled Vocabularies

A traditional controlled vocabulary operates by choosing a preferred way of expressing a concept and then making certain that synonymous ways of expressing the concept will be connected to the preferred terminology. Traditionally, the nonused terminology appears in the controlled vocabulary listed under the preferred terminology and is often preceded by the abbreviation **UF** meaning "used for." For example:

> **Maintenance**
> > **UF** Preventive maintenance
> > Upkeep

The reverse of this entry in a list is an entry at each of the unused terms that refers the user to the preferred term:

> Preventive maintenance   *use*   **Maintenance**
> Upkeep   *use*   **Maintenance**

A traditional controlled vocabulary also keeps track of the hierarchical relationships of a concept. The preferred term is shown in relationship to its broader term(s), narrower term(s), and related term(s), if any. These are often designated by the abbreviations **BT**, **NT**, and **RT**, respectively. For example:

> **Maintenance**
> > **BT** Maintainability (Engineering)
> > **RT** Repairing
> > **NT** Grounds maintenance

(This example is not exhaustive, but only illustrative.) These relationships are reciprocal: under "Maintainability (Engineering)," "Maintenance" would be listed as a narrower term; under "Repairing," "Maintenance" would be listed as a related term; and under "Grounds maintenance," "Maintenance" would be listed as a broader term.

There are different kinds of hierarchical relationships that may be designated as simply broader and narrower terms in a general vocabulary, but which may be designated more specifically in some thesauri. These include: genus/species or class/class member (e.g., the class of all *buildings* includes *houses, apartment buildings,* etc.); whole/part (e.g., *fingers* are part of a *hand*); generic topic/named example or "instance" (e.g., *San Francisco* is an instance of a *city*). Likewise, there are different kinds of related relationships. These include: one term needed in the definition of the other (e.g., *stamps* is needed in the definition of *philately*); meanings of two terms overlap, or two terms may be used interchangeably, yet are not synonyms (e.g., *carpets* and *rugs*); linking of persons and their fields of endeavor (e.g., *attorneys* and *law*).

Relationships are also expressed in ontologies. Relationships shown in *WordNet*®[9] (see also discussion below), for example, are the following:

- *Synonyms* have the same, or nearly the same, meanings and often can be substituted for each other. A synonym is like the "used for" relationship in traditional controlled vocabularies.

- *Coordinate terms* might be called siblings; they all have the same parent term. A coordinate term is like the "related term" relationship in traditional controlled vocabularies.

- A *hypernym* is the parent term of all the instances that are "kinds of" the hypernym (e.g., "family" is a hypernym for "nuclear family," "extended family," "foster home," etc.). A hypernym is like the "broader term" relationship in traditional controlled vocabularies.

- A *hyponym* designates a member of a class (e.g., "nuclear family" is a hyponym of the class "family"). A hyponym is like the "narrower term" relationship in traditional controlled vocabularies.

- A *holonym* is the name of the whole of which the meronym (see below) is a part. With a holynym one has the name of a whole that has parts (e.g., a family has members: child, parent, sibling, etc.). A holonym is also like the "broader term" relationship.

- With a *meronym* one has a constituent part or a member of something (e.g., "sister" is a meronym of "family"). A meronym is also like the "narrower term" relationships in traditional controlled vocabularies.

- *Antonyms* have opposite meanings (e.g., "hot" is the antonym of "cold"). Antonyms are not dealt with in traditional controlled vocabularies.

Another example comes from OWL Web Ontology Language[10] (see also discussion below). Some relationships provided for in OWL are:

- subClassOf—"x" is a subset of the class "y" (e.g., the class "Mammals" is a subset of the class "Animals")

- oneOf—the enumerated thing is an instance of the class (e.g., Asia is one of the class "Continents")

- equivalentClass—two class descriptions have exactly the same set of individuals (e.g., the class "U.S. President" is equivalent to the class "Principal Resident of White House")

- intersectionOf—a class can belong to two other classes (e.g., the class "Student" can be both "Person" and "University Asset")

- disjointWith—two classes have no individuals in common (e.g., the class "Cats" does not include any individuals of the class "Dogs")

Some controlled vocabularies also give hierarchical listings of the vocabulary terms. In these lists the terms are placed in juxtaposition to each other so that one can visualize broader and narrower relationships. Such lists are helpful in seeing where a term fits within an entire hierarchy, not just its relationship to the terms above and below it. These are often called "tree structures," visualizing branches growing from branches of a trunk, an excellent example of which is the "MeSH Tree Structures."[11] Hierarchical listings in search engine directories can resemble tree structures if shown as levels rather than being presented in a single string at the top of the screen.

Subject Heading Lists

Among the best-known and most-used subject heading lists are *Library of Congress Subject Headings (LCSH)*, *Sears List of Subject Headings (Sears)*, and *Medical Subject Headings (MeSH)*. A brief description of each follows, but more detailed descriptions can be found in other sources, some of which are suggested at the end of this chapter.

Library of Congress Subject Headings (LCSH)

Starting in 1988 with the eleventh edition, new print versions of *LCSH* have been produced once a year. *LCSH* is updated continuously, and a fully updated electronic version is available by subscription through *Classification Web*,[12] and through various bibliographic utilities such as OCLC and RLIN. *LCSH* covers the world of knowledge. It is used by all kinds of libraries in many different kinds of settings, including countries other than the United States. In the indexing process *LCSH* is used in conjunction with the *Subject Cataloging Manual: Subject Headings.*[13] The manual gives the policies and practices of the Library of Congress, which is responsible for the maintenance of the list; it is an essential tool if one wishes to apply *LCSH* correctly. A sample from *LCSH* is shown as Figure 10.1. The MARC-encoded authority records for the headings in Figure 10.1 are shown in Figure 10.2. (MARC records from LC do not contain narrower terms.)

Sears List of Subject Headings (Sears)

Sears is still published in print form with a new edition coming out every few years. It is also updated continuously, and updates are periodically available in electronic form. This list is intended for small collections used by persons with general needs. Its main users are public libraries (usually small to medium-sized) and school libraries. For most of its existence *Sears* has followed the lead of *LCSH* in format and in terminology choices, although in the last couple of editions *Sears* has taken the initiative to make changes that were later followed by *LCSH*. For example, the change of "Afro-American" to "African American" was made first by *Sears*. In its use of *LCSH* terminology, though, *Sears* has used only the more general terms and has not included the more specific terms or the ones geared for research audiences. In addition, *Sears* has fewer subdivisions. A sample from *Sears* is shown as Figure 10.3.

Medical Subject Headings (MeSH)

The National Library of Medicine calls *MeSH* a thesaurus,[14] and in the sense that it provides a strict hierarchical structure and it is subject-oriented, it is a thesaurus. But in the sense that it precoordinates phrases (e.g., "Sensitivity Training Groups"; "Life Change Events") it is a subject heading list. It also has a subdivision list from which terms are taken to be used with the terms and phrases found in the list proper.

MeSH is used for providing subject access points on every bibliographic record created at the National Library of Medicine, whether it be MEDLINE, the Library's catalog, or *Index Medicus*. In print form *MeSH* has three volumes: a hierarchical listing; an alphabetical arrangement that includes scope notes; and a permuted alphabetical listing, in which every

Hair
          [GN193 (Physical Anthropology)]
          [QL942 (Comparative anatomy)]
          [QM488 (Human anatomy)]
    BT   Body covering (Anatomy)
          Head
    RT   Scalp
    NT   Beards
          Bristles
          Eyebrows
          Eyelashes
          Gray hair
          Guard hair
          Horsehair
          Long hair
          Molting
          Mustaches
          Sale of human hair
          Whiskers
          Wigs
          Wool
          . . .
Hair--Coloring
          USE Hair--Dyeing and bleaching
          . . .

Hair dyes (May Subd Geog)
          [TP984 (Chemical technology)]
          [TT969 (Hairdressing)]
    UF   Dyes and dyeing--Hair
          Hair tints
          Tints, Hair
    BT   Hair preparations

Hair dyes--Law and legislation (May Subd Geog)

Fig. 10.1. Sample entries from *Library of Congress Subject Headings (LCSH)*, as found in *Classification Web* (June 2003). Available: http://classweb.loc.gov/ (by subscription).

word of a phrase heading is brought into the lead position and arranged alphabetically. It is updated annually and is available from the National Technical Information Service.[15] In machine-readable form *MeSH* is provided free on the Web.[16] A sample from *MeSH* is shown as Figure 10.4.

Rec stat	c	Entered	19860211	Replaced	19930608105447.9			
Type	z	**Upd status**	a	**Enc lvl**	n	**Source**		
Roman	|	**Ref status**	b	**Mod rec**		**Name use**	b	
Govt agn	|	**Auth status**	a	**Subj**	a	**Subj use**	a	
Series	n	**Auth/ref**	a	**Geo subd**	|	**Ser use**	b	
Ser num	n	**Name**	n	**Subdiv tp**	n	**Rules**	n	

010	sh 85058305
040	DLC ‡c DLC ‡d DLC
053	GN193 ‡c Physical anthropology
053	QL942 ‡c Comparative anatomy
053	QM488 ‡c Human anatomy
150	Hair
550	Body covering (Anatomy) ‡w g
550	Head ‡w g
550	Scalp

Rec stat	c	Entered	19860211	Replaced	19870903094434.7			
Type	z	**Upd status**	a	**Enc lvl**	n	**Source**		
Roman	|	**Ref status**	b	**Mod rec**		**Name use**	b	
Govt agn	|	**Auth status**	a	**Subj**	a	**Subj use**	a	
Series	n	**Auth/ref**	a	**Geo subd**	i	**Ser use**	b	
Ser num	n	**Name**	n	**Subdiv tp**	n	**Rules**	n	

010	sh 85058317
040	DLC ‡c DLC ‡d DLC
053	TP984 ‡c Chemical technology
053	TT969 ‡c Hairdressing
150	Hair dyes
450	Dyes and dyeing ‡x Hair
450	Hair tints
450	Tints, Hair
550	Hair preparations ‡w g

Fig. 10.2. Sample authority records for headings shown in Figure 10.1. (Source: OCLC Connexion, Authorities, record numbers 02051217 and 02051346.)

Thesauri

There are many, many thesauri for different subject areas. Representative of thesauri are *Art & Architecture Thesaurus, Thesaurus of ERIC Descriptors,* and the *INSPEC Thesaurus.* Brief descriptions follow; suggested readings giving more detailed information are given at the end of the chapter.

Hair   612.7; 646.7
Use for general materials on hair as well as
for materials on hairdressing and haircutting.
UF   Barbering
        Coiffure
        Haircutting
        Hairdressing
        Hairstyles
        Hairstyling
BT   **Head**
        Personal Grooming
NT   **Wigs**

Fig. 10.3. Sample entry from *Sears List of Subject Headings (Sears)*, 17th ed., 2000.

Art & Architecture Thesaurus (AAT)

The *AAT* is intended to assist in verbal access to all kinds of cultural heritage information.[17] Terms are provided for describing objects, textual materials, images, architecture, and material culture. *AAT* is widely used in several communities: archives, libraries, museums, visual resources collections, and conservation agencies. In structure it is arranged in seven facets (categories) that progress from the abstract to the concrete: Associated concepts, Physical attributes, Styles and periods, Agents, Activities, Materials, and Objects. The facets are divided into subfacets, each of which gives a hierarchical listing of all terms in that subfacet.

AAT is available as a searchable Web resource that provides full access.[18] It can be licensed as either a file of ASCII records in fielded format or as a file of MARC authority records. Electronic versions are constantly updated. User's manuals are available. A sample from *AAT* is shown as Figure 10.5.

Thesaurus of ERIC Descriptors

ERIC is an acronym for the Educational Resources Information Center, which is a national information system designed to provide access to a large body of education-related literature. Among the documents that ERIC indexes besides journal articles are descriptions and evaluations of programs, research reports, curriculum and teaching guides, instructional materials, position papers, computer files, and resource materials. These materials are indexed using terms from the *Thesaurus of ERIC Descriptors*.[19]

Sample entries of MeSH Descriptor Data:

MeSH Heading	Hair
Tree Number	A17.360
Annotation	abnormally pulling at one's hair = TRICHOTILLOMANIA; HAIR FOLLICLE is available
Scope Note	A filament-like structure consisting of a shaft which projects to the surface of the SKIN from a root which is softer than the shaft and lodges in the cavity of a HAIR FOLLICLE. It is found on most surfaces of the body.
Entry Term	Animal Fur
Entry Term	Fetal Hair
Entry Term	Hair, Fetal
Entry Term	Lanugo
Allowable Qualifiers	AB AH CH CY DE EM EN GD IM ME MI PA PH PP PS RA RE RI TR UL US VI
Online Note	use HAIR to search LANUGO 1966-78
History Note	LANUGO was see under HAIR 1963-78
Unique ID	D006197

MeSH Heading	Hair Dyes
Tree Number	D26.175.430.430
Annotation	D25-26 qualif
Scope Note	Dyes used as cosmetics to change hair color either permanently or temporarily.
Entry Term	Coloring Agents, Hair
Entry Term	Dyes, Hair
Entry Term	Hair Colorants
Allowable Qualifiers	AE AN CH CL CS CT DU EC HI IP ME PD PK PO RE SD ST TO
Registry Number	0
Previous Indexing	Cosmetics (1966-1978)
Previous Indexing	Dyes (1966-1978)
Previous Indexing	Hair (1966-1978)
Previous Indexing	Hair Color (1976-1978)
History Note	91(79); was see under HAIR PREPARATIONS 1980-90; was see under COSMETICS 1979
Unique ID	D006202

Sample entries of MeSH Tree Structures:

```
Integumentary System
[A17]
                  ▶ Hair [A17.360]
                              Eyebrows [A17.360.296]
                              Eyelashes [A17.360.421]
                              Hair Follicle [A17.360.710]
                  Nails [A17.600]
                  Skin
                  [A17.815] ±
Specialty Chemicals and Products [D26]
    Cosmetics [D26.175]
        Hair Preparations [D26.175.430]
                  ▶ Hair Dyes [D26.175.430.430]
```

Fig. 10.4. Sample entries from National Library of Medicine, *Medical Subject Headings, 2003 MeSH.* **(Source: http://www.nlm.nih.gov/mesh/meshhome. html.)**

ID: 300013029

Record Type: concept

> **dye** (colorant, <materials by function>, ... Materials)

Note: A colored substance that dissolves or is suspended in a liquid and imparts its color by staining or being absorbed, or by serving as a pigment.

Terms:

> **dye** (preferred, C,U,D,English, American-P)
> **dyes** (C,U,AD,English, American)
> **dyestuff** (C,U,UF,English, American)
> **dyestuffs** (C,U,UF,English, American)

Facet/Hierarchy Code: M.MT

Hierarchical Position:

> Materials Facet
> .... Materials
> .... materials
> .... <materials by function>
> .... colorant
> .... dye

Related concepts:

> activity/event needing/producing .... dyeing
> .... (coloring, <additive and joining processes and techniques>, ... Processes and Techniques) [300053049]
>
> materials required/produced .... dyeing
> .... (coloring, <additive and joining processes and techniques>, ... Processes and Techniques) [300053049]
>
> related to .... dyeing
> .... (coloring, <additive and joining processes and techniques>, ... Processes and Techniques) [300053049]

ID: 300011814

Record Type: concept

> **hair** (<hair and hair components>, <keratinous material>, ... Materials)

Note: The fibrous outgrowths of the skins of various animals, composed of the protein keratin, used, among other things, for making fabrics, as stuffing, and for making brushes.

Terms:

> hair (preferred, C,U,D,English, American-P)

Facet/Hierarchy Code: M.MT

Hierarchical Position:

Materials Facet
.... Materials
.... materials
.... <materials by origin>
.... animal material
.... <keratinous material>
.... <hair and hair components>
.... hair

Related concepts:

related to .... hairstyling
.... (<processes and techniques by material>, <processes and techniques by specific type>, ...
Processes and Techniques) [300261971]

Fig. 10.5. Sample entries from *Art & Architecture Thesaurus On Line*. (Source: http://www.getty.edu/research/tools/vocabulary/aat/.)

The thesaurus consists of four parts: the main Alphabetical Display, the Rotated Display, the Hierarchical Display, and the Descriptor Group Display. The Alphabetical Display is like the display in *LCSH*. The Rotated Display provides an alphabetical index to every word in the thesaurus, including access to unused terms as well as main terms. The Hierarchical Display shows broader and narrower terms in their relationships to each other. The Descriptor Group Display offers a kind of table of contents by placing all descriptors into a set of broad categories. The alphabetical display from the ERIC thesaurus is available on the Web.[20] A sample from the alphabetical display from the ERIC thesaurus is shown as Figure 10.6.

INSPEC Thesaurus

The *INSPEC (Information Services for the Physics and Engineering Communities) Thesaurus* was designed for use in the INSPEC database. It contains controlled terms and cross-reference terms, shows relationships between terms, and shows the dates on which the terms were added. If there was a formerly authorized term for the same concept, the dates of use of that term are given. The thesaurus is available on CD-ROM and can also be licensed for single-site use in an SGML version or in an ISO 2709 version (i.e., ASCII or EBCDIC).[21]

The subject access interface takes the user directly into the the-

COLOR   *Oct. 1969*
      Postings: 973   GC: 490
UF   Color Presentation (1969 1980)
      Color Television (1969 1980) #
      Hue
RT   Art
      Color Planning
      Contrast
      Dimensional Preference
      Light
      Painting (Visual Arts)
      Visual Environment
      Visual Perception

Fig. 10.6. Sample entry from *Thesaurus of ERIC Descriptors*, **14th ed., 2001.**

saurus when a word or phrase is entered. The user is shown where the word or phrase lies (or would lie if present) in the thesaurus, and allows the choice of that word or phrase or any other shown on the screen. Clicking on the term chosen initiates the search of the database. Linking between the thesaurus and the INSPEC Classification is provided. An example of an *INSPEC Thesaurus* listing is shown in Figure 10.7.

Ontologies

In the computer science field an "intelligent agent" (e.g., robot) is only able to perceive the part of the world that is allowed by its ontology. The broadest usage of ontology is for formal representations of what, to a human, is common sense. Categories in this sense are such things as space, time, and structure of physical objects. Such formal representations are useful in creating intelligent agents that can perform certain tasks (e.g., vacuum a floor). Such an ontology is a nonlinguistic ontology.

There have been attempts to formalize abstract concepts, as well. An ontology that will work for organizing and retrieving documents must formalize the reality of using language for communication. These are sometimes called *linguistic ontologies* and may include realities of grammar, semantics, syntax, and the like. The parts that deal with semantics may be called *lexicons* or *lexical dictionaries,* but as noted above, they are also called *ontologies.*

Natalya Noy and Deborah McGuinness point out that in the Artificial Intelligence literature, ontologies have been defined in many ways,

dynamic braking
USE   braking

dynamic nuclear polarisation
   UF   dynamic nuclear polarization
         solid effect
   NT   CIDNP
         Overhauser effect
   BT   magnetic double resonance
   TT   resonance
   RT   nuclear polarisation
   CC   A0758   A3335D   A7670E
   DI   January 1977
   PT   magnetic double resonance

Fig. 10.7. Sample entry from the *INSPEC Thesaurus*. (Source: *INSPEC Thesaurus*, 1999 [ed.] [London: Institution of Electrical Engineers, 1999].)

some of which contradict each other.[22] Some definitions indicate a strong underpinning of categorization/classification. Others emphasize vocabulary and definitions. This is obviously an evolving area that bears watching.

An OWL Web Ontology Language document defines ontology:

> An ontology defines the terms used to describe and represent an area of knowledge. Ontologies are used by people, databases, and applications that need to share domain information. . . . Ontologies include computer-usable definitions of basic concepts in the domain and the relationships among them. . . . They encode knowledge in a domain and also knowledge that spans domains. In this way, they make that knowledge reusable.[23]

The vision for the Semantic Web requires that information have explicit meaning so that machines can automatically process information found on the Web. Ontologies providing such meaning are building blocks for the Semantic Web, to be used with XML, the XML Schema, RDF, and the RDF Schema. Ontologies are important if "agents" on the Web are to be able to search and/or merge information from diverse communities. This is because the same term may be used in different contexts with different meanings, and the same meaning may be represented by different terms in different contexts. In order to standardize the means for creating ontologies that can be used on the Web, the Web Ontology Working Group of the W3C has developed the OWL Web Ontology Language. It is, as it is named, a "language" for creating interoperable ontologies that can be extensions of RDF.

Ontologies have different degrees of structure. Some ontologies are taxonomies (i.e., classifications or hierarchical listings) of terminology of a particularly narrow subject area (see discussion of taxonomies in Chapter 11). Some are specifications of sets of conceptual characteristics. For example, metadata schemas are ontologies that specify elements to be used, what those elements mean, and what kinds of attributes and values those elements can have. Other ontologies appear to be categorized controlled vocabularies. These include semantic analysis of words, putting them into categories such as nouns, verbs, adjectives, and adverbs, as is done in *WordNet*® (described further below). This is in contrast to subject heading lists and thesauri that tend to give only noun forms of the terminology contained within them (along with modifiers in other than noun form).

Another example of an ontology is the Unified Medical Language System (UMLS).[24] This system does not call itself an ontology, but it has many of the characteristics that distinguish ontologies from thesauri. The UMLS is comprised of three "knowledge sources": a "metathesaurus," a lexicon, and a semantic network. The metathesaurus pulls together terminology from more than 100 biomedical vocabularies and classifications, linking many different names for the same concepts, without designating one as a preferred term. The lexicon contains syntactic information for words, including verbs, that do not appear in the metathesaurus. The network contains information about the categories to which the metathesaurus concepts have been assigned and describes the relationships among them. It can be seen, then, that the three parts together fit the definition of an ontology.

NATURAL LANGUAGE PROCESSING (NLP)

Although there has been some work in computer processing of spoken words, most work has been done on the processing of written words. Therefore, in discussing Natural Language Processing (NLP), we are concentrating on written language processing. One goal of NLP is to be able to create Information Retrieval (IR) systems that can accomplish three things: (1) interpret users' information needs as expressed in free text; (2) represent the complete range of meaning conveyed in documents; and (3) "understand" when there is a match between the user's information need and all (and no more than) the documents that meet it. In order to do this, certain language problems have to be addressed:[25]

- English sentences are often incomplete descriptions of what they mean. For example, "The door opened" does not tell whether the door was opened by a person, the wind, or its own weight. If the next sentence is "Susan walked in," then the implication is that Susan opened the door.

- The same expression can mean different things in different contexts. For example, "Where's the water?" can mean that one is thirsty; or it can mean that one wants to know which way it is to the beach.

- Natural language is constantly gaining new words, usages, expressions, and meanings. During the 1998 Olympics one could hear that "The United States has not yet medaled." Most people had not heard "medal" used as a verb before that.

- There are many ways to say the same thing. For example, "Mary registered for two summer courses" and "Mary signed up for two courses for the summer term" mean essentially the same thing.

- Sentences that are constructed identically can mean different things. In the two sentences "Jennifer took the course with Professor Jones" and "Jennifer took the course with Mary," the first indicates that the professor taught the course Jennifer took. But the second could mean that Jennifer and Mary are both students and took a course together, or it could mean that Professor Mary Jones likes to be addressed by her first name. Such ambiguities can often be sorted out through the context of surrounding sentences.

Elaine Rich and Kevin Knight identify the following steps as necessary for NLP:[26]

- Morphological analysis—separate components of words (e.g., prefixes, suffixes, possessive endings, etc.) and separate punctuation from words.

- Syntactic analysis—analyze the linear sequences of words

to show how the words relate to each other; the computer converts the flat sequence of words into a structure. For those who learned to diagram sentences in grammar classes, diagramming is essentially what is done in this step.

- Semantic analysis—map individual words into appropriate places in the knowledge base; create a structure to indicate how the meanings of the individual words combine with each other (e.g., the sentence "She wants to print a Web page" indicates a wanting event in which "she" wants a printing event to occur wherein she must have access to a Web browser and a printer).

- Discourse integration—determine the meaning of an individual sentence in relation to the sentences that precede and follow it. For example, the meaning of pronouns such as "it," "them," "her," can be given individual meanings only if what or who they refer to can be determined.

- Pragmatic analysis—reinterpret the structure that represents what was said to show what was actually meant. For example, the question "Do you have the time?" should not be answered with "yes," but should be interpreted as a request to be told the time. In the case of an IR system, the result of such analysis should be a translation to a command to be executed by the system. If the system is asked a question such as "Do you have anything on artificial intelligence?" the response should be a list of sources on artificial intelligence, not the word "Yes."

Semantic analysis includes as its first step looking up individual words in an ontology to determine which of a word's meanings or nuances is meant in the sentence at hand. Such a resource must give not only definitions, but also must give semantic markers. For example, the word "at" requires a time or a location as its object. Identification of this fact is a semantic marker. Others might be: physical object, abstract concept, animate object, and so forth.

Keywords

One of the first approaches used by NLP researchers was the manipulation of keywords. The success of keyword searching depends upon at least two assumptions: (1) that authors writing about the same concepts will use the same words in their writings, and (2) that searchers will be able to guess what words those authors used for the concept. A 1993 study of journal articles in the pure sciences and social sciences looked at articles that shared common references.[27] An assumption was made that if articles shared common references they dealt with the same or a related subject. It was found that few articles with common references shared common keywords. Another study the same year reported difficulty in choosing keywords for a literature search due to the use of multiple terms representing the same concepts.[28]

Among other problems discovered with keyword searching were that not all related information was retrieved, and searches often led to the extraction of irrelevant materials. A synonym list approach was tried. Synonym lists were databases consisting of groupings of synonymous terms. When a keyword search was done, the synonym list was tapped to provide synonyms without the searcher having to be the one to think of all of them. This approach also failed for several reasons. The lists were not large or general enough; they were implemented in very small and specialized domains. Also, the lists did not attempt any level of word role assignment; for example, although one could substitute "aircraft" for "planes" and "big" for "large," it was not possible to substitute "big aircraft" for "large planes" because the system had no "knowledge" of adjectives and nouns and which kinds of words could be used together to make a phrase.[29]

WordNet®

There has also been much work with full-text analysis. Again, though, tests have been conducted in limited specialized domains. Results have not been transferable to general, multiple domain searches. Textual analysis typically is not done in real-time, especially as the amounts of data grow. Texts are analyzed and "indexed" when they are entered into the system; changes in the indexing mechanism require reindexing every document. Although full-text analysis retrieval systems are being marketed, many systems (e.g., distributed networks, the Web) cannot transmit the complete text of hundreds of documents in response to a search query. Sujata Banerjee and Vibhu Mittal proposed an indexing system using keyword searching combined with a well-developed linguistic ontology. They used *WordNet*®[30] as an example of a linguistic ontology that could be used in this way.[31]

WordNet® calls itself an "on-line lexical reference system whose design is inspired by current psycholinguistic theories of human lexical memory."[32] It allows five categories of words: nouns, adjectives, adverbs, verbs, and function words. Relationships between words and their meanings are "many to many"; that is, some words have different meanings *(polysemy)*, and some meanings have several different ways of being expressed *(synonyms)*. A word can be placed into as many of the five categories as are appropriate, and in each category there can be as many different meanings (or senses) as are appropriate. For each sense all synonyms are grouped together in "synsets," and unlike thesauri, none of the synonyms is designated as the "used" term with all others designated as "unused." At the main screen that shows all the senses (see Figure 10.8), one can ask for screens that show coordinate terms, hyponyms, hypernyms, meronyms, holonyms, and antonyms.

Banerjee and Mittal have proposed the following model[33] (enhanced by the author): For each query (e.g., "family crisis") of an IR system that uses *WordNet®*, results of an exact match would be given first. If there were insufficient matches the system would prompt the user for other options. It could first substitute adjective synonyms and present a list to the user who would choose the combinations that make sense. (The user would be involved also at each of the following stages.) Our example would yield the search terms: household crisis, house crisis, home crisis, and so forth. Then the system would substitute noun synonyms, resulting in a search for family emergency. The system would then drop adjectives, resulting in "crisis" being searched. Then the noun would be generalized to its hypernyms, resulting in: family situation, family state of affairs, family juncture, family occasion. Then the adjective synonyms could be combined with the noun hypernyms, resulting in: household situation, household state of affairs, home situation, home state of affairs, and so forth. Also, the hyponyms of both noun and adjective could be searched, resulting in: family challenge, family complication, family nightmare, foster home crisis, couple crisis, marriage crisis, and so forth. Thus, a very large lexical ontology covering many fields of knowledge could be used to enhance keyword searching of full-text documents.

CONCLUSION

This chapter has addressed verbal approaches to provision of subject access to information packages. The process of determining what information packages are about was addressed in the preceding chapter as a crucial first step in providing subject access. In the provision of verbal subject approaches, the determination of aboutness is followed by translation

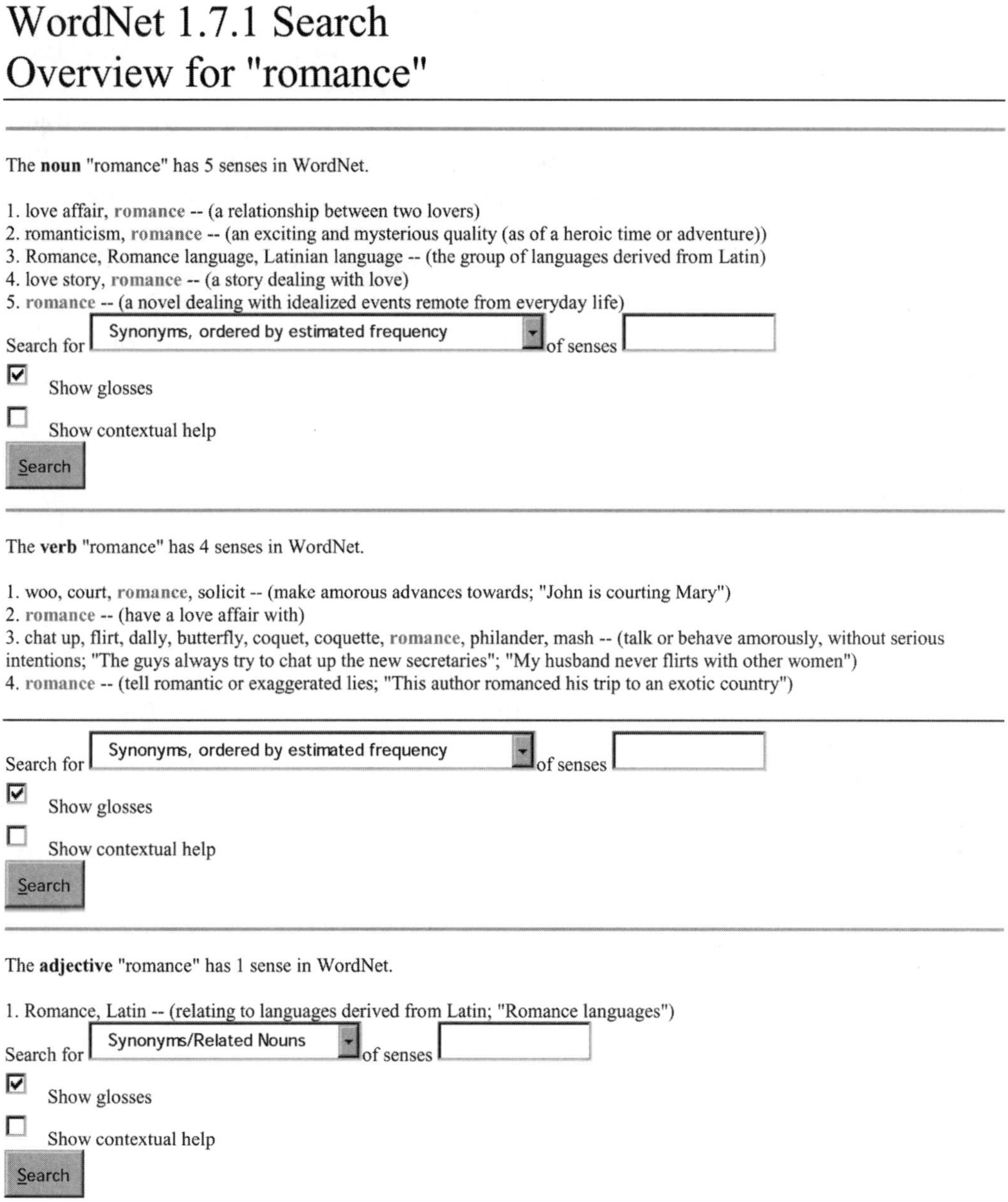

WordNet 1.7.1 Search
Overview for "romance"

The **noun** "romance" has 5 senses in WordNet.

1. love affair, romance -- (a relationship between two lovers)
2. romanticism, romance -- (an exciting and mysterious quality (as of a heroic time or adventure))
3. Romance, Romance language, Latinian language -- (the group of languages derived from Latin)
4. love story, romance -- (a story dealing with love)
5. romance -- (a novel dealing with idealized events remote from everyday life)

Search for [Synonyms, ordered by estimated frequency ▼] of senses [   ]

☑ Show glosses

☐ Show contextual help

[Search]

The **verb** "romance" has 4 senses in WordNet.

1. woo, court, romance, solicit -- (make amorous advances towards; "John is courting Mary")
2. romance -- (have a love affair with)
3. chat up, flirt, dally, butterfly, coquet, coquette, romance, philander, mash -- (talk or behave amorously, without serious intentions; "The guys always try to chat up the new secretaries"; "My husband never flirts with other women")
4. romance -- (tell romantic or exaggerated lies; "This author romanced his trip to an exotic country")

Search for [Synonyms, ordered by estimated frequency ▼] of senses [   ]

☑ Show glosses

☐ Show contextual help

[Search]

The **adjective** "romance" has 1 sense in WordNet.

1. Romance, Latin -- (relating to languages derived from Latin; "Romance languages")

Search for [Synonyms/Related Nouns ▼] of senses [   ]

☑ Show glosses

☐ Show contextual help

[Search]

Fig. 10.8. Screen from *WordNet*® showing all the "senses" of the term *romance*. (Source: http://cogsci.princeton.edu/wn/.)

of that aboutness into index terms, usually controlled vocabulary. Controlled vocabularies all have to deal with issues and problems during their construction; understanding these issues contributes to making the best use of the vocabulary, as does understanding the general principles. Subject heading lists, thesauri, and ontologies make up three kinds of controlled vocabularies in use today. Subject heading lists were the first, created by libraries. Thesauri are more strictly hierarchical and, for the most part, grew up in subject-specific situations and/or commercial indexing services. Ontologies have evolved as a way to help humans and computers share knowledge about a particular subject area. Ontologies have grown out of Natural Language Processing (NLP), which holds promise for sophisticated keyword approaches. The next chapter is also concerned with subject access, but from the point of view of categorization and classification.

NOTES

All URLs accessed July 2003.

1. Thomas Mann, " 'Cataloging Must Change!' and Indexer Consistency Studies: Misreading the Evidence at Our Peril," *Cataloging & Classification Quarterly* 23, nos. 3/4 (1997): 3–45.

2. Hans H. Wellish, "Aboutness and Selection of Topics," *Key Words* 4, no. 2 (March/April 1996): 9.

3. Mann, " 'Cataloging Must Change!' " pp. 9–10.

4. Library of Congress, *Library of Congress Authorities*. Available: http://authorities.loc.gov/.

5. The Getty, *Union List of Artist Names On Line*. Created 2000. Available: http://www.getty.edu/research/tools/vocabulary/ulan/.

6. The Getty, *Getty Thesaurus of Geographic Names On Line*. Created 2000. Available: http://www.getty.edu/research/tools/vocabulary/tgn/.

7. National Information Standards Organization, *Guidelines for the Construction, Format, and Management of Monolingual Thesauri* (Bethesda, Md.: NISO Press, 1994). "ANSI/NISO Z39.19-1993."

8. Elin K. Jacob, "Ontologies and the Semantic Web," *Bulletin of the American Society for Information Science and Technology* 29, no. 4 (April/May 2003): 22. Available: http://www.asis.org/Bulletin/Apr-03/BulletinAprMay03.pdf.

9.   Cognitive Science Laboratory, Princeton University, *WordNet®—A Lexical Database for English.* Available: http://www.cogsci.princeton.edu/~wn.

10.   *OWL Web Ontology Language Overview,* W3C Working Draft 31 March 2003. Available: http://www.w3.org/TR/owl-features/.

11.   National Library of Medicine, *MeSH Tree Structures—2003.* Available: http://www.nlm.nih.gov/mesh/MBrowser.html (click on "Navigate from tree top").

12.   Library of Congress, *Classification Web.* Available (by subscription): http://classweb.loc.gov/.

13.   *Subject Cataloging Manual: Subject Headings,* prepared by The Cataloging Policy and Support Office, Library of Congress, 5th ed. (Washington, D.C.: Cataloging Distribution Service, Library of Congress, 1996).

14.   National Library of Medicine, *Fact Sheet: Medical Subject Headings (MeSH®).* Last updated 4 December 2002. Available: http://www.nlm.nih. gov/pubs/factsheets/mesh.html.

15.   National Technical Information Service (NTIS), "Products>New Products>MeSH." Available: http://www.ntis.gov/products/mesh.asp.

16.   National Library of Medicine, *Medical Subject Headings: MeSH Browser.* Available: http://www.nlm.nih.gov/mesh/MBrowser.html.

17.   The Getty, *Art & Architecture Thesaurus On Line: About the AAT.* Created 2000. Available: http://www.getty.edu/research/tools/vocabulary/aat/about. html.

18.   The Getty, *The Art & Architecture Thesaurus On Line.* Available: http:// www.getty.edu/research/tools/vocabulary/aat/.

19.   Educational Resources Information Center (ERIC), *Thesaurus of ERIC Descriptors,* 14th ed. (Phoenix, Ariz.: Oryx Press, 2001).

20.   Educational Resources Information Center (ERIC), Processing and Reference Facility, *Search Thesaurus.* Available: http://www.ericfacility.net/ extra/pub/thessearch.cfm.

21.   INSPEC, *Thesaurus* [Web page description only]. Created 2003. Available: http://www.iee.org/Publish/Support/Inspec/Document/Thes/index. cfm.

22.   Natalya Fridman Noy and Deborah L. McGuinness, "Ontology Development 101: A Guide to Creating Your First Ontology" (Knowledge Systems

Laboratory, Stanford University, 2000), p. 3. Available: http://www.ksl. stanford.edu/people/dlm/papers/ontology-tutorial-noy-mcguinness.pdf.

23.   *Web Ontology Language (OWL) Use Cases and Requirements*, W3C Working Draft 31 March 2003. Available: http://www.w3.org/TR/webont-req/.

24.   National Library of Medicine, *Unified Medical Language System®* *(UMLS®)*. Last updated 1 July 2003. Available: http://www.nlm.nih.gov/ research/umls/.

25.   Elaine Rich and Kevin Knight, *Artificial Intelligence*, 2nd ed. (New York: McGraw-Hill, 1991), pp. 377–379.

26.   Ibid., pp. 379–380.

27.   S. N. Ali, "Subject Relationship Between Articles Determined by Co-occurrence of Keywords in Citing and Cited Titles," *Journal of Information Science* 19, no. 3 (1993): 225–231.

28.   R. B. Bush, "A Bibliography of Monographic Works on Biomaterials and Biocompatibility," *Journal of Applied Biomaterials* 4, no. 2 (1993): 195–209.

29.   Sujata Banerjee and Vibhu O. Mittal, "On the Use of Linguistic Ontologies for Accessing and Indexing Distributed Digital Libraries," in *Digital Libraries '94: Proceedings of the First Annual Conference on the Theory and Practice of Digital Libraries, June 19–21, 1994, College Station, Texas*. Available: http:// www.csdl.tamu.edu/DL94/paper/banerjee.html.

30.   *WordNet®*. Available: http://www.cogsci.princeton.edu/~wn/.

31.   Banerjee and Mittal, "On the Use of Linguistic Ontologies."

32.   *WordNet®*. Available: http://www.cogsci.princeton.edu/~wn/.

33.   Banerjee and Mittal, "On the Use of Linguistic Ontologies," p. 3.

SUGGESTED READINGS

Cleveland, Donald B., and Ana D. Cleveland. *Introduction to Indexing and Abstracting*. 3rd ed. Englewood, Colo.: Libraries Unlimited, 2001. Chapter 8: "Indexing and Abstracting a Document" and Chapter 11: "Indexing Special Subject Areas and Formats."

Koch, Traugott. *Controlled Vocabularies, Thesauri and Classification Systems Available in the WWW. DC Subject.* Last updated 27 September 2001. Available: http://www.lub.lu.se/metadata/subject-help.html.

Lancaster, F. W. *Indexing and Abstracting in Theory and Practice.* 3rd ed. Champaign: University of Illinois, Graduate School of Library and Information Science, 2003. Chapter 2: "Indexing Principles", Chapter 4: "Precoordinate Indexes", Chapter 5: "Consistency of Indexing", Chapter 6: "Quality of Indexing", Chapter 16: "Indexing and the Internet", and Chapter 17: "The Future of Indexing and Abstracting."

Olson, Hope A., and John J. Boll. *Subject Analysis in Online Catalogs.* 2nd ed. Englewood, Colo.: Libraries Unlimited, 2001. Chapter 3: Language in Information Retrieval", Chapter 4: "Managing Information Retrieval Languages", Chapter 5: "Subject Indexing Process and Policy", and Chapter 6: "Subject Headings and Descriptors."

Svenonius, Elaine. *The Intellectual Foundation of Information Organization.* Cambridge, Mass.: The MIT Press, 2000. Chapter 8: "Subject Languages: Introduction, Vocabulary Selection, and Classification" and Chapter 9: "Subject Languages: Referential and Relational Semantics."

Taylor, Arlene G. *Wynar's Introduction to Cataloging and Classification.* 9th ed., with the assistance of David P. Miller. Englewood, Colo.: Libraries Unlimited, 2000. Chapter 14: "Verbal Subject Analysis."

LCSH

Berman, Sanford. *Joy of Cataloging.* Phoenix, Ariz.: Oryx Press, 1981.

Chan, Lois Mai. *Library of Congress Subject Headings: Principles and Applications.* 3rd ed. Englewood, Colo.: Libraries Unlimited, 1995.

Mann, Thomas. *Doing Research at the Library of Congress: A Guide to Subject Searching in a Closed Stacks Library.* Washington, D.C.: Library of Congress, Humanities and Social Sciences Division, 1994.

Pugh, Mary Jo. "The Illusion of Omniscience: Subject Access and the Reference Archivist." *American Archivist* 45, no. 1 (Winter 1982): 33–44.

Taylor, Arlene G. *Wynar's Introduction to Cataloging and Classification.* 9th ed., with the assistance of David P. Miller. Englewood, Colo.: Libraries Unlimited, 2000. Chapter 15: "Library of Congress Subject Headings."

Sears

Miller, Joseph, ed. *Sears List of Subject Headings.* 17th ed. Bronx, N.Y.: H. W. Wilson, 2000, pp. xv–xl. [18th ed. forthcoming 2004]

Taylor, Arlene G. *Wynar's Introduction to Cataloging and Classification.* 9th ed., with the assistance of David P. Miller. Englewood, Colo.: Libraries Unlimited, 2000. Chapter 16: "Sears List of Subject Headings."

MeSH

"*MeSH* Introduction." In *Medical Subject Headings: Annotated Alphabetic List.* Bethesda, Md.: National Library of Medicine, 1998, pp. I–3 to IL–166.

National Library of Medicine. *Fact Sheet: Medical Subject Headings* (*MeSH*®). Last updated 4 December 2002. Available: http://www.nlm.nih.gov/pubs/factsheets/mesh.html.

———. *Fact Sheet: UMLS*® *Metathesaurus*®. Last updated 13 January 2003. Available: http://www.nlm.nih.gov/pubs/factsheets/umlsmeta.html.

Taylor, Arlene G. *Wynar's Introduction to Cataloging and Classification.* 9th ed., with the assistance of David P. Miller. Englewood, Colo.: Libraries Unlimited, 2000. Chapter 17: "Other Types of Verbal Analysis."

AAT

Barnett, Patricia J., and Toni Petersen. "Extending MARC to Accommodate Faceted Thesauri: The *AAT* Model." In *Beyond the Book: Extending MARC for Subject Access,* edited by Toni Petersen and Pat Molholt. Boston: G. K. Hall, 1990, pp. 7–23.

The Getty. *Art & Architecture Thesaurus On Line: About the AAT.* Created 2000. Available: http://www.getty.edu/research/tools/vocabulary/aat/about.html.

ERIC

"ERIC's Indexing and Retrieval: 2001 Update" and "Thesaurus Construction and Format." In *Thesaurus of ERIC Descriptors,* edited by James E. Houston. 14th ed. Phoenix, Ariz.: Oryx Press, 2001, pp. xiv–xxxi.

Ontologies

Jacob, Elin K. "Ontologies and the Semantic Web." *Bulletin of the American Society for Information Science and Technology* 29, no. 4 (April/May 2003): 19–22. Available: http://www.asis.org/Bulletin/Apr-03/BulletinAprMay 03.pdf.

Noy, Natalya F., and Deborah L. McGuinness. *Ontology Development 101: A Guide to Creating Your First Ontology.* Knowledge Systems Laboratory, Stanford University, 2000. Available: http://www.ksl.stanford.edu/ people/dlm/papers/ontology-tutorial-noy-mcguinness-abstract.html.

OWL Web Ontology Language Overview, W3C Working Draft. 31 March 2003. Available: http://www.w3.org/TR/owl-features/.

WordNet®. Available: http://www.cogsci.princeton.edu/~wn.

NLP

Banerjee, Sujata, and Vibhu O. Mittal. "On the Use of Linguistic Ontologies for Accessing and Indexing Distributed Digital Libraries." In *Digital Libraries '94: Proceedings of the First Annual Conference on the Theory and Practice of Digital Libraries, June 19–21, 1994, College Station, Texas.* Available: http://www.csdl.tamu.edu/DL94/paper/banerjee.html.

Harris, Mary Dee. *Introduction to Natural Language Processing.* Reston, Va.: Reston, 1985, pp. 3–12.

Rich, Elaine, and Kevin Knight. *Artificial Intelligence.* 2nd ed. New York: McGraw-Hill, 1991. Chapter 15: "Natural Language Processing."

CHAPTER 11

SYSTEMS FOR CATEGORIZATION

The previous chapter discussed verbal methods of providing subject access to information packages. Another kind of subject access is provided by classification. Classification has a much longer history than that of controlled vocabularies. Philosophers have tried to categorize knowledge for many centuries. Classification basically is categorizing, but during the twentieth century, classification has come to be associated with assigning some kind of notation to physical information packages, and in the thinking of many persons, the connection to categorizing has been lost. However, the categories devised by philosophers in past centuries are the basis for the major classification schemes in use today.

Classification theory has not received as much attention in the United States as it has in other places such as European countries. There has been a tendency in the United States to see classification only as a way to arrange physical information packages. But there is great potential use for categorizing electronic resources. This chapter addresses this potential along with answering the following questions: How do humans categorize? How is subject content expressed symbolically in surrogate/metadata records? What conflicts arise in the application of classification to information packages? What is the role of automatic classification in organizing information?

THEORY OF CATEGORIZATION

It was mentioned in Chapter 1 that human beings seem to have a basic drive to organize and that children begin early to categorize images.

Children must learn early to distinguish between things that are edible and things that are not edible, for example. At later stages of development children categorize toys by color or by shape. Adults, too, seem to have a need for categories. Most people arrange their homes with quite different things in kitchens from those found in bedrooms, for example. Theory of categories goes back at least as far as the ancient Greeks. For example, Pythagoras (582?–500? B.C.E.) categorized the cycle of life as consisting of birth, growth, decay, death, absorption, and metamorphosis. Empedocles (490?–430? B.C.E.) placed every physical thing into one of four elements: earth, air, fire, and water.

Classical Theory of Categories

The roots of current classification systems can be traced back to Aristotle's theory of categories. He espoused the idea that things are placed into the same category on the basis of what they have in common. Aristotle's theory, the "classical theory of categories," went essentially unchallenged until the middle of the twentieth century, because, George Lakoff says, categories were thought to be well understood. A category was like an abstract container with things either inside or outside the container. The properties the things inside the container had in common were what defined the category.[1] Aristotle's categories, it should be noted, were arranged in a hierarchical fashion, the belief seeming to be that there was a perfect hierarchy for the world—all we had to do was find it.

A brief history of the research of the second half of the twentieth century will serve to illuminate the process of categorizing and its relationship to classification. This history is summarized from Lakoff.[2] Cracks began to appear in the classical theory of categories in 1953, when Ludwig Wittgenstein showed that a category like *game* does not fit the classical mold. This category has no single collection of common properties. For example, a game may be for education, amusement, or competition, and it may involve luck or skill. The game category has no fixed boundary, because new kinds of games such as video games and interactive computer games can be added to it. Wittgenstein proposed the idea that *family resemblances,* not a set of common properties, are what unites games into what we call a category. Just as members of a family have similarities, so do games.

J. L. Austin, in a paper published in 1961, extended Wittgenstein's analysis to the study of words. He wondered why we call different things by the same name (e.g., foot of a mountain, foot of a list, person's foot). Should not *mountain, list,* and *person* be in the same category if they all have a foot? But there are times when words do belong in the same category even though they share no common properties (e.g., *ball, bat,* and *umpire* can all go into the category *baseball*). Austin, like Wittgenstein, helped to show that traditional views of categories were inadequate.

Lotfi Zadeh contributed *fuzzy set theory* to the chipping away of the classical theory of categories. He noted that some categories are well defined while others are not. One either is or is not a member of a club, but whether one is tall or not depends to some extent upon the observer. The category of "tall" is graded—one may be neither clearly tall or clearly short; and a short person, looking at someone of medium height, would probably say that the person is tall. In 1965 Zadeh devised a form of set theory to deal with graded categories.

Floyd Lounsbury's studies of Native American kinship systems also chipped away at the classical theory. He found that among various groups, the same name is used to express the kinship relationships of several relatives. For example, in one group, uncles, great-uncles, and nephews on one's mother's side of the family are all called by the same word. (Perhaps they find it strange that in the dominant culture there is no verbal distinction between uncles who are the mother's brothers and uncles who are the father's brothers.) A challenge to classical theory here is that what seem to be definite and distinct categories in one culture and language are not the same categories in another culture and language.

Brent Berlin and Paul Kay (also mentioned in the preceding chapter) published their work on color in 1969. They found that in different languages there can be expressions for two to eleven basic colors. Although people speaking languages that have fewer than the eleven basic color names of English can conceptually differentiate all the colors, they cannot express them as different words. For example, red, orange, and yellow may all be expressed as the same word. Again it is shown that language and culture play a major role in the establishment of categories.

Paul Kay of the previous team and Chad McDaniel did follow-up work with colors and reported it in 1978. They drew on work that had been done in neurophysiology to conclude that human biology influences perception of color. They drew on fuzzy set theory to determine that in all cultures that have fewer than eleven basic colors, "cold" colors always include green, blue, and black, while "warm" colors always include red, orange, yellow, and white. Thus, color categories are not quite as arbitrary as might have been implied by the Berlin/Kay studies.

Roger Brown began the study of "basic-level categories." His work published in 1965 observed that there is a first level at which children learn categories (e.g., flower [for any variety of flower]). Yet there are many names that can be used for such categories, some more specific (e.g., rose, daffodil) and some more general (e.g., plant). Brown considered the child-level to be "natural," while the specific and general levels were viewed as "achievements of the imagination."

Brent Berlin and associates, in research on naming plants and animals, published from 1969 to 1977, showed that there seems to be a universal level at which humans name things, and for plants and animals it is more likely to be at the genus level (e.g., *oak*, not *tree* and not *white oak;* although this might not hold true for someone with experience only in an urban culture or for someone whose training has led to a more precisely honed level). It can be suggested that certain basic levels of categories have to do with being human and will be the same across cultures.

Prototype Theory

A major crack in classical theory of categories came when Eleanor Rosch developed "prototype theory" with her work between 1973 and 1981. She theorized that if, as classical theory states, categories are defined only by properties that all members share, then no members should be better examples of the category than any other members. She further theorized that if categories are defined only by properties that all members share, then categories should be independent of the humans doing the categorizing. She found that, contrary to classical theory, categories *do* have best examples (i.e., prototypes). For example, Rosch found that people in her research thought that *robin* was a better example of *bird* than was *ostrich.* And she found that human capacities *do* play a role in categorization (e.g., for someone 5 feet tall, there are many more "tall people" in the world than there are for someone 6 feet tall). This is the *fuzzy set theory,* mentioned earlier. *Ad hoc* categories also figure in here. Ad hoc categories are those that are made up on the spur of the moment. Different people will put different things into a category such as "things to take camping," depending upon their experience, where they are going, how they will camp, and so forth.

Because the most widely used classification schemes in the United States are based upon the classical theory of categories, classifiers using them are sometimes quite frustrated to find that they have a subject concept that does not fit neatly into one of the categories. They are often relieved to learn that classical theory has major cracks; so it is not unusual to run into nonprototypes and fuzzy sets.

BIBLIOGRAPHIC CLASSIFICATION

Bibliographic classification came into being for the purpose of arranging and retrieving information packages, and later became used for the purpose of arranging surrogate records for those information packages. Classification schemes as we know them are relatively new in the history of organization. Early depositories of recorded information usually had some arrangement: title, broad subject, chronology, author, order of acquisition, or size. Callimachus's *Pinakes* had at least ten broad categories (or main classes). Arrangement within the classes tended to be by author. This seemed to be a model for arrangement of catalogs and bibliographies into the early Middle Ages.

During the mid–Middle Ages, when monastery libraries became the keepers of books, there was little need for classification because the libraries were so small. The universities of the late Middle Ages divided their books according to the Trivium (Grammar, Rhetoric, Logic) and the Quadrivium (Arithmetic, Music, Geometry, Astronomy), the seven subject fields taught. But within the seven classes, the books had fixed shelf locations.

Starting in the sixteenth century, librarians devised many different classification schemes. Often these were based upon philosophers' systems of knowledge. However, none caught on, and fixed locations continued to predominate. With the rapid growth of libraries in the nineteenth century, librarians felt a need for better arrangement so that the content of the collections would be more apparent to the user. Philosopher Francis Bacon in the early seventeenth century divided knowledge into three basic "faculties": history (natural, civil, literary, ecclesiastical); philosophy (including theology); and works of imagination (poetry, fables, etc.). This scheme had widespread influence, and numerous classification schemes were based upon it. The most famous was that of Thomas Jefferson, who classified his own library before he eventually gave it to the Library of Congress as the basis of a new collection in 1815.

Some history of the development of specific classification schemes in the nineteenth and twentieth centuries is discussed in Chapter 3 and need not be repeated in full here. Very briefly, in 1876 Melvil Dewey devised his Dewey Decimal Classification (DDC), and shortly afterward, Charles Cutter began work on his Expansive Classification. Otlet and La-Fontaine began development of the Universal Decimal Classification (UDC), based on the fifth edition of DDC, in 1895. At the beginning of the twentieth century the Library of Congress created its own classification (LCC), based loosely on Cutter's Expansive Classification. S. R. Ranganathan created his Colon Classification (CC) in the early 1930s and adapted the word *facet* as a term to indicate the various subparts of the whole classification notation.

Hierarchical, Enumerative, and Faceted Classifications

As all of the schemes just mentioned were devised before anyone challenged the classical theory of categories, these schemes were (except for CC) firmly based in *hierarchical* arrangements. And even CC is hierarchical at its main starting level. Hierarchical schemes follow classical theory, creating categories from general to specific. For example, DDC starts with ten main classes, divides each of those into ten divisions (one hundred), divides each of the divisions into ten sections (one thousand), divides each of those into ten subsections (ten thousand), and so on into potential infinity (see Figure 11.1).

The same classification schemes were also fairly *enumerative.* Enumerative schemes attempt to assign a designation for every subject concept (both single and composite) needed in the system. All schemes have elements that are enumerative, but some much more than others. LCC is much more enumerative than is DDC (see Figure 11.2). UDC started out based on DDC, and so was hierarchical and enumerative at its base; it has now developed more into what we call a *faceted* scheme.

If one thinks of each of the faces of a cut and polished diamond as a *facet* of the whole diamond, one can picture a classification notation that has small notations standing for subparts of the whole topic strung together to create a complete classification notation. This concept was named first by S. R. Ranganathan in explanation of his classification. CC provides lists of designations for single concepts, with rules for combining them for complex concepts.

Ranganathan posed five fundamental categories that can be used to illustrate the facets of a subject: personality (i.e., the focal or most specific subject); material; energy (i.e., an activity, operation, or process); space (i.e., place); and time. Using the first letters of the five words, he called this the "PMEST" formula. For example, "the design of wooden furniture in eighteenth-century America" has all five facets. Furniture is the focal subject, or personality; wood is the material facet; design is an activity and so constitutes the energy facet; the space is America; and the time is the eighteenth century. If each facet has a specific notation (e.g., let's say P28 for furniture, M16 for wood, etc.), then these notations can be strung together according to the rules of the system.

Both CC and UDC use punctuation marks and symbols between

The Ten Main Classes

000	Computer science, information & general works
100	Philosophy & psychology
200	Religion
300	Social sciences
400	Language
500	Science
600	Technology
700	Arts & recreation
800	Literature
900	History & geography

The Hundred Divisions

. . .

600	**Technology**
600	Technology
610	Medicine & health
620	Engineering
630	Agriculture
640	Home & family management
650	Management & public relations
660	Chemical engineering
670	Manufacturing
680	Manufacture for specific uses
690	Building & construction

. . .

Detailed hierarchy for 646.724

600	Technology
640	Home & family management
646	Sewing, clothing, management of personal and family life
646.7	Management of personal and family life
646.72	Care of hair, face, skin, nails
646.724	**Care of hair**
646.7240, . . .	Standard and Special Subdivisions
646.7247	Braiding
646.7248	Wigs

Fig. 11.1. Illustration of hierarchical arrangement in the Dewey Decimal Classification (DDC), 22nd ed. (Source: WebDewey through OCLC Connexion.)

A – General Works
B – Philosophy. Psychology. Religion
C – Auxiliary Sciences of History
D – History: General and Old World
E – History: America
F – History: America
   . . .
S – Agriculture
T – Technology

TT1-999	Handicrafts. Arts and crafts
	Including mechanic trades

	Hairdressing, barbering, beauty culture, cosmetology, etc.
	Including beauty shop practice
TT950	Periodicals, societies, collections, etc.
TT951	Dictionaries and encyclopedias
	Documents
	United States
TT952	General works
TT953.A-.W	States, A-W

   . . .

TT960	Barbers' manuals
TT963	Hair styles for men
TT964	Shaving

   . . .

TT970	Haircutting (General)
	Cf. TT960 Barber's manuals
TT971	Study and teaching
	Hairdressing for women
TT972	General works
TT973	Hair tinting and bleaching
	Hairwork
TT975	Braids, wigs, toupees, etc.

Fig. 11.2. Illustration of the hierarchical and enumerative arrangement of the Library of Congress Classification (LCC). (Source: Classification Web. Available: http://classweb.loc.gov/ [by subscription].)

the notations as "facet indicators." These help to identify the relationships among the facets. In the earliest versions of the scheme, CC used the "colon" (:) in significant positions; thus the name of the scheme. By the middle of the twentieth century, though, Ranganathan realized that a more elaborate system of facet indicators was needed to avoid confusion, and additional pieces of punctuation were adopted for this purpose. The long notations created in faceted schemes are not easy to use for arranging physical information packages on shelves. However, in online catalogs they have the potential to be quite helpful, as each facet may be searched independently.

LCC has limited faceting capabilities. There are tables of geographic areas in some schedules, for example, that can be used to build notations that show place. Many of the table numbers, however, are literally mathematically added to a number in the schedule; the resulting notation does not show the geographic area as a facet. Only the geographic area notations that are "cutter numbers," consisting of the first letter of the geographic area name and one or more numerical digits, are recognizable as facets. (See discussion of cutter numbers in Chapter 12.)

DDC has many faceting capabilities and gains more with each new edition. There are six tables that can be used at various places in the schedules. The notations from tables are attached to the end of the notation from the schedule so that the facet is intact. In some cases, the end of the schedule notation and the beginning of the table notation are not demarcated; but most of the time the table notation is preceded by digit "0" or "1." As new editions create new faceting arrangements, they are using "0" and "1" to indicate the beginning of a facet

Major Bibliographic Classification Schemes

The major bibliographic classification schemes (i.e., DDC, LCC, UDC) have certain components in common. These have been outlined by Hope Olson and John Boll as follows:

- A verbal description, topic by topic, of the things and concepts that can be represented in or by the scheme.

- An arrangement of these verbal descriptions in classed or logical order that is intended to permit a meaningful arrangement of topics and that will be convenient to users.

- A notation that appears alongside each verbal description, which is used to represent it and which shows the order. The entire group of verbal descriptions and notations form the schedules.

- References within the schedules to guide the classifier and the searcher in different aspects of a desired topic or to other related topics (like the related term references in alphabetical lists).

- An alphabetical index of terms used in the schedules, and of synonyms of those terms, that leads to the notations.

- Instructions for use. General instructions (with examples) are usually to be found at the beginning of the scheme, and instructions relating to particular parts of the schedules are, or should be, given in the parts to which they relate.

- An organization that will ensure that the classification scheme is maintained, that is, revised and republished. This is external to the scheme, but an important factor in evaluating its comparative usefulness.[3]

In addition to the *schedules* mentioned in the third point above, the schemes have *tables* that are independent listings of notations for concepts that can be attached or added to the notations from the schedules. The tables comprise listings of such concepts as form/genre, geographic area, and language. In addition to the instructions in the schemes themselves, these major bibliographic classifications have separate manuals that give further instructions and many examples of the use of the schemes. Manuals can be written by either the organizations responsible for the maintenance of the schemes, by independent parties, or by both.

Traugott Koch has suggested that there are four broad varieties of classification schemes:

- Universal schemes—examples include the Dewey Decimal Classification (DDC), the Universal Decimal Classification (UDC), and the Library of Congress Classification (LCC);

- National general schemes—universal in subject coverage but usually designed for use in a single country. Examples include the Nederlandse Basisclassificatie (BC) and the Sveriges Allmäma Biblioteksförening (SAB);

- Subject specific schemes—designed for use by a particular subject community. Examples include Iconclass for art resources, the National Library of Medicine (NLM) scheme for medicine and Engineering Information (Ei) for engineering subjects;

- Home-grown schemes—schemes devised for use in a particular service. An example from the Internet is the "ontology" developed for the Yahoo! search service.[4]

At Koch's Web site there is a description of each of the major schemes he mentions. Koch also has created a useful list of many classification systems, as well as controlled vocabularies, available on the Web.[5] In addition, there are a number of homegrown schemes in print that are interesting and useful in particular contexts. One example is *A Classification System for Libraries of Judaica*, now in its third edition.[6] It is kept up-to-date by people who make use of it. For example, after the publication of the third edition, a synagogue librarian created a Holocaust Expansion that is posted with the home page of the authors of the third edition.[7]

There are many more classification schemes not mentioned here. Much has been written about each of the classification schemes mentioned, as well as many not mentioned. At the end of the chapter are suggestions for places to read about the schemes and, in some cases, manuals for use in applying them.

CLASSIFICATION CONCEPTS

A number of classification concepts and issues affect the use of classification schemes. Some of these apply to the application of a scheme regardless of how the classification is going to be used (e.g., as a way of arranging physical information packages; as a way of identifying subject content in metadata; as a way of organizing and/or presenting virtual information packages; etc.). Others are issues particularly in the use of classification as a device for arranging physical information packages. The following sections are arranged from general to specific.

Broad vs. Close Classification

Broad classification is classification that uses only the main classes and divisions of a scheme and perhaps only one or two levels of subdivisions. *Close classification* is classification that uses all the minute subdivisions that are available for very specific subjects. This is somewhat like the "specific vs. general" issue in controlled vocabularies. It is necessary to decide when beginning to use a classification scheme whether one is only going to use the top levels of the scheme or whether one is going to use the scheme at the deepest level possible.

One issue here is that if the intent of using the scheme is to collocate topics, then broad vs. close may depend upon the size of the collection that is being classified. If the collection is very large, then using only the top levels of the scheme means that very large numbers of information packages, or the surrogate records for them, will be collocated at the same notation. On the other hand, if the collection is very small, then using close classification may mean that most notations are assigned to only one or two information packages, with the result that collocation is minimal (unless one is using a scheme like DDC where one can drop digits off the end of the notation to get to the next broader level of the concept being sought).

It might be observed that what is considered close classification for a small collection may be broad classification for a large collection. That is, for a small collection, DDC's 612.1, meaning the concept of "blood and circulation" in medicine, is a very specific level; but in a medical collection there may be a thousand or more information packages on blood and circulation, and for that collection, close classification would mean going to 612.112, meaning "white corpuscles."

Another issue has to do with the globalization of organization of information. Even if a collection in a particular place is small, its metadata may be combined with that of many collections, producing a mega-collection. If some of the metadata has been created using close classification, and some has been created using broad classification, the combined effect will be confusing and less helpful. It may be necessary in today's world to use the closest classification available in the scheme being used. This is problematic in some institutions where the classification is used for arranging physical items. Close classification often produces very long notations, which sometimes have to be placed on very small items. Michael Gorman has suggested that this problem be solved by using shorter notations for *call numbers* but using close classification for the purposes of intellectual retrieval.[8] (See discussion of call numbers in Chapter 12.) This, of course, is objected to in many quarters because of the extra cost of providing two notations; but there is a cost to the user who is trying to retrieve information when classification is not usable for collocating topics.

Classification of Knowledge vs. Classification of a Particular Collection

Classification of knowledge is the concept that a classification system can be created that will encompass all knowledge that exists. DDC began as a classification of knowledge (at least Western knowledge as understood by Melvil Dewey). Classification of a particular collection is the concept that a classification system should only be devised for the information packages that are being added to collections, using the concept of *literary warrant*. Literary warrant is the name applied to the concept that new notations are created for a classification scheme and new terms are added to a controlled vocabulary only when information packages actually exist that are about a new concept. (See previous comments on literary warrant in Chapter 10.) LCC began as a classification of a particular collection.

Even though DDC began as a classification of knowledge, it has been forced to use literary warrant for updates and revisions. Some areas of knowledge that have developed in the twentieth century need significantly more space in the scheme than originally given, if indeed they existed and were given any at all. Dewey devoted a whole division to the artificial waterways called "canals," but the concept has been moved to allow expansion of other areas such as engineering, canals no longer being given the attention they were given in Dewey's day. And this is one value of the approach taken by LCC. The alphabet has twenty-six letters. In most places in LCC letters are doubled, and in the last revisions letters have been tripled, giving the potential for up to 1,352 divisions versus the 100 available to DDC. LCC has not come close to using this amount of space.

It can be seen that if a scheme has been devised using literary warrant, it can be more flexible than one devised on the basis of classification of knowledge. This issue may come down to preference as to the logical approach of a classification of knowledge versus the practical approach of a classification of what is being studied, created, or written about at the present time.

Integrity of Numbers vs. Keeping Pace With Knowledge

Integrity of numbers is the concept that in the creation and maintenance of a classification scheme, a notation, once assigned, should always retain the same meaning and should never be used with another meaning. *Keeping pace with knowledge* is the concept that in the creation and maintenance of a classification scheme, it is recognized that knowledge changes, and therefore it is necessary to be able to move concepts, insert new concepts, and to change meanings of numbers.

Melvil Dewey was a strong advocate of the concept of integrity of numbers. He did not want the users of his system ever to have to change a number because its meaning had been changed in the system. He wanted new concepts to be assigned to new numbers. As the twentieth century went forward, however, it became impossible to keep pace with new knowledge without sometimes changing the older notations. For example, in the field of mathematics the understanding of the field changed with new research. So it became necessary to change Dewey's arrangement of the basic sections of mathematics, with the following result:

DDC 1st edition	*DDC 22nd edition*
510 Mathematics	510 Mathematics
511 Arithmetic	511 General principles of mathematics
512 Algebra	512 Algebra
513 Geometry	513 Arithmetic
514 Trigonometry	514 Topology
515 Conic sections	515 Analysis
516 Analytical geometry	516 Geometry
517 Calculus	517 [Unassigned]
518 Quaternions	518 Numerical analysis [formerly 515]
519 Probabilities	519 Probabilities and applied mathematics

Such changing of meanings of numbers always involves soul-searching on the part of classifiers. As cost is an ever-present issue, there is a desire not to have to change notations, because this can be expensive. On the other hand, if changes are not made, the system exists with, for example, 513 meaning both *geometry* and *arithmetic.* Collocation is compromised. Searches on classification notations produce confusing results. On the other hand, it has been argued that leaving the older materials in the older numbers accurately reflects their contents, while newer materials reflect the new thinking that prompted the change in the scheme. This only works if the different schemes are kept separate both in arranging and in searching.

At the level of the classification scheme itself, its keepers must update it periodically or it will not continue to serve its purpose. If the scheme is flexible enough, updates can be accomplished by inserting new notations. LCC, for example, accomplishes most of its updating in this fashion. If the scheme is less flexible, as with DDC, some inserting can be done, but sometimes meanings of numbers must also be changed.

It was mentioned earlier that some classification issues are general, but others mainly are issues for the use of classification for arranging physical items. Integrity of numbers versus keeping pace with knowledge is an issue that has both general and physical implications and gives us a transition into the issues regarding physical entities. In this case reclassification of physical items when meanings of numbers have been changed is an expensive process. In most collections complete reclassification is not done. Instead there often is some kind of process set up to reclassify items as they are used. Items needing reclassification are taken care of as they are returned after the first use after a change in a number's meaning. Or sometimes a whole collection affected by a change of numbers in a whole section of the scheme will be reclassified on a project basis. Changing only some of a collection, of course, ignores the use of classification as a search key in an online system. Searching a system where certain notations bring up surrogate records for information packages on different subjects is not satisfactory.

Fixed vs. Relative Location

The term *fixed location* signifies a set place where a physical information package will always be found or to which it will be returned after having been removed for use. A fixed location identifier can be an accession number; or a designation made up of room number, stack number, shelf number, position on shelf, and so on; or other such designations.

The term *relative location* is used to mean that an information package will be or might be in a different place each time it is reshelved; that is, it is reshelved relative to what else has been acquired, taken out, returned, and so forth, while it was out for use. The method for accomplishing this is usually a *call number* with the top line or two being a classification notation. (See discussion of call numbers in Chapter 12.)

Fixed location is often used for the purpose of saving space. If fixed location is used, space does not have to be left at the end of each shelf for potential new acquisitions in a particular area of the classification. This is particularly useful for remote storage facilities where space must be saved. Relative location, however, is desirable in a situation where users have access to the stacks and can browse (see discussion of closed versus open stacks below).

It is often argued that the cost of fixed location is much less than that of relative location. If classification notations do not have to be assigned, and if space can be used to the fullest, then cost of fixed location is less to the agency involved. However, especially in libraries, the cost is passed on to the user who loses the collocation provided by classification and the serendipity of being able to browse in the stacks.

Closed vs. Open Stacks

Closed stacks is the name given to the situation where information package storage areas are accessible only to the staff of the library, archives, or other place that houses information packages. *Open stacks* is the name given to the opposite situation where patrons of the facility have the right to go into the storage areas themselves. In closed stack situations users must call for items at a desk and then wait for them to be retrieved and delivered. This eliminates any possibility of what is called *browsing*. Browsing is a process of looking, usually based on subject, at all the items in a particular area of the stacks, or in a listing in an online retrieval tool, in order to find, often by serendipity, the items that best suit the needs of the browser.

In most cases where remote storage is used for older and less-used materials, compact shelving is used. This means that in order to make the most efficient use of space, items are shelved using every inch of shelf space, usually with fixed location. In such situations the storage areas are closed. A number of large research libraries have for a long time had closed stacks. There are various reasons for this, including tradition, vandalism, and precedence of certain classes of users over others. In such libraries a proposal to stop classifying resurfaces every so often. The question asked is, "Why classify if readers cannot browse?" Such a proposal includes data about how costs will be lowered if classification is stopped. However, classification is a major form of subject access, and if browsing of the stacks is not allowed, then browsing of the classification listing in the catalog becomes even more important. Reference librarians often use classification to assist users in finding subject-related material.[9]

In archives the storage areas are almost always closed. This hardly matters as far as classification goes because classification has not been found to be particularly useful for archives in any case. A collection of records can have individual pieces that are on diverse subjects, and dividing and separating these out to classify would violate the principle of provenance. It is conceivable that whole collections could be classified, but usually the classification in such a case would be so broad as to be nearly meaningless.

Location Device vs. Collocation Device

Another controversy surrounding classification is that of whether classification serves as a collocation device or whether it is simply a location device. A *location device* is a number or other designation on an item to tell where it is located physically. It can be an accession number, a physical location number, or a call number, among other designators. A *collocation device* is a number or other designation on an item used to place it next to (i.e., collocate with) other items that are like it. It is usually a classification notation.

Those responsible for the costs of organizing collections tend to take the location device view. They believe that any call number is all right as long as the notation placed on the physical item matches the notation on the surrogate record for the item. The argument is that if the notations on item and surrogate record match, the user will be able to find the item. However, this assumes that the subject headings are sufficient for finding subject-related material in a catalog. Thomas Mann, cited above, and others have shown that both subject headings and classification are required for the most effective retrieval of subject-related material.[10]

It is not clear whether the same notation is adequate to serve both the collocation and the location functions. Gorman, as mentioned above, has suggested that a fully detailed classification be assigned for the purpose of collocation, while a shortened version of it be used for a location device.[11] (This would not really be helpful in the case of LCC, because most notations, even for complex subjects, are relatively short.) In most of the United States, one classification notation has served for both collocation and location for many decades. In some other places, especially where classified catalogs are used, the functions of collocation and location have been served by different notations for decades.

A recent point for discussion has been classification of Internet resources. Cost managers often believe that classification is mainly for location, and because Internet resources have location devices in the form of URLs, no classification is needed. However, from the viewpoint of the user, classification can be an effective means of organizing Internet information packages for subject retrieval (see discussion below).

Classification of Serials vs. Alphabetic Order of Serials

Serials are sometimes called journals or magazines. A *serial* may be defined as a publication issued in successive parts (regularly or irregularly) that is intended to continue indefinitely. Classification of serials means that a classification notation is assigned to a serial, and this classification notation is placed on each bound volume and/or each issue of that serial. Alphabetic order of serials means that the serials are placed in order on shelves or in a listing according to the alphabetical order of the titles of the serials. The issues involved in the classification/alphabetic order dilemma apply to runs of printed serials. Serials now produced only on the Internet have issues and problems, but classification is not yet one of these.

With serials it is sometimes quite difficult to discern the intended title because of its placement (e.g., following a corporate body name that is in larger type than the title). In addition, serials are apt to have title changes, sometimes several times. They also can merge or split, and can be absorbed by another serial, all of which result in title changes. This is one of the most persuasive arguments against alphabetic order of serials. What to do with runs of serials when there has been a title change is not a resolved issue. Some institutions move the whole run and place at the alphabetic position of the old title(s) a "dummy block" that gives the new title. It is argued in this situation that users will expect to find all of that serial together in spite of the title change. Other institutions divide the serial at the point of the new title. It is argued here that when a title changes, it does so because of a change of emphasis in the serial; therefore, the two runs are almost like two different serials.

Classification of serials provides a solution to the title change dilemma. The new title can be given the same classification as the old. It also has the advantage of allowing the serial to be placed with monographs on the same subject; this is beneficial for browsing purposes. However, classification requires two look-ups. That is, a user comes to the collection with a citation to an article in a journal. If the serial collection is classified, the user must look for the journal title in the catalog, note its call number, and then go to the stacks to find that call number. If serials are placed alphabetically, the user goes to the serials stacks with the citation and finds the journal title. Classification also requires more cataloging/indexing time and thus seems to cost more, although the maintenance of title changes in an alphabetically arranged situation may offset some of the cost that would be incurred by classifying.

One other consideration is the arrangement of serials in a "special library." Many such libraries are subject area–specific. In some of these situations, most of the serials are on the same or closely related subjects, which could mean that their classification notations would be very near each other, resulting in a semi-alphabetic order. Such libraries often choose alphabetic arrangement in the first place. The actual arrangement of serials in all libraries in the United States is about 50 percent alphabetic and 50 percent classified.

Classification of Monographic Series (Classified Separately vs. Classified as a Set)

First, let us define monograph. A *monograph* is a complete bibliographic unit or information package. It is often a single work, but may also be one work or more than one work issued in successive parts; but unlike a serial, it is not intended to be continued indefinitely. A work intended to be complete in, let's say, twenty-eight volumes, is a monograph. A *monographic series* is a hybrid of monograph and serial. In a monographic series each work that is issued as a part of the series is a monograph but is identified as one work in the series. The series itself may or may not be intended to be continued indefinitely. For example, the *Library Science Text*

Series published by Libraries Unlimited, Inc., continues to have new works added to it as appropriate works are identified by the publisher.

The difficulty with classification of monographic series is whether to classify each work in the series separately with a specific class number representing its particular subject matter, or to treat the series as if it were a multivolume monograph and give all parts of the series the same (usually broad) classification notation representing the subject matter of the entire series. Classification of the series as a set results in the loss of collocation of the specific subjects contained in each of the works.

On the other hand, especially in public libraries, classification of the series as a set may meet with resounding approval by the users. There are readers who wish to go through a series one by one and find it satisfactory to have them classified together. It is obviously the intention of some publishers that some series be shelved together, especially those series that are bound alike. In some cases the situation is handled by acquiring duplicates, and then classifying one with the set and the other in its specific subject area. The cost of doing this usually is not supported, however, and sometimes cost is the deciding factor for classifying a series as a set—it is cheaper to slap on an already-conceived classification notation than to do the subject analysis necessary for specific classification.

TAXONOMIES

Definitions of *taxonomy* abound in the literature, and some of those definitions contradict each other. Amy Warner says that the terms *taxonomies, thesauri,* and *classification systems* are synonyms that are "organized lists of words and phrases, or notation systems, that are used to initially tag content, and then to find it through navigation or search."[12] She goes on to say that definitions of terms are currently in flux and that one hopes that definitions will soon be standardized. Similar confusion is indicated in the *Montague Institute Review:*

> Taxonomies have recently emerged from the quiet backwaters of biology, book indexing, and library science into the corporate limelight. They are supposed to be the silver bullets that will help users find the needle in the intranet haystack, reduce "friction" in electronic commerce, facilitate scientific research, and promote global collaboration. But before this can happen, practitioners need to dispel the myths and confusion, created in part

by the multi-disciplinary nature of the task and the hype surrounding content management technologies.[13]

The article continues by saying that the confusion begins with definitions and gives the following very broad definition: "A taxonomy is a system for naming and organizing things into groups that share similar characteristics."[14] These definitions do not include the necessity for hierarchy, but Thomas Wason says that "A taxonomy is a controlled vocabulary of terms and or phrases . . . an orderly classification of information according to presumed natural relationships. . . . The most typical form of a taxonomy is a hierarchy."[15]

F. W. Lancaster, in decrying the "rediscovery of wheels" he sees in today's "new" concepts says, "My biggest complaint, however, is the fact that the noun 'classification' has virtually been replaced by (shudder!) 'taxonomy,' (double shudder!!) 'ontology,' or even (triple shudder!!!) 'taxonomized set of terms.' The way these terms are defined in recent articles clearly shows that they are used synonymously with 'classification scheme.' "[16]

Taxonomy comes from the Greek *taxis* (arrangement, order) and *nomos* (law). Taxonomies have existed in the strict, hierarchical world of science at least since 1735, when Linnaeus published his *Systema Naturae*, a classification of plants and animals. The taxonomies being constructed today for use in intranets, though, do not follow such strict rules, nor are they always hierarchical. What they do seem to have in common is categories. Therefore, the discussion of categorization above is also applicable to taxonomies.

Lists of taxonomies that one finds on the Web often include traditional classification schemes, subject heading lists, and Internet directories and gateways, as well as subject-specific tools that actually call themselves taxonomies. Examples of the last are the "Taxonomy of Educational Technology"[17] and "GRIN Taxonomy."[18] (GRIN is The Germplasm Resources Information Network.) A number of taxonomies are proprietary to the organizations that created them and are under copyright so that they may not be freely used in other situations, even if the subject matter is identical.

CLASSIFICATION ON THE INTERNET

Although classification has an obvious role in organizing tangible (physical) information packages, the role that classification can play in organizing the Internet is less well understood. Research has shown that browsing is quite useful for information discovery in a variety of environments.[19] Classification gives the ability to browse and also to narrow and broaden searches, another activity valued by users. In a physical arrangement, the relationship of classification to browsing is obvious to the user, but this need not be true with Internet resources. A hierarchical or faceted arrangement can be exploited without the user seeing any classification notations. In this environment the concept might be better understood if it were called categorization.

Categorization is apparent in Yahoo![20] where Web sites are placed into categories that have been created by the catalogers at Yahoo!; the categories can be viewed in hierarchical fashion. However, the hierarchies are not true hierarchies in the sense that categories at the same hierarchical level are narrower concepts of the concept at the next level up, nor are the subcategories at an equivalent level with each other. For example, under *Recreation & Sports* one finds the following subcategories (as of August 9, 2003):

- Automotive

- Aviation

- Chats and Forums

- Employment

- Events

- Gambling

- Games

- etc.

interfiled with references for:

- Amusement and Theme Parks (categorized under *Entertainment*)

- Booksellers (categorized under *Business and Economy > Shopping and Services > Books > Bookstores*)

- Cooking (categorized under *Society and Culture > Food and Drink*)

- Dance (categorized under *Arts > Performing Arts*)

- Fitness (categorized under *Health*)

- etc.

In comparing the terms in the list, one can see that "Automotive" and "Aviation" might be seen as kinds of "Recreation," but "Chats and Forums" and "Events" are about recreation, and "Employment" identifies opportunities in recreation.

Under *Automotive* one finds that there is a "top category" of "Makes and Models," followed by "Additional Categories":

- Accessories

- Alternative fuel vehicles

- British cars

- Buyer's Guides

- Charitable Vehicle Donation

- Chats and Forums

- Classic Cars

- Clubs and Organizations

- etc.

interfiled with references for:

- Auto-free Transportation (categorized under *Recreation > Travel > Transportation*)

- Booksellers (categorized under *Business and Economy > Shopping and Services > Books > Bookstores*)

- Buses (categorized under *Recreation > Travel > Transportation*)

- Business to Business (categorized under *Business and Economy*)

- Car Art (categorized under *Arts: Visual Arts*)

- Classifieds (categorized under *Business and Economy > Shopping and Services > Automotive*)

- etc.

"Accessories" seems not to be at the same level of specificity as "British cars" and "Classic Cars." "Buyer's Guides," "Chats and Forums," and "Clubs and Organizations" are not kinds of "Automotive," but are entities that concern themselves with the topic. The references for "Auto-free Transportation" and "Classifieds" appear to have strayed somewhat from the idea of "Recreation."

It is unfortunate that Yahoo! chose not to take advantage of an already-existing classification or at least use classification theory. The subcategories in each category of the "hierarchy" cannot all be viewed on one screen, and as more categories need to be added, and the lists take more and more screens, users will be more and more dependent upon the terminology chosen to represent the categories. All of the keyword issues found in the various search engines will need to be addressed. An already-existing classification has several advantages: it provides consistent levels in a hierarchy; it is kept up-to-date through consultation with many users; and it also is well known to many users.

As already mentioned, classification of sites on the Internet can give assistance with browsing and with narrowing or broadening of searches. It can also assist with context for searches of concepts that can appear in more than one field of knowledge. For example, the concept of "children" can be seen in relation to psychology, religion, education, language, medicine, art, and others. Classification can let one know which context applies. In addition, on the Internet, an information package can be placed into as many categories as are appropriate. If a work discusses "children" in relation to both education and art, it can be placed in both categories. What one has, then, is essentially a classified catalog in electronic form.

Classification is a useful way to divide large databases logically. It offers an alternative to alphabetical subdivision, which is quite useful for known-item searches but not so useful for subject searches (unless the letters of the alphabet take one to a thesaurus instead of to titles arranged alphabetically). And if the same classification scheme is chosen by several database sites, it is possible to enable searching across databases.

Finally, classification can be used as a switching language among many languages. The notations of a classification are not language-specific, and therefore the meanings of the notations can be given in whatever language is appropriate for the setting. For DDC, for example, translations into a number of languages either already exist or are being worked on: for example, Arabic, French, Greek, Hebrew, Italian, Persian, Russian, and Spanish. The Universal Decimal Classification (UDC) is also multilingual. There are full editions in English, French, German, Japanese, Russian, and eight other languages. Abridged editions exist in seventeen languages and five alphabets. Unfortunately, LCC has not yet moved in a multilingual direction.

A criticism of using classification for the Internet is that humans often need to determine the categories, and the sheer number of information packages makes the task daunting. Research is being conducted on automatic classification. One such project is at OCLC. When cataloging Internet resources through Connexion, one can ask for automatic classification. Software developed by OCLC researchers analyzes the text of a Web site, compares text words to words available in headings and notes found in the DDC, and then assigns DDC numbers based on the comparisons. The software is available for use or evaluation by others.[21] Another project, conducted by Microsoft researchers, automatically organizes Web search results into hierarchical categories.[22]

Many subject search services on the Internet use a classification scheme for organization. An excellent list of sites that use classification schemes or subject headings is one created by Gerry McKiernan called *Beyond Bookmarks.*[23]

ARTIFICIAL NEURAL NETWORKS (ANNs)

An artificial neural network (ANN) is a computer system inspired by the architecture of the human biological nervous system. Artificial neural networks have been used in a variety of applications such as pattern and handwriting recognition. They have also been used for automatic categorization. Automatic categorization with ANNs has been used in some Information Retrieval (IR) applications.

One of the most widespread artificial neural network models used for categorization is a browsing tool called a self-organizing map (SOM) based on the work of Teuvo Kohonen.[24] SOMs can be compared to the IR methodology of clustering. Clustering brings related items together, which allows for browsing by subject area.

Researchers at the Neural Networks Research Centre of the Helsinki University of Technology have developed an exploratory full-text information retrieval method and browsing tool called the WEBSOM,[25] which uses ANNs to categorize automatically a variety of Web documents. The result is a map that provides visual representation of a collection of documents or other kinds of information. Not only are similar documents clustered together, but the map also displays subjects located near similar subjects. The size of an area in the map corresponds to the frequencies of word occurrence in the document set (see Figure 11.3). Such maps allow one to zoom in on a particular subject to obtain more specific subsets.

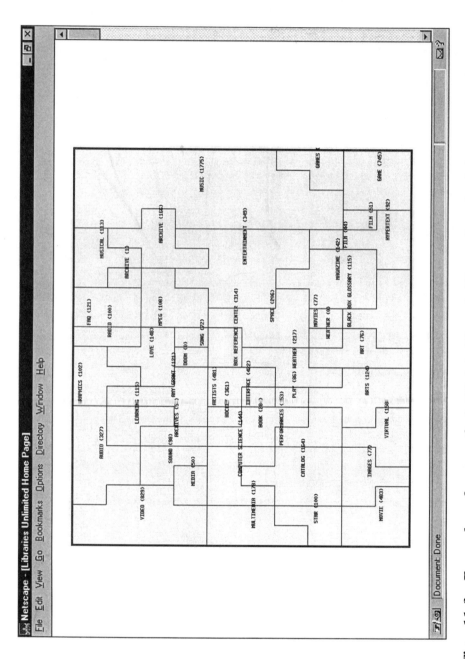

Fig. 11.3. Example of use of Artificial Neural Network principles to provide visual representation of the subject matter in a collection of documents. This SOM clusters words in an "entertainment" document set.

Then, often, zooming in again reveals dots, each of which will retrieve a document when clicked.

Another example of a visual presentation of information is the map one can see at Smartmoney.com (http://www.smartmoney.com/market map/). It shows activity of groups of stocks during the last trading session. Individual stocks are grouped into broad categories (e.g., Communication, Energy, Health care, Technology, etc.). Within the categories blocks of different sizes and colors represent the various stocks. Bright green blocks represent stocks that did well. Mousing over a block brings up identification of the stock and how much it gained or lost.

CONCLUSION

This chapter has addressed categorization and classification as a way to provide subject access to information packages. An understanding of classification theory has been shown to be helpful in understanding classification schemes in use today. Arrangement of classification schemes (i.e., hierarchical, enumerative, and faceted) is based in classification theory. Specific classifications are numerous and run from universal schemes to home-grown schemes. Regardless of which scheme is used, there are classification concepts and controversies that must be addressed in the application of any scheme. Some concepts apply to physical packages, while others apply both to physical and nontangible resources. Large numbers of sites of Internet resources are being organized with classification, often called taxonomies in this environment. The future holds the potential for the use of Artificial Neural Networks for a kind of automatic categorization, especially the visualization of topics and relationships among those topics.

One of the most important factors in information retrieval is to have information packages and surrogate records arranged or displayed in a logical fashion. Classification often plays a major role in such arrangement or display, which is the topic discussed in the next chapter.

NOTES

All URLs accessed July 2003.

1. George Lakoff, *Women, Fire, and Dangerous Things: What Categories Reveal About the Mind* (Chicago: University of Chicago Press, 1987), p. 6.

2. Ibid., pp. 16–57.

3.   Hope A. Olson and John J. Boll, *Subject Analysis in Online Catalogs*, 2nd ed. (Englewood, Colo.: Libraries Unlimited, 2001), pp. 155–156.

4.   From "Executive Summary" in Traugott Koch, *The Role of Classification Schemes in Internet Resource Description and Discovery*. Last updated 14 May 1997. Available: http://www.ukoln.ac.uk/metadata/desire/classification/class_su.htm.

5.   Traugott Koch, *Controlled Vocabularies, Thesauri and Classification Systems Available in the WWW. DC Subject.* Last updated 27 September 2001. Available: http://www.lub.lu.se/metadata/subject-help.html.

6.   David H. Elazar and Daniel J. Elazar, *A Classification System for Libraries of Judaica*, 3rd ed., with the assistance of Rachel K. Glasser and Rita C. Frischer (Northvale, N.J.: Jason Aronson, 1997). Home page for this work is available at: http://www.geocities.com/Athens/Acropolis/6527/class.html.

7.   Carylyn Gwyn Moser, *Elazar Classification System Holocaust Expansion*, 1997. Available: http://www.geocities.com/Athens/Acropolis/6527/holocaust.html.

8.   Michael Gorman, "The Longer the Number, the Smaller the Spine; or, Up and Down with Melvil and Elsie," *American Libraries* 12, no. 8 (September 1981): 498–499.

9.   Thomas Mann, *Doing Research at the Library of Congress. A Guide to Subject Searching in a Closed Stacks Library* (Washington, D.C.: Library of Congress, Humanities and Social Sciences Division, 1994).

10.   Ibid.

11.   Gorman, "The Longer the Number," pp. 498–499.

12.   Amy J. Warner, *A Taxonomy Primer* (Lexonomy, 2002). Available: http://www.lexonomy.com/publications/aTaxonomyPrimer.html.

13.   "Ten Taxonomy Myths," *Montague Institute Review*. November 2002; updated 29 April 2003. Available: http://www.montague.com/review/myths.shtml.

14.   Ibid.

15.   Thomas D. Wason, "Dr. Tom's Taxonomy Guide: Description, Use and Selections," IMS Global Learning Consortium, Inc., 10 August 2000. Available: http://www.imsglobal.org/drtomtaxonomiesguide.cfm.

16. F. W. Lancaster, *Indexing and Abstracting in Theory and Practice*, 3rd ed. (Champaign: University of Illinois, Graduate School of Library and Information Science, 2003), p. xiii.

17. Bertram C. Bruce and James A. Levin, "Educational Technology: Media for Inquiry, Communication, Construction, and Expression," *Journal of Educational Computing Research* 17, no. 1 (1997): 79–102. Also available: http://www.lis.uiuc.edu/~chip/pubs/taxonomy/index.html.

18. Agricultural Research Service, *GRIN Taxonomy*. Last updated 22 August 2000. Available: http://www.ars-grin.gov/npgs/tax/.

19. Gary Marchionini, *Information Seeking in Electronic Environments* (Cambridge; New York: Cambridge University Press, 1995).

20. Yahoo! Available: http://www.yahoo.com/.

21. OCLC, *Scorpion*. Available: http://www.oclc.org/research/software/scorpion/.

22. Hao Chen and Susan Dumais, "Bringing Order to the Web: Automatically Categorizing Search Results," Microsoft Research Publications, 2000. Available: http://research.microsoft.com/~sdumais/chi00.pdf.

23. Gerry McKiernan, *Beyond Bookmarks: Schemes for Organizing the Web*. 22 March 2001. Available: http://www.public.iastate.edu/~CYBERSTACKS/CTW.html.

24. Teuvo Kohonen, *Self-Organizing Maps*, 3rd ed. (Berlin, N.Y.: Springer-Verlag, 2001).

25. Timo Honkela, Samuel Kaski, Krista Lagus, and Teuvo Kohonen, "Self-Organizing Maps of Document Collections," *Alma* 2 (1996).

SUGGESTED READINGS

Classification in General

Bowker, Geoffrey C., and Susan Leigh Star. *Sorting Things Out: Classification and Its Consequences*. Cambridge, Mass.: MIT Press, 1999. Introduction: "To Classify Is Human", Chapter 9: "Categorical Work and Boundary Infrastructures: Enriching Theories of Classification", and Chapter 10: "Why Classifications Matter."

Classification Research Group. "The Need for a Faceted Classification as the Basis of All Methods of Information Retrieval." In *Theory of Subject*

Analysis: A Sourcebook, edited by Lois Mai Chan, Phyllis A. Richmond, and Elaine Svenonius. Littleton, Colo.: Libraries Unlimited, 1985, pp. 154–167.

Gorman, Michael. "The Longer the Number, the Smaller the Spine; or, Up and Down with Melvil and Elsie." *American Libraries* 12, no. 8 (September 1981): 498–499.

Hunter, Eric J. *Classification Made Simple.* 2nd ed. Aldershot, England; Brookfield, Vt.: Gower, 2002.

Intner, Sheila S., and Jean Weihs. *Standard Cataloging for School and Public Libraries.* 3rd ed. Englewood, Colo.: Libraries Unlimited, 2001. Chapter 10: "Classification Systems."

Lakoff, George. *Women, Fire, and Dangerous Things: What Categories Reveal About the Mind.* Chicago: University of Chicago Press, 1987. Chapter 1: "The Importance of Categorization."

Langridge, D. W. *Classification: Its Kinds, Elements, Systems, and Applications.* London: Bowker-Saur, 1992.

Leise, Fred. "Using Faceted Classification to Assist Indexing." *Key Words* 9, no. 6 (November/December 2001): 178–179.

Mann, Thomas. *Doing Research at the Library of Congress: A Guide to Subject Searching in a Closed Stacks Library.* Washington, D.C.: Library of Congress, Humanities and Social Sciences Division, 1994.

———. *Library Research Models: A Guide to Classification, Cataloging, and Computers.* New York: Oxford University Press, 1993. Chapter 3: "The Traditional Library Science Model, Part One: The Classification Scheme" and Chapter 5: "The Traditional Library Science Model, Part Three: Published Bibliographies and Indexes."

Marcella, Rita, and Arthur Maltby, eds. *The Future of Classification.* Aldershot, England; Brookfield, Vt.: Gower, 2000.

Marcella, Rita, and Robert Newton. *A New Manual of Classification.* Aldershot, England; Brookfield, Vt.: Gower, 1994.

Olson, Hope A., and John J. Boll. *Subject Analysis in Online Catalogs.* 2nd ed. Englewood, Colo.: Libraries Unlimited, 2001. Chapter 7: "Bibliographic Classification."

Soergel, Dagobert. "The Rise of Ontologies or the Reinvention of Classification." *Journal of the American Society for Information Science* 50, no. 12 (October 1999): 1119–1120.

Taylor, Arlene G. *Wynar's Introduction to Cataloging and Classification*. 9th ed., with the assistance of David P. Miller. Englewood, Colo.: Libraries Unlimited, 2000. Chapter 9: "Classification of Library Materials."

Specific Classification Schemes

Dewey Decimal Classification

Chan, Lois Mai, and Joan S. Mitchell. *Dewey Decimal Classification: Principles and Application*. 3rd ed. Dublin, Ohio: OCLC, 2003.

Dewey Decimal Classification Homepage. Available: http://www.oclc.org/dewey/index.htm.

Foskett, A. C. *The Subject Approach to Information*. 5th ed. London: Library Association Publishing, 1996. Chapter 17: "The Dewey Decimal Classification."

Olson, Hope A., and John J. Boll. *Subject Analysis in Online Catalogs*. 2nd ed. Englewood, Colo.: Libraries Unlimited, 2001. Chapter 8: "Online Catalogs and the Dewey Decimal and Library of Congress Classifications."

Taylor, Arlene G. *Wynar's Introduction to Cataloging and Classification*. 9th ed., with the assistance of David P. Miller. Englewood, Colo.: Libraries Unlimited, 2000. Chapter 10: "Decimal Classification."

Universal Decimal Classification

Foskett, A. C. *The Subject Approach to Information*. 5th ed. London: Library Association Publishing, 1996. Chapter 18: "The Universal Decimal Classification."

Taylor, Arlene G. *Wynar's Introduction to Cataloging and Classification*. 9th ed., with the assistance of David P. Miller. Englewood, Colo.: Libraries Unlimited, 2000. Chapter 10: "Decimal Classification." (UDC specifically discussed on pp. 300–301.)

UDC Consortium. "About Universal Decimal Classification and the UDC Consortium." Available: http://www.udcc.org/about.htm.

LC Classification

Chan, Lois Mai. *A Guide to the Library of Congress Classification.* 5th ed. Englewood, Colo.: Libraries Unlimited, 1999.

Foskett, A. C. *The Subject Approach to Information.* 5th ed. London: Library Association Publishing, 1996. Chapter 22: "The Library of Congress Classification."

Library of Congress, Cataloging Policy and Support Office. "Library of Congress Classification." Available: http://lcweb.loc.gov/catdir/cpso/cpso. html#class.

Taylor, Arlene G. *Wynar's Introduction to Cataloging and Classification.* 9th ed., with the assistance of David P. Miller. Englewood, Colo.: Libraries Unlimited, 2000. Chapter 11: "Library of Congress Classification."

Colon Classification

Foskett, A. C. *The Subject Approach to Information.* 5th ed. London: Library Association Publishing, 1996. Chapter 21: "The Colon Classification."

Ranganathan, S. R. *Prolegomena to Library Classification.* 3rd ed. London: Asia Publishing House, 1967.

Steckel, Mike. "Ranganathan for IAs. An Introduction to the Thought of S.R. Ranganathan for Information Architects." *Boxes and Arrows* (October 7, 2002). Available: http://www.boxesandarrows.com/archives/ ranganathan_for_ias.php.

Other Classification Schemes

Foskett, A. C. *The Subject Approach to Information.* 5th ed. London: Library Association Publishing, 1996. Chapter 19: "The Bibliographic Classification" and Chapter 20: "The Broad System of Ordering."

Hearst, Marti A. "Interfaces for Searching the Web." *Scientific American* 276, no. 3 (March 1997): 68–72. Also available: http://www.hackvan.com/ pub/stig/articles/trusted-systems/0397hearst.html.

Taylor, Arlene G. *Wynar's Introduction to Cataloging and Classification.* 9th ed., with the assistance of David P. Miller. Englewood, Colo.: Libraries Unlimited, 2000. Chapter 13: "Other Classification Systems."

Taxonomies

Bertolucci, Katherine. "Happiness Is Taxonomy: Four Structures for Snoopy." *Information Outlook* 7, no. 3 (March 2003): 36–44.

Nash, Lisa, and Aaron Press. "Taxonomies: Structuring Today's Knowledge Management Systems." *Information About Information Briefing* 4, no. 26 (July 18, 2001): 1–18.

"Ten Taxonomy Myths." *Montague Institute Review* (November 2002). Last updated 29 April 2003. Available: http://www.montague.com/review/myths.shtml.

Warner, Amy J. *A Taxonomy Primer.* Lexonomy, 2002. Available: http://www.lexonomy.com/publications/aTaxonomyPrimer.html.

Wason, Thomas D. "Dr. Tom's Taxonomy Guide: Description, Use and Selections." IMS Global Learning Consortium, Inc., 10 August 2000. Available: http://www.imsglobal.org/drtomtaxonomiesguide.cfm.

Classification and the Internet

Chen, Hao, and Susan Dumais. "Bringing Order to the Web: Automatically Categorizing Search Results." Microsoft Research Publications, 2000. Available: http://research.microsoft.com/~sdumais/chi00.pdf.

Koch, Traugott. *The Role of Classification Schemes in Internet Resource Description and Discovery.* Last updated 25 March 1998. Available: http://www.ukoln.ac.uk/metadata/desire/classification/class_ti.htm.

McKiernan, Gerry. *Beyond Bookmarks: Schemes for Organizing the Web.* Last updated 22 March 2001. Available: http://www.public.iastate.edu/~CYBERSTACKS/CTW.html.

Vizine-Goetz, Diane. "Online Classification: Implications for Classifying and Document[-like Object] Retrieval." In *Knowledge Organization and Change: Proceedings of the Fourth International ISKO Conference, 15–18 July 1996, Washington, D.C.,* edited by Rebecca Green. Frankfurt/Main: IN-DEKS Verlag, 1996. Also available: http://orc.rsch.oclc.org:6109/dvgisko.htm.

———. "Using Library Classification Schemes for Internet Resources." Last edited 23 November 1999. Available: http://staff.oclc.org/~vizine/Intercat/vizine-goetz.htm.

Artificial Neural Networks (ANNs)

Anderson, James A. *An Introduction to Neural Networks.* Cambridge, Mass.: MIT Press, 1995, pp. vii–xi, 1–15.

Doszkocs, Tamas, James Reggia, and Xia Lin. "Connectionist Models and Information Retrieval." In *Annual Review of Information Science and Technology,* Vol. 25, edited by Martha E. Williams. Amsterdam: Elsevier Science, 1990, pp. 212–214, 222–230.

Kohonen, Teuvo. *Self-Organizing Maps.* 3rd ed. Berlin, N.Y.: Springer-Verlag, 2001.

"What Is a Neural Network?" NeuroDimension, Inc., 2002. Available: http://www.nd.com/welcome/whatisnn.htm.

CHAPTER 12
ARRANGEMENT AND DISPLAY

$\mathscr{S}$*helving* and *filing* were the names traditionally given to the topics of this chapter. That is, books were shelved and cards were filed. In today's information environment there is still a great deal of shelving of physical information packages (their numbers have not diminished as predicted), and some filing of cards is still done. Some institutions still maintain card shelflists; and some smaller institutions still have no local online systems. Archives shelve collection boxes, but within the boxes archivists may file papers if the collection arrives with no discernible order.

In addition to shelving and filing, though, we have arrangement and display of nontangible resources and the order of displays on screens to be concerned about. This chapter addresses the following questions: How are information packages arranged? How are surrogate/metadata records arranged and displayed? How is categorization used in the arrangement of information packages and surrogate records? What is the significance of arrangement in the electronic environment?

ARRANGEMENT OF PHYSICAL INFORMATION PACKAGES

Libraries

Arrangement of physical information packages has been of concern to libraries for centuries. Since the early 1980s, there has been increasing concern about arrangement of electronic resources contained in physical packaging (e.g., CD-ROMs, videodiscs, music CDs, etc.). For the

331

last few years, there has been increasing concern about arrangement of intangible electronic resources.

Physical information packages in libraries are usually shelved by *call number*. A call number is a notation on an information package that matches the same notation in the surrogate/metadata record. It is the number used to "call" for an item in a closed stack library—thus, the source of the name *call number*. A call number usually consists of at least two lines on a label placed on the outside of the packaging. The top line is usually a classification notation. With long notations, the classification notation may continue onto a second line. The next line is usually a *cutter number*. Cutter numbers were devised by Charles A. Cutter more than a century ago for the purpose of alphabetizing all works that had exactly the same classification notation. Cutter devised a table in which letters of the alphabet were listed in one column and equivalent numerals were listed in an adjoining column.[1] For example:

Fonti	684
Fontr	685
Foo	686

A Cutter line for an author named Fontrain, for example, might be F685d. The small "d" is a *work mark* assigned to help keep the works of a particular author who writes on the same subject in alphabetical order. The work mark usually stands for the first word, not an article, of the title of the work; although for biographies, the work is usually "cuttered" for the name of the person the work is about, and the work mark stands for the last name of the author of the biography. This kind of Cutter number is most often used with Dewey Decimal Classification (DDC) notations. Library of Congress Classification (LCC) also uses cutter numbers (with a small "c"). LC borrowed Charles Cutter's idea, but created its own table that takes only a few lines.[2] A third line for a call number is often the date. Examples of call numbers are:

DDC	**LCC**
378.4	QE22.D25
F685d	S65
1998	1997

There are also alphabetical arrangements, accession order arrangements, and fixed location arrangements for physical information packages. In public libraries, in particular, fiction is often grouped together, subarranged in alphabetical order by author. Other uses for alphabetical order include arrangements of biographies and serials. Biographies may be arranged in alphabetical order by the last name of the person the biography is about. And, as discussed in Chapter 11, serials are often arranged in alphabetical order by title. Accession order arrangements may be used for materials waiting to be cataloged, and sometimes for more "permanent" backlogs. They may also be used for fixed location settings, such as remote storage.

In most libraries there is more than one sequence of the A–Z or 0–9 or other arrangement that is the basic one. There is usually a reference collection, for example, that has information packages from all classes. These are kept separately from the regular circulating collection. In academic libraries there is often a collection of reserve items for use for certain courses. In many libraries some kinds of information packages are separated by format. Microforms, CD-ROMs, sound recordings, videocassettes, and the like, are arranged in their own groups with their own sequences. This is often for housing and preservation purposes. Some media centers have tried to interfile all formats in classification order, but the idea has never really caught on.

Archives

Archives seldom use classification. As mentioned in Chapter 1, the principles for arrangement are *provenance* and *original order*. That is, to the extent possible, archival collections are arranged by their source, and within each source group, by the order in which they were kept by the person or corporate body from whence they came to the archives. The principle is based on evidence that the original order made some sense to the creator, and that order is important in any research that may be conducted where an understanding of the person or corporate body is important.

When an archive receives a new collection, it is assessed and a processing plan is made. This includes such things as determining what descriptive products will be created (e.g., finding aid, catalog record, etc.); whether samples from the collection will be scanned so that they can be viewed electronically; what kind of appraisal the collection will receive; what preservation measures will be taken; and whether the inventory will be created at the box level, the file level, or the item level.

The person responsible for description also determines what *series* are present. The word *series* is used very differently in archives than in libraries. In archival collections a series is a logically grouped set of files, books, correspondence, or other such set. For example, in the personal papers of a university professor, one might find files grouped in such a way that files for each of the professor's courses are together, files relating to the person's research and writing are together, and files relating to administrative issues (e.g., student advisees, doctoral comprehensive examinations, etc.) are together. Each of these groupings would be a series.

If a collection arrives in no discernible order, then the person responsible for its description must impose an order upon it. Such a situation almost always involves personal papers. The describer tries to put papers that have to do with the person's life in one grouping, manuscripts in another, correspondence in another, and so forth.

The physical placing of the boxes is by fixed location in closed stacks. An entire collection does not necessarily have to have all its boxes shelved together. The record in the shelflist gives the fixed locations of boxes, whether they are shelved together or not.

ARRANGEMENT OF INTANGIBLE INFORMATION PACKAGES

Internet resources are literally organized by protocol (e.g., http://), server address (e.g., www.pitt.edu/), path (e.g., agtaylor/ala/papers/), and file name (e.g., blfictio.html). Stringing these together creates the Uniform Resource Locator (URL) for the information package. This is not useful in collocating resources by any of the usual measures: creator, title, subject matter, form/genre. In fact, to do a specific search by URL, one has to have all the above pieces of the URL exactly right even to capitalization.

In the organization of Internet resources we have to, first, accept that the entire Internet will never be organized. And why should it be? Libraries, archives, and museums have always chosen what they will organize based upon collection development policies. Seldom did the collection include advertisements, ephemera, and the like. There has been an attempt to organize materials of lasting value. The same should be true of the Internet. An advantage we have with the Internet is that we do not have to duplicate each other's efforts. With a little effort, organization can be divided up by, perhaps, subject area, geographic area, or some other means.

Currently, much organization of the Internet is being accomplished by individual persons or organizations pulling together materials of lasting value, and usually on a particular subject or person or related in some other fashion. These resources are not literally pulled together, of course, but are hot-linked to a gathering page. The arrangement may be in the form of a large bibliography, as, for example, the International Federation of Library Association's bibliography "Digital Libraries: Metadata Resources."[3] Other pages are arranged using classification/categorization (see discussion in Chapter 11). With some of the latter the classification notations are explicit; with others notation is not visible to the user, but browsing and the ability to narrow and broaden searches is much appreciated by users. A list of sites that use classification schemes or subject headings is one created by Gerry McKiernan called *Beyond Bookmarks: Schemes for Organizing the Web,* which is itself an example of a site where organization is evident.[4] Organization is also being done by search engines, directories, gateways, and other such entities, as discussed in Chapters 2 and 11.

ARRANGEMENT OF SURROGATES (METADATA)

For most of the twentieth century, catalogs were in card, book, or COM formats. In card catalogs the arrangement of surrogate records was by a filing arrangement achieved by humans. Persons doing the filing had rules to follow that would lead to an arrangement that was deemed to be conducive to helping users find what they were looking for. In early book catalogs, the same was true because book catalogs often were made from cards or "slips" created by catalogers and placed in order by filers.

As computers entered the picture, book and then COM catalogs began to be created in electronic databases where the actual "filing" was done according to computer algorithms. Finally, Online Public Access Catalogs (OPACs) came into use. The records were stored sequentially or randomly within the computer, but in order to display the results of a search to a user, the subset of records retrieved had to be arranged and then displayed on the screen in some order. Early computer algorithms dictated an order of characters: sometimes numerals preceded letters, sometimes not; and there was (and still is) great difficulty in even displaying diacritical marks, let alone arranging them to display in some meaningful order.

OPACs and other electronic databases continue to be arranged on screen by computer algorithm. A few systems have been developed to make use of MARC tags and subfield codes to create more logical arrangements. And, whatever the algorithm, no computer can make up for a typographical error the way a filer can. In a card catalog an alert filer would see such a "typo" as *Salve rebellions* and file it properly as *Slave rebellions*. In a computer, which would see "salve" as a properly spelled word in any spelling checker, the title with the typo would be arranged before all other entries for the correctly spelled title. Intervening between *Salve* and *Slave* would be *Scarlet letter, Search for sanity, Silent world,* and many hundreds of other titles. Note also that retrieval of known items is not possible when a typo is involved.

Filing History

Charles A. Cutter included filing rules in his cataloging code.[5] There have been separate filing codes, not connected with cataloging rules, ever since Cutter. Earlier filing codes reflected the influence of the classified catalog. They presorted catalog entries into categories. For example, entries beginning with the word "orange" were sorted into: personal names (separating single surname entries from compound surname entries); geographic entities; corporate bodies; subject headings (separating the fruit from the color); and titles. Even though the rules were for *dictionary* catalogs, the categories were to be filed one after another instead of being interfiled alphabetically. The earlier codes also reflected the many variant local practices that existed. The 1942 *A.L.A. Rules for Filing Catalog Cards*[6] had many rules with two or three "correct" alternatives for a particular filing dilemma. One library could use rules 1.a. and 2.b., while another library could use rules 1.b. and 2.a. Both could claim to be following the American Library Association (ALA) filing rules. Users going from one library to another had to learn new filing rules for each catalog.

By the mid-1960s frustration was mounting. People in ALA decided to create a consistent code of filing rules derived from one basic principle. The resulting 1968 *ALA Rules for Filing Catalog Cards*[7] recommended straight alphabetical order, but there were exceptions. For example, personal surname entries (for single surnames only) were to be arranged before other entries beginning with the same word. Also, a filer had to spell out numerals and abbreviations in the language of the item and then file the card in the place where the spelled-out form would go in the catalog.

In 1980 ALA again published a code of filing rules,[8] and this time they were so different that they were not called a third edition. They called for straightforward filing according to principles, but still, alphabetical order was not absolute. A brief review of these rules serves to highlight some of the problems that keep people from finding what they want in computer displays, especially when a displayed set takes up more than one or two screens.

General Rules for Arrangement

Traditional arrangement in catalogs is word-by-word. This means that everything beginning with a particular word should precede other entries beginning with a word that has the same beginning letters as the first word (e.g., New York files before Newark). Not all information retrieval tools use this arrangement. Some encyclopedias and dictionaries, for example, use letter-by-letter arrangement. The difference is that in word-by-word arrangement, a space between words is treated according to the principle: "nothing files before something." That is, a space is "nothing," and it should be filed before a character, which is "something." According to the *ALA Filing Rules,* spaces, dashes, hyphens, diagonal slashes, and periods are all considered to be "nothing." Arrangements using the letter-by-letter approach ignore spaces and some of the punctuation marks just mentioned, and the entry files as if it is all run together into one word (e.g., New York is treated as Newyork and follows Newark). A longer example may assist in clarifying the distinction:

Word-by-Word	**Letter-by-Letter**
A book about myself	A book about myself
Book bytes	Bookbinding
Book-making (Betting)	Book bytes
Book of bells	Booker T. Washington
Book reports	Booker, William, 1905–
Bookbinding	Bookfinder
Booker T. Washington	Bookkeeping made simple
Booker, William, 1905–	Book-making (Betting)
Bookfinder	Book of bells
Bookkeeping made simple	Book reports
Books that changed the world	Booksellers and bookselling
Booksellers and bookselling	Books that changed the world

Another principle of arrangement is that numerals precede letters. Formerly, numerals were filed as spoken and spelled out, e.g.,

> Twenty-four dramatic cases . . .
> 24 ways to . . .
> XXIVth Congress of . . .

However, in the 1980 filing rules the difficulties of mentally spelling out something like "24" in French, German, Russian, and so on, for both filers and users were recognized. Numerals were to go first, but in numerical order, and Roman numerals filed with Arabic numerals. Thus, "1/2" (the fraction) was to file before "1" (the first integer). But computers have difficulty with this. The computer sees *one-slash-two,* not *one-half,* in "1/2." In the following example one can see that numerical order for a computer is based upon column by column matching and Roman numerals are seen as letters:

Manual Filing	**Machine Arrangement**
6 concerti grossi	10 times a poem
9 to 5	1984
10 times a poem	6 concerti grossi
XIXth century drawings	9 to 5
90 days to a better heart	90 days to a better heart
1984	XIXth century drawings

Among other principles of manual filing are: letters in the English alphabet precede letters of nonroman alphabets; ampersands (&) may be ignored, or optionally, may be spelled out in their language equivalents; and punctuation, nonalphabetic signs, and symbols are ignored. Computers generally treat these the same way except that they cannot follow the option of spelling out ampersands in their language equivalents. Ampersands are problematic for retrieval because a user who has heard a title but has not seen it does not know whether "and" is spelled out or represented by an ampersand, and usually does not know to try the other way if one way does not work. Recently, catalogers have often made additional title access points for the spelled-out form when ampersands or numerals have been used in titles.

Filing/Display Dilemmas

There are quite a few situations that cannot be resolved by human intellect as was done in the past. It seems impossible to program computers to handle all these situations so that the outcome is logical. For example, when titles are transcribed from chief sources of information in the process of creating metadata, the title is taken character by character as it appears. This results in some titles that begin with or contain the same words appearing to a computer to contain different words. Names beginning with prefixes, for example, are sometimes written with a space preceding the prefix (e.g., De Gaulle and DeGaulle). Another case arises from words that began as two words and are in the process of becoming one word (e.g., on line, on-line, and online). Here is another case where a user, having heard a title spoken, would not know which way to look for it.

Another spacing problem comes from punctuation marks. As mentioned above, the *ALA Filing Rules* says that spaces, dashes, hyphens, diagonal slashes, and periods are all considered to be "nothing." However, this is not true in all computer systems. Such marks might be replaced by a space, or they might not even be replaced by a space, resulting in words being run together inappropriately (e.g., "surrogate/metadata records" might become "surrogatemetadata records").

Computers also have difficulty with abbreviations. A human or a Natural Language Processing system can tell whether *Co.* means "County" or "Company"; whether *St.* means "Street" or "Saint"; whether *Dr.* means "Doctor" or "Doktor." Most systems cannot tell the difference, however, and arrangement is simply done by the letters that are there. A retrieval challenge here is that even if users know the titles they are searching for word-for-word, if they have only heard the titles and have not seen them, they do not know if certain words are abbreviated or spelled out.

Dates in subject headings present yet another challenge. In traditional manual practice, dates are to be arranged in chronological order. With *Library of Congress Subject Headings (LCSH)*, however, some dates are preceded by a verbal phrase identifying a name for the particular period of time. These headings can be placed in chronological order by a human, but a computer can't see "1775–1783" until it has arranged "Revolution" preceding or following all other numerals. For example:

Dates (Manual Filing)	Dates (Machine Arrangement)
United States—History—Revolution, 1775–1783	United States—History—1800–
United States—History—1800–	United States—History—1801–1809
United States—History—1801–1809	United States—History—1900–
United States—History—War of 1812	United States—History—1945–
United States—History—Civil War, 1861–1865	United States—History—Civil War, 1861–1865
United States—History—1900–	United States—History—Revolution, 1775–1783
United States—History—1945–	United States—History—War of 1812

Some machine systems place numerals after letters, but in any case the letters would be all together and the numerals would be all together. How many users know that in a long list of time periods for the history of a country, the named periods come last or the dates alone all come last? For that matter, how many know the names of time periods?

Initials and acronyms present yet another arrangement and retrieval challenge. If they are written with periods or spaces between them, they are filed as if each letter is a word (e.g., "A B C" files as if the first word is "A," the second is "B," and the third is "C"; while "ABC" files as a single word). For example:

> A.A.
> A.A.U.W.
> A apple pie
> A B C programs
> AAA
> Aabel, Marie
> Abacus calculating
> ABCs of collecting

Users are at a loss to know whether periods or spaces have been used. This kind of situation requires the assistance of someone to see that access points are provided both with and without spaces.

A final arrangement problem that we will discuss is the one surrounding such things as articles and elisions. Articles ("a," "an," "the" and their equivalents in other languages) that come at the beginning of a heading are supposed to be ignored in filing. This can only happen in all languages if the system is using an encoding scheme like MARC, wherein a human can give in an indicator the number of characters that the computer should ignore before beginning the arrangement order. Even in the MARC format there is no provision for indicating articles for every possible title access point. In *MARC 21,* for example, Uniform titles and titles in subfield "t" of several access point fields do not have indicators for articles. In addition, if a system is programmed to give access to subtitles, those beginning with articles will be arranged under the articles.

A system cannot just have a stoplist of all articles in all languages. First, some articles are ordinary words in other languages (e.g., the German *die*). Second, if the article is part of a proper name, it should be arranged under the article. For example:

> Los angeles custodios *[title in A]*
> Los Angeles in fiction *[title in L]*
> Los Angeles Bar Association *[corporate body in L]*
>
> L'enfant abandonee *[title in E]*
> L'Enfant, Edouard *[person in L]*

The main concern in the issues discussed above is that in online systems, when searchers retrieve responses that take more than two screens to display, they have to understand the arrangement. If they think that responses are in alphabetical order, and if they expect, for example, an acronym to be at the beginning of the listing, they might not even go to the screen that actually has the entry. Although arrangement is done by the computer system, some profiling can be done by humans to enable displays to be more predictable.

CONCLUSION

Arrangement and display have evolved in the online world from shelving and filing in the paper world. Physical information packages continue to need to be shelved in fashions that allow them to be found again. The methods for doing this are well worked out. We also face the need to arrange virtual information packages in ways that allow them to be found easily. This is a task that requires imaginative approaches and experimentation, just as organizing physical information packages once did.

Arrangement of surrogate/metadata records is also evolving. The first online catalogs were automated card catalogs, but without the sophisticated filing arrangements that could be accomplished in card catalogs. Display of search results has had many improvements, but problems still abound. An appropriate display is highly dependent upon system design, as discussed in Chapter 5.

NOTES

All URLs accessed July 2003.

1. The various editions of the Cutter tables (including the Cutter-Sanborn tables) are available from Libraries Unlimited, Inc.

2. For more explanation of call numbers, see Arlene G. Taylor, *Wynar's Introduction to Cataloging and Classification*, 9th ed., with the assistance of David P. Miller (Englewood, Colo.: Libraries Unlimited, 1992), pp. 324–331.

3. International Federation of Library Associations and Institutions, *Digital Libraries: Metadata Resources*. Latest revision 3 February 2003. Available: http://www.ifla.org/II/metadata.htm.

4. Gerry McKiernan, *Beyond Bookmarks: Schemes for Organizing the Web*, 22 March 2001. Available: http://www.public.iastate.edu/~CYBERSTACKS/CTW.html.

5.   Charles A. Cutter, *Rules for a Dictionary Catalog*, 4th ed. (Washington, D.C.: Government Printing Office, 1904; reprint, London: The Library Association, 1962), p. 12.

6.   *A.L.A. Rules for Filing Catalog Cards* (Chicago: American Library Association, 1942).

7.   *ALA Rules for Filing Catalog Cards*, 2nd ed. (Chicago: American Library Association, 1968).

8.   *ALA Filing Rules* (Chicago: American Library Association, 1980).

SUGGESTED READINGS

Arrangement of Information Packages

Petroski, Henry. *The Book on the Bookshelf.* New York: Knopf, 1999. Appendix: "Order, Order," pp. 233–252.

Libraries

Taylor, Arlene G. *Wynar's Introduction to Cataloging and Classification.* 9th ed., with the assistance of David P. Miller. Englewood, Colo.: Libraries Unlimited, 2000. Chapter 12: "Creation of Complete Call Numbers."

Archives

Fox, Michael J., and Peter Wilkerson. *Introduction to Archival Organization and Description: Access to Cultural Heritage.* The Getty Information Institute, 1998. Section entitled "What is Processing?" Available: http://www.schistory.org/getty/index.html.

Miller, Fredric M. *Arranging and Describing Archives and Manuscripts.* Chicago: Society of American Archivists, 1990. Chapter 1: "Introduction" and Chapter 7: "Title," pp. 77–78.

Internet

McKiernan, Gerry. *Beyond Bookmarks: Schemes for Organizing the Web.* 22 March 2001. Available: http://www.public.iastate.edu/~CYBERSTACKS/CTW.htm.

Arrangement of Bibliographic/Surrogate Records

Buckland, Michael K., Barbara A. Norgard, and Christian Plaunt. "Filing, Filtering and the First Few Found." *Information Technology and Libraries* 12, no. 3 (September 1993): 311–319.

Taylor, Arlene G. *Wynar's Introduction to Cataloging and Classification.* 9th ed., with the assistance of David P. Miller. Englewood, Colo.: Libraries Unlimited, 2000. Appendix: "Arrangement Dilemmas and Filing Rules."

CONCLUSION

In the preceding chapters we have discussed the past and present of organization of information. Organizing has been going on, I suspect, since the first appearance of humans, because it seems to be such an innate need. Even some nonhuman animals, birds, and insects are organizers (e.g., ants have highly organized societies with certain responsibilities assigned to various individuals). The organization of information among humans began as soon as language developed sufficiently for information to be passed from person to person. In oral traditions information was organized in people's minds, and, in recorded information traditions, ways of identifying information packages were developed at least as early as clay tablets.

Current retrieval tools, including bibliographies, catalogs, indexes, finding aids, museum registers, and search engines, represent the highest state of progress in organizing information that humans have achieved so far. These tools are far from perfect, though, and there is much room for organizers to improve metadata and for system designers to provide more helpful retrievals and more logical displays. Development of seamless interfaces among these tools is also a possibility.

Arrival at this current state of organization has taken centuries. Progress in the Western world was given impetus by printing with moveable type, but even then, movement toward bibliographic control was slow as printing moved through the stage of imitating manuscript production to the stage of creating new type fonts just for printing. We are experiencing a similar stage now as we use computers to imitate our previous print culture. Alan Kay, the first person to conceive of the laptop computer, has said that the computer revolution has not yet begun:

> The printing press was invented in the middle of the 15th century, yet it took 100 years before a book was considered dangerous enough to be banned, 150 years before science was invented, almost 200 years before a new kind of political essay was invented, and more than 300 years before a country with an invented political system (the

US) could be argued into existence via the press and a citizenry that could understand the arguments. Schooling and general literacy were also fruits of the press, and also took many centuries to become established. The commercial computer is now about 50 years old and is still imitating the paper culture that came before it, just as the printing press did with the manuscript culture it gradually replaced. No media revolution can be said to have happened without a general establishment of "literacy": fluent "reading" and "writing" at the highest level of ideas that the medium can represent. With computers we are so far from that fluent literacy—or even understanding what that literacy should resemble—that we could claim that the computer revolution hasn't even started.[1]

While it seems that much has happened in the five years since Kay said this, we still have not accomplished the literacy of which he spoke. Therefore, we cannot know what organized information will look like in another fifty years or even twenty-five years. I believe, however, that the principles of organization that have developed over the last several hundred centuries will not be thrown out but will continue to evolve into the organizing principles of the future.

NOTE

1. Alan Kay, "The Computer Revolution Hasn't Happened Yet," lecture in the SCS Distinguished Lecture Series, presented at Carnegie Mellon University, 29 April 1998.

APPENDIX: SUBJECT ANALYSIS APPLICATION

A way to use the subject analysis concepts presented in Chapter 9 is to follow an outline of the subconcepts to be identified. Such an outline might be:

A. Identify concepts and determine what is the purpose of the information package (e.g., who the intended users are) in the following:

   1. Title and subtitle.

   2. Table of contents or equivalent.

   3. Preface and/or introduction (etc.).

   4. Illustrations and their captions.

B. Identify names used as subject concepts.

C. Identify role(s) of any geographic name(s) present.

D. Identify chronological elements.

E. Identify form of the item being analyzed.

F. Construct a sentence giving analysis of what this information package is about.

   1. Identify index terms from the sentence to be searched in the controlled vocabulary.

   2. Translate the terms into specific headings from the controlled vocabulary list.

G. Construct the hierarchy (discipline/subdiscipline/concept/topic, etc.) into which the "aboutness" falls.

   1. Convert the hierarchy into a classification notation.

EXAMPLE

The summarization-level analysis of the Web site *JGarden: The Japanese Garden Database* (see Figures A.1 and A.2) created and maintained by Robert Cheetham, might proceed as follows:

    A.   Identify concepts in:

        1.   Title and subtitle.

Note that the title contains the word "Database." It will be necessary to determine if this Web site fits the *LCSH* definition of "database."

        2.   Table of contents or equivalent.

Note use of several terms that seem not necessarily to be related to the concept of "Japanese Garden": for example, "Administrative."

        3.   Preface and/or introduction.

Note that the Introduction states that the site was originally intended for professionals in the field of landscape architecture and garden history, but has been broadened to be made available to the general public through the Internet.

        4.   Illustrations and their captions.

Note that illustrations are of various gardens, some at varying times of year, and that there are also topographical and location maps. However, these do not constitute a large proportion of the work.

    B.   Identify names used as subject concepts.

The personal names involved are names of designers of gardens. There are too many to index separately at the summarization level. A few corporate names are given in lists such as bibliographies or lists of related sites; the work is not about these corporate bodies, however.

    C.   Identify role(s) of any geographic name(s) present.

The geographic area Japan provides the context for the topic of this work. The work is not about Japan, but the gardens discussed are of a type originally designed in Japan, and at this particular site, all the individual gardens discussed actually are in Japan.

    D.   Identify chronological elements.

The time periods involved here are from several centuries B.C.E. to the present, much too long a time to be meaningful in a subject heading string.

what's new

▶ JGarden Newsletter--Volume 3, Number 3

▶ JOJG Announces Results of Australian Garden Survey

▶ New/Updated Features

▶ Join Mailing List

E-mail Address

gardens

garden-of-the-month

UNESCO Headquarters
Paris, France
Photo: Robert Cheetham

tools

▶ Forum

▶ Calendar

▶ Search

⌄⌄

▶ Zip Code Search

⌄⌄

resources

NEW! JOJG articles
web articles
features archive
plants
books, etc.
designers, etc.
suppliers
organizations
biographies
glossary
timeline
links

about JGarden.org

Site Index >>

the japanese garden database

Fig. A.1. View of first screen of Robert Cheetham's *JGarden: The Japanese Garden Database*, found at http://www.jgarden.org.

E.   Identify form of the item being analyzed.

This item consists of many different kinds of form: text, pictures, maps, bibliographies, and the like. Note that "database" is included in the subtitle, but the work does not fit the usual definition of a database.

F.   Construct a sentence giving analysis of what this electronic resource is about.

This resource is about the history and design of Japanese gardens as a concept and also the history and design of major Japanese gardens in the country of Japan.

1.   Identify index terms from the sentence to be searched in the controlled vocabulary.

Japan, Japanese

Gardens

History, Historic

Design

2.   Translate the terms into specific headings from the controlled vocabulary list.

LCSH:

Gardens, Japanese—Japan—History

Gardens—Japan—Design

Historic gardens—Japan

G.   Construct the hierarchy (discipline/subdiscipline/concept/ topic, etc.) into which the "aboutness" falls.

Arts / design / landscaping / gardens / Japanese

1.   Convert the hierarchy into a classification notation.

LC Classification: SB466.J3

Dewey Decimal Classification: 712.0952

gardens   tools   resources

About JGarden

The Japanese Garden Database is intended as a repository of information on the historical and contemporary gardens of Japan as well as the gardens located outside Japan that have been inspired by the culture. It is a non-profit, educational web site that seeks to provide information on a selection of outstanding examples of garden art found in Japan while juxtaposing a diversity of media related to them. This juxtaposition is intended to bring about fresh insight to a body of discourse that can often be mired in romanticized and exoticized notions of Asia and the cultures therein.

For further information about the site, please refer to the following pages:

> ▸How to support JGarden
>
> ▸Linking to JGarden
>
> ▸Copyright information
>
> ▸Contact JGarden
>
> ▸Content Submissions
>
> ▸Suggestions

search

--Entire Site--   ▼

>>

JGarden.org Background

What you see on the screen is now the fifth iteration of the site. In some ways it is the closest to what I had originally conceived. What began simply as a proof-of-concept for a more comprehensive multimedia reference work on the gardens of Japan, this web site has since taken on a life of its own. Many of the changes have also come about due to changing technology. For the past several years the World Wide Web has transformed itself about every twelve months and to both push myself and to keep the site fresh, I have done my best to keep up.

shop

Koi and Garden Pools : A Complete Introduction
Axelrod, Herbert R.
[JGarden Bibliography]

Since Josiah Condor's *Landscape Gardening in Japan* (1912) and particularly in the post-World War II era, the gardens of Japan have received a great deal of attention in both popular and professional design literature. A small number of gardens have become almost iconic. The *karesansui* garden of Ryoanji, the shrine at Ise and the Katsura and Shugakuin imperial villas are ubiquitous in writings from Walter Gropius to John Cage.

browse

gardens
tools
JOJG articles NEW!
web articles
features archive
plants
books, etc.
designers
suppliers
organizations
biographies
glossary
timeline
links

However, with a few exceptions, discussion of the gardens of Japan has tended to be generic and superficial, often grouping them into an amorphous category called 'Japanese gardens' devoid of the social, historical and cultural context within which they were constructed. The language barrier coupled with a persistent romanticization of the 'mysterious, enigmatic Orient' often encouraged by the Japanese themselves, has contributed to this situation.

Fig. A.2. First page of the "about" page of the *JGarden* Web site.

GLOSSARY

AAAF (Anglo-American Authority File). File implemented at the British Library using the USNAF (U.S. Name Authority File) and the BLNAL (British Library Name Authority List).

AACR2 (Anglo-American Cataloguing Rules, 2nd ed.). A set of rules, published in 1978, for producing the descriptive and name-and-title access points part of a surrogate record for an information package; the creation of these rules was the result of collaboration among representatives from Canada, Great Britain, and the United States.

AACR2R (Anglo-American Cataloguing Rules, Second Edition, 1988 Revision). A revision of *AACR2*; rules are monitored by the Joint Steering Committee (JSC) for *AACR*, which is made up of representatives from Australia, Canada, Great Britain, and the United States.

AACR2R (Anglo-American Cataloguing Rules, Second Edition, 2002 Revision). A revision of *AACR2* that incorporates rewritten chapters for the description of cartographic materials, electronic resources, and continuing resources.

AAT (Art & Architecture Thesaurus). A thesaurus of terms in hierarchical arrangement that cover content and materials in the disciplines of art and architecture.

Aboutness. The subject of an information package. *See also* **Subject analysis.**

Access control. (1) The results of the process of doing authority work, but without the necessity of choosing one form of name or title and one subject term to be the "authorized" selection. In access control every variant name, title, or term is given equal status, with one form chosen for default display; however, a searcher may use any of the forms to gain access to information packages related to the name, title, or subject (*see also* **Authority control; Authority work**). (2) In the technical world of computers access control refers to an operating system feature that controls the access that certain categories of users have to files and to functions.

Access point. Any word or phrase used to obtain information from a retrieval tool or other organized system; in cataloging and indexing, "access points" are specific names, titles, and subjects chosen by the cataloger or indexer, when creating a surrogate/metadata record, to allow for the retrieval of the record. *See also* **Added entry; Primary access point**.

Accession number. A notation assigned to an information package that is unique to the package; the notations are often based upon the order in which information packages are acquired.

Added entry. Any access point in a metadata record other than the primary access point.

A-G Canada. A computer-based bibliographic network offering its database and services to a variety of Canadian libraries and also to a few libraries in the northeastern United States; formerly Utlas International, and then ISM/LIS.

Aggregation. Collection of publications in electronic form (also called "Aggregator database" or "Aggregator"). Aggregations come in many forms (e.g., publisher-based aggregations in which all the journals in the collection are from one publisher; subject-based aggregations that usually include publications from numerous publishers but that share the same broad subject; vendor-based aggregations in which full-text publications can be accessed through vendors who have aggregated journals of many publishers).

Alphabetical catalog. Catalog in which the surrogate records are arranged or displayed in the order of the alphabet that is used in the institution that houses the catalog.

Alphabetico-classed catalog. Catalog in which subject categories are used for arrangement of surrogate records; broad categories are subdivided by narrower categories that are placed alphabetically within each broad category.

Analytical entry. An entry made for each of the works in a volume, as opposed to making only one entry for the entire volume.

ANN (Artificial Neural Network). *See* **Artificial neural network**.

Annotation. A brief note indicating the subject matter or commenting on the usefulness of information in a particular information package.

ANSI (American National Standards Institute). A body that takes responsibility for establishing voluntary industry standards; works closely with NISO (q.v.).

APPM (Archives, Personal Papers, and Manuscripts). A standard based on *AACR2R* for the description of archival materials; has been accepted as a standard by most of the archival community.

Archival description. The process of establishing intellectual control over the holdings of an archive through the preparation of finding aids.

Archival series. A logical group of files, books, correspondence, or other such set.

Archive. Organization that preserves records of enduring value that document activities of organizations or persons and are accumulated in the course of daily activities.

Art & Architecture Thesaurus. See AAT.

Artificial neural network (ANN). A computer system inspired by the architecture of the human biological nervous system.

ASCII (American Standard Code for Information Interchange). A standard code that assigns specific bit patterns to letters, numbers, and symbols; used for exchange of textual data in instances where programs are incompatible, because ASCII can be read almost universally by any computing machine.

Asynchronous responsibility. The situation in which the persons or corporate bodies involved in the creation of an information package have made different kinds of contributions to the creation of the work (e.g., author and illustrator; performer, conductor, choreographer, and producer; etc.).

Attribute. In metadata, a named value or relationship that is associated with a property or an element of an information package; in searching, a characteristic of a search query.

Author. A person who is responsible for all or some of the intellectual content of a text. *See also* **Creator**.

Author entry. The place in a retrieval tool where a surrogate record beginning with the name of the creator of an information package may be found.

Author/title access point. Access point that includes both the author and the title of a work in the construction of a single access point.

Authority control. The results of the process of maintaining consistency of forms of headings and the further process of showing relationships among headings—all for the purpose of collocation. Following this process means that headings in surrogate records are consistent with the character strings for those headings established in the authority file.

Authority file. A collection of authority records.

Authority record. A means for recording all the decisions made in the process of authority work.

Authority work. The process of determining and maintaining the form of a name, title, or subject concept to be used in creating access points. In the name and title areas, the process includes identifying all variant names or titles and relating the variants to the name or title forms chosen to be access points. In some cases it may also include relating names and/or titles to each other. In the verbal subject area, the process includes identifying and maintaining relationships among terms—relationships such as synonyms, broader terms, narrower terms, and related terms.

Bibliographic control. The process of describing items in the bibliographic universe and then providing name, title, and subject access to the descriptions, resulting in records that serve as surrogates for the actual items of recorded information. Bibliographic control further requires that surrogate records be placed into retrieval systems where they act as pointers to the actual information packages.

Bibliographic data. Information gathered in the process of creating bibliographic records.

Bibliographic database. A collection of bibliographic records held in the format of a database (q.v.).

Bibliographic network. A corporate entity that has as its main resource a bibliographic database; access to the database is available for a price, and members of the network can contribute new records and download existing ones.

Bibliographic record. Description of an information package; later terms used for descriptions of information packages are "surrogate record" and "metadata record."

Bibliographic tool. *See* **Retrieval tool**.

Bibliographic universe. A concept that encompasses all instances of recorded information.

Bibliography. A list of information packages; bibliographies bring together lists of sources based on subject matter, on authors, by time periods, and the like.

Book catalog. Catalog in which surrogate records are printed on pages that are bound into book form.

Boolean operators. The terms AND, OR, and NOT as used to construct search topics through postcoordinate indexing.

Boolean searching. The process of searching with individual index terms or keywords that are linked with Boolean operators (either using actual operators, or using a system where operators are implied if not specified).

Broad classification. Classification that uses only the main classes and divisions of a scheme and perhaps only one or two levels of subdivisions. *See also* **Close classification**.

Broader term (BT). A term one level up from the term being examined in a listing where terms for subject concepts have been conceived in relationships that are hierarchical.

Browsing. A process of looking, usually based on subject, at all the items in a particular area of the stacks in order to find, often by serendipity, the items that best suit the needs of the browser. In online systems browsing is the process of looking at all the surrogate records that are displayed under a certain subject, in a particular classification, or under a certain name or title.

Call number. A notation on an information package that matches the same notation in the surrogate/metadata record; it is the number used to "call" for an item in a closed stack library—thus the source of the name *call number.*

Card catalog. Catalog in which surrogate records are written, typed, or printed on cards (usually measuring 3 by 5 inches) that are placed in file drawers in a particular order (usually alphabetical or classified order).

Catalog. Retrieval tool that provides access to individual items within collections of information packages (e.g., physical entities such as books, videos, and CDs in a library; artists' works in an art museum; Web pages on the Internet; etc.).

Catalog gateway. *See* **Gateway**.

Catalog record. *See* **Surrogate record**.

Cataloger. Person in an archive, a library, or other such organization who creates surrogate records for the information packages collected by the organization and who works to maintain the system through which those surrogate records are made available to users; the person may also be an independent contractor. *See also* **Indexer**.

Cataloging. The acts of creating surrogate records for information packages, choosing appropriate access points, and maintaining the system through which the records are made available. Such work done in nonprofit agencies is usually called *cataloging,* while such work done for commercial enterprises is usually called *indexing.*

CD-ROM (Compact Disc–Read Only Memory). A computer storage medium that is "read" with a laser beam and can store 680 megabytes of data on a single disc.

Character-by-character filing. *See* **Letter-by-letter filing**.

Checksum. A value computed for a block of data, based on the contents of the block; used to detect corruption of the data.

Chief source of information. The location from which much of the information is to be taken that is used to create the descriptive part of a surrogate record (e.g., title page of a book, title screen of a motion picture, label on a sound recording tape or disc).

CIP (Cataloging-in-Publication). A program in which cataloging is provided by an authorized agency to the publisher or producer of an information package so that the cataloging can be issued with the information package; ordinarily the phrase is applied in the case of cataloging provided by the Library of Congress to the publishers of books.

Classical theory of categorization. Theory based on Aristotle's theory that categories contain items based on what they have in common and that categories are like abstract containers with things either in or out of the container.

Classification. The placing of subjects into categories; in organization of information, classification is the process of determining where an information package fits into a given hierarchy and often then assigning the notation associated with the appropriate level of the hierarchy to the information package and to its surrogate.

Classification notation. A set of numbers, letters, symbols, or a combination of these that is assigned to a certain level of hierarchy in a classification scheme.

Classification schedule. A listing of the hierarchy of a classification scheme along with the notation for each level.

Classification scheme. A specification of a systematic organization of knowledge. *See also* **Taxonomy**.

Classification table. Supplementary part of a classification scheme in which notations are assigned for concepts that can be applied in conjunction with many different topical subjects. Tables commonly exist for geographic locations, time periods, standard subdivisions (e.g., dictionaries, theory, serial publications, historical treatment, etc.), ethnic and national groups, and the like.

Classified catalog. Catalog in which surrogate records are arranged or displayed in the order of the classification scheme used in the institution that houses the catalog.

Close classification. Classification that uses all the minute subdivisions that are available in a particular classification for very specific subjects. *See also* **Broad classification**.

Closed stacks. The name given to the situation where information package storage areas are accessible only to the staff of the library, archives, or other place that houses information packages. *See also* **Open stacks**.

Code (as a noun). (1) A set of rules. (2) A specific designation in an encoding standard that defines and limits the kinds of data that can be stored at that point.

Code (as a verb). The process of assigning the appropriate specified designations of an encoding standard.

Codification. The process of creating sets of rules to govern such things as the making of surrogate records.

Coextensive subject entry. A subject heading or a set of headings that covers all, but no more than, the concepts or topics covered in the information package.

Collocation. The bringing together of records and/or information packages that are related in some way (e.g., same author, same work [different titles or different editions], same subject, etc.).

Collocation device. A number or other designation on an item used to place it next to (i.e., collocate with) other items that are like it.

Colon Classification. Classification scheme devised by S. R. Ranganathan in the early 1930s; it was the first fully faceted classification scheme.

Colophon. A set of data at the end of a "document" that gives varying kinds of bibliographic data. It might give information usually found on a title page, and, in items after the invention of printing with moveable type, it gives such information as date of printing, printer, typeface used, and the like.

COM (Computer Output Microform) catalog. Catalog in which surrogate records are produced on either microfiche or microfilm and require a microform reader in order to be able to use them.

Command searching. The process of searching in which a "code" (e.g., "a" or "au" for "author," "t" or "ti" for "title," etc.) is followed by an exact string of characters that are matched against the system's internal index.

Content. The intellectual information transmitted in or by a resource, information package, or metadata; content is distinguished from the encoding, packaging, or framework used for transmission.

Continuing resource. A work that is issued in parts, sometimes as separate entities, and sometimes with new information integrated into the existing information package. *See also* **Integrating resource; Serial (as opposed to "monographic" work).**

Contract cataloging. An institution's use of a contractual relationship with a person or agency to provide surrogate records that represent the institution's acquisitions for its collection. *See also* **Outsourcing.**

Controlled vocabulary. A list or database of subject terms in which all terms or phrases representing a concept are brought together. Often a preferred term or phrase is designated for use in surrogate records in a retrieval tool; the terms not to be used have references from them to the chosen term or phrase, and relationships (e.g., broader terms, narrower terms, related terms, etc.) among used terms are identified. There may also be scope notes for the terms and hierarchical listings.

Copy cataloging. The process of adapting for use in a catalog a copy of the original cataloging created by another library. *See also* **Original cataloging.**

CORC (Cooperative Online Resource Catalog). *See* **OCLC Connexion.**

Core Record. Standard set by the Program for Cooperative Cataloging (PCC) that presents the minimum requirements for elements to be included in a nationally acceptable *AACR2* record.

Corporate body. A group of persons who have a group name and who act as an entity.

Creator. Person who is responsible for the intellectual content of an information package.

Cross reference. *See* **Reference**.

Crosswalks. Visual instruments for showing equivalent values in two or more schemes; for example, a crosswalk could be used to show which value in one metadata standard matches a particular value in another standard, or it could be used to show which classification notation in, say, DDC, is equivalent to a notation in LCC.

CSDGM (FGDC Content Standards for Digital Geospacial Metadata). A specification that provides a common set of terminology and definitions for metadata about digital geospatial data. *See also* **FGDC (Federal Geographic Data Committee) metadata standard**.

Cutter number. A designation that has the purpose of alphabetizing all works that have exactly the same classification notation; named for Charles Ammi Cutter, who devised such a scheme. *See also* **Call number**.

Cyberspace. The intangible place in which some electronic documents, such as Web pages or e-mail messages, exist.

Data administration. The terminology applied to the control of the explosion of electronic information in offices and other administrative settings. *See also* **Records management**.

Data modeling. The process of designing a system for managing office and administrative records; the process involves developing a conceptual model of an activity in a particular setting, followed by a logical model that includes much more detail, which is then translated into a physical data model that can be implemented as a database management system.

Database. A set of records that are all constructed in the same way and are often connected by relationship links; the structure underlying retrieval tools.

DDC (Dewey Decimal Classification). *See* **Dewey Decimal Classification**.

Depth indexing. Indexing that extracts all the main concepts dealt with in an information resource, recognizing many subtopics and subthemes. *See also* **Exhaustivity; Summarization**.

Description. *See* **Descriptive data**.

Descriptive cataloging. The process of providing the descriptive data and access points (other than subject) for surrogate records that are to be part of a catalog.

Descriptive data. Data that describes an information package, such as its title, its associated names, its edition, its date of publication, its extent, and notes identifying pertinent features.

Descriptor. Subject concept term, representing a single concept, usually found in thesauri and used in indexes. *See also* **Subject heading**.

Dewey Decimal Classification (DDC). Classification devised by Melvil Dewey in 1876; it divides the world of knowledge hierarchically into ten divisions, which are in turn divided into ten sections, and so on, using the ten digits of the Arabic numeral system. DDC is enumerative but with many faceting capabilities, especially in its later editions.

Diacritic. Modifying mark over, under, or through a character to indicate that pronunciation is different from that of the character without the diacritic.

Dictionary catalog. Catalog in which surrogate records are arranged in alphabetical order by access point, intermixing name, title, and subject access points.

Digital library. A collection of information packages in digital form that are selected, brought together, organized, preserved, and to which access is provided over digital networks for a particular community of users.

Direct entry. A principle in the *formulation* of controlled vocabularies that stipulates the entry of a concept directly under the term that names it, rather than as a subdivision of a broader concept (e.g., Child rearing, *not* Children—Development and guidance). *See also* **Specific entry.**

Divided catalog. Catalog in which surrogate records are arranged or displayed in separate files or displays, separated by name access points, title access points, and subject access points.

Document. An information package; often associated in people's minds with text and illustrations having been produced on paper, but increasingly associated with a video, a CD music disc, a computer file, or other such manifestation.

Document retrieval vs. Information retrieval. A dichotomy that is created by the level of exhaustivity used in subject indexing; summarization allows for retrieval of a document which can, itself, then be searched for relevant information, while depth indexing allows for retrieval of information at a much more specific level than the whole document.

Domain. (1) A sphere of knowledge, influence, or activity. (2) In networking, a group of computers whose host names share a common name (i.e., the domain name).

DTD (Document Type Definition). An SGML or XML application; defines the structure of a particular type of document.

Dublin Core (shortened form of Dublin Core Metadata Element Set). An internationally agreed-upon set of elements that can be "filled in" by the creator of an electronic document in order to create a metadata record for the document.

EAD (Encoded Archival Description). An XML DTD created specifically to encode finding aids.

EAD Header. Descriptive data about the metadata in the rest of the EAD record. It is based heavily on the TEI Header, and the content is based on the rules in the *APPM.*

Edition. Specific manifestation of the intellectual content (work) found in an information package.

Electronic resource. Information package that requires the use of a computer to access its intellectual contents.

Element. An individual category or field that holds an individual piece of description of an information package; typical metadata elements include title, creator, creation date, subject identification, and the like.

Encoding. The setting off of each part of a record so that the part can be displayed in certain positions according to the wishes of those creating a display mechanism, and so that certain parts of a record can be searchable.

Entity. (1) A "thing" (resource, person, name, address, etc.). (2) A term used in the field of organization of information to indicate an item; both "entity" and "item" are used in order to avoid using "book" or other such specific designation.

Entry. The place in a print retrieval tool where a surrogate record is found.

Entry word. The first word of a *heading.*

Enumerative classification. A subject concept arrangement that attempts to assign a designation for every subject concept (both single and composite) needed in the system.

ERIC thesaurus. A commonly used term for the *Thesaurus of ERIC Descriptors,* a thesaurus for indexing and searching documents indexed by the Educational Resources Information Center.

Exemplar. A typical or standard model or example.

Exhaustivity. The number of concepts that will be considered in the process of providing subject analysis; two basic degrees of exhaustivity are *depth indexing* and *summarization.*

Expansive classification. A scheme in which a set of coordinated schedules gives successive development possibilities from very simple (broad) to very detailed (close) subdivisions.

Expression. Level in describing works where the work can actually be seen or heard or felt.

Faceted classification. A subject concept arrangement that has small notations standing for subparts of the whole topic, which, when strung together, usually in prescribed sequence, create a complete classification notation for a multipart concept.

FGDC (Federal Geographic Data Committee) metadata standard. Provides a common set of terminology and definitions for metadata about geospatial data (e.g., maps) that are in digital form. *See also* **CSDGM.**

Field. A separately designated part of an encoded record; it may contain one or more subfields.

Filing. The process of placing paper records (e.g., catalog cards, acquisition forms, etc.) in order, usually in drawers.

Finding aid. A long, inventory-like description of an archival collection; it describes a whole collection rather than individual pieces of the collection. A catalog record may be made for the finding aid.

Fixed field. A field of an encoded record that is always the same length from record to record.

Fixed location. A set place where a physical information package will always be found or to which it will be returned after having been removed for use.

Full entry. *See* **Main entry (record)**.

Fuzzy set theory of categorization. A theory that holds that some categories are not well defined and sometimes depend upon the observer, rather than upon a definition (e.g., people under five feet tall think the category of "tall people" is larger than do people over six feet tall).

Gateway. A computer system or a Web location that provides access to many different databases or other resources through the same interface.

GILS (Government [or Global] Information Locator Service) record. Metadata that describes the information holdings of a U.S. federal agency.

GMD (General Material Designation). In an *AACR2* record, an indication of the class of item being described (e.g., art original, electronic resource, motion picture, text, etc.).

Granularity. In metadata description, the level and depth at which information packages are described; in database design, a measure of the size or number of segments into which memory is divided.

GUI (Graphical User Interface). A computer interface that uses icons and other such graphics to make a screen more intuitive for users.

Heading. (1) An access point printed at the top of a copy of a surrogate record or at the top of a listing of related works in an online retrieval tool. (2) The exact string of characters of the authorized form of the access point as it appears in the authority record.

Hierarchical classification. A subject concept arrangement that follows the classical theory of categorization, creating categories from general to specific. *See also* **Taxonomy**.

Hierarchy. An arrangement by which categories are grouped in such a way that a concept (e.g., class or discipline) is subdivided into subconcepts of an equal level of specificity, each of those subconcepts are further subdivided into subcategories, and so on. In science, for example, living organisms are in the hierarchy: phylum, class, order, family, genus, species.

HTML (HyperText Markup Language). A scheme for encoding text, pictures, and the like, so that they can be displayed using various programs because the coding is totally made up of ASCII text.

HTTP (HyperText Transfer Protocol). The part of a URL that lets the browser know that a Web page is being sought; the protocol itself defines how messages are formatted and is the protocol most often used to transfer information from World Wide Web servers to browsers.

Hyperlink. An electronic connection between two separate pieces of information: it may be between two Web pages, between two parts of an electronic information package, between text and an image, and so forth.

Hypertext. Document in which words, pictures, references, and the like, may be linked to other locations or documents so that clicking on one of the links takes a person to related information.

IFLA (International Federation of Library Associations and Institutions). International organization for the promotion of library standards and the sharing of ideas and research.

ILL (Interlibrary loan). The process of acquiring a physical information package or a copy of it from a library that owns it by a library that does not own it.

ILS (Integrated Library System). Computer system that includes various modules to perform different functions while sharing access to the same database.

Imprint. The information in a textual publication that tells where it was published, who published it, and when it was published.

Index. A bibliographic tool that provides access to the analyzed contents of information packages (e.g., articles in a journal, short stories in a collection, papers in a conference proceeding, etc.). Back-of-the-book indexes provide access to the analyzed contents of one work.

Indexer. A person who determines access points (usually subject terms, but may be authors or titles) that are needed in order to make surrogate records available to searchers; an indexer also may create surrogate records. *See also* **Cataloger**.

Indexing. The process of creating surrogate records, especially the access points, for information packages; such work done in commercial enterprises is often called *indexing*, while similar work done in nonprofit agencies is usually called *cataloging*.

Indexing language. A rule-based means for choosing and structuring terms, either controlled or noncontrolled, that can assist in providing access to an information package.

Indexing vocabulary. *See* **Controlled vocabulary**.

Indicators. In the MARC encoding standards, indicators for a field contain coded information that is needed for interpreting or supplementing data in the field.

Information architecture. A methodology for planning, designing, building, organizing, and maintaining an information system (usually associated with systems on the Web).

Information package. An instance of recorded information (e.g., book, article, video, Internet document or set of "pages," sound recording, electronic journal, etc.). *See also* **Item**; **Work**.

Information retrieval vs. Document retrieval. *See* **Document retrieval vs. Information retrieval**.

Interface design. The part of a system design that controls the interaction between the computer and the user.

Integrating resource. In *AACR2R* (2002 revision), a bibliographic resource that is added to or changed by means of updates that are integrated into the whole resource (includes updating loose-leafs and updating Web sites).

Interlibrary Loan. *See* **ILL**.

Internet. A global network comprised of thousands of interconnected computer networks; it allows access to such services as electronic mail, remote login, file transfer services, and the World Wide Web; the networks all use TCP/IP (Transmission Control Protocol/Internet Protocol).

Interoperability. The compatibility of two or more systems such that they can exchange information and data and can use the exchanged information and data without any special manipulation.

Inventory. A tool whose purpose is to provide a record of what is owned.

ISBD (International Standard Bibliographic Description). A standard that was designed in the early 1970s to facilitate the international exchange of cataloging records by standardizing the elements to be used in the description, assigning an order to these elements, and specifying a system of symbols to be used in punctuating the elements.

ISBN (International Standard Book Number). A number that is accepted as an international standard for a unique number for a monographic item.

ISM/LIS (Information Systems Management/Library Information Services). *See* **A-G Canada**.

ISO (International Standards Organization). A corporate body that oversees the creation and approval of standards.

ISSN (International Standard Serial Number). A number that is accepted as an international standard for a unique number for a serial.

Item (as opposed to "work"). One copy of a manifestation of a work, focusing on the packaging of an information package rather than its contents.

Keyword. A term that is chosen, either from actual text or from a searcher's head, that is considered to be a "key" to finding certain information.

Keyword searching. The use of one or more keywords as the intellectual content of a search command.

Knowledge management. The attempt to capture, evaluate, store, and reuse what the employees of an organization know.

LCRIs (Library of Congress Rule Interpretations). A collection of the decisions that have been made by the Library of Congress's Cataloging Policy and Support Office as to how catalogers at the Library of Congress will interpret and apply *AACR2*.

LCSH. *See* ***Library of Congress Subject Headings***.

Letter-by-letter filing. An arrangement of entries in a retrieval tool in which spaces and some punctuation marks are ignored so that the entry files as if it is all run together into one word (e.g., "New York" is treated as "Newyork" and follows "Newark"). *See also* **Word-by-word filing**.

Library of Congress Classification (LCC). Classification scheme created by the Library of Congress beginning in the late 1890s; it divides the world of knowledge hierarchically into categories using letters of the English alphabet and then using Arabic numerals for further subdivisions. LCC is basically an enumerative scheme, allowing only a limited amount of faceting.

Library of Congress Rule Interpretations. See LCRIs.

Library of Congress Subject Headings (LCSH). A list of terms to be used as controlled vocabulary for subject headings created by the Library of Congress and used by any agency that wishes to provide controlled subject access to surrogate records.

Literary warrant. The concept that new notations are created for a classification scheme and new terms are added to a controlled vocabulary only when information packages actually exist about new concepts.

Location device. A number or other designation on an item to tell where it is physically located.

Main entry (access point). The access point that is chosen as the main or primary one.

Main entry (record). A copy of the surrogate record that contains a complete set of all elements of the record as provided by the cataloger.

Manifestation. Any one of the formats in which one of the expressions of a work can be found.

Manuscripts. Papers created by an individual (not organizational papers); original handwritten or typed documents that usually exist in single copies (unless they have been carbon-copied or photocopied).

MARC (Machine-Readable Cataloging). A standard prescribing codes that precede and identify specific elements of a catalog record, allowing the record to be "read" by machine and thus to be displayed in a fashion designed to make the record intelligible to users.

MARC 21. A MARC standard agreed upon by Canadian and U.S. representatives; *MARC 21* represents a consolidation of USMARC and CAN/MARC, the two previous national MARC schemes. *MARC 21* has been adopted by Great Britain as well as by Canada and the United States.

Markup language. A scheme that allows the tagging and describing of individual structural elements of text for the purpose of digital storage, appropriate layout display, and retrieval of individual components.

Medical Subject Headings (MeSH®). A list of terms to be used as controlled vocabulary for subject headings created by the National Library of Medicine and used by any agency that wishes to provide controlled subject access to surrogate records in the field of medicine.

Menu searching. A process of searching that allows one to navigate by making choices, not by giving commands.

Metadata. An encoded description of an information package (e.g., an *AACR2* record encoded with MARC, a Dublin Core record, a GILS record, etc.); the purpose of metadata is to provide a level of data at which choices can be made as to which information packages one wishes to view or search, without having to search massive amounts of irrelevant full text.

Metalanguage. A language for describing markup languages.

Meta-metadata. Data describing metadata (e.g., administrative data used to track metadata).

METS (Metadata Encoding and Transmission Standard). A standard for encoding descriptive, administrative, and structural metadata for objects in a digital library.

MODS (Metadata Object Description Schema). A schema for a bibliographic element set that has been particularly developed for library applications; a subset of MARC expressed in XML.

Monographic (as opposed to "serial") work. A complete bibliographic unit or information package. It is often a single work, but may also be one work or more than one work issued in successive parts; but unlike serials, it is not intended to be continued indefinitely.

Museum accession record. A record used as a surrogate for an object acquired by a museum; it contains many kinds of information about the object, such as its provenance, financial history, location in the museum, historical significance, and the like.

Museum registration. *See* **Registration**.

Namespace. A collection of element type and attribute names; the collection (i.e., namespace) is identified by a unique name (i.e., a URI). In a traditional namespace each name must be unique within that namespace; however, the same name can be used in more than one namespace with different meanings. An XML namespace identifies each element type or attribute name uniquely by a two-part name that includes the URI of its XML namespace and its local name.

Narrower term (NT). A term one level down from the term being considered in a listing where terms for subject concepts have been conceived in relationships that are hierarchical.

National Union Catalog (NUC). A publication of the Library of Congress that cumulated cataloging records from many libraries and indicated by "NUC symbol" those libraries that owned a particular item.

Natural language. The language used by a person when expressing a concept about which information is desired.

Natural language processing (NLP). Computer analysis of written or spoken language in order to interpret meaning in a way that can allow the computer to "understand" and "respond."

Neural network. *See* **Artificial neural network (ANN)**.

NISO (National Information Standards Organization). A corporate body that oversees the creation and approval of standards to be used in information processing; an American counterpart to ISO (q.v.).

NLP (Natural language processing). *See* **Natural language processing**.

Nonbook materials. Terminology used for any information package that is not text in book form.

Notation. A representation in a system, such as a classification system, with a set of marks, usually consisting of letters, numbers, and/or symbols.

OCLC (Online Computer Library Center). A bibliographic network, based in Dublin, Ohio, that is the largest and most comprehensive bibliographic network in the world.

OCLC Connexion. A Web-based interface to OCLC's database; it began as CORC, a system that helped libraries provide access to Web resources.

ONIX International (ONline Information eXchange). The book industry standard for representing and communicating product information in e-format; designed to carry the kind of information traditionally carried on jacket covers and, optionally, also to carry excerpts, book reviews, cover images, author photos, and the like.

Online catalog. Catalog in which surrogate records are encoded for computer display and are stored in computer memory or on CD-ROM discs; arrangement within the memory or on disc is irrelevant to the user, as arrangement is created in response to a query.

Online index. An index in which surrogate records for the analyzed contents of information packages are encoded for computer display and are stored in computer memory or on CD-ROM discs.

On-the-fly record. A record created electronically for an information package between the request by a searcher and the display of responses.

Ontology. In the field of artificial intelligence, a formal representation of what, to a human, is common sense; in NLP, a formal representation of language that identifies specific terms, usually from a defined subject area, and lays out the relationships that exist between the terms.

OPAC (Online Public Access Catalog). *See* **Online catalog**.

Open stacks. The name given to the situation where patrons of the facility have the right to go into the storage areas themselves. *See also* **Closed stacks**.

Original cataloging. Cataloging in which a surrogate/metadata record for an information package is created wholly by a cataloger without the use of cataloging data for the package that may have been created by someone else first. *See also* **Copy cataloging.**

Original order. The order in which records in a collection were originally kept when they were in active use.

Outsourcing. A management technique whereby some activities, formerly conducted in-house, are contracted out for completion by a contracting agency; technical services operations are sometimes outsourced. *See also* **Contract cataloging.**

Paris Principles. The conventional name of the Statement of Principles agreed upon by attendees at the International Conference on Cataloguing Principles in Paris, October 9–18, 1961.

Pathfinder. A subject bibliography that uses a systematic approach to lead a user to find the resources a library has available on a specific topic; a pathfinder may be in print or online, and the resources listed may be physical or digital.

PCC (Program for Cooperative Cataloging). An international cooperative program coordinated jointly by the Library of Congress and participants around the world; effort is aimed at expanding access to collections through useful, timely, cost-effective cataloging that meets internationally accepted standards.

Portals. Transactional Internet gateways targeted to a specific audience.

Postcoordinate indexing. The assigning of single concept terms from a controlled vocabulary to surrogate records so that the searcher of the system is required to coordinate the terms through such techniques as Boolean searching.

Precoordinate indexing. The assigning of subject terms to surrogate records in such a way that some concepts, subconcepts, place names, time periods, and form concepts are put together in subject strings, and searchers of the system do not have to coordinate these particular terms themselves.

Primary access point. Access point that is chosen as the main or primary one; usually referred to as "main entry" in the library and archival worlds.

Property. A characteristic of a resource, such as the title, the description, or the author of an information package; or the address or the affiliation of a person.

Protocol. A standard set of rules that determines how computers communicate with each other across networks (e.g., HTTP and Z39.50 are protocols); it describes the format that a message must take and the way in which computers must exchange a message.

Prototype theory of categorization. The theory that categories have prototypes (i.e., best examples; e.g., most people think a robin is a better example of a bird than is an ostrich).

Provenance. The origin of an archival document or collection, or of a museum object. In the case of an archival collection the origin may be an organization, office, or person that created, received, or accumulated and used the item or the records in the collection. In the case of a museum object, the origin may be a person, family, or other prior owner of the object, or it may be an archaeological expedition, or it may be the location where a natural history specimen was found.

Proximity (in searching). The concept of "nearness" of search terms to one another in a text.

Publisher. The person or corporate body responsible for issuing information packages to make them available for public use.

RDF (Resource Description Framework). An infrastructure that enables the encoding, exchange, and reuse of structured metadata; it uses XML as the means for exchanging and processing the metadata. RDF is based on the premise that resources have properties, properties have values, some values can be other resources with their own properties and values, and all these relationships can be linked within the framework.

Record. *See* **Bibliographic record; Metadata; Surrogate record.**

Records management. The process of maintaining records for an organization; it includes such functions as making decisions about what records should be created, saving necessary records, establishing effective systems for retrieval of records, and archiving important records for posterity.

Reference (cross reference). An instruction in a retrieval tool that directs a user to another place in the tool.

Register (accession log). Primary control tool for a museum; it functions like a catalog with a number of additional kinds of access points (e.g., donor, style, provenance, etc.).

Registration. The process of creating a surrogate record that uniquely identifies an object belonging to a museum; the records form the register for the museum.

Related term (RT). A term at the same level of specificity or bearing a nonhierarchical relationship to another term in a listing where terms for subject concepts have been conceived in relationships that are hierarchical.

Relational database. A database in which records are structured in such a way that information is not all stored in the same file; files for different kinds of information are created (e.g., a bibliographic file, a personal name file, a corporate name file, a subject file, a classification file, etc.); records in the bibliographic file contain pointers to records in the other files and vice versa. A relational database structure conserves storage space, allows for faster searching, and allows for easier modification of records. Pointers establish "relationships" among records.

Relative location. The situation in which an information package will be or might be in a different place each time it is reshelved because it is shelved in relation (usually classificatory) to entities already shelved.

Reprint. A new printing of an item either by photographic methods or by resetting unchanged text.

Resource discovery. The process of locating, accessing, retrieving, and bringing together relevant information from widely distributed networks.

Retrieval tool. Device such as a catalog, an index, a search engine, and the like, created for use as an information retrieval system.

Retrospective conversion. The process of changing information in eye-readable surrogate records into machine-readable form.

RLIN (Research Libraries Information Network). A bibliographic network that is particularly aimed at academic/research libraries and is especially important for special collections.

Schedule. *See* **Classification schedule**.

Schema. A document or piece of code that controls a set of terms in another document or piece of code; similar in function to a master checklist.

Scope note. A statement delimiting the meaning and associative relations of a subject heading, index term, or classification notation.

Search engine. A computerized retrieval tool that, in general, matches keywords input by a user to words found in documents of the site being searched; the more sophisticated search engines may allow other than keyword searching.

Sears List of Subject Headings (Sears). A controlled vocabulary of terms and phrases that is used mostly in small libraries to provide subject access to information packages available from that library.

Semantics. The meaning of a string of characters, as opposed to the syntax, which dictates the structure, independent of meaning.

Serial record file. A group of records that contains information about receipt of specific issues of serials or other continuing resources.

Serial (as opposed to "monographic") work. A publication issued in successive parts (regularly or irregularly) that is intended to continue indefinitely. *See also* **Continuing resource**; **Integrating resource**.

Series. A group of separate works that are related in subject or form and are published by the same entity.

Series (archives). A logically grouped set of files, books, correspondence, or other such set.

SGML (Standard Generalized Markup Language). An international standard for document markup for machine readability.

Shelflist. Originally, a list of physical information packages owned by an institution in the order in which they appeared on the shelves of the institution in which they were housed; in time the meaning has developed to indicate classification order display of surrogate records for information packages, which now allows for intangible as well as physical information packages.

Shelving. The process of placing physical information packages on shelves in the order of the arrangement of their call numbers or other notations that indicate their appropriate locations.

Specific entry. A principle observed in *application* of controlled vocabularies, by which a cataloger and/or an indexer assigns to an information package the most precise term available in the controlled vocabulary (or allowed to be created by the rules of the vocabulary), rather than assigning some broader heading. *See also* **Direct entry**; **Specificity.**

Specificity. The level of subject analysis that is addressed by a particular controlled vocabulary (e.g., *LCSH* has greater specificity in its established headings than does *Sears*, as, for example, in the greater depth of subdivisions that are established under main headings by *LCSH*). *See also* **Specific entry.**

Standard. Something established by authority or custom as a model or example; in the information field, standards are approved by national and/or international bodies after discussion and voting by representatives.

Structure. Arrangement in a definite pattern of the parts of a whole.

Subfield. A separately designated segment of a field in an encoded record.

Subject access. The provision to users of the means of locating information using subject terminology and/or classification notations.

Subject analysis. The part of indexing or cataloging that deals with the conceptual analysis of an information package; the translation of that conceptual analysis into a framework for a particular classification, subject heading, or indexing system; and then using the framework to assign specific notations or terminology to the information package and its surrogate record.

Subject authority file. A record of choices made in the development of a controlled vocabulary. The authority file contains such things as justification for the choice of one synonym over another; references from unused synonyms or near-synonyms; references for broader terms, narrower terms, and related terms; scope notes; citations for references used; and the like. *See also* **Subject heading list**.

Subject cataloging. The process of providing subject analysis, including subject headings and classification notations, when creating catalog records for archives, libraries, museums, and the like.

Subject entry. The place in a retrieval tool where a surrogate record containing a particular controlled vocabulary term is found.

Subject heading. Subject concept term or phrase found in a subject heading list and used in catalog records; sometimes used in indexes. *See also* **Descriptor**.

Subject heading list. A list of authorized controlled vocabulary terms or phrases together with any references, scope notes, and subdivisions associated with each term or phrase. *See also* **Subject authority file**; **Thesaurus**.

Subject indexing. The process of determining the aboutness of an information package and determining appropriate subject terminology to express the aboutness in an indexing language.

Subject subdivision. A method of precoordinating subject headings by using terms or phrases following main concepts to show special treatment of a subject.

Summarization. Indexing that identifies only a dominant, overall subject of an information package, recognizing only concepts embodied in the main theme. *See also* **Depth indexing**; **Exhaustivity**.

Surrogate record. A presentation of the characteristics (e.g., title, creator, physical description if appropriate, date of creation, subject[s], etc.) of an information package.

Switching language. A mediation language used to establish equivalencies between or among different subject indexing languages or classification schemes.

Synchronous responsibility. The situation in which all persons or corporate bodies involved in the creation of an information package have made the same kind of contribution to the creation of the work (e.g., joint authors).

Syndetic structure. The system of controlled vocabulary with all its references as used in a catalog or other retrieval tool.

Synonym. A term with the same meaning as another term; often, in controlled vocabularies, used for a term that has nearly the same meaning as well as for a term that has the same meaning.

Syntax. The combination of symbols, regardless of their meaning, into a structure; metadata's syntax is described by its encoding schema (e.g., MARC, XML), just as a language's syntax is described by its grammar.

System design. The specification of the working relations among all parts of a system; important design concepts include small testable components, user friendly operation, and attractive functionality.

Table. *See* **Classification table**.

Tag. A number, set of letters, certain set of punctuation marks, and so forth, that designates the kind of field in an encoding standard.

Taxonomy. A classification, usually in a restricted subject field, that is arranged to show presumed natural relationships. *See also* **Classification scheme**.

Technical services. The group of activities in an institution that involves acquiring, organizing, housing, maintaining, and conserving collections and automating these activities. In some places circulating collections is also considered to be a technical service.

TEI (Text Encoding Initiative). Refers to both the corporate organization with that name and to the encoding standard created by that group. The encoding standard was originally intended for the encoding of literary texts, although it has expanded to be used for other types of texts.

TEI Header. A set of encoded metadata at the beginning of a TEI document that describes the document, its contents, and its origins.

Thesaurus. A list of authorized controlled vocabulary terms representing single concepts together with any references, scope notes, and subdivisions associated with each term, and organized so that the relationships between concepts are made explicit. *See also* **Subject heading list**.

Title entry. The place in a retrieval tool where a surrogate record containing the name of an information package may be found.

Tracing. On printed surrogate records (e.g., catalog cards, records in book catalogs), the set of name, title, and subject access points, other than the main entry, that appear at the bottom of the record and are used to "trace" the additional copies of the surrogate record.

UBC (Universal Bibliographic Control). *See* **Universal Bibliographic Control**.

UCS (Universal Character Set). ISO standard for encoded representation of characters in computers; has the purpose of including all characters in all written languages of the world.

UDC (Universal Decimal Classification). *See* **Universal Decimal Classification**.

Unicode. An American industry counterpart to UCS, which permits computers to be able to handle the large number of character sets used in various languages. Both UCS and Unicode provide a unique number for every character to be used regardless of platform or format; a number of countries have adopted it as their national format.

Uniform title. A title chosen for a work so that all manifestations will be displayed together under the same main entry and also will be displayed together among all the entries for that main entry. Uniform titles also are used to distinguish between and among different works that have the same title.

UNIMARC (UNIversal MARC). Originally conceived as a conversion format, in which capacity it requires that each national agency create a translator to change records from UNIMARC to the particular national format and vice versa; a number of countries have adopted it as their national format.

Union catalog. A catalog that represents the holdings of more than one institution or collection.

Universal Bibliographic Control. The concept that it will someday be possible to have access to surrogate records for all the world's important information packages.

Universal Decimal Classification (UDC). A classification devised by Otlet and LaFontaine in the late 1890s. It was originally based on DDC, but has evolved into a much more faceted scheme than DDC.

URI (Uniform Resource Identifier). A way (such as use of a name or number) used on the Web to identify things such as people, corporations, books, abstract concepts, or network-accessible things; not limited to things that have network locations.

URL (Uniform Resource Locator). One form of URI: the address of an information package on the Internet; it indicates what protocol to use (e.g., "http," "telnet") and then gives the IP address or the domain name where the resource is located: most often server address, directory path, and file name.

USMARC (United States MARC). The version of MARC used in the United States until it was superseded by *MARC 21*.

USNAF (United States Name Authority File). A file housed at the Library of Congress (LC), containing not only the authority records created by LC and its cooperating U.S. contributors, but also records contributed from Australia, Canada, Great Britain, and others.

Value. A specific attribute of a property of a resource; for example, the value of an "author" property might be "Jane Smith," or the value of a "subject" property might be "Information organization."

Variable field. A field of an encoded record that can be as long or as short as the data to be placed into that field.

Vocabulary control. The process of creating and using a controlled vocabulary.

VRA (Visual Resources Association) Core Categories. A set of guidelines for describing visual documents depicting works of art, architecture, and artifacts or structures from material, popular, and folk culture.

Web. *See* **WWW**.

WLN (Western Library Network). Formerly a bibliographic network that served western North America, while its software was used in Australia, Canada, and other places; now absorbed by OCLC.

Word-by-word filing. An arrangement of terms in a retrieval tool in such a way that spaces between words take precedence over any letter that may follow (e.g., "New York" appears before "Newark"). *See also* **Letter-by-letter filing**.

Work (as opposed to "item"). A distinct intellectual or artistic creation; an abstract instance of content or ideas, regardless of the packaging in which the content or ideas may be expressed.

Work mark. A designation added to a cutter number in a call number that usually stands for the first word, not an article, of the title of the entity, but may stand for other entities, such as the name of a biographee, depending upon the circumstances.

Wrapper. In programming or in an encoding scheme (e.g., XML), a code or element that can have subcodes or subelements nested within it.

WWW (World Wide Web). A nonlinear, multimedia, flexible system to provide information resources on the Internet and to gain access to such resources; based on hypertext and HTTP.

XML (eXtensible Markup Language). A subset of SGML, designed specifically for Web documents, that omits some features of SGML and includes a few additional features (e.g., a method for reading non-ASCII text); it allows designers to create their own customized tags, thus overcoming many of the limitations of HTML.

XML Schema. A definition, like the Document Type Definition (DTD), that provides the constraints of XML document instances and provides a mechanism for their validation. Unlike a DTD, an XML Schema is expressed in XML syntax itself, and follows XML rules. Moreover, XML Schemas support Namespaces, Inheritance, and are capable of defining Data Types.

Z39. The standards section of ANSI/NISO that is devoted to libraries, information science, and publishing.

Z39.50. A national standard that provides for the exchange of information, such as surrogate records or full text, between otherwise noncompatible computer systems.

Z39.50 protocol. A standard applications level tool that allows one computer to query another computer and transfer search results without the user having to know the search commands of the remote computer.

ZING (Z39.50-International: Next Generation). Name for a number of initiatives by Z39.50 implementers to try to make the intellectual/semantic content of Z39.50 more broadly available and more attractive to information providers by making it easier to implement.

SELECTED BIBLIOGRAPHY

Ahronheim, Judith R. "Descriptive Metadata: Emerging Standards." *Journal of Academic Librarianship* 24, no. 5 (September 1998): 395–403.

Akeroyd, John, and Andrew Cox. "Integrated Library Management Systems: Overview." *Vine* 115 (2000): 3–10.

ALA/ALCTS/CCS Committee on Cataloging: Description and Access. Task Force on Metadata and the Cataloging Rules. *Metadata and the Cataloging Rules.* Last updated 3 April 1998. Available: http://www.libraries. psu.edu/tas/jca/ccda/tf-tei2.html.

———. *The Future of AACR.* Last updated April 2003. Available: http:// www.libraries.psu.edu/tas/jca/ccda/future1.html.

Anderson, James A. *An Introduction to Neural Networks.* Cambridge, Mass.: MIT Press, 1995.

Anderson, James D. *Guidelines for Indexes and Related Information Retrieval Devices.* Bethesda, Md.: NISO Press, 1997.

Arant, Wendi, and Leila Payne. "The Common User Interface in Academic Libraries: Myth or Reality?" *Library Hi Tech* 19, no. 1 (2001): 63–76.

Arms, William Y. *Digital Libraries.* Cambridge, Mass.: MIT Press, 2000.

Atherton, Jay. "From Life Cycle to Continuum: Some Thoughts on the Records Management-Archives Relationship." *Archivaria* 21 (Winter 1985–1986): 43–51.

Baca, Murtha. "A Picture Is Worth a Thousand Words: Metadata for Art Objects and Their Visual Surrogates." In *Cataloging the Web: Metadata, AACR, and MARC 21*, edited by Wayne Jones, et al. Lanham, Md.: Scarecrow Press, 2002, pp. 131–138.

————, ed. *Introduction to Metadata: Pathways to Digital Information.* Version 2.0, 2000. Available: http://www.getty.edu/research/institute/stan dards/intrometadata/.

Baca, Murtha, Patricia Harpring, Elisa Lanzi, Linda McRae, and Ann White-side. *Cataloguing Cultural Objects: A Guide to Describing Cultural Works and Their Images.* Bronx, N.Y.: Visual Resources Association, 2003. Available: http://www.vraweb.org/CCOweb/index.html.

Baker, Nicholson. "Discards." *New Yorker* 70, no. 7 (4 April 1994): 64–86.

Banerjee, Sujata, and Vibhu O. Mittal. "On the Use of Linguistic Ontologies for Accessing and Indexing Distributed Digital Libraries." In *Digital Libraries '94: Proceedings of the First Annual Conference on the Theory and Practice of Digital Libraries, June 19–21, 1994, College Station, Texas.* Available: http://www.csdl.tamu.edu/DL94/paper/banerjee.html.

Barnett, Patricia J. "Indexing with the *AAT*." In *Guide to Indexing and Cataloging with the Art & Architecture Thesaurus,* edited by Toni Petersen and Patricia J. Barnett. New York: Oxford University Press, 1994, pp. 33–40.

Barnett, Patricia J., and Toni Petersen. "Extending MARC to Accommodate Faceted Thesauri: The AAT Model." In *Beyond the Book: Extending MARC for Subject Access,* edited by Toni Petersen and Pat Molholt. Boston, Mass.: G. K. Hall, 1990, pp. 7–23.

Barnhart, Linda. "Access Control Records: Prospects and Challenges." In *Authority Control in the 21st Century: An Invitational Conference: Proceedings,* sponsored by OCLC, 31 March–1 April 1996. Available: http://www. oclc.org/oclc/man/authconf/barnhart.htm.

Bates, Marcia J. "The Design of Browsing and Berrypicking Techniques for the Online Search Interface." *Online Review* 13, no. 5 (October 1989): 407–424.

————. "Subject Access in Online Catalogs: A Design Model." *Journal of the American Society for Information Science* 37, no. 6 (1986): 357–376.

Bearman, David. "Archives and Manuscript Control with Bibliographic Utilities: Challenges and Opportunities." *American Archivist* 52 (Winter 1989): 26–39.

———. "Functional Requirements for Collections Management Systems." *Archival Informatics Technical Report* 1, no. 3 (Fall 1987): 1–87.

Beheshti, Jamshid. "The Evolving OPAC." *Cataloging & Classification Quarterly* 24, no. 1/2 (1997): 163–185.

Berman, Sanford. *Joy of Cataloging.* Phoenix, Ariz.: Oryx Press, 1981.

Berner, Richard C. "Historical Development of Archival Theory and Practices in the United States." *Midwestern Archivist* 7, no. 2 (1982): 103–117.

Berners-Lee, Tim, James Hendler, and Ora Lassila. "The Semantic Web." *Scientific American* 284, no. 5 (May 2001): 34–38, 40–43. Available: http://www.scientificamerican.com/article.cfm?articleID=00048144-10D 2-IC70-84A9809EC588EF21&catID=2.

Bertolucci, Katherine. "Happiness Is Taxonomy: Four Structures for Snoopy." *Information Outlook* 7, no. 3 (March 2003): 36–44.

Bhatt, G. D. "Knowledge Management in Organizations: Examining the Interactions Between Technologies, Techniques, and People." *Journal of Knowledge Management* 5, no. 1 (2001): 68–75.

Bierbaum, Esther Green. "Records and Access: Museum Registration and Library Cataloging." *Cataloging & Classification Quarterly* 9, no. 1 (1988): 97–111

Bolin, Mary K. "Catalog Design, Catalog Maintenance, Catalog Governance." *Library Collections, Acquisitions, & Technical Services* 24 (2000): 53–63.

Borgman, Christine L. *From Gutenberg to the Global Information Infrastructure: Access to Information in the Networked World.* Cambridge, Mass.: MIT Press, 2000.

———. "Why Are Online Catalogs Hard to Use? Lessons Learned from Information Retrieval Studies." *Journal of the American Society for Information Science* 37, no. 6 (June 1986): 387–400.

———. "Why Are Online Catalogs *Still* Hard to Use?" *Journal of the American Society for Information Science* 47, no. 7 (July 1996): 493–503.

Bowker, Geoffrey C., and Susan Leigh Star. *Sorting Things Out: Classification and Its Consequences.* Cambridge, Mass.: MIT Press, 1999.

Bowman, J. H. "The Catalog as Barrier to Retrieval—Part 1: Hyphens and Ampersands in Titles." *Cataloging & Classification Quarterly* 29, no. 4 (2000): 39–60.

Bray, Tim. "What is RDF?" Last updated January 24, 2001. Available: http://www.xml.com/pub/a/2001/01/24/rdf.html.

Brown, A. G., in collaboration with D. W. Langridge and J. Mills. *An Introduction to Subject Indexing.* 2nd ed. London: Bingley, 1982.

Bryan, Martin. "An Introduction to the Extensible Markup Language (XML)." *Bulletin of the American Society for Information Science* 25, no. 1 (October/November 1998): 11–14. Also available: http://www.personal.u-net.com/~sgml/xmlintro.htm.

———. "An Introduction to the Standard Generalized Markup Language (SGML)." The SGML Centre, 1992. Available: http://www.personal.u-net.com/~sgml/sgml.htm.

Buck, Rebecca A., and Jean Allman Gilmore, eds. *The New Museum Registration Methods.* Washington, D.C.: American Association of Museums, 1998.

Buckland, Michael K. "What is a 'Document'?" *Journal of the American Society for Information Science* 48, no. 9 (September 1997): 804–809. Available: http://www.sims.berkeley.edu/~buckland/whatdoc.html.

Buckland, Michael K., Barbara A. Norgard, and Christian Plaunt. "Filing, Filtering and the First Few Found." *Information Technology and Libraries* 12, no. 3 (September 1993): 311–319.

Burke, Frank G. "Archives: Organization and Description." In *World Encyclopedia of Library and Information Services.* 3rd ed. Chicago: American Library Association, 1993, pp. 63–68.

Burnard, Lou, and C. M. Sperberg-McQueen. *TEI Lite: An Introduction to Text Encoding for Interchange.* June 1995, revised May 2002. Available: http://www.tei-c.org/Lite/.

Bush, Vannevar. "As We May Think." *Atlantic Monthly* 176 (July 1945): 101–108. Available: http://www.theatlantic.com/unbound/flashbks/computer/bushf.htm. Also available: http://www.ps.uni-sb.de/~duchier/pub/vbush/vbush.shtml.

Calhoun, Karen, and Bill Kara. "Aggregation or Aggravation? Optimizing Access to Full-Text Journals." In *From Catalog to Gateway: Briefings from the CFFC*, paper no. 15. *ALCTS Newsletter Online* 11, no. 1 (Spring 2000). Available: http://www.pitt.edu/~agtaylor/ala/papers/Calhoun Aggregation.pdf.

Caplan, Priscilla. *Metadata Fundamentals for All Librarians*. Chicago: American Library Association, 2003.

Carlyle, Allyson. "Fulfilling the Second Objective in the Online Catalog: Schemes for Organizing Author and Work Records into Usable Displays." *Library Resources & Technical Services* 41, no. 2 (April 1997): 79–100.

Chan, Lois Mai. *Cataloging and Classification: An Introduction*. New York: McGraw-Hill, 1994.

———. *A Guide to the Library of Congress Classification*. 5th ed. Englewood, Colo.: Libraries Unlimited, 1999.

———. *Library of Congress Subject Headings: Principles and Applications*. 3rd ed. Englewood, Colo.: Libraries Unlimited, 1995.

Chan, Lois Mai, and Joan S. Mitchell. *Dewey Decimal Classification: Principles and Application*. 3rd. ed. Dublin, Ohio: OCLC, 2003.

Chen, Hao, and Susan Dumais. "Bringing Order to the Web: Automatically Categorizing Search Results." Microsoft Research Publications, 2000. Available: http://research.microsoft.com/~sdumais/chi00.pdf.

Chepesiuk, Ron. "Organizing the Internet: The 'Core' of the Challenge." *American Libraries* 30, no. 1 (January 1999): 60–63.

Classification Research Group. "The Need for a Faceted Classification as the Basis of All Methods of Information Retrieval." In *Theory of Subject Analysis: A Sourcebook*, edited by Lois Mai Chan, Phyllis A. Richmond, and Elaine Svenonius. Littleton, Colo.: Libraries Unlimited, 1985, pp. 154–167.

Clayton, Mark. "Library Stacks? No, That's My Office." *Christian Science Monitor* (16 July 2002). Available: http://www.csmonitor.com/2002/0716/p16s01-lehl.html.

Cleveland, Donald B., and Ana D. Cleveland. *Introduction to Indexing and Abstracting*. 3rd ed. Englewood, Colo.: Libraries Unlimited, 2001.

Coffman, Steve. "Building Earth's Largest Library: Driving into the Future."

Searcher 7, no. 3 (March 1999). Available: http://www.infotoday.com/searcher/mar99/coffman.htm.

Crawford, Walt. "The Card Catalog and Other Digital Controversies: What's Obsolete and What's Not in the Age of Information." *American Libraries* 30, no. 1 (January 1999): 52–58.

———. "Gutting America's Local Libraries: Informal Comments on 'Building Earth's Largest Library.' " 30 August 1999; edited 26 August 2000. Available: http://home.att.net/~wcc.libmedx/gutting.htm.

Crawford, Walt, and Michael Gorman. *Future Libraries: Dreams, Madness, & Reality.* Chicago: American Library Association, 1995.

Cutter, Charles A. *Rules for a Dictionary Catalog.* 4th ed. Washington, D.C.: Government Printing Office, 1904; Reprint, London: The Library Association, 1962.

Day, Michael. *Metadata: Mapping Between Metadata Formats.* Last updated 22 May 2002. Available: http://www.ukoln.ac.uk/metadata/interoperability.

Digital Library Technology Trends. Santa Clara, Calif.: Sun Microsystems, 2002. Available: http://www.sun.com/products-n-solutions/edu/whitepapers/pdf/digital_library_trends.pdf.

Dillon, Andrew. "Information Architecture in JASIST: Just Where Did We Come From?" *Journal of the American Society for Information Science and Technology* 53, no. 10 (2002): 821–823. Also available: http://www.gslis.utexas.edu/~adillon/publications/jasisintro.pdf.

Dixson, Larry E. "Z39.50 and Its Use in Library Systems (Part One)." In *From Catalog to Gateway: Briefings from the CFFC*, paper no. 3. *ALCTS Newsletter* 5, no. 6 (1994): A–D.

———. "Z39.50 and Its Use in Library Systems (Part Two)." In *From Catalog to Gateway: Briefings from the CFFC*, paper no. 4. *ALCTS Newsletter* 6, no. 1 (1995): A–D.

Dooley, Jackie M. "Subject Indexing in Context." *American Archivist* 55, no. 2 (Spring 1992): 344–354.

Dorner, Dan. "Cataloging in the 21st Century—Part 1: Contextual Issues." *Library Collections, Acquisitions, & Technical Services* 23, no. 4 (1999): 393–399.

———. "Cataloging in the 21st Century—Part 2: Digitization and Information Standards." *Library Collections, Acquisitions, & Technical Services* 24 (2000): 73–87.

Doszkocs, Tamas, James Reggia, and Xia Lin. "Connectionist Models and Information Retrieval." In *Annual Review of Information Science and Technology*, Vol. 25, edited by Martha E. Williams. Amsterdam: Elsevier Science, 1990, pp. 212–214, 222–230.

Drabenstott, Karen M., and Marjorie S. Weller. "Failure Analysis of Subject Searches in a Test of a New Design for Subject Access to Online Catalogs." *Journal of the American Society for Information Science* 47, no. 7 (July 1996): 519–537.

Dunkin, Paul S. *Cataloging U.S.A.* Chicago: American Library Association, 1969.

Ellis, Judith, ed. *Keeping Archives.* 2nd ed. Port Melbourne, Australia: Thorpe, in association with the Australian Society of Archivists, 1993.

El-Sherbini, Magda. "Metadata and the Future of Cataloging." *Library Trends* 50, no. 1 (2001): 16–27.

"ERIC's Indexing and Retrieval: 2001 Update" and "Thesaurus Construction and Format." In *Thesaurus of ERIC Descriptors*, edited by James E. Houston. 14th ed. Phoenix, Ariz.: Oryx Press, 2001, pp. xiv–xxxi.

Farb, Sharon. "Universal Design and the Americans with Disabilities Act: Not All Systems Are Created Equal—How Systems Design Can Expand Information Access." In *From Catalog to Gateway: Briefings from the CFFC*, paper no. 16. *ALCTS Newsletter Online* 11, no. 1 (Spring 2000). Available: http://www.pitt.edu/~agtaylor/ala/papers/FarbUniversalDesign.pdf.

Fidel, Raya, and Michael Crandall. "The AACR2 as a Design Schema for Bibliographic Databases." *Library Quarterly* 58, no. 2 (April 1988): 123–142.

Fishbein, Meyer H. "Archives: Records Management and Records Appraisal." In *World Encyclopedia of Library and Information Services.* 3rd ed. Chicago: American Library Association, 1993, pp. 60–63.

Foskett, A. C. *The Subject Approach to Information.* 5th ed. London: Library Association Publishing, 1996.

Fox, Michael J., and Peter Wilkerson. *Introduction to Archival Organization and Description: Access to Cultural Heritage.* The Getty Information Institute, 1998. Available: http://www.schistory.org/getty/index.html.

Fritz, Deborah A., and Richard J. Fritz. *MARC 21 for Everyone: A Practical Guide.* Chicago: American Library Association, 2003.

Furrie, Betty. *Understanding MARC Bibliographic: Machine-Readable Cataloging.* 7th ed. Library of Congress, Cataloging Distribution Service, 2003. Available: http://www.loc.gov/marc/umb.

Gaynor, Edward. "From MARC to Markup: SGML and Online Library Systems." In *From Catalog to Gateway: Briefings from the CFFC,* paper no. 7. *ALCTS Newsletter* 7, no. 2 (1996): A–D. Also available (archival copy): http://xml.coverpages.org/gaynorMARC96.html.

The Getty. *Art & Architecture Thesaurus On Line: About the AAT.* 2000. Available: http://www.getty.edu/research/tools/vocabulary/aat/about.html.

Gilliland-Swetland, Anne J. "Setting the Stage." In *Introduction to Metadata: Pathways to Digital Information.* Version 2.0, edited by Murtha Baca. 2000. Available: http://www.getty.edu/research/institute/standards/intrometadata/2_articles/index.html.

Gilster, Paul. *Digital Literacy.* New York: Wiley, 1997.

Gladwell, Malcolm. "The Social Life of Paper: Looking for Method in the Mess." *The New Yorker* (25 March 2002). Available: http://www.newyorker.com/printable/?critics/020325crbo_books.

Gorman, Michael. *The Concise AACR2: 1998 Revision.* Chicago: American Library Association, 1999.

———. "The Longer the Number, the Smaller the Spine; or, Up and Down with Melvil and Elsie." *American Libraries* 12, no. 8 (September 1981): 498–499.

Guenther, Rebecca S. "MODS: The Metadata Object Description Schema." *Portal: Libraries and the Academy* 3, no. 1 (2003): 137–150.

Hagler, Ronald. *The Bibliographic Record and Information Technology.* 3rd ed. Chicago: American Library Association, 1997.

Harris, Mary Dee. *Introduction to Natural Language Processing.* Reston, Va.: Reston, 1985.

Harris, Michael H. *History of Libraries in the Western World.* 4th ed. Metuchen, N.J.: Scarecrow Press, 1995.

Hearst, Marti A. "Interfaces for Searching the Web." *Scientific American* 276, no. 3 (March 1997): 68–72. Also available: http://www.hackvan.com/pub/stig/articles/trusted-systems/0397hearst.html.

Heery, Rachel, and Manjula Patel. "Application Profiles: Mixing and Matching Metadata Schemes." *Ariadne* 25 (24 September 2000). Available: http://www.ariadne.ac.uk/issue25/app-profiles/intro.html.

Hemmasi, Harriette, David Miller, and Mary Charles Lasater. "Access to Form Data in Online Catalogs." In *From Catalog to Gateway: Briefings from the CFFC*, edited by Arlene G. Taylor, paper no. 13. *ALCTS Newsletter Online* 10, no. 4 (July 1999). Available: http://www.pitt.edu/~agtaylor/ala/papers/HemmasiFormData.pdf.

Hildreth, Charles R. "Online Catalog Design Models: Are We Moving in the Right Direction? A Report Submitted to Council on Library Resources August, 1995." Available: http://phoenix.liu.edu/~hildreth/clr-opac.html.

———. "The Use and Understanding of Keyword Searching in a University Online Catalog." *Information Technology and Libraries* 16, no. 2 (June 1997): 52–62.

Hodge, Gail. *Metadata Made Simpler.* Bethesda, Md.: National Information Standards Organization, 2001. Available: http://www.niso.org/news/Metadata_Simpler.pdf.

———. *Systems of Knowledge for Digital Libraries: Beyond Traditional Authority Files.* Washington, D.C.: Digital Library Federation, Council on Library and Information Resources, 2000.

Holm, Liv Aasa. "Authority Control in an International Context in the New Environment." *International Cataloguing and Bibliographic Control* 28, no. 1 (January/March 1999): 11–12.

Honkela, Timo, Samuel Kaski, Krista Lagus, and Teuvo Kohonen. "Self-Organizing Maps of Document Collections." *Alma* 2 (1996).

Hopkins, Judith. "The 1791 French Cataloging Code and the Origins of the Card Catalog." *Libraries & Culture* 27, no. 4 (Fall 1992): 378–404.

Hsieh-Yee, Ingrid. *Organizing Audiovisual and Electronic Resources for Access: A Cataloging Guide.* Englewood, Colo.: Libraries Unlimited, 2000.

Hudgins, Jean, Grace Agnew, and Elizabeth Brown. *Getting Mileage out of Metadata: Applications for the Library.* Chicago: American Library Association, 1999.

Humbert, de Romans. *Regulations for the Operation of a Medieval Library.* St. Paul: Associates of the James Ford Bell Library, University of Minnesota, 1980.

Hunter, Eric J. *Classification Made Simple.* 2nd ed. Aldershot, Eng.; Brookfield, Vt.: Gower, 2002.

Hurley, Bernard J., John Price-Wilkin, Merrilee Proffitt, and Howard Besser. *The Making of America II Testbed Project: A Digital Library Service Model.* Washington, D.C.: The Digital Library Federation, Council on Library and Information Resources, 1999.

Ince, A. Nejat, Cem Evrendilek, Dag Wilhelmsen, and Fadil Gezer. *Planning and Architectural Design of Modern Command Control Communications and Information Systems: Military and Civilian Applications.* Boston: Kluwer Academic, 1997.

International Federation of Library Associations and Institutions. *Digital Libraries: Metadata Resources.* Latest revision 3 February 2003. Available: http://www.ifla.org/II/metadata.htm.

International Federation of Library Associations and Institutions, IFLA Study Group. *Functional Requirements for Bibliographic Records (FRBR).* München: Saur, 1998. Available: http://www.ifla.org/VII/s13/frbr/frbr.pdf or http://www.ifla.org/VII/s13/frbr/frbr.htm.

Intner, Sheila S., Sally C. Tseng, and Mary Lynette Larsgaard, eds. *Electronic Cataloging: AACR2 and Metadata for Serials and Monographs.* Binghamton, N.Y.: Haworth Information Press, 2003.

Intner, Sheila S., and Jean Weihs. *Standard Cataloging for School and Public Libraries.* 3rd ed. Englewood, Colo.: Libraries Unlimited, 2001.

Inventories and Registers: A Handbook of Techniques and Examples. Chicago: Society of American Archivists, 1976.

Jackson, Sidney L. *Libraries and Librarianship in the West: A Brief History.* New York: McGraw-Hill, 1974.

Jacob, Elin K. "Ontologies and the Semantic Web." *Bulletin of the American Society for Information Science and Technology* 29, no. 4 (April/May 2003): 19–22. Also available: http://www.asis.org/Bulletin/Apr-03/Bulletin AprMay03.pdf.

Jacsó, Péter, and F. W. Lancaster. *Build Your Own Database.* Chicago: American Library Association, 1999.

Johnson, Bruce Chr. "XML and MARC: Which Is 'Right'?" *Cataloging & Classification Quarterly* 32, no. 1 (2001): 81–90.

Jones, Wayne, Judith R. Ahronheim, and Josephine Crawford, eds. *Cataloging the Web: Metadata, AACR, and MARC 21.* (ALCTS Papers on Library Technical Services and Collections, no. 10.) Lanham, Md.: Scarecrow Press, 2002.

Kelly, Brian. "What Is . . . XML?" Last updated May 18, 1998. Available: http://www.ariadne.ac.uk/issue15/what-is/.

Koch, Traugott. *Controlled Vocabularies, Thesauri and Classification Systems Available in the WWW. DC Subject.* Last updated 27 September 2001. Available: http://www.lub.lu.se/metadata/subject-help.html.

———. *The Role of Classification Schemes in Internet Resource Description and Discovery.* Last updated 25 March 1998. Available: http://www.ukoln. ac.uk/metadata/desire/classification/class_ti.htm.

Kohonen, Teuvo. *Self-Organizing Maps.* 3rd ed. Berlin, N.Y.: Springer-Verlag, 2001.

Kwasnik, Barbara H. "How a Personal Document's Intended Use or Purpose Affects Its Classification in an Office." In *Proceedings of the 12th Annual International ACM SIGIR Conference on Research and Development in Information Retrieval.* New York: ACM, 1989[?], pp. 207–210.

Lagoze, Carl. "Accommodating Simplicity and Complexity in Metadata: Lessons from the Dublin Core Experience." Presented at Seminar on Metadata Organized by Archiefschool, Netherlands Institute for Archival Education and Research, 8 June 2000. Available: http://www.cs. cornell.edu/lagoze/Papers/dc.pdf.

Lakoff, George. *Women, Fire, and Dangerous Things: What Categories Reveal about the Mind.* Chicago: University of Chicago Press, 1987.

Lancaster, F. W. *Indexing and Abstracting in Theory and Practice.* 3rd ed. Champaign: University of Illinois, Graduate School of Library and Information Science, 2003.

―――. *Vocabulary Control for Information Retrieval.* 2nd ed. Arlington, Va.: Information Resources Press, 1986.

―――. "Whither Libraries? or Wither Libraries." *College & Research Libraries* 39, no. 5 (September 1978): 345–357; also reprinted in *College & Research Libraries* 50, no. 4 (July 1989): 406–419.

Langridge, D. W. *Classification: Its Kinds, Elements, Systems and Applications.* London: Bowker-Saur, 1992.

―――. *Subject Analysis: Principles and Procedures.* London: Bowker-Saur, 1989.

Larson, Ray R. "Classification Clustering, Probabilistic Information Retrieval, and the Online Catalog." *Library Quarterly* 6, no. 2 (April 1991): 133–173.

Larson, Ray R., Jerome McDonough, Paul O'Leary, and Lucy Kuntz. "Cheshire II: Designing a Next-Generation Online Catalog." *Journal of the American Society for Information Science* 47, no. 7 (July 1996): 555–567.

Lazinger, Susan S. *Digital Preservation and Metadata: History, Theory, Practice.* Englewood, Colo.: Libraries Unlimited, 2001.

Lee-Smeltzer, Kuang-Hwei (Janet). "Finding the Needle: Controlled Vocabularies, Resource Discovery, and Dublin Core." *Library Collections, Acquisitions & Technical Services* 24 (2000): 205–215.

Leise, Fred. "Using Faceted Classification to Assist Indexing." *Key Words* 9, no. 6 (November/December 2001): 178–179.

Levy, David M. "Cataloging in the Digital Order." In *Digital Libraries '95: The Second Annual Conference on the Theory and Practice of Digital Libraries, June 11–13, 1995, Austin, Texas.* Available: http://www.csdl.tamu.edu/DL95/papers/levy/levy.html.

―――. *Scrolling Forward: Making Sense of Documents in the Digital Age.* New York: Arcade Publishing, 2001.

Lynch, Clifford. "The Battle to Define the Future of the Book in the Digital

World." *First Monday* 6, no. 6 (June 2001). Available: http://www.firstmonday.org/issues/issue6_6/lynch/index.html.

Lynch, Clifford A. "Future Developments in Metadata and Their Role in Access to Networked Information." In *Cataloging the Web: Metadata, AACR, and MARC 21*, edited by Wayne Jones, et al. Lanham, Md.: Scarecrow Press, 2002, pp. 183–187.

Mann, Thomas. *Doing Research at the Library of Congress: A Guide to Subject Searching in a Closed Stacks Library*. Washington, D.C.: Library of Congress, Humanities and Social Sciences Division, 1994.

———. *Library Research Models: A Guide to Classification, Cataloging, and Computers*. New York: Oxford University Press, 1993.

"The MARC 21 Formats: Background and Principles." Prepared by MARBI in conjunction with Network Development and MARC Standards Office, Library of Congress. Washington, D.C.: Library of Congress, 1996. Available: http://lcweb.loc.gov/marc/96principl.html.

Marcella, Rita, and Arthur Maltby, eds. *The Future of Classification*. Aldershot, Eng.; Brookfield, Vt.: Gower, 2000.

Marcella, Rita, and Robert Newton. *A New Manual of Classification*. Aldershot, Eng.; Brookfield, Vt.: Gower, 1994.

Matthews, Joseph R. "Time for New OPAC Initiatives: An Overview of Landmarks in the Literature and Introduction to WordFocus." *Library Hi Tech* 15 (1997): 111–122.

———. "The Value of Information: The Case of the Library Catalog." *Technical Services Quarterly* 19, no. 2 (2001): 1–16.

McKiernan, Gerry. *Beyond Bookmarks: Schemes for Organizing the Web*. March 22, 2001. Available: http://www.public.iastate.edu/~CYBERSTACKS/CTW.htm.

Meghabghab, Dania Bilal. *Automating Media Centers and Small Libraries: A Microcomputer-Based Approach*. Englewood, Colo.: Libraries Unlimited, 1997.

"*MeSH* Introduction." In *Medical Subject Headings: Annotated Alphabetic List*. Bethesda, Md.: National Library of Medicine, 1998, pp. I-3–IL-166.

"Metadata Standards, Crosswalks, and Standard Organizations." In *Cataloger's Toolbox*. Memorial University of Newfoundland Libraries. Last revised June 19, 2003. Available: http://staff.library.mun.ca/staff/tool box/standards.htm.

Miller, Eric. "An Introduction to the Resource Description Framework." *Bulletin of the American Society for Information Science* 25, no. 1 (October/ November 1998): 15–19.

Miller, Fredric M. "Archival Description." In *Reference Services for Archives and Manuscripts*, edited by Laura B. Cohen. Binghamton, N.Y.: Haworth Press, 1997, pp. 55–66.

———. *Arranging and Describing Archives and Manuscripts*. Chicago: Society of American Archivists, 1990.

Miller, Joseph. "Principles of the Sears List of Subject Headings." In *Sears List of Subject Headings*. 17th ed. Bronx, N.Y.: H. W. Wilson, 2000, pp. xv–xl. [18th ed. forthcoming, 2004.]

Miller, Paul. "Z39.50 for All." *Ariadne* 21 (September 20, 1999). Available: http://www.ariadne.ac.uk/issue21/z3950/.

Milsap, Larry. "A History of the Online Catalog in North America." In *Technical Services Management, 1965–1990: A Quarter Century of Change, A Look to the Future: A Festschrift for Kathryn Luther Henderson*, edited by Linda C. Smith and Ruth C. Carter. Binghamton, N.Y.: Haworth Press, 1996, pp. 79–91.

Milstead, Jessica, and Susan Feldman. "Metadata: Cataloging by Any Other Name . . ." *Online* (January 1999). Available: http://www.onlinemag. net/OL1999/milstead1.html.

———. "Metadata Projects and Standards." *Online* (January 1999). Available: http://www.onlinemag.net/OL1999/milstead1.html#projects.

Moen, William E. "Resource Discovery Using Z39.50: Promise and Reality." In *Proceedings of the Bicentennial Conference on Bibliographic Control for the New Millennium, November 15–17, 2000*. Washington, D.C.: Library of Congress Cataloging Distribution Service, 2001, pp. 185–206. Also available: http://lcweb.loc.gov/catdir/bibcontrol/moen_paper.html.

Mullins, Craig. *Database Administration: The Complete Guide to Practices and Procedures*. Boston: Addison-Wesley, 2002.

Nash, Lisa, and Aaron Press. "Taxonomies: Structuring Today's Knowledge Management Systems." In *Information About Information Briefing* (Outsell, Inc.) 4, no. 26 (July 18, 2001): 1–18.

National Center for Supercomputing Applications. "A Beginner's Guide to HTML." Last updated 24 January 2001. Available: http://archive.ncsa.uiuc.edu/General/Internet/WWW/HTMLPrimer.html.

National Library of Medicine. *Fact Sheet: Medical Subject Headings (MeSH®)*. Last updated December 4, 2002. Available: http://www.nlm.nih.gov/pubs/factsheets/mesh.html.

———. *Fact Sheet: UMLS® Metathesaurus®*. Last updated: January 13, 2003. Available: http://www.nlm.nih.gov/pubs/factsheets/umlsmeta.html.

Needleman, Mark H. "RDF: The Resource Description Framework." *Serials Review* 27, no. 1 (December 10, 2001): 58–61.

Norton, M. Jay. "Knowledge Discovery in Databases." *Library Trends* 48, no. 1 (Summer 1999): 9–21.

Noy, Natalya Fridman, and Deborah L. McGuinness. *Ontology Development 101: A Guide to Creating Your First Ontology*. Knowledge Systems Laboratory, Stanford University, 2000. Available: http://www.ksl.stanford.edu/people/dlm/papers/ontology-tutorial-noy-mcguinness-abstract.html.

OCLC. *Bibliographic Formats and Standards*. 3rd ed. 2002. Available: http://www.oclc.org/bibformats/.

Oder, Norman. "Cataloging the Net: Can We Do It?" *Library Journal* 123, no. 16 (October 1, 1998): 47–51.

———. "Cataloging the Net: Two Years Later." *Library Journal* 125, no. 16 (October 1, 2000): 50–51.

Olson, Hope A., and John J. Boll. *Subject Analysis in Online Catalogs*. 2nd ed. Englewood, Colo.: Libraries Unlimited, 2001.

"Organizing Internet Resources: Metadata and the Web." *Bulletin of the American Society for Information Science* 24, no. 1 (October/November 1997).

Osborn, Andrew D. "The Crisis in Cataloging." In *Foundations of Cataloging: A Sourcebook*, edited by Michael Carpenter and Elaine Svenonius. Littleton, Colo.: Libraries Unlimited, 1985, pp. 90–103. Originally published in *Library Quarterly* 11, no. 4 (October 1941): 393–411.

OWL Web Ontology Language Overview, W3C Working Draft. 31 March 2003. Available: http://www.w3.org/TR/owl-features/.

Petroski, Henry. *The Book on the Bookshelf.* New York: Knopf, 1999.

Pettee, Julia. "The Subject Approach to Books and the Development of the Dictionary Catalog." In *Theory of Subject Analysis: A Sourcebook,* edited by Lois Mai Chan, Phyllis A. Richmond, and Elaine Svenonius. Littleton, Colo.: Libraries Unlimited, 1985, pp. 94–98.

Pitti, Daniel V. "Creator Description: Encoded Archival Context." In the Proceedings of *International Conference [on] Authority Control: Definition and International Experiences.* Florence, Italy, 12–23 February 2003. Available: http://www.unifi.it/universita/biblioteche/ac/relazioni/pitti_eng.pdf.

Program for Cooperative Cataloging. *Introduction to the Program for Cooperative Cataloging BIBCO Core Record Standard.* Available: http://lcweb.loc.gov/catdir/pcc/bibco/coreintro.html.

Pugh, Mary Jo. "The Illusion of Omniscience: Subject Access and the Reference Archivist." *American Archivist* 45, no. 1 (Winter 1982): 33–44.

Ranganathan, S. R. *Prolegomena to Library Classification.* 3rd ed. London: Asia Publishing House, 1967.

"Report of the Working Group on Standards for Archival Description." *American Archivist* 52, no. 4 (Fall 1989): 440–461.

Reynolds, Dennis. *Library Automation: Issues and Applications.* New York: Bowker, 1985.

Rich, Elaine, and Kevin Knight. *Artificial Intelligence.* 2nd ed. New York: McGraw-Hill, 1991.

Robins, David. "Information Architecture, Organizations, and Records Management." *Records and Information Management Report* 17, no. 3 (March 2001): 1–14.

Roe, Kathleen. "Enhanced Authority Control: Is It Time?" *Archivaria* 35 (Spring 1993): 119–129.

Rogers, JoAnn V., and Jerry D. Saye. *Nonprint Cataloging for Multimedia Collections.* 2nd ed. Littleton, Colo.: Libraries Unlimited, 1987.

Rosenfeld, Louis, and Peter Morville. *Information Architecture for the World Wide Web.* 2nd ed. Cambridge, Mass.: O'Reilly, 2002.

Rowley, Jennifer, and John Farrow. *Organizing Knowledge: An Introduction to Managing Access to Information.* 3rd ed. Aldershot, Eng.; Burlington, Vt.: Ashgate, 2000.

Russell, Beth M. "Hidden Wisdom and Unseen Treasure: Revisiting Cataloging in Medieval Libraries." *Cataloging & Classification Quarterly* 26, no. 3 (1998): 21–30.

Sauperl, Alenka. *Subject Determination during the Cataloging Process.* Lanham, Md.: Scarecrow Press, 2002.

Schulze, Anna Noakes. "User-Centered Design for Information Professionals." *Journal of Education for Library and Information Science* 42, no. 2 (Spring 2001): 116–122.

Shepherd, Elizabeth, and Geoffrey Yeo. *Managing Records: A Handbook of Principles and Practice.* London: Facet Publishing, 2003.

Smalley, Joseph. "The French Cataloging Code of 1791: A Translation." *Library Quarterly* 61, no. 1 (January 1991): 1–14.

Smiraglia, Richard P. *The Nature of "A Work": Implications for the Organization of Knowledge.* Lanham, Md.: Scarecrow Press, 2001.

Snowden, Dave. "Complex Acts of Knowing: Paradox and Descriptive Self-Awareness." *Bulletin of the American Society for Information Science and Technology* 29, no. 4 (April/May 2003): 23–28. Available: http://www.asis.org/Bulletin/Apr-03/BulletinAprMay03.pdf. This version is extracted and condensed from one that first appeared in *Journal of Knowledge Management* 6, no. 2 (May 2003): 100–111. A copy of the original is also available: http://www-1.ibm.com/services/files/complex.pdf.

Soergel, Dagobert. "The Rise of Ontologies or the Reinvention of Classification." *Journal of the American Society for Information Science* 50, no. 12 (October 1999): 1119–1120.

Steckel, Mike. "Ranganathan for IAs: An Introduction to the Thought of S. R. Ranganathan for Information Architects." *Boxes and Arrows* (October 7, 2002). Available: http://www.boxesandarrows.com/archives/ranganathan_for_ias.php.

Stoll, Clifford. *Silicon Snake Oil: Second Thoughts on the Information Highway.* New York: Doubleday, 1995.

St. Pierre, Margaret and William P. LaPlant. *Issues in Crosswalking Content Metadata Standards.* Released October 15, 1998. Available at: http://www.niso.org/press/whitepapers/crsswalk.html.

Strout, Ruth French. "The Development of the Catalog and Cataloging Codes." *Library Quarterly* 26, no. 4 (October 1956): 254–275.

Svenonius, Elaine. *The Intellectual Foundation of Information Organization.* Cambridge, Mass.: The MIT Press, 2000.

Taylor, Arlene G. "Authority Control: Where It's Been and Where It's Going." In *Authority Control: Why It Matters.* Conference held at College of the Holy Cross, Worcester, Mass., sponsored by the NELINET Cataloging and Technical Services Advisory Committee, November 1, 1999. Available: http://www.nelinet.net/conf/cts/cts99/taylor.htm.

———. "Cataloguing." In *World Encyclopedia of Library and Information Services.* 3rd ed. Chicago: American Library Association, 1993, pp. 177–181.

———. "The Information Universe: Will We Have Chaos or Control?" *American Libraries* 25, no. 7 (July/August 1994): 629–632.

———. "On the Subject of Subjects." *Journal of Academic Librarianship* 21, no. 6 (November 1995): 484–491.

———. *Wynar's Introduction to Cataloging and Classification.* 9th ed., with the assistance of David P. Miller. Englewood, Colo.: Libraries Unlimited, 2000.

"Ten Taxonomy Myths." *Montague Institute Review*, November 2002; updated April 29, 2003. Available: http://www.montague.com/review/myths.shtml.

Thiele, Harold. "The Dublin Core and Warwick Framework: A Review of the Literature, March 1995–September 1997." *D-Lib Magazine* (January 1998). Available: http://www.dlib.org/dlib/january98/01thiele.html.

Thomas, David. "The Effect of Interface Design on Item Selection in an Online Catalog." *Library Resources & Technical Services* 45, no. 1 (January 2001): 20–45.

Tillett, Barbara B. "Authority Control: State of the Art and New Perspectives." In the proceedings of *International Conference [on] Authority Control: Definition and International Experiences.* Florence, Italy, 12–23 February 2003. Available: http://www.unifi.it/universita/biblioteche/ac/relazioni/tillett_eng.pdf.

————. "Authority Control on the Web." In *Proceedings of the Bicentennial Conference on Bibliographic Control for the New Millennium, November 15–17, 2000.* Washington, D.C.: Library of Congress Cataloging Distribution Service, 2001, pp. 207–220. Also available: http://lcweb.loc.gov/catdir/bibcontrol/tillett_paper.html.

————. "Bibliographic Relationships." In *Relationships in the Organization of Knowledge,* edited by Carole A. Bean and Rebecca Green. Dordrecht: Kluwer Academic Publishers, 2001, pp. 9–35.

————. "International Shared Resource Records for Controlled Access." In *From Catalog to Gateway: Briefings from the CFFC,* paper no. 12. *ALCTS Newsletter Online* 10, no. 1 (December 1998). Available: http://www.pitt.edu/~agtaylor/ala/papers/TillettInternationalShared.pdf.

————. "Problems and Solutions in Cataloging Electronic Resources." *International Cataloguing and Bibliographic Control* 29, no. 1 (January/March 2000): 14–15.

————. "A Taxonomy of Bibliographic Relationships." *Library Resources and Technical Services* 30, no. 2 (April 1991): 156.

UDC Consortium. "About Universal Decimal Classification and the UDC Consortium." Available: http://www.udcc.org/about.htm.

"User Guidelines for Dublin Core Creation." Version 1.0. 29 May 1997. Last updated 22 November 1999. Available: http://www.sics.se/~preben/DC/DC_guide.html.

"The Value of Metadata." Last updated 8 July 2003. Available: http://www.fgdc.gov/publications/documents/metadata/metabroc.html.

Vellucci, Sherry L. "Herding Cats: Options for Organizing Electronic Resources." *Internet Reference Services Quarterly* 1, no. 4 (1996): 9–30.

————. "Metadata and Authority Control." *Library Resources & Technical Services* 44, no. 1 (January 2000): 33–43.

————. "Options for Organizing Electronic Resources: The Coexistence of Metadata." *Bulletin of the American Society for Information Science* 24, no. 1 (October/November 1997): 14–17.

Vickery, B. C. "Ontologies." *Journal of Information Science* 23, no. 4 (1997): 277–286.

Vizine-Goetz, Diane. "Online Classification: Implications for Classifying and Document[-like Object] Retrieval." In *Knowledge Organization and Change: Proceedings of the 4th International ISKO Conference, July 15–18, 1996, Washington, D.C.*, edited by Rebecca Green. Frankfurt/Main: IN-DEKS Verlag, 1996. Also available: http://orc.rsch.oclc.org:6109/dvgisko.htm.

————. "Using Library Classification Schemes for Internet Resources." Last updated November 23, 1999. Available: http://staff.oclc.org/~vizine/Intercat/vizine-goetz.htm.

Warner, Amy J. *A Taxonomy Primer.* Lexonomy, 2002. Available: http://www.lexonomy.com/publications/aTaxonomyPrimer.html.

Wason, Thomas D. "Dr. Tom's Taxonomy Guide: Description, Use and Selections." IMS Global Learning Consortium, Inc., 10 August 2000. Available: http://www.imsglobal.org/drtomtaxonomiesguide.cfm.

Weinberg, Bella Hass. *Can You Recommend a Good Book on Indexing? Collected Reviews on the Organization of Information.* Medford, N.J.: Information Today, 1998.

————. "Exhaustivity of Indexes: Books, Journals, and Electronic Full Text." *Key Words* 7, no. 5 (September/October 1999): 1, 6–19.

————, ed. *Indexing: The State of Our Knowledge and the State of Our Ignorance: Proceedings of the 20th Annual Meeting of the American Society of Indexers, New York City, May 13, 1988.* Medford, N.J.: Learned Information, 1989.

Weldon, J. L. "A Career in Data Modeling." *Byte* 22, no. 6 (June 1997): 103–106.

Wellish, Hans H. "Aboutness and Selection of Topics." *Key Words* 4, no. 2 (March/April 1996): 7–9.

Wells, Amy Tracy, Susan Calcari, and Travis Koplow, eds. *The Amazing Internet Challenge: How Leading Projects Use Library Skills to Organize the Web.* Chicago: American Library Association, 1999.

"What Is a Neural Network?" NeuroDimension, Inc., 2002. Available: http://www.nd.com/welcome/whatisnn.htm.

Williamson, Nancy. "Classification in the Millennium." *Online & CDROM Review* 21, no. 5 (October 1997): 298–301.

Wilson, Patrick. "The Catalog as Access Mechanism: Background and Concepts." In *Foundations of Cataloging: A Sourcebook*, edited by Michael Carpenter and Elaine Svenonius. Littleton, Colo.: Libraries Unlimited, 1985, pp. 253–268.

———. *Two Kinds of Power: An Essay on Bibliographical Control.* Berkeley: University of California Press, 1968.

Wool, Gregory J. "Bibliographical Metadata; or, We Need a Client-Server Cataloging Code!" In *Finding Common Ground: Creating the Library of the Future without Diminishing the Library of the Past*, edited by Cheryl LaGuardia and Barbara S. Mitchell. New York: Neal-Schuman, 1998, pp. 398–401.

———. "A Meditation on Metadata." *The Serials Librarian* 33, no. 1/2 (1998): 167–178.

Wyllys, R. E. "Information Architecture." Reading prepared for Information Technologies and the Information Profession, Graduate School of Library & Information Science, University of Texas at Austin, 2000. Last updated 28 June 2003. Available: http://www.ischool.utexas.edu/~wyllys/ITIPMaterials/InfoArchitecture.html.

Yee, Martha M. "Guidelines for OPAC Displays." In *From Catalog to Gateway: Briefings from the CFFC*, paper no. 14. *ALCTS Newsletter Online* 10, no. 6 (December 1999). Available: http://www.pitt.edu/~agtaylor/ala/papers/YeeOPACGuidelines.pdf.

———. "What Is a Work?" *Cataloging & Classification Quarterly* 19, nos. 1–2 (1994); 20, nos. 1–2 (1995). Four-part series.

Yee, Martha M., and Sara Shatford Layne. *Improving Online Public Access Catalogs.* Chicago: American Library Association, 1998.

INDEX

About the Author

ARLENE G. TAYLOR is Professor, School of Information Sciences, University of Pittsburgh, Pennsylvania, and author of several works on cataloging and classification. She has received ALA's Margaret Mann Citation in Cataloging and Classification.